Jaguar Books on Latin A

Series Editors

WILLIAM H. BEEZLEY, Neville G. Penrose Chair of Latin
  American Studies, Texas Christian University
COLIN M. MACLACHLAN, Professor and Chair, Department
  of History, Tulane University

Volumes Published

John E. Kicza, ed., *The Indian in Latin American History: Resistance,
  Resilience, and Acculturation* (1993). Cloth ISBN 0-8420-2421-2
  Paper ISBN 0-8420-2425-5

Susan E. Place, ed., *Tropical Rainforests: Latin American Nature and
  Society in Transition* (1993). Cloth ISBN 0-8420-2423-9
  Paper ISBN 0-8420-2427-1

Paul W. Drake, ed., *Money Doctors, Foreign Debts, and Economic
  Reforms in Latin America from the 1890s to the Present* (1994).
  Cloth ISBN 0-8420-2434-4   Paper ISBN 0-8420-2435-2

John A. Britton, ed., *Molding the Hearts and Minds: Education,
  Communications, and Social Change in Latin America* (1994).
  Cloth ISBN 0-8420-2489-1   Paper ISBN 0-8420-2490-5

Darién J. Davis, ed., *Slavery and Beyond: The African Impact on Latin
  America and the Caribbean* (1995). Cloth ISBN 0-8420-2484-0
  Paper ISBN 0-8420-2485-9

David J. Weber and Jane M. Rausch, eds., *Where Cultures Meet: Frontiers
  in Latin American History* (1994). Cloth ISBN 0-8420-2477-8
  Paper ISBN 0-8420-2478-6

Gertrude M. Yeager, ed., *Confronting Change, Challenging Tradition:
  Women in Latin American History* (1994). Cloth ISBN 0-8420-2479-4
  Paper ISBN 0-8420-2480-8

Linda Alexander Rodríguez, ed., *Rank and Privilege: The Military and
  Society in Latin America* (1994). Cloth ISBN 0-8420-2432-8
  Paper ISBN 0-8420-2433-6

Gilbert M. Joseph and Mark D. Szuchman, eds., *I Saw a City Invincible:
  Urban Portraits of Latin America* (1996). Cloth ISBN 0-8420-2495-6
  Paper ISBN 0-8420-2496-4

Roderic Ai Camp, ed., *Democracy in Latin America: Patterns and Cycles* (1996). Cloth ISBN 0-8420-2512-X   Paper ISBN 0-8420-2513-8

Oscar J. Martínez, ed., *U.S.-Mexico Borderlands: Historical and Contemporary Perspectives* (1996). Cloth ISBN 0-8420-2446-8 Paper ISBN 0-8420-2447-6

William O. Walker III, ed., *Drugs in the Western Hemisphere: An Odyssey of Cultures in Conflict* (1996). Cloth ISBN 0-8420-2422-0 Paper ISBN 0-8420-2426-3

Democracy in
Latin America

Democracy in Latin America
Patterns and Cycles

Roderic Ai Camp
Editor

Jaguar Books on Latin America
Number 10

A Scholarly Resources Inc. Imprint
Wilmington, Delaware

© 1996 by Scholarly Resources Inc.
All rights reserved
First published 1996
Printed and bound in the United States of America

Scholarly Resources Inc.
104 Greenhill Avenue
Wilmington, DE 19805-1897

Library of Congress Cataloging-in-Publication Data

Democracy in Latin America : patterns and cycles / Roderic Ai Camp,
  editor.
       p.   cm. — (Jaguar books on Latin America ; no. 10)
    Includes bibliographical references.
    ISBN 0-8420-2512-X (cloth : alk. paper). — ISBN 0-8420-2513-8
(paper : alk. paper)
    1. Democracy—Latin America. 2. Latin America—Politics and
government—1980–   I. Camp, Roderic Ai. II. Series.
JL966.D454   1995
320.98'09'049—dc20   95-30776
                                                           CIP

♾ The paper used in this publication meets the minimum requirements
of the American National Standard for permanence of paper for printed
library materials, Z39.48, 1984.

To my students

in Latin American politics

Acknowledgments

I would like to thank Bill Beezley and Colin MacLachlan, the editors of the Jaguar Books on Latin America series, for insisting that I contribute to their project with this edited volume. It has been a challenging and informative experience. In particular, I would also like to offer gratitude to the individual contributors and editors who, by waiving their own personal royalties, facilitated the publication of this collection and, as a consequence, the enhancement of knowledge about Latin American politics.

Contents

Foreword

Scholarly interest in Latin America's politics has intensified in the last two decades, often in association with its role in international relations. As is true with respect to other parts of the world, public concern with the region tends to rise and fall in direct relation to the degree to which U.S. foreign policy issues are linked to the area. During President Ronald Reagan's administrations in the 1980s, a period of intense conflicts in Central America, the U.S. government deeply involved itself in the resolution of those hostilities, both in El Salvador—embroiled in a civil war involving the military and guerrilla forces—and Nicaragua—where a socialist, revolutionary government had come to power, opposed by a well-armed group.

Interest in the Latin American states has much deeper roots, of course. Given the geographic proximity, shared colonial experiences, and economic and cultural ties of those states, the region is seen in the United States as deserving of special attention. Yet, as these nations evolved economically and politically in the nineteenth and twentieth centuries, observers increasingly began to note the differences in their developmental processes, and their social and political achievements, from those found in the United States. These differences were highlighted by the fact that after World War II, when the United States assumed the status of a world power, the contrast between it and its southern neighbors became sharper.

The international political events of the last decade have made it imperative for students in the United States to understand the origins and future directions of Latin American development, political or otherwise. Just as England was forced to come to grips with European societies and their complex social and economic problems, as economic integration among the members of the European Economic Community inextricably tied their fates to that of the continent, the United States has linked itself economically with Mexico and, in the immediate future, with other Latin American countries through the North American Free Trade Agreement (NAFTA). The imminent membership of Chile, one of the southernmost countries in Latin America, suggests the rapidity of regional economic integration and the linking of the futures of various countries in the Western Hemisphere.

This hemispheric pattern of economic integration is part of a larger global trend toward regional trading blocs. It is also the result of the tremendous technological changes that have led to a smaller planet—that is, a reduction in the barriers of physical geography and communication. The shrinking size of the Earth has increased cultural and commercial exchange as individuals, ideas, and goods have moved freely from one society to another. Given the historic cultural and economic ties between the United States and Latin American states, increased contact was to be expected.

The heated debate about whether or not the United States should join a trade pact with Canada and Mexico focused not only on the bread-and-butter issues of trade surpluses and employment but also on Mexico's political system, which differs substantially from that found in its two northern neighbors. The primary focus of the debate was on Mexico's lack of democracy and the political evils associated with a less representative system.

Unlike Mexico, most of Latin America has moved since the mid-1980s toward more democratic forms of political participation. Like Mexico, however, nearly all Latin American countries typically have been characterized by more authoritarian forms of government; indeed, many witnessed extreme forms of state-sponsored repression and terrorism during the 1970s and 1980s. To those analysts with a sharper historical eye, Latin America has appeared to alternate between more or less authoritarian regimes for decades.

The wave of democracy that currently characterizes Latin American countries and other nations that were formerly under authoritarian regimes has a cyclical history in the Western Hemisphere. Many students of Latin American politics are not optimistic about the persistence of the overt features of democratization in the region, most notably competitive elections and increased citizen participation. It is well to remember that among these countries, the U.S. political model and culture have been the exception, not the rule.

If the pattern is cyclical, and one has only to recall the phrase used in the late 1950s describing the winds of democracy in Latin America, why bother to examine what is happening? There are three major reasons why such a focus deserves attention. First, although the pattern has been cyclical, features may exist in the present cycle that distinguish it from past experiences. For example, the major actors in the political process may have changed. It is also reasonable to believe that the 1980s and 1990s have introduced new actors, with differing agendas and, perhaps more important, different means of achieving their goals. As physical space declines in significance, peer support or influence outside the domestic political arena becomes more important. The most obvious form of this type of support, explicit and implicit, is global public opinion, expressed in the mass media and through official statements by world leaders. Other influences increasingly act on the minds and behaviors of individual actors. For example, international interest groups, ranging from human rights to environmental organizations, bring pressure to bear on behalf of their goals. Domestic actors sharing similar concerns seek out their support financially and intellectually. Another variable that has changed dramatically is behaviors associated with the Cold War—that is, the conflict between the United States and the Soviet Union for supremacy, especially in their specific spheres of influence.

A second reason for examining the changing face of Latin American politics is that the future of the United States is linked increasingly with that of Latin America. The process of economic integration has focused on the economic interdependency of each country on its neighbors, nearby or across the globe. What is not so clear to the average citizen is the linking of international social and political conditions with domestic policy issues. In the last months of 1994 and the beginning of 1995 alone, the problems of Haitian immigration, and its association with a repressive military regime, led to an overwhelming U.S. presence in this Caribbean nation. The Hispanic and Mexican immigration to the Southwest emerged as a major issue of California politics in the gubernatorial and congressional elections, resulting in the approval of Proposition 187, a strongly anti-immigrant bill. Finally, political instability in southern Mexico, combined with a devaluation of the peso, led to a major financial crisis, requiring the United States and Canada to provide a multibillion-dollar package to support the Mexican currency. No state or community is immune to the effects of regional affairs on the American economic or political landscape. The fate of the United States as a nation is going to be increasingly determined by what happens outside its borders, in particular in this hemisphere.

Finally, a third reason why students should be interested in examining Latin American politics in the 1990s is the linkage that both politicians and scholars are drawing between politics and development. An intellectual and popular argument often offered in the United States is that capitalism is the product of a democratic political model, or that democracy is inextricably tied to capitalism. In fact, defenders of NAFTA argue that it will help push Mexico, and therefore any future member, farther and faster on the path to democracy. Whether or not such a link-age exists is debatable, as one can find concrete examples of capitalism without democracy.

A more important issue for students to consider in reading the fol-lowing essays is the potential implications of such an association for po-litical ideology. Neoliberal advocates proclaimed the death of socialism, economic and political. Yet, societies in North, Central, and South America are faced with tasks that are tremendously challenging. The burdens placed on the capitalist economic system to solve structural inequities and re-duce exploitation are in some cases nearly insurmountable. If the nations of the Americas fail to resolve their fundamental problems, the dominant political and economic model of the decade, democratic capitalism, is likely to be delegitimized. If democratic capitalism fails in Latin America, it may find itself in the same state of disrepute as is socialism now. If that occurs, what lies ahead?

R.A.C.

I

What Is Democratization in Latin America?

1

Democracy and Development: An Overview

Shannan Mattiace and Roderic Ai Camp

Democracy and development are two widely discussed and debated themes in political science. After World War II, many observers of Latin American politics believed that the region would not achieve democracy until socioeconomic development had reached a certain level. For example, some modernization theorists suggested that low levels of literacy, urbanization, and industrial development explained democracy's failure to take root in a region or country.[1] It came as a surprise to many observers, therefore, when high levels of economic growth in some Latin American countries during the 1960s and 1970s did not lead to democracy. Not only did military governments revive and persist in most of the region during these decades but also authoritarianism increased its repressiveness and use of violence, especially in Argentina, Brazil, and Chile, which are among the most economically developed countries. Latin American political analysts were particularly dismayed when Chile, a country with a long history of democratic government, regular elections, and a tradition of strong political parties, succumbed to military rule in 1973.

The return of civilian rule in many Latin American countries during the 1980s, termed the "lost decade" because of the prolonged economic recession that many societies experienced, challenged the conventional wisdom that democracy is linked to socioeconomic development. Despite the poor economic performance of many regimes throughout the region, more freely elected governments in Latin America existed at the end of the 1980s than at any other time in recent history.

As the 1990s began, developments in the Soviet Union led to its demise and to a political rebirth of Eastern Europe. A wave of political liberalization akin to American-style democratization, emphasizing free elections, competitive political parties, and a revival of capitalism,

appeared to be sweeping the globe. In both Mexico and Brazil, governments began to limit and circumscribe the role of the state in the economy,
subscribing to an equally popular wave of economic liberalization.

Faced with sweeping economic and political changes worldwide,
scholars began to rethink the interrelationship between social and economic development, capitalism, and democracy. The authors of the selections in this book attempt to address this relationship, thereby providing
a timely focus for students of Latin American politics as they examine
the recent surge of democratization throughout the region. This study also
presents a significant topic for students interested in the consequences of
recently adopted neoliberal economic policies for long-term political liberalization.[2] The fragility of many of these regimes in Latin America suggests the uncertainty of the direction of democracy.[3]

It is necessary to lay out, as done in Part I, several definitions of
democracy, from the procedural to the more substantive, because all the
chapters in this volume deal with the theme of democracy and the process
of democratization from different perspectives. Part II examines the tension between arguments favoring political culture and those stressing the
role of structures in explaining the democratization process. Part III explores some of the potential agents of political change—religion, militarism, electioneering, and nongovernmental organizations (NGOs)—and
focuses on the tension between elite and grass-roots representatives in
the process of fostering democratic practices and attitudes. The selections on elections and civil-military relations stress the importance of elites
in political development, while those on the church and nongovernmental organizations emphasize the significance of grass-roots democracy.
Part IV uses case studies to examine the consequences of democratization in the region. The overarching theme of the three selections highlighted in this section is the relationship between politics and economics.
In different ways, the authors challenge the assumption held by many
scholars that economic change causes political change, stressing the importance of politics in the democratization process. Finally, these three
authors conclude by discussing several dilemmas of democratization or
key challenges currently facing Latin American democracies.

Two caveats are in order. First, any study aspiring to deal with an
entire region must necessarily fall prey to generalizations that distort national and local realities. Although scholars might discuss Latin America
as if it were a homogeneous unit, it is clearly diverse and heterogeneous.
The fact that the majority of Latin Americans share a common language
(Spanish), religion (Catholicism), and colonial history often masks tremendous diversity within the continent. For example, geographically,
South and Central America, the interior and coasts, the highlands and

lowlands, differ sharply; culturally, many qualities separate the indigenous and mestizo; linguistically, Portuguese, Spanish, and a multitude of indigenous languages are spoken; and as for religion, Catholicism, folk Catholicism, and evangelical Protestantism cover the region. Second, students who approach this volume in an effort to discover a general theory of democratization will be disappointed. Decades of work by scholars on democratic theory and transitions to democracy suggest that no one set of causes—economic, social, psychological, or international—definitively explains democracy.

I What Is Democratization in Latin America?

Key to any discussion of transitions to democracy is a precise and rigorous definition of democracy itself. Joseph Schumpeter defines it as a representative polity that includes free and universal suffrage, civil liberties, competitive parties, selection of alternative candidates for office, and the presence of political institutions that regulate and guarantee the roles of government and opposition.[4] In a similar vein, Samuel P. Huntington claims that a twentieth-century political system is democratic to the extent that its most powerful collective decisionmakers are selected through fair, honest, and periodic elections in which candidates compete freely for votes and in which virtually the entire adult population is eligible to vote. Thus defined, democracy involves two dimensions: contestation and participation. It also implies the existence of civil and political freedoms to speak, publish, assemble, and organize, thereby guaranteeing political debate and the conduct of electoral campaigns. For Huntington, democratic systems have a common institutional core that establishes their identity.[5]

Another scholar, Francis Hagopian, goes further than the procedural definitions of either Schumpeter or Huntington. He argues that democracy must be understood not only in terms of the institutions that limit state power and hold those who govern accountable to the governed but also in terms of the distribution of political power, which requires that subordinate groups be able to frame interests and demands autonomously and to engage in political action based on those interests and demands.[6] Hagopian insists that mechanisms must be present to frame those interests and demands if a country is to be considered a democracy.

Robert Dahl also has built this requirement into his definition of democracy. In order for government to be responsive to the preferences of its citizens, they must have "unimpaired opportunities to formulate their preferences; to signify their preferences to their fellow citizens and the government by individual and collective action; and to have their preferences weighed equally in the conduct of government."[7] This can be accomplished concretely by arguing that democracy requires programmatic political parties in order to guarantee the opportunity to voice citizen preferences.[8]

Other scholars also go beyond procedural definitions as sufficient indicators of democracy. Valerie Bunce, for example, emphasizes governance as an indispensable requirement of a liberal democracy. "Democratic elections, in short, are nice, but democratic governance is crucial."[9] She identifies five requirements of a liberal democracy: (1) dominance of rule of law; (2) extensive civil liberties guaranteed by law; (3) representative government—that is, a government that is simultaneously representative, accountable, and powerful; (4) a Weberian bureaucracy—that is, a bureaucracy that is rational, rule-bound, merit-based, and subject to control by elected officials so that the administrative apparatus is accountable to the public; and (5) some dispersion of economic resources.[10] Bunce's definition is important in that it identifies the establishment of democratic and representative institutions as vital parts of the process of democratization. In the Latin American case, one also can make the argument, as does Terry Lynn Karl (Chapter 2), that civilian supremacy over the military is an essential requisite of democracy.[11]

II The Political Heritage: Culture, Structures, and Authoritarianism

After World War II, modernization theorists looked to levels of literacy, urbanization, and industrial development to explain democracy's failure to take root in a particular region or country. Popular among modernization theorists was the "stages of growth" thesis, which held that every country was similar at the traditional stage and needed to pass through a prescribed set of changes in order to become "modern." Some authors argue that these changes were primarily economic in nature. In contrast, political culture theorists contend that these changes were to be found in the sphere of values.[12] Political culture theory stresses the importance of a country's values and its historical political experiences to explain democracy's success or failure. For example, it has been suggested that a capacity for empathy and a willingness to participate in the political system are characteristics that typically make democracy possible.[13] Still other scholars combine both historical and cultural variables in identifying obstacles to democratization.[14]

Analysts who focus on political culture and its relationship to democratization attempt to move away from what they perceive to be an excessive focus on economic factors to explain the process of democratization. A leading scholar commenting on the question of the origins of stable democracy stated that "there is no question that economic factors are politically important, but they are only part of the story."[15] In his extensive work on political culture, Ronald Inglehart has focused on a specific subset of norms and attitudes supportive of democracy. His conclusion from a two-decade study of fifteen nations is that "a long-term commitment to democratic institutions among the public is . . . required, in order to sustain democracy when conditions are dire."[16]

Those who stress the importance of political culture argue that the norms and attitudes adopted and practiced by the citizens of a particular polity contribute significantly to the potential success or failure of democracy to take root. They often look to attitudes concerning freedom of speech and assembly, tolerance of protest, levels of mass versus elite tolerance, levels of support for the existing political system, levels of trust, and tolerance of critics who wish to run for political office.

In Chapter 3, Glen Caudill Dealy argues that political culture not only mediates other factors important to democracy's emergence but also is actually determinative. For him, the civic virtues cherished by Latin Americans are essentially those perfections prized by classical, especially Roman, civilization. He infers that many virtues and values have changed little over the centuries and that Latin Americans hold values not particularly auspicious for democratic government. He claims, for example, that classical grandeur is frequently displayed in Latin oratory as a means of attracting followers, a prerequisite for political endeavor, and, probably most discouraging for democracy, that Latin Americans reject "process" society and rigid procedural government. Those who hope for a U.S.-style democracy in Latin America also would be dismayed with Dealy's assertion that "endless alliances, coups, and rigged elections leading to surface political instability and uncertainty should be interpreted as the logical outcome of a status-seeking order where each ambitious male consciously endeavors to impress himself upon a theatrically inspired world through the tangible media of words and deeds."

Dealy does not paint a rosy picture of the future for democracy in Latin America. While he argues that North Americans have much to learn from Latin Americans in the familial and public spheres, he believes that Latin Americans have not had success in building the norms and attitudes necessary for democracy, a view shared by many political culture theorists.[17]

In contrast to Dealy, Mitchell A. Seligson (Chapter 4) advocates political culture research as one way to assess democracy's success or failure in a specific country or region. He rejects scholarship that focuses exclusively on economic factors to explain the democratization process, arguing that in Latin America crossing the economic threshold may be a necessary condition for democratization, but it is clearly far from a sufficient condition. Seligson, however, does not conclude that democratic attitudes produce democratic systems, but he insists on the complexity of this question and leaves it open for future researchers to probe.

Chapters 5 and 6 by Peter F. Klarén and James M. Malloy, respectively, illustrate the tension between cultural and structural variables to help understand Latin American underdevelopment. Klarén focuses on four main approaches to the study of development in Latin America: modernization theory, dependency theory and Marxism, corporatism, and bureaucratic authoritarianism. While all but dependency and Marxism discuss the role of certain values in creating and maintaining specific political, economic, and social structures, they particularly stress structural explanations for the region's underdevelopment. Beginning with a discussion of modernization theory, as applied to Latin America, Klarén summarizes the works of leading theorists. He argues that modernization theory is ultimately insufficient in explaining Latin American underdevelopment, noting that one key problem involves its use of evolutionary theory and the assumption by modernization theorists that all societies move in a linear, developmental continuum from traditional to modern, as occurred in the West, thus passing through distinct stages. Critics of modernization theory, as Klarén demonstrates, also attack the idea, implicit in this theory, that all preindustrial societies are alike. These critics note the great variation in social structures around the world, arguing that there is no reason to assume that feudal, tribal, or bureaucratic societies will all change in the same way.

Probably the most vehement critics of modernization theory are members of the dependency school. Of the four arguments that Klarén discusses, dependency is clearly the most structuralist in orientation. Dependency theorists argue that Latin Americans are adversely affected by their trade relationship with the First World. According to this group, Latin America, as part of the periphery of the international system, is forced to supply raw materials (whose prices fluctuate greatly on the world market) to the core (the industrialized nations), which turns these raw materials into finished goods and then sells them back to the periphery for a profit. They urge structural improvements such as land reform and income redistribution to expand the internal market for local industry by increasing the purchasing power of peasants and workers.

Dependency theorists also advocate a policy of import substitution industrialization (manufacturing products in-country to reduce imports) to protect domestic industries from damaging competition from abroad. Neo-Marxists added to the debate by arguing that industrialized nations actually need underdevelopment in the Third World to maintain their prosperity. Paul Baran, a neo-Marxist, argues that Western imperialism, rather than initiating the global transition from feudalism to capitalism, according to Marxist-Leninist theory, "actually stunted the growth of capitalism in the third world by draining off capital and killing native industry through unequal competition."[18] For dependency theorists and neo-Marxists, it was not cultural factors that led to underdevelopment but structures of dependency that caught Third World countries in a vicious cycle of underdevelopment.

Both Klarén and Malloy focus on the legacy of Latin American corporatism, or the relationship between the state and specific groups. The debate over corporatism illustrates the tension between cultural and structural factors as explanatory variables. Klarén points out that the core of corporatist theory lies in the organic-state tradition (which stresses the political community and the central role of the state in achieving the common good), claiming that it originated with Aristotle and runs through Roman law, medieval natural law, and contemporary Catholic social philosophy. He notes that other scholars suggest similarities between modernization theory and corporatism and argues that both heavily emphasize cultural values.

Malloy, in contrast to Klarén, argues that structural factors explain why authoritarian and corporatist regimes have been more common in the region than democratic ones. He focuses not on the norms and attitudes among the populace but on the historical political, economic, and social forces that have led to these conditions. While he acknowledges the argument that accounts for Latin American corporatism by pointing to the Hispanic-Catholic tradition, he concludes that it alone does not explain the emergence of authoritarian corporate regimes in Latin America. He believes that structural factors are crucial to their presence, stating that two important processes are linked to the emergence of these regimes: delayed, dependent development and populism. Malloy does not dismiss cultural explanations in accounting for authoritarian governments but instead focuses his attention on structural and historically based explanations. In short, he argues that Latin American populism was a general regional response to the first crisis of delayed, dependent development since 1930.

Klarén's and Malloy's discussions of bureaucratic authoritarianism also highlight differences between cultural and structural explanations. Klarén argues that bureaucratic authoritarianism owes much to Max Weber's theory of bureaucracy and politics, especially Weber's concern with values and roles. To be fair, Klarén also points out the more structural explanations that these theorists employ to explain the emergence of bureaucratic authoritarianism in Latin America. He particularly acknowledges Guillermo O'Donnell's argument that economic stagnation, coupled with increasing political demands, led to the breakdown of the progressive populist coalitions of the 1930s and 1940s. In comparison, Malloy explains the emergence of blatant authoritarian regimes in Latin America beginning in the mid-1960s by noting a new structural crisis that developed with the exhaustion of import substitution growth and the reality of economic penetration by multinational corporations. He notes that an orientation toward state-sponsored rapid industrial development has continued to be paramount in these regimes.

The selections in Part II help to provide insight into the central tension existing between cultural and structural explanations of Latin America's political heritage. Although many questions are left unanswered in assessing which variables have the greatest explanatory power, when comparing the differences between cultural and structural explanations, students might want to examine the extent of their overlap. Do cultural values emerge from previous structural positions? How, in fact, do cultural values change? Are cultural values immutable? How, if at all, do value orientations shape structure? Are political structures the product of behavior or the end result?

III Agents of Political Change? Religion, Militarism, Electioneering, and Nongovernmental Organizations

This section examines these four potential agents of political change and focuses on the tension between the elite and grass-roots levels in the democratization process. Democratic attitudes and practices must be fostered on both levels if democracy is to be maintained. Much of the literature on transitions to democracy stresses the significance of elite cooperation or conflict during the formative process of building democratic regimes. Some elite theorists assert that democratic stability depends on agreements, or "pacts," that can be struck only among elites representing rival organizations and popular groupings.[19]

In a way similar to elite theorists, Guillermo O'Donnell emphasizes the significance of pact making, arguing that regime transitions occur either by "collapse" of the authoritarian regime or by a "transaction" in which a decisive set of incumbents of an authoritarian regime decides to open or "depressurize" the situation. In the latter, elites are very much in control of the situation that typically results in the making of pacts among key political and economic elites. Pact transitions are defined as a series of agreements made and renegotiated between the authoritarian incumbents and the opposition during what is usually a significantly longer process than occurs in the case of transitions by collapse.[20] Dankwart Rustow, another political scientist, notes the importance of pact making during the transition period, arguing that this phase is concluded by a deliberate decision by political leaders to accept the existence of diversity in unity and to institutionalize some crucial aspect of the democratic procedure.[21] He concludes that a small circle of leaders is likely to play a disproportionate role during this political shift.

In Latin America the relationship between civil and military elites is crucial in the literature on democratic transitions. Augusto Varas (Chapter 7) argues that theoretical and empirical research on the relations among the armed forces, society, and the state has become an absolutely critical issue for Latin American democracy. He identifies a set of structural and cultural variables that facilitate the withdrawal of the military from government. He suggests that weak institutionalization of political parties and other formal civilian political organizations facilitates military intervention. Vargas believes that the armed forces' withdrawal from politics occurs during periods of crisis resulting from the contradiction between the functions of defense and domestic police tasks and from a management crisis in government.[22] This withdrawal, however, is only the first step toward the restoration of democracy. Varas points to several factors necessary to normalize civil-military relations after the military's retreat to the barracks, noting the importance of mass support for civilian rule and changes in civilian political culture.

Another variable crucial to the democratization process is elections. Elections are a way for the electorate to demonstrate not just its preference between parties and policies but also its commitment to the democratic process. Electoral reform in many Latin American countries means more than improving the system—it may be necessary to the system's very survival. Elite theorists also recognize the pivotal importance of elections in the democratization process. Several have concluded that the most common path to a democratic regime is through an elite convergence, which occurs when opposing factions within disunified elites discover that they can mobilize a reliable majority of voters, win elections repeatedly, and thereby protect their interests by dominating government executive power.[23] In cases of elite convergence, the electoral system is utilized to unify the elite before arriving at a formal understanding by signing an official agreement. Alan Angell, Maria D'Alva Kinzo, and Diego Urbaneja (Chapter 9) corroborate this argument by noting that the political right in Latin America is now committed to seeking power through elections, whereas in the past it frequently sought power through support for military intervention.

After the transitional period is over, elections become an essential component of the consolidation process. According to Angell, Kinzo, and Urbaneja, they serve not only as expressions of popular choice but also as evidence that both the left and the right, whose attachment to democracy in the past has been conditional at best, now accept the rules of pluralistic democracy. To illustrate modern electioneering tactics used in Latin America, these authors examine three case studies: Brazil, Chile, and Venezuela. Although these countries vary widely in several key respects, electioneering has developed in a similar fashion. Both Varas and the authors of Chapter 9 note the Americanization of the electioneering as one point of convergence. They also note the widespread use of television for election campaigning in these three countries, arguing that most electioneering in Latin America today is conducted on television with techniques as modern as those found in the United States. Finally, they reveal the increasing use in recent years of public opinion polls in electoral campaigns.

So far, then, it has been suggested that the democratization process is primarily constructed and controlled by elites, particularly in the transitional period. Although many authors in the field point to the significance of elite pact making and top-down liberalization, civil society and the popular sectors are by no means insignificant. Although recent examples of Western authoritarian rule demonstrate that civil society often takes a backseat in the process of democratization, citizens turned out to be the surprising protagonist in East European transitions.[24] O'Donnell insists that civil society's resurrection cannot be exaggerated in the transitional period and that mobilization of the citizenry and the intense demands that it places on all political actors greatly strengthen the position of the democratic opposition.[25] Other scholars also emphasize the influence of civil society under authoritarian regimes and during the transition. Fernando Henrique Cardoso [president-elect of Brazil], for instance, argues that it is decisive in the difficult task of extending the frontiers of what could or could not be done under authoritarian regimes.[26]

Much of the literature on democratic transitions suggests that most successful regime transitions are initiated by the political elite through a complete "collapse" of the authoritarian regime or a "transaction," in which a pact or agreement is signed by key elites or alternatively by a gradual process of liberalization leading to eventual democratization. In fact, Terry Lynn Karl and Philippe Schmitter argue that democracies that have endured appear to be characterized by relatively strong elite actors who engage in strategies of compromise. They conclude that "transitions by pact are the most likely to lead to political democracy."[27]

Thus, it appears that most authors within this literature view the transitional period as being controlled largely by elites. Civil society, they assert, becomes most important as the transition consolidates itself and as channels of participation are institutionalized. It is to this latter period that the Levine and Landim essays are directed.

It is imperative that democratic attitudes and practices be fostered on the level of formal institutions and on the grass-roots level. Toward this end, Daniel H. Levine concentrates on the grass-roots organizations necessary to sustain viable democracy (Chapter 8). Instead of exclusively focusing on religious and political activism in the realm of formal institutions (such as the Catholic Church) and traditional elites, he stresses the emergence of new popular groups and movements, arguing that their emergence has shifted the discussion from "church and state" to "religion and politics" in an effort to make scholarly analysis more dynamic and broader in scope. Levine notes that traditional concerns over education, marriage, divorce, state subsidies, and the like have yielded center stage to discussions of human rights, justice, social criticism, and the proper role and place of popular classes in the social order. Despite these reorientations, Levine claims that the prevailing research remains centered on formal structures and institutions rather than on how people perceive various institutions. According to Levine, in the past, resistance by popular groups and movements was seen primarily as a reaction to repression.

Since Vatican II (1961–1964) and the Medellín Conference (1968), the Church in Latin America has moved from being an unquestioned supporter of the established order to a current posture of neutrality. Levine suggests that the variations between national and local Catholic churches throughout the region be examined. He advocates a systematic analysis of how different models of the Catholic Church are worked into normal practice and experienced on a day-to-day basis by real men and women.

In discussing the future of the Catholic Church in Latin America, Levine further argues that the centrality of religious groups in political organization and action will fade if recent democratizing trends continue simply because there will be more channels for popular participation under democratic rule than exist under authoritarian regimes. Nevertheless, he insists that churches and religion generally will remain important to the formulation of political issues and phenomena and is hopeful that, although Christian Base Communities (CEBs, from the Spanish, *comunidades eclesiales de base*) may become less visible in explicitly political matters, they will continue to play a subtle, long-term role by eliciting and promoting new sources and styles of leadership.

While Levine contends that the centrality of CEBs and other popular organizations within the Catholic Church in Latin America will fade if recent democratizing trends continue, the opposite seems to be true for nongovernmental organizations. In Chapter 10, Leilah Landim defines NGOs as private, nonprofit organizations that are publicly registered— that is, they have legal status—and whose principal function is to implement development projects favoring the popular sectors, which receive financial support. She argues that the current period of redemocratization sweeping across the continent has given NGOs an "extra boost." Developed in Latin America during periods of political authoritarianism, when they served to denounce and resist repression, NGOs have always had a strong orientation to civil society rather than to the state. According to Landim, they are organizations that stress their direct relationships with social groups and movements within which they act. Because of their origins under authoritarian regimes, NGOs largely distanced themselves from the state, focusing on society's grass-roots level.

How will Latin American democratization alter the stance of NGOs toward the state? Landim notes that one of the current debates among these organizations revolves around the question: Should we work in cooperation with state programs? At present, NGOs in Latin America are rethinking their relationship to the state in a new atmosphere of democratization. The contribution that NGOs have made to the democratization process and to the deepening of democracy has been discussed in large conferences of NGO leaders in Latin America and remains an open question. It does appear certain, however, that NGOs do contribute to democracy's consolidation through their vocation of pluralism and autonomy.

As mentioned, civil society's role is vital during the consolidation period. Whereas elites often take the lead during the transitional phase, political organizations and NGOs concerned with grass-roots democracy, government accountability, and citizen participation play a significant role in regime consolidation. In the case of Brazil, the development of citizen groups outside government and the organization of locally based social movements facilitated citizen support of the new democracy.[28] Scholars suggest that new social movements have become especially important in the process of consolidating Brazil's democratic regime following the 1985 presidential elections. Because the decades-long process of military rule rendered ineffective and eliminated many of the traditional patterns of political organization and mobilization, the popular strata were forced to adopt new forms of struggle and contestation. Howard Winant states that the new social movements expanded the terrain of politics, addressing issues that had been seen as personal or private as public, social, and legitimate areas for mobilization. NGOs' direct link with these locally based social movements can be crucial in the consolidation period.[29]

IV Consequences of Democratization: Case Studies in Change

Thus far, this brief overview of democracy and development has looked at the tension between cultural and structural explanations and the need for fostering democratic attitudes and practices on both the elite and grassroots levels. This final section attempts to balance these democratic theories with concrete case studies in order to examine the consequences of democratization in Latin America. Case studies are important in the field of comparative politics in orienting and testing our theories, as well as in helping scholars to learn which theories illuminate reality and which confuse and distort it.

This most recent wave of redemocratization sweeping across Latin America began in the early 1980s. However, there are no guarantees that many of these "new" democracies will be maintained over the long run. Ben Ross Schneider, Peter H. Smith, and Karen L. Remmer highlight challenges that Latin American countries currently face under democratic rule. Many of these challenges to political democratization are economic in nature. In particular, in Chapter 11, Schneider points out that in Brazil the runaway inflation, high level of external debt, and lack of macroeconomic stability are key challenges under the "new" democratic government of Fernando Collor de Mello (who was removed from office for corruption before completing his term). Smith discusses the link between free trade and democracy in Mexico, while Remmer compares the performance of authoritarian regimes, older democracies, and newer democracies in dealing with economic crises. Likewise, political crises also impede economic development. Schneider and Smith note the lack of programmatic political parties in both Brazil and Mexico as a debilitating factor in the consolidation of democracy in these two countries. All three authors illustrate the inseparability of politics and economics.

Smith challenges the conventional wisdom that a free-trade agreement will accelerate the process of democratization in Mexico (Chapter 12). This view, according to Smith, rests on the assumption that economic change causes political change.[30] In examining the Mexican case, some writers insist on making the distinction between regime liberalization and genuine democracy. Soledad Loaeza, for example, argues that economic liberalization is much less predictable than democratization because under liberalization an authoritarian elite does not necessarily give up its privileges and power. Consequently, during economic liberalization, elites may or may not submit themselves to the rule of laws and institutions. Loaeza concludes that a low level of institutionalization is what distinguishes the process of economic liberalization from that of democratization. Democracy therefore requires a marked separation between the party in power and the state.[31]

Smith highlights the political implications of free trade. In his view, contemporary discussions on free trade in Mexico have been too economistic in substance, too technocratic in tone, and in the political realm, too simplistic and imprecise. After laying out various alternative scenarios concerning free trade and democracy in Mexico, Smith focuses on several political variables necessary to strengthen democracy in the Mexican context: participation, competition, and accountability. He also notes that strengthening political parties would broaden the possibilities for authentic interparty competition, thereby giving citizens real choices and enhancing their participation in the political process.

Schneider also points to the lack of programmatic parties as an obstacle to the consolidation of democracy in Brazil. For example, when Collor ran for president in 1990 without a party coalition and refused endorsements from organizations, not only did he not campaign under a party banner but his "reformist" program also included cutting out intermediaries such as business groups, unions, parties, and other organizations so that he could relate directly to the masses. Without a political coalition or a focused political agenda, Collor made it impossible to cope effectively with the myriad economic problems that he and his administration faced: runaway inflation, high levels of external debt, and a lack of macroeconomic stability. Schneider argues that political and business elites could not reach a negotiated settlement to handle these key issues.

Schneider also identifies Brazil's frayed social fabric as another difficulty in the consolidation of its democracy. Brazilian civil society's lack of organization, combined with tremendous levels of social and economic inequality, makes democratic consolidation questionable. Moreover, poverty is a threat to democracy in Brazil.

In Chapter 13, Remmer challenges the conventional wisdom that authoritarianism has been repeatedly linked with the successful management of economic crises and democracy with failure. She suggests that comparative research indicates that new democracies may be at a distinct advantage in dealing with these issues, claiming that they often enjoy a special reserve of political support and trust that carries them through difficult periods. After studying eleven Latin American regimes from 1982 to 1988 (ten South American nations and Mexico), Remmer writes that newly established democracies have outperformed authoritarian regimes in promoting growth, containing fiscal deficits, and limiting debt burdens. Ultimately, she concludes, the way in which a country responds to economic crisis is not a function of regime characteristics.

On a hopeful note, Remmer challenges those who view new democracies as severely threatened by economic crises, arguing that they are more resilient than conventional thinking indicates. Her assertion does not diminish the many difficulties currently facing democratic regimes in Latin America: the possibility of military intervention, extreme poverty, lack of interparty competition, fraudulent elections, economic austerity, and social inequality. However, despite these many challenges, democracy appears to be surviving, if only tenuously, although no definitive answers explain its future in Latin America. As is often the case, the tools of social science are better at describing what occurs than at predicting future events.

Conclusion

At present, no consensus exists among scholars as to which conditions, variables, or characteristics are most essential to constructing and consolidating a democratic regime. Furthermore, scholars seem unable to develop a general theory to explain democracy's emergence and persistence and continue to disagree on the significance played by political culture, structure, formal democratic institutions, grass-roots democratic practices, and economic crisis management. Yet, progress in the field of democratic theory has been made.

Although the literature is voluminous, many questions remain open for future research: What is the relationship between cultural and structural variables? How do the choices made in the transitional period influence the democratic consolidation? What is the nature of the relationship between politics and economics, generally, and democracy and capitalism specifically? Does economic liberalization establish the foundation for political democracy? This is an exciting time for students of democracy. It is hoped that this volume will provide a useful historical context for current developments in Latin America.

Notes

1. Seymour Martin Lipset, "Some Social Requisites of Democracy: Economic Development and Political Legitimacy," *American Political Science Review* 53 (March 1959): 69–105.

2. Terry Lynn Karl and Philippe C. Schmitter suggest that this is a fourth wave of global democracy and that, unlike its predecessors, it is the product of many causes and its reach is far broader, including Europe, Africa, Asia, and Latin America. They discuss the potential consequences and risks of these dynamic patterns on global politics. See "Democratization Around the Globe: Opportunities and Risks," in *World Security: Challenges for a New Century*, ed. Michael T. Klare and Daniel C. Thomas (New York: St. Martin's Press, 1994), 43–62.

3. For a brief overview of the difficulties facing democratic Latin America, see Peter Hakim and Abraham F. Lowenthal, "Latin America's Fragile Democracies," *Journal of Democracy* 2, no. 3 (Summer 1991): 16–29.

4. Giuseppe Di Palma, *To Craft Democracies: An Essay on Democratic Transitions* (Berkeley: University of California Press, 1990), 16.

5. Samuel P. Huntington, *The Third Wave: Democratization in the Late Twentieth Century* (Norman: University of Oklahoma Press, 1991), 7.

6. Francis Hagopian, "Democracy by Undemocratic Means?: Elites, Political Pacts, and Regime Transition in Brazil," *Comparative Political Studies* 23, no. 2 (July 1990): 151–52.

7. Robert A. Dahl, *Polyarchy: Participation and Opposition* (New Haven: Yale University Press, 1971), 1–2.

8. Hagopian, "Democracy by Undemocratic Means?," 152.

9. Cited in Tamara J. Resler and Roger E. Kanet, "Democratization: The National-Subnational Linkage," *In Depth*, 3, no. 1 (Winter 1993): 12.

10. Ibid. For an excellent discussion of the principles that make democracy feasible, see Philippe C. Schmitter and Terry Lynn Karl, "What Democracy Is . . . and Is Not," *Journal of Democracy* 2, no. 3 (Summer 1991): 75–88.

11. Terry Lynn Karl, "Dilemmas of Democratization in Latin America," *Comparative Politics* 23, no. 1 (October 1990): 1–21.

12. Gabriel Almond and Sydney Verba, eds., *The Civic Culture: Political Attitudes and Democracy in Five Nations* (Princeton: Princeton University Press, 1963).

13. Dankwart A. Rustow, "Transitions to Democracy: Towards a Dynamic Model," *Comparative Politics* 2, no. 3 (April 1970): 343.

14. For example, see Kendall W. Brown and Lissa Roche, eds., *Political and Economic Pluralism in the Third World* (Hillsdale, MI: Hillsdale College Press, 1986), 85–102.

15. Ronald Inglehart, "The Renaissance of Political Culture: Central Values, Political Economy and Stable Democracy" (paper presented at the American Political Science Association Annual Meeting, Chicago, September 2–5, 1987), p. 2, published as "The Renaissance of Political Culture," *American Political Science Review* 82 (November 1988): 1203–30.

16. Ibid., p. 7.

17. See, for example, the work of Lawrence E. Harrison, *Underdevelopment Is a State of Mind: The Latin American Case* (Lanham, MD: Madison Books, 1985). Remarkably, André Gunder Frank, one of the foremost dependency theorists, recanted his views in 1993. See *LACC News* 13, no. 2 (Fall 1993): 3.

18. Cited in Peter F. Klarén, "Lost Promise: Explaining Latin American Underdevelopment," in *Promise of Development: Theories of Change in Latin America*, ed. Peter F. Klarén and Thomas J. Bossert (Boulder, CO: Westview Press, 1986), 17.

19. Michael G. Burton, Richard Gunther, and John Higley, "Introduction: Elite Transformations and Democratic Regimes," in *Elites and Democratic Consolidation in Latin America and Southern Europe*, ed. Michael G. Burton, Richard Gunther, and John Higley (New York: Cambridge University Press, 1991), 10.

20. Guillermo O'Donnell, "Transitions to Democracy: Some Navigation Instruments," in *Democracy in the Americas: Tipping the Pendulum*, ed. Robert Pastor (New York: Holmes and Meier, 1989), 63.

21. Rustow, "Transitions to Democracy," 355.

22. Augusto Varas, "Civil-Military Relations in a Democratic Framework," in *The Military and Democracy: The Future of Civil-Military Relations in Latin America*, ed. Louis W. Goodman et al. (Lexington, KY: Lexington Books, 1990), 199.

23. Burton et al., "Elite Transformations and Democratic Regimes," 24.

24. Di Palma, *To Craft Democracies*, 63.

25. O'Donnell, "Transitions to Democracy," 67.

26. Fernando Henrique Cardoso, "Democracy in Latin America," *Politics and Society* 15, no. 1 (1986–87): 33.

27. Terry Lynn Karl and Philippe Schmitter, "Modes of Transition in Latin America, Southern and Eastern Europe," *International Social Science Journal* 128 (May 1991): 272.

28. Lawrence S. Graham, "Rethinking the Relationship Between the Strength of Local Institutions and the Consolidation of Democracy: The Case of Brazil," *In Depth* 3, no. 1 (Winter 1993): 185.

29. Howard Winant, "The Other Side of the Process: Racial Formation in Contemporary Brazil" (paper presented at the Latin American Studies Association meeting, January 1989), p. 36.

30. For numerous perspectives on the interrelationship between political and economic liberalization generally, see Gabriel Almond, "Capitalism and Democracy," *PS, Political Science and Politics* 24, no. 3 (September 1991): 467–73; for Mexico specifically, see Riordan Roett, ed., *Political and Economic Liberalization in Mexico* (Boulder, CO: Lynne Rienner, 1993).

31. Soledad Loaeza, "La incertdumbre política mexicana," *Nexos* 16, no. 186 (1993): 49.

2

Dilemmas of Democratization in Latin America

Terry Lynn Karl

One of the most difficult problems facing students interested in analyzing the influences of political liberalization and democracy in Latin America is ascertaining the meaning of democracy. Individuals throughout the region and in U.S. policy and academic communities use the word in their discussions, but it does not have the same meaning in different political cultures. Terry Lynn Karl, director of the Center for Latin American Studies at Stanford University, who has written widely in the 1990s on democratization, copes here with the difficulties of conceptualizing democracy, identifying deficiencies in traditional definitions and suggesting some variations appropriate to the Latin American states. She also describes some of the characteristics found in countries making the transition to democracy, including Chile, Brazil, Argentina, and Nicaragua, thereby providing a useful context from which to understand trends in the last decade.

The demise of authoritarian rule in Argentina, Bolivia, Brazil, Chile, Ecuador, Peru, and Uruguay, when combined with efforts at political liberalization in Mexico and the recent election of civilian presidents in Guatemala, El Salvador, Honduras, and Nicaragua, represents a political watershed in Latin America. This wave of regime changes in the 1980s places a number of questions on the intellectual and political agenda for the continent. Will these newly emergent and fragile democracies in South America be able to survive, especially in the context of the worst economic recession since the 1930s? Can the liberalization of authoritarian rule in Central America and the possible prospect of honest competitive elections in Mexico be transformed into genuine democratic transitions?

From *Comparative Politics* 23 (October 1990): 1–21. Reprinted by permission of *Comparative Politics* and the author. Figures omitted.

Will previously consolidated political democracies such as Venezuela and Costa Rica be able to extend the basic principles of citizenship into economic and social realms, or will they be "deconsolidated" by this challenge and revert to a sole preoccupation with survivability?[1]

Behind such questions lies a central concern expressed by Dankwart A. Rustow almost twenty years ago: "What conditions make democracy possible and what conditions make it thrive?"[2] This article addresses Rustow's query by arguing the following. First, the manner in which theorists of comparative politics have sought to understand democracy in developing countries has changed as the once-dominant search for prerequisites of democracy has given way to a more process-oriented emphasis on contingent choice. Having undergone this evolution, theorists should now develop an interactive approach that seeks explicitly to relate structural constraints to the shaping of contingent choice. Second, it is no longer adequate to examine regime transitions writ large, that is, from the general category of authoritarian rule to that of democracy. Such broad-gauged efforts must be complemented by the identification of different types of democracy that emerge from distinctive modes of regime transition as well as an analysis of their potential political, economic, and social consequences. Before these issues and their implications for the study of Latin America can be addressed, however, a definition of democracy must be established.

Defining Democracy

Defining democracy is no simple task because the resolution of a number of disputes over both its prospects and evaluation rests on how the term itself is operationalized. If, for example, democracy is defined in a Schumpeterian manner as a polity that permits the choice between elites by citizens voting in regular and competitive elections, the militarized countries of Central America could be classified as political democracies by many scholars, just as they are (with the exception of Sandinista Nicaragua) by U.S. policymakers.[3] But if the definition is expanded to include a wider range of political conditions—from lack of restrictions on citizen expression, to the absence of discrimination against particular political parties, to freedom of association for all interests, to civilian control over the military—these same countries (with the exception of Costa Rica) could scarcely be classified under this rubric.

The problem is compounded when a number of substantive properties—such as the predominance of institutions that faithfully translate individual preferences into public policy through majoritarian rule, the incorporation of an ever-increasing proportion of the population into the process of decision making, and the continuous improvement of economic equity through the actions of governing institutions—are included as either components or empirical correlates of democratic rule.[4] Approaches that stipulate socioeconomic advances for the majority of the population and active involvement by subordinate classes united in autonomous popular organizations as defining conditions intrinsic to democracy are hard-pressed to find "actual" democratic regimes to study. Often they are incapable of identifying significant, if incomplete, changes toward democratization in the political realm. Moreover, they are cut off from investigating empirically the hypothetical relationship between competitive political forms and progressive economic outcomes because this important issue is assumed away by the very definition of regime type. While these substantive properties are ethically desirable to most democrats, such conceptual breadth renders the definition of democracy virtually meaningless for practical application.[5]

For these reasons, I will settle for a middle-range specification of democracy. It is defined as "a set of institutions that permits the entire adult population to act as citizens by choosing their leading decision makers in competitive, fair, and regularly scheduled elections which are held in the context of the rule of law, guarantees for political freedom, and limited military prerogatives." Specified in this manner, democracy is a political concept involving several dimensions: (1) contestation over policy and political competition for office; (2) participation of the citizenry through partisan, associational, and other forms of collective action; (3) accountability of rulers to the ruled through mechanisms of representation and the rule of law; and (4) civilian control over the military. It is this latter dimension, so important in the Latin American context, which sets my definition apart from Robert Dahl's classic notion of a "procedural minimum."[6] A middle-range definition of this sort avoids the Scylla of an overly narrow reliance on the mere presence of elections without concomitant changes in civil-military relations and the Charybdis of an overly broad assumption of social and economic equality. While perhaps less than fully satisfactory from a normative perspective, it has the advantage of permitting a systematic and objective investigation of the relationship between democratic political forms and the long-range pursuit of equity.

The Futile Search for Democratic Preconditions

If the questions raised by democratization remain relatively unchanged from the past, the answers that are offered today come from a different direction. This becomes evident through a brief comparison of the divergent theories about the origins of democratic regimes that have dominated the study of Latin America. The scholarship that preceded the new wave of democratization in the 1980s argued that a number of preconditions were necessary for the emergence of a stable democratic polity.

First, a certain degree of wealth or, better said, level of capitalist development was considered a prerequisite of democracy. Market economies in themselves were not enough; a country had to cross (and remain beyond) a minimum threshold of economic performance before political competition could be institutionalized. "The more well-to-do a nation," Seymour Martin Lipset claimed, "the greater the chances that it will sustain democracy."[7] A wealthy economy made possible higher levels of literacy, education, urbanization, and mass media exposure, or so the logic went, while also providing resources to mitigate the tensions produced by political conflict.[8]

A second set of preconditions that underlay traditional approaches to democracy was derived from the concept of political culture, that is, the system of beliefs and values in which political action is embedded and given meaning. The prevalence of certain values and beliefs over others was said to be more conducive to the emergence of democracy. Thus, for example, Protestantism allegedly enhanced the prospects for democracy in Europe while Catholicism, with its tradition of hierarchy and intolerance, was posited to have the opposite effect in Latin America.[9] Although arguments based only on the link between different religious systems and experiences with democracy have been dismissed by most scholars, more sophisticated claims sought to identify political cultures characterized by a high degree of mutual trust among members of society, a willingness to tolerate diversity, and a tradition of accommodation or compromise because such cultures were considered necessary for the subsequent development of democratic institutions. That a "civic culture" of this sort necessarily rested on a widely differentiated and articulated social structure with relatively autonomous social classes, occupational sectors, and ethnic, religious, or regional groups was an unspoken assumption. In other words, a prodemocratic consensus and set of values was considered the main prerequisite of political democracy.[10]

Third, specific domestic historical conditions and configurations were said to be prerequisites of democracy. Theorists of "crises and sequences" argued that the order in which various crises of modernization appeared and were settled determined whether economic and social transformations were conducive to the development of democracy. Democratic regimes were more likely to emerge if problems of national identity were resolved prior to the establishment of a central government and if both of these events preceded the formation of mass parties.[11]

In a different, yet still historically grounded vein, Barrington Moore, Jr., contended that democracies were more likely to appear where the social and economic power of the landed aristocracy was in decline relative to that of the bourgeoisie and where labor-repressive agriculture was not the dominant mode of production. When this occurred as a result of the commercialization of agriculture that transformed a traditional peasantry into either a class of small farmers or a rural proletariat, the prognosis for democracy was strong indeed.[12] A version of Moore's approach has been used to explain the different political trajectories in Central America. Specifically, democracy is said to have emerged in Costa Rica because of the creation of a yeoman farmer class, while the persistence of authoritarian rule in Guatemala and El Salvador is attributed to the continued dominance of the landed aristocracy.[13]

Finally, some scholars treated external influences as another set of preconditions on the grounds that these could be decisive in determining whether a polity became democratic or authoritarian. Dependency theorists in Latin America and the United States contended that the continent's particular insertion into the international market made democratization especially problematic at more advanced stages of import-substituting capitalist development and even enhanced the necessity for authoritarian rule under specific circumstances. In a logic that ran counter to Lipset's "optimistic equation," both Guillermo O'Donnell and Fernando Henrique Cardoso argued that, as dependent economies became more complex, more penetrated by foreign capital and technology, and more reliant upon low wages to maintain their competitive advantage in the international economy, professional militaries, technocrats, and state managers moved to the forefront of the decision-making process, forcibly replacing unruly, "populist" parties and trade unions in order to establish a supposedly more efficient form of rule.[14]

Inversely, using an argument based on external influences of a qualitatively different sort, proponents of an aggressive U.S. foreign policy toward the region declared that the rise and decline of democracy was directly related to the rise and decline of the global power of the United States rather than to market mechanisms or accumulation processes. In Samuel Huntington's view, the dramatic increase in authoritarian rule during the 1960s and 1970s was a direct reflection of the waning of U.S. influence. Specifically, it was due to the decreased effectiveness of efforts by U.S. officials to promote democracy as a successful model of development. Concomitantly, he argued, the spate of democratic transitions in the 1980s could be credited to the Reagan administration's renewed effort to "restore American power" throughout the rollback of revolutions and the promotion of electoral reforms. This position, so ideologically convenient for policymakers, located the roots of democracy outside Latin America.[15]

The experience of Latin American countries in the 1980s challenged all of these presumptions about preconditions. The hypothetical association between wealth and democracy might be called upon to "explain" the transition to democracy in Brazil after a protracted economic boom, but it could hardly account for the case of Peru, whose transition was characterized by stagnant growth rates, extreme foreign debt, persistent balance of payments problems, and a regressive distribution of income. Nor could it explain the anomaly of Argentina, where relatively high levels of per capita GDP [gross domestic product] were persistently accompanied by authoritarian rule. If the political cultures of Argentina, Uruguay, and Brazil all tolerated, admittedly to varying degrees, the practice of official state terror and widespread violations of human rights, how could they suddenly become sufficiently "civic" and "tolerant" to support a democratic outcome? As the Catholic Church took an increasingly active role in opposing authoritarian rule, especially in Brazil, Chile, Peru, Central America, and Panama, the argument about the so-called antidemocratic bias of Catholicism became increasingly implausible.[16]

The predictability of approaches emphasizing the influence of the international system fared little better. While the manner of a country's insertion into the world capitalist economy is now considered essential in explaining its subsequent political and economic development, as dependency theorists claimed, criticisms of other scholars plus the democratic transitions in Brazil and Chile demonstrated that there was no direct or inevitable correlation between capital deepening and authoritarian rule.[17] The general trends toward recession in export earnings, debt crises, diminishing U.S. support for human rights, and the frequent resort to military instruments under the foreign policy of the Reagan administration boded ill for the emergence of democracies in the 1980s, yet emerge they did. The pattern of their appearance presented an undeniable challenge to Huntington's thesis linking democratization with the rise of U.S. power. In the Southern Cone, where influence from the north is not especially high, military rulers generally made way for civilian authority. In Central America, Panama, and Haiti, where the overriding historical role of the United States is indisputable, militaries either permitted elections to occur without limiting their own prerogatives or refused to leave power altogether. Indeed, where the decline in U.S. hegemony was greatest, democracy seemed to appear even though dictatorship "should" have been the more appropriate response!

These anomalies suggest the pressing need for important revisions, even reversals, in the way democratization in contemporary Latin America is understood. First, there may be no single precondition that is sufficient to produce such an outcome. The search for causes rooted in economic, social, cultural/psychological, or international factors has not yielded a general law of democratization, nor is it likely to do so in the near future despite the proliferation of new cases.[18] Thus, the search for a set of identical conditions that can account for the presence or absence of democratic regimes should probably be abandoned and replaced by more modest efforts to derive a contextually bounded approach to the study of democratization.

Second, what the literature has in the past considered the preconditions of democracy may be better conceived in the future as the outcomes of democracy. Patterns of greater economic growth and more equitable income distribution, higher levels of literacy and education, and increases in social communication and media exposure may be better treated as the products of stable democratic processes rather than as the prerequisites of its existence. A "civic" political culture characterized by high levels of mutual trust, a willingness to tolerate diversity of opinion, and a propensity for accommodation and compromise could be the result of the protracted functioning of democratic institutions that generate appropriate values and beliefs rather than a set of cultural obstacles that must be initially overcome. There is evidence for this contention in the fact that most democracies in Europe and Latin America's oldest democracy in Costa Rica have emerged from quite "uncivic" warfare. In other words, what have been emphasized as independent variables in the past might be more fruitfully conceived as dependent variables in the future.

From Contingent Choice to Structured Contingency

The failure to identify clear prerequisites, plus the hunch that much of what had been thought to produce democracy should be considered as its product, has caused theorists of comparative politics to shift their attention to the strategic calculations, unfolding processes, and sequential patterns that are involved in moving from one type of political regime to another, especially under conditions of nonviolence, gradualism, and social continuity. For Guillermo O'Donnell and Philippe Schmitter, democratization is understood as a historical process with analytically distinct, if empirically overlapping, stages of transition, consolidation, persistence, and eventual deconsolidation.[19] A variety of actors with different followings, preferences, calculations, resources, and time horizons come to the fore during these successive stages. For example, elite factions and social movements seem to play the key roles in bringing about the demise of authoritarian rule; political parties move to center stage during the transition itself; and business associations, trade unions, and state agencies become major determinants of the type of democracy that is eventually consolidated.[20]

What differentiates these stages above all, as Adam Przeworski points out, is the degree of uncertainty which prevails at each moment. During regime transitions, all political calculations and interactions are highly uncertain. Actors find it difficult to know what their interests are, who their supporters will be, and which groups will be their allies or opponents. The armed forces and the civilian supporters of the incumbent authoritarian regime are characteristically divided between "hard-line" and "soft-line" factions. Political parties emerge as privileged in this context because, despite their divisions over strategies and their uncertainties about partisan identities, the logic of electoral competition focuses public attention on them and compels them to appeal to the widest possible clientele. The only certainty is that "founding elections" will eliminate those who make important miscalculations.

The absence of predictable "rules of the game" during a regime transition expands the boundaries of contingent choice. Indeed, the dynamics of the transition revolve around strategic interactions and tentative arrangements between actors with uncertain power resources aimed at defining who will legitimately be entitled to play in the political game, what criteria will determine the winners and losers, and what limits will be placed on the issues at stake. From this perspective, regime consolidation occurs when contending social classes and political groups come to accept some set of formal rules or informal understandings that determine "who gets what, where, when, and how" from politics. In so doing, they settle into predictable positions and legitimate behaviors by competing according to mutually acceptable rules. Electoral outcomes may still be uncertain with regard to person or party, but in consolidated democracies they are firmly surrounded by normative limits and established patterns of power distribution.

The notion of contingency (meaning that outcomes depend less on objective conditions than subjective rules surrounding strategic choice) has the advantage of stressing collective decisions and political interactions that have largely been underemphasized in the search for preconditions. But this understanding of democracy has the danger of descending into excessive voluntarism if it is not explicitly placed within a framework of structural-historical constraints. Even in the midst of the tremendous uncertainty provoked by a regime transition, where constraints appear to be most relaxed and where a wide range of outcomes appears possible, the decisions made by various actors respond to and are conditioned by the types of socioeconomic structures and political institutions already present. These can be decisive in that they may either restrict or enhance the options available to different political actors attempting to construct democracy.

For example, certain social structures seem to make the emergence of political democracy highly improbable; inversely, it is reasonable to presume that their absence may make accommodative strategies more viable and reinforce the position of democratic actors. Political democracies have lasted only in countries where the landed class, generally the most recalcitrant of interests, has played a secondary role in the export economy—for example, Venezuela and Chile—or where non-labor-repressive agriculture has predominated—for example, Costa Rica, Argentina, and Uruguay. Thus, the survivability of political democracy does seem to depend on a structural space defined in part by the absence of a strong landowner elite engaged in labor-repressive agriculture or its subordination to interests tied to other economic activities.[21]

The cases of Venezuela and Chile better make the point. In Venezuela, dependence upon petroleum as the leading source of foreign exchange had the (unintended) effect of hastening the decline of that country's already stagnant agriculture and, with it, the landowning elite. Faced with overvalued exchange rates that hurt agro-exports and abundant foreign reserves for importing cheap foodstuffs, landowners sold their property to oil companies and converted themselves into a commercial and financial urban bourgeoisie. This largely voluntary self-liquidation removed the incentive for them to commercialize rural areas, to subordinate the peasantry through repressive means, and eventually to maintain authoritarian rule. It also removed the social base for an antisystem party of the right. Thus, actors designing pact-making strategies in Venezuela during the regime transition in 1958 did not face powerfully organized antidemocratic rural elites.[22] Social dynamics in Chile, though different, had the same effect. Conservative elements based in a system of labor-repressive agriculture eventually supported the expansion of the suffrage in the nineteenth century as a means of combating the rising power of industrialists and *capas medias*, who were tied to the state and supported by revenues from copper.[23] In effect, the social impact of the dominant presence of mineral exports meant that, when compared to the cases of Central America, both Venezuela and Chile were able to institutionalize democratic agreements with relative ease.

These cases illustrate the limits, as well as the opportunities, that social structures place upon contingent choice. If the focus in explaining the emergence of democracy had been solely on the forging of institutional compromises, that is, conceptualizing the establishment of democracy as only the product of strategic interactions, the pact-making that characterized the Venezuelan transition and the gradual expansion of the suffrage in Chile would appear to be simply the result of skillful bargaining by astute political leaders.[24] Instead, by focusing on the internal social dynamics produced by a mineral-based insertion into the international economy, it becomes evident how oil- or copper-induced structural change makes such "statecraft" possible. This is not to argue that individual decisions made at particular points in time or all observable political outcomes can be specifically and neatly linked to preexisting structures, but it is claimed that historically created structures, while not determining which one of a limited set of alternatives political actors may choose, are "confining conditions" that restrict or in some cases enhance the choices available to them. In other words, structural and institutional constraints determine the range of options available to decision makers and may even predispose them to choose a specific option.

What is called for, then, is a path-dependent approach which clarifies how broad structural changes shape particular regime transitions in ways that may be especially conducive to (or especially obstructive of) democratization. This needs to be combined with an analysis of how such structural changes become embodied in political institutions and rules which subsequently mold the preferences and capacities of individuals during and after regime changes. In this way, it should be possible to demonstrate how the range of options available to decision makers at a given point in time is a function of structures put in place in an earlier period and, concomitantly, how such decisions are conditioned by institutions established in the past. The advantages of this method are evident when compared to a structural approach alone, which leads to excessively deterministic conclusions about the origins and prospects of democracy, or to a sole focus on contingency, which produces overly voluntaristic interpretations.[25]

Modes of Transition to Democracy

Once the links between structures, institutions, and contingent choice are articulated, it becomes apparent that the arrangements made by key political actors during a regime transition establish new rules, roles, and behavioral patterns which may or may not represent an important rupture with the past. These, in turn, eventually become the institutions shaping the prospects for regime consolidation in the future. Electoral laws, once adopted, encourage some interests to enter the political arena and discourage others. Certain models of economic development, once initiated through some form of compromise between capital and labor, systematically favor some groups over others in patterns that become difficult to change. Accords between political parties and the armed forces set out the initial parameters of civilian and military spheres. Thus, what at the time may appear to be temporary agreements often become persistent barriers to change, barriers that can even scar a new regime with a permanent "birth defect."

These observations have important implications for studying democracy in Latin America. Rather than engage in what may be a futile search for new preconditions, they suggest that scholars would do well to concentrate on several tasks: (1) clarifying how the mode of regime transition (itself conditioned by the breakdown of authoritarian rule) sets the context within which strategic interactions can take place; (2) examining how these interactions, in turn, help to determine whether political democracy will emerge and survive; and (3) analyzing what type of democracy will eventually be institutionalized.

Thus, it is important to begin to distinguish between possible modes of transition to democracy. First, we can differentiate cases in which democracies are the outcome of a strategy based primarily on overt force from those in which democracies arise from compromise. . . . Second, we can distinguish between transitions in which incumbent ruling groups, no matter how weakened, are still ascendant in relation to mass actors and those in which mass actors have gained the upper hand, even temporarily, vis-à-vis those dominant elites. . . . These distinctions produce four ideal types of democratic transition: reform, revolution, imposition, and pact.

Latin America, at one time or another, has experienced all four modes of transition. To date, however, *no* stable political democracy has resulted from regime transitions in which mass actors have gained control, even momentarily, over traditional ruling classes. Efforts at reform from below, which have been characterized by unrestricted contestation and participation, have met with subversive opposition from unsuppressed traditional elites, as the cases of Argentina (1946–1951), Guatemala (1946–1954), and Chile (1970–1973) demonstrate.[26] Revolutions generally produce stable forms of governance (Bolivia is an obvious exception), but such forms have not yet evolved into democratic patterns of fair competition, unrestricted contestation, rotation in power, and free associability, although developments in Nicaragua and Mexico may soon challenge this assertion.[27]

Thus far, the most frequently encountered types of transition, and the ones which have most often resulted in the implantation of a political democracy, are "transitions from above." Here traditional rulers remain in control, even if pressured from below, and successfully use strategies of either compromise or force—or some mix of the two—to retain at least part of their power.

Of these two modes of transition, democratization by pure imposition is the least common in Latin America—unless we incorporate cases in which force or the threat of force is applied by foreign as well as domestic actors. This is not the case for both Europe and Asia, where democratization through imposition often followed in the wake of World War II. [For example, cases of] imposition include Brazil and Ecuador, where the military used its dominant position to establish unilaterally the rules for civilian governance. Cases on the margin include Costa Rica (where in 1948 an opposition party militarily defeated the governing party but then participated in pact-making to lay the foundation for stable democratic rule), Venezuela (1945–1948) and Peru (where the military's control over the timing and shape of the transition was strongly influenced by a mass popular movement),[28] and Chile (where the military's unilateralism was curbed somewhat by its defeat in the 1988 plebiscite).[29]

Where democracies that have endured for a respectable length of time appear to cluster is in [a] cell defined by relatively strong elite actors who engage in strategies of compromise. This cell includes the cases of Venezuela (1958–), Colombia (1958–), the recent redemocratization in Uruguay (1984–), and Chile (1932–1970).[30] What unites all of these diverse cases, except Chile, is the presence of foundational *pacts*, that is, explicit (though not always public) agreements between contending actors, which define the rules of governance on the basis of mutual guarantees for the "vital interests" of those involved. Chile appears to be an exception because there was no explicit pact or agreement among elites in 1932, when the democratic regime was simply "restored" on the basis of preexisting constitutional rules left over from the first democratic transition in 1874. While the Chilean case suggests that elite-based democracies can be established in the absence of foundational pacts, this may be more difficult in the contemporary period, which is characterized by more developed organized interests, the presence of mass politics, stronger military capabilities, and a tighter integration into the international market. Under such conditions, *pactismo* may prove to be essential.[31]

Foundational pacts are well exemplified by the case of Venezuela. Here a series of agreements negotiated by the military, economic, and party leaders rested on explicit institutional arrangements.[32] The military agreed to leave power and to accept a new role as an "apolitical, obedient, and nondeliberative body" in exchange for an amnesty for abuses committed during authoritarian rule and a guaranteed improvement of the economic situation of officers. Political parties agreed to respect the electoral process and share power in a manner commensurate with the voting results. They also accepted a "prolonged political truce" aimed at depersonalizing debate and facilitating consultation and coalitions. Capitalists agreed to accept legal trade unions and collective bargaining in exchange for significant state subsidies, guarantees against expropriation or socializing property, and promises of labor peace from workers' representatives. This arrangement changed what could have become potentially explosive issues of national debate into established parameters by removing them from the electoral arena.

The foundational pacts underlying some new democracies have several essential components. First, they are necessarily comprehensive and inclusive of virtually all politically significant actors. Indeed, because pacts are negotiated compromises in which contending forces agree to forego their capacity to harm one another by extending guarantees not to threaten each other's vital interests, they are successful only when they include all significantly threatening interests. Thus, the typical foundational pact is actually a series of agreements that are interlocking and dependent upon each other; it necessarily includes an agreement between the military and civilians over the conditions for establishing civilian rule, an agreement between political parties to compete under the new rules of governance, and a "social contract" between state agencies, business associations, and trade unions regarding property rights, market arrangements, and the distribution of benefits.

Second, while such pacts are both substantive (about the main tenets of policy) and procedural (about the rules of policymaking), they initially emphasize rule making because "bargaining about bargaining" is the first and most important stage in the process of compromise. Only after all contending forces have agreed to bargain over their differences can the power-sharing which leads to consensual governance result. This initial bargain can begin to lay the basis for mutual trust if only by building up reserves of familiarity between opposing groups. Subsequently, the very decision to enter into a pact can create a habit of pact making and an accommodative political style based on a "pact to make pacts."

Such foundational pacts must be differentiated from smaller, more partial "managerial" accords.[33] These include the neofunctional arrangements frequently found in social democratic polities in Europe, for example, the annual corporatist negotiations among capital, labor, and the state in postwar Austria for setting wages and social policy as well as the frequent mini-accords hammered out between political opponents in Latin America. Unlike foundational pacts, managerial accords are partial rather than comprehensive, exclusionary rather than inclusionary, and substantively oriented rather than rule making in content. These characteristics of comprehensiveness, inclusion, and rule making are critical in identifying the presence of a foundational pact. They help distinguish between basic agreements, like those present in Venezuela in 1958, and more transitory political deals, like the Pact of Apaneca, which was forged in El Salvador in 1983 between the Christian Democratic Party and ARENA [Alianza Republícana Nacionalista].[34]

Finally, these pacts serve to ensure survivability because, although they are inclusionary, they are simultaneously aimed at restricting the scope of representation in order to reassure traditional dominant classes that their vital interests will be respected. In essence, they are antidemocratic mechanisms, bargained by elites, which seek to create a deliberate socioeconomic and political contract that demobilizes emerging mass actors while delineating the extent to which all actors can participate or wield power in the future. They may accomplish this task by restricting contestation (as Colombian parties did in 1958 by agreeing to alternate in power regardless of the outcome of elections), by restricting the policy agenda itself (as Venezuelan parties did in 1958 by agreeing to implement the same economic program), or by restricting the franchise (as Chilean elites did beginning with the electoral law of 1874). Regardless of which strategic option is chosen, the net effect of these options is the same: the nature and parameters of the initial democracy that results is markedly circumscribed.

Types of Democracies and Their Prospects in the Contemporary Period

What are the implications of this excursus into preconditions and modes of transition for the prospects of democratization in contemporary Latin America? To begin with, the notion of unfolding processes and sequences from regime breakdown to transition to consolidation and persistence is fundamental in understanding the two concurrent realities of democratization in Latin America today. On the one hand, most of the newly emergent civilian or militarized civilian regimes—Argentina, Chile, Peru, Ecuador, Guatemala, Honduras, El Salvador, and Nicaragua—face the overwhelming problem of sheer survivability. What threatens their survival is the omnipresent specter of a military coup, a coup which may be provoked by intense partisan political disagreements, by the inability of political parties to manage the current profound economic crisis of the region, by the actions of antisystem elites, by a mass mobilization of labor, peasants, or the urban poor that escapes the control of traditional dominant classes, by the actions of a foreign power, or by threats to the vital corporate interests of the military itself. Significant uncertainty over the rules of the game still prevails in these fragile democracies.

What becomes important in maintaining civilian rule is to find mechanisms—other than rigged or unpredictable elections—that can limit this
uncertainty, especially by reducing incentives for civilians on the losing
end to appeal to the military for salvation. This suggests that there are
two critical tasks initially facing Latin American democratizers: first, to
arrive at a sufficiently strong consensus about the rules of the game (including institutional formalities guaranteeing respect for certain crucial
but minoritarian concerns) so that no major elite is tempted to call upon
the military to protect its vital interests and, second, to begin to design
conscious strategies for the establishment of qualitatively new civil-
military relations appropriate to future stable civilian rule. This is probably easier to accomplish in the more developed regions of the continent,
where the armed forces have learned the importance of cooperating with
capitalist and managerial elites, than in the less developed ones (Bolivia,
Central America, and the Caribbean), where the military still retains relatively confident notions of its ability to manage the economy and polity
or is simply too corrupt to worry about such matters.[35]

On the other hand, other types of democracies in the region—
Venezuela, Costa Rica, and, more recently, Brazil and Uruguay—are relatively consolidated in that actors are not so preoccupied by the overriding
concern with survivability. Rather, the challenge that confronts most of
these polities (and that will certainly confront newer democracies as preoccupation with mere survivability recedes) is providing some new and
better resolution to the ancient question of *cui bono*. This issue of "who
benefits" from democracy is singularly problematic in Latin America,
where the pattern of dependent capitalist development has been especially
ruthless in its historic patterns of exploitation.[36] This means that the
extension of citizenship and equal political rights must take place in a
context of extreme inequality, which is unparalleled even in Africa or
Asia.[37] It must also take place during *la decada perdida*, that is to say, in
the midst of the most severe and prolonged economic crisis since the
Depression.[38]

The relationship between the problematics of survivability and *cui
bono* may well represent the central dilemma of democratization in Latin
America. The choices made by key political actors to ensure the survivability of a fragile democracy—the compromises they make, the agreements they enter into—will necessarily and even irrevocably affect who
gains and who loses during the consolidation of a new regime. Subsequent "populist" decisions to redistribute gains without regard for losses
may affect the durability of the regime itself, regardless of how consolidated it may appear to be. At the same time, decisions *not* to redistribute
or inaction on this front may also influence regime durability because the

commitment to democracy in part rests on the widely held (if sometimes inaccurate) conviction that economic benefits will be more fairly distributed or the welfare of the general population improved under this type of polity. Hence the current concern with both survivability and "who benefits" merely underlines the significance of choices made during the founding moments of democracies and highlights some potential relationships between political democracy and economic outcomes for future research. It also produces some not-so-promising scenarios for the emergence of different types of democracies.

First, political democracy in Latin America may be rooted in a fundamental paradox: the very modes of transition that appear to enhance initial survivability by limiting unpredictability may preclude the future democratic self-transformation of the economy or polity further down the road. Ironically, the conditions that permit democracies to persist in the short run may constrain their potential for resolving the enormous problems of poverty and inequality that continue to characterize the continent. Indeed, it is reasonable to hypothesize that what occurs in the phase of transition or early consolidation may involve a significant trade-off between some form of political democracy, on the one hand, and equity, on the other. Thus, even as these democracies guarantee a greater respect for law and human dignity when compared to their authoritarian predecessors, they may be unable to carry out substantive reforms that address the lot of their poorest citizens. If this scenario should occur, they would become the victims of their successful consolidation, and the democratic transitions of the 1980s that survive could prove to be the "frozen" democracies of the 1990s.

Second, while this may be the central dilemma of elite-ascendant processes of democratization, there may be important differences between countries like Uruguay, a pacted transition, and Brazil, a unilaterally imposed transition. Pacted democracies, whatever their defects, have been honed through compromise between at least two powerful contending elites. Thus, their institutions should reflect some flexibility for future bargaining and revision over existing rules. In Uruguay, for example, while the agreed-upon rules made it very difficult to challenge agreements between the military and the parties on the issue of amnesty for crimes committed during authoritarian rule, the left opposition, excluded from this agreement, was nevertheless able to force the convocation of a plebiscite on this major issue, which it subsequently lost. It is difficult to imagine that anything similar could occur in Brazil. Because the military exerted almost complete control over the transition, it never curtailed its own prerogatives or fully agreed to the principle of civilian control, and it has not been compelled to adopt institutional rules reflecting the need for compromise.

The contrast between the cases of Uruguay and Brazil raises a hypothesis that merits investigation: to the extent that transitions are unilaterally imposed by armed forces who are not compelled to enter into compromises, they threaten to evolve into civilian governments controlled by authoritarian elements who are unlikely to push for greater participation, accountability, or equity for the majority of their citizens. Paradoxically, in other words, the heritage left by "successful" authoritarian experiences, that is, those characterized by relatively moderate levels of repression and economic success which has left the military establishment relatively intact, may prove to be the major obstacle to future democratic self-transformation.[39] This danger exists, albeit to a lesser extent, in civilian-directed unilateral transitions, for example, Mexico, because the institutional rules that are imposed are likely to favor incumbents and permit less scope for contestation.

Third, the attempt to assess possible consequences of various modes of transition is most problematic where strong elements of imposition, compromise, and reform are simultaneously present, that is to say, where neither incumbent elites nor newly ascendant power contenders are clearly in control and where the armed forces are relatively intact. This is currently the case in Argentina and Peru. Given the Argentine military's defeat in the Falklands/Malvinas war, the high level of mass mobilization during the transition, and the absence of pacts between civilian authority and the armed forces, on the one hand, and trade unions and employers, on the other, Argentina combines elements of several modes of transition. Such a mixed scenario, while perhaps holding out the greatest hope for political democracy and economic equity, may render a consistent strategy of any type ineffectual and thus lead to the repetition of Argentina's persistent failure to consolidate any type of regime. The prospects for failure are even greater in Peru. Given the absence of explicit agreements between the leading political parties, the possibility of mass mobilizations in the midst of economic depression, the presence of an armed insurgency, and a unified military, Peru is currently the most fragile democracy in South America.

Fourth, because political democracies generally arise from a compromise between contending organized elites that are unable to impose their will unilaterally or the unilateral action of one dominant group, usually the armed forces, this does not bode well for democratization in situations in which the armed forces are inextricably tied to the interests of a dominant (and antidemocratic) agrarian class. Guatemala and

El Salvador in particular are characterized by a landowning elite whose privileged position is based on labor-repressive agriculture and on a virtual partnership with the armed forces, thereby making it unlikely that their militaries (as currently constituted) will tolerate comprehensive political competitiveness, civil liberties, or accountability. Regardless of the profound differences between these two Central American countries, the extraordinary pressure of U.S. intervention as well as international diffusion means that, at minimum, they can be expected to adhere to "electoralism," meaning the regularized holding of elections, even as they continue to restrict the other political rights and opportunities of their citizens. This hybrid mix of electoral forms and authoritarianism, which has been dubbed "electocratic rule" by one observer,[40] is likely to emerge in other developing areas wherever the spread of elections under foreign inspiration either precedes or is intended to co-opt strong domestic pressures for democratization.

These observations can be distilled into types of democracies, which, at least initially, are largely shaped by the mode of transition in Latin America. They suggest that democratization by imposition is likely to yield conservative democracies that cannot or will not address equity issues. To the extent that imposition originates from outside, however, the result is likely to be some form of electoral authoritarian rule, which cannot be considered democracy at all. Pacted transitions are likely to produce corporatist or consociational democracies in which party competition is regulated to varying degrees determined, in part, by the nature of foundational bargains. Transition through reform is likely to bring about competitive democracies, whose political fragility paves the way for an eventual return to authoritarianism. Finally, revolutionary transitions tend to result in one-party dominant democracies, where competition is also regulated. These types are characterized by different mixes and varying degrees of the chief dimensions of democracy: contestation, participation, accountability, and civilian control over the military.

Such predictions are discouraging, but they may be offset by more hopeful observations that affect the contingent choices of contemporary democratizers. On the one hand, the Cold War features of the international system have changed remarkably, and this may offer new opportunities for the reformist mode of transition in Latin America. The failure of two of the three cases cited in this category, Guatemala (1946–1954) and Chile (1970–1973), was profoundly affected by U.S. intervention, motivated in large part by the ideological identification of mass-based reforms with the spread of Soviet influence in the Western Hemisphere. U.S. intervention against peasant-based movements in Central America has been justified in the same manner. To the extent that the global state system loses its "bipolarity," the credibility of such accusations becomes increasingly difficult to sustain, thus potentially creating more space for mass ascendant political movements. The fact that this mode of transition failed in the past in Latin America does not mean that it will not succeed in the future.[41]

On the other hand, this discussion of modes of transition and varying probabilities for survival has not presumed that democracies will benefit from superior economic performance, which is fortunate given the state of contemporary Latin American economies. Most observers assume that crises in growth, employment, foreign exchange earnings, and debt re-payments necessarily bode ill for the consolidation of democratic rule, and few would question the long-run value of an increasing resource base for stability. But austerity may have some perverse advantages, at least for initial survivability. In the context of the terrible economic conditions of the 1980s, the exhaustion of utopian ideologies and even of rival policy prescriptions has become painfully evident. Neither the extreme Right nor the extreme Left has a plausible alternative system to offer—to them-selves or to mass publics. Though populism, driven by diffuse popular expectations and *desencanto* [disenchantment] with the rewards of com-promised democracy, is always a possibility—witness the experience of Peru and the recent elections in Argentina—it cannot deliver the immedi-ate rewards that have been its sustenance in the past.

To the extent that this situation diminishes both the expected benefits and rewards from antisystem activity, it enhances the likelihood of de-mocracies to endure. This suggests a possible hypothesis for future ex-ploration. The relationship between democratization and economic performance, rather than rising or falling in tandem, may be parabolic. Conditions to strike bargains may be most favorable in the midst of pro-tracted austerity, as well as in the midst of sustained plenty. They may be worse when the economy is going through stop-and-go cycles or being hit with sudden windfalls or scarcities. If true, this provides a ray of hope for the otherwise unpromising decade ahead.

Finally, there is no a priori reason why one type of democracy cannot be transformed into another, that is to say, why electoral authoritarian regimes, for example, cannot evolve into conservative or competitive democracies, or corporatist democracies into more competitive ones. Given the frequency of *pactismo* and the gravity of the equity problem in Latin America, the latter scenario is especially important. While pacted transi-tions establish an improvisational institutional framework of governance that may become a semipermanent barrier to change, this framework is subject to further modification in the future. Such modification may be brought about preemptively when some ruling groups, having experienced the advantages of democratic rule, become more inclined over time to seek to accommodate potential pressures from below rather than suppress them, or it may occur through the direct pressure of organized social groups.[42] In either case, democratization can prove to be an ongoing process of renewal.

The notion that one type of democracy may gradually evolve into a qualitatively different type suggests that the dynamics of democratic consolidation must differ in important ways from the transition if "freezing" is to be avoided. Because the overriding goal of the transition is to reach some broad social consensus about the goals of society and the acceptable means to achieve them, successful transitions are necessarily characterized by accommodation and compromise. But if this emphasis on caution becomes an *overriding* political norm during consolidation, democracies may find it difficult to demonstrate that they are better than their predecessors at resolving fundamental social and economic problems. Thus, consolidation, if it is to be successful, should require skills and commitments from leading actors which are qualitatively different from those exhibited during the transition. In this latter phase, these actors must demonstrate the ability to differentiate political forces rather than to draw them all into a grand coalition, the capacity to define and channel competing political projects rather than seek to keep potentially divisive reforms off the agenda, and the willingness to tackle incremental reforms, especially in the domains of the economy and civil-military relations, rather than defer them to some later date. If the cycle of regime change that has plagued Latin America is to be broken and replaced by an era of protracted democratic rule, democratizers must learn to divide as well as to unite and to raise hopes as well as to dampen expectations.

Notes

1. These questions underlie a number of new studies on democracy. See, for example, Guillermo O'Donnell, Philippe Schmitter, and Laurence Whitehead, eds., *Transitions from Authoritarian Rule*, 4 vols. (Baltimore: The Johns Hopkins University Press, 1986); Paul W. Drake and Eduardo Silva, eds., *Elections and Democratization in Latin America, 1980–1985* (San Diego: Center for Iberian and Latin American Studies, University of California, 1986); Enrique A. Baloyra, *Comparing New Democracies: Transition and Consolidation in Mediterranean Europe and the Southern Cone* (Boulder, CO: Westview Press, 1987); Carlos Huneeus, *Para Vivir La Democracia* (Santiago: Editorial Andante, 1987); and Larry Diamond, Juan J. Linz, and Seymour Martin Lipset, eds., *Democracy in Developing Countries*, 4 vols. (Boulder, CO: Lynne Rienner, 1988–1990).

2. See Dankwart A. Rustow, "Transitions to Democracy: Towards a Dynamic Model," *Comparative Politics* 2 (April 1970).

3. This statement requires some qualification. J. A. Schumpeter defines democracy as "that institutional arrangement for arriving at political decisions in which individuals acquire the power to decide by means of a competitive struggle for the people's vote" in *Capitalism, Socialism and Democracy* (London: Geo. Allen and Unwin, 1943), 269. Under this definition the competition for leadership through free elections is the distinctive feature of democracy. But Schumpeter, unlike Jeane Kirkpatrick and other U.S. policymakers in the 1980s, considered civil liberties a necessary condition for the operation of democracy. Thus, it cannot be assumed that he would have shared the current emphasis on the mere presence of elections, which I have elsewhere referred to as "electoralism," that is, "the faith that merely holding elections will channel political action into peaceful contests among elites and accord public legitimacy to the winners in these contests." See Terry Lynn Karl, "Imposing Consent? Electoralism Versus Democratization in El Salvador," in Drake and Silva, eds., 34.

4. For an example of this approach, see Suzanne Jonas, "Elections and Transitions: The Guatemalan and Nicaraguan Case," in *Elections and Democracy in Central America*, ed. John Booth and Mitchell Seligson (Chapel Hill: University of North Carolina Press, 1989). Jonas and Stein argue against separating political democracy from socioeconomic equity and support "a broader view that meaningful 'transitions to democracy' [in Central America] involve more sweeping social change on the scale of the major bourgeois and socialist revolutions historically." See Suzanne Jonas and Nancy Stein, "Democracy in Nicaragua," in *Democracy in Latin America*, ed. Suzanne Jonas and Nancy Stein (New York: Bergin and Garvey Publishers, 1990), 43.

5. In examining the problem of constructing institutions that can translate the preferences of majorities into public policy, for example, social choice theorists have demonstrated the difficulty of designing decision-making procedures that give equal weight to the preferences of all citizens and that permit the aggregation of these preferences into governmental policies without violating any of the other basic tenets of democratic theory. See, for example, William H. Riker, *Liberalism Versus Populism: A Confrontation Between the Theory of Democracy and the Theory of Social Choice* (San Francisco: W. H. Freeman and Co., 1982), and the review by Jules Coleman and John Ferejohn, "Democracy and Social Choice," *Ethics* 97 (October 1986). Theorists of democracy have long grappled with other dilemmas involving notions of social justice and equity. See, for example, Peter Bachrach, *The Theory of Democratic Elitism: A Critique* (Washington, DC: University Press of America, 1980); and Carole Pateman, *Participation and Democratic Theory* (New York: Cambridge University Press, 1970).

6. I have drawn the first two dimensions and, to some extent, the third from Robert A. Dahl, *Polyarchy: Participation and Opposition* (New Haven: Yale University Press, 1971). But Dahl, like other democratic theorists, does not emphasize the establishment of civilian control over the military through the limitation of military prerogatives. Indeed, this dimension often appears to be an assumed condition or even an unstated prerequisite in other definitions of democracy. Alfred Stepan, *Rethinking Military Politics: Brazil and the Southern Cone* (Princeton: Princeton University Press, 1988), is an important corrective in this regard. Stepan defines the military's institutional prerogatives as "those areas where, whether challenged or not, the military as an institution assumes they have an acquired right or privilege, formal or informal, to exercise effective control over its internal governance, to play a role within extra-military areas within

the state apparatus, or even to structure relationships between the state and political or civil society" (p. 93). The clear determination and limitation of these areas are a measure of civilian control and, in my view, are also a measure of democratization.

7. This formulation originally appeared in Seymour Martin Lipset, "Some Social Requisites of Democracy: Economic Development and Political Legitimacy," *American Political Science Review* 53 (March 1959).

8. Some proponents of this view often measured the prospects for democracy by per capita gross domestic product, leading the occasional political observer to await the moment when a particular country would cross "the threshold" into democracy. This supposed threshold has varied from country to country. Spain's López Redo once predicted that his country would not become democratic until it reached a per capita income of $2,000. More recently, Mitchell Seligson has argued that Central America needs to approach a per capita income of $250 (in 1957 dollars) and a literacy rate of over 50 percent as a necessary precondition for democratization. See James M. Malloy and Mitchell A. Seligson, eds., *Authoritarians and Democrats: Regime Transition in Latin America* (Pittsburgh: University of Pittsburgh Press, 1987), 7–9.

9. For example, Howard Wiarda, "Toward a Framework for the Study of Political Change in the Iberic-Latin Tradition: The Corporative Model," in *Corporatism and National Development in Latin America*, ed. Howard Wiarda (Boulder, CO: Westview Press, 1981), argued that Latin America possessed "a political culture and a sociopolitical order that at its core is essentially two-class, authoritarian, traditional, elitist, patrimonial, Catholic, stratified, hierarchical and corporate." A similar argument can be found in Richard N. Morse, "The Heritage of Latin America," in *Politics and Social Change in Latin America*, ed. Howard Wiarda (Amherst: University of Massachusetts Press, 1974).

10. The notion of "civic culture," first introduced by Gabriel Almond and Sidney Verba in *The Civic Culture* (Princeton: Princeton University Press, 1963), sought to analyze the relationship between the political attitudes of a population and the nature of its political system. It was the forerunner of the works on Latin America cited above.

11. This was the basic argument put forward by Leonard Binder et al., eds., *Crises and Sequences in Political Development* (Princeton: Princeton University Press, 1971), and by Eric Nordlinger, "Political Development, Time Sequences and Rates of Change," in *Political Development and Social Change*, 2nd ed., ed. Jason L. Finkle and Robert W. Gable (New York: John Wiley, 1971).

12. See Barrington Moore, Jr., *Social Origins of Dictatorship and Democracy* (Boston: Beacon Press, 1966).

13. See John Weeks, "An Interpretation of the Central American Past," *Latin American Research Review* 21 (1986); Enrique Baloyra-Herp, "Reactionary Despotism in Central America," *Journal of Latin American Studies* 15 (1983); and Jeffrey Paige, "Coffee and Politics in Central America," in *Crisis in the Caribbean Basin*, ed. Richard Tardanico (Beverly Hills: Sage Publications, 1987). In a more recent work, Paige seeks to differentiate his argument from that of Moore. He correctly contends that there is no collision between an industrial bourgeoisie and a landed class in either Costa Rica, El Salvador, or Nicaragua and that the agrarian aristocracy has successfully transformed itself into a modern capitalist class, both conditions that belie Moore's argument. Nonetheless, in Guatemala and El Salvador a landed class continues to exercise domination, and the com-

mercialization of agriculture has not replaced a labor-repressive mode of production, thus providing some important confirmation of Moore. See Jeffrey Paige, "The Social Origins of Dictatorship, Democracy and Socialist Revolution in Central America" (paper presented at the annual meeting of the American Sociological Association, San Francisco, August 8, 1989).

14. See Guillermo O'Donnell, *Modernization and Bureaucratic-Authoritarianism* (Berkeley: University of California, Institute for International Studies, 1973), and Fernando Henrique Cardoso, "Associated-Dependent Development: Theoretical and Practical Implications," in *Authoritarian Brazil*, ed. Alfred Stepan (New Haven: Yale University Press, 1973): 142–78.

15. See Samuel P. Huntington, "Will More Countries Become Democratic?" *Political Science Quarterly* 99 (1984).

16. Furthermore, through the Church's active promotion of "base communities," it could even be argued that contemporary Catholicism contributes to the creation of a uniquely democratic culture by encouraging participation among previously unorganized groups of the urban and rural poor. See Philip Oxborn, "Bringing the Base Back In: The Democratization of Civil Society under the Chilean Authoritarian Regime" (Ph.D. diss., Harvard University, 1989).

17. For criticism of the O'Donnell hypothesis linking capital deepening to authoritarian rule, see David Collier, ed., *The New Authoritarianism in Latin America* (Princeton: Princeton University Press, 1979), and Karen Remmer and Gilbert Merkx, "Bureaucratic-Authoritarianism Revisited," *Latin American Research Review* 17 (1982).

18. Albert Hirschman has even claimed that this search can be pernicious. In his view, to lay down strict preconditions for democracy—"dynamic growth *must* be resumed, income distribution *must* be improved, . . . political parties *must* show a cooperative spirit"—may actually encourage the deconsolidation of existing democracies. Hirschman argues that this will almost certainly obstruct constructive thinking about the ways in which democracies may be formed, survive, and even become stronger in the face of and in spite of continuing adversity. See Albert Hirschman, "Dilemmas of Democratic Consolidation in Latin America" (unpublished notes for the São Paulo Meeting on Democratic Consolidation in Latin America and Southern Europe, 1986).

19. See especially Guillermo O'Donnell and Philippe C. Schmitter, *Tentative Conclusions about Uncertain Transitions* (Baltimore: The Johns Hopkins University Press, 1986); Adam Przeworski, "Some Problems in the Study of the Transition to Democracy," in *Transitions from Authoritarian Rule*, vol. 3, and Adam Przeworski, "Democracy as a Contingent Outcome of Conflicts," in *Constitutionalism and Democracy*, ed. Rune Slagsted and Jon Elster (New York: Cambridge University Press, 1989).

20. See Philippe Schmitter, "Democratic Consolidation of Southern Europe," unpublished manuscript.

21. Evelyne Huber Stephens makes a similar observation in "Economic Development, Social Change and Political Contestation and Inclusion in South America" (paper prepared for the Latin American Studies Association, New Orleans, 1988).

22. See Terry Lynn Karl, "Petroleum and Political Pacts: The Transition to Democracy in Venezuela," *Latin American Research Review* 22 (1986).

23. See Arturo Valenzuela and Samuel Valenzuela, "Los Origines de la Democracia: Reflexiones Teoricas sobre el Caso de Chile," *Estudios Publicos* 12 (Spring 1983).

24. This is the general thrust of Daniel Levine's analysis of Venezuela, which attributes the emergence of a democratic regime primarily to statecraft and the ability of political actors to compromise. See Daniel Levine, "Venezuela since 1958: The Consolidation of Democratic Politics," in *The Breakdown of Democratic Regimes: Latin America*, ed. Juan Linz and Alfred Stepan (Baltimore: The Johns Hopkins University Press, 1978).

25. An approach of this sort treats regime changes as critical junctures and carries an implicit assumption of patterns of political change characterized by gradualism punctuated by sharp discontinuities. It has a long tradition in the study of politics, but it is especially important in recent work on the "new institutionalism." See, for example, J. G. March and J. P. Olson, "The New Institutionalism: Organizational Factors in Political Life," *American Political Science Review* 78 (September 1984): 734–49, and Stephen D. Krasner, "Sovereignty: An Institutional Perspective," *Comparative Political Studies* 21 (April 1988): 66–94. Krasner, though emphasizing political institutions alone rather than the combination of social structures and institutions, also argues that institutions established in the past constrain present choices, that the preferences of individual actors are conditioned by institutional structures, and that historical trajectories are path-dependent. The most recent comparative analysis of patterns of South American and Mexican development adopts a similar framework. Ruth Berins Collier and David Collier, *Shaping the Political Arena: Critical Junctures, the Labor Movement and Regime Dynamics in Latin America* (Princeton: Princeton University Press, 1991), is the most ambitious effort to utilize this sort of path-dependent approach. In their comparative analysis, they examine the different trajectories that result from the initial patterns of incorporation of the labor movement into political life.

26. Strictly speaking, the case of Chile from 1970 to 1973 is not an effort of regime transition from authoritarian rule in the sense considered here. Rather, it is better understood as an attempt to move from one type of democracy to another, that is, a move . . . toward a reformist democracy.

27. There are interesting moves in this direction in the processes taking place in both Nicaragua and Mexico. Nicaragua is the first revolutionary regime on the continent to hold national elections in which a number of political parties have been able to compete. In 1984, the traditional Liberal and Conservative parties and several small leftist parties competed with the Sandinista National Liberation Front (FSLN) and won almost 35 percent of the vote. In 1990, the UNO (Unión Nacional Opositova), a coalition of fourteen anti-Sandinista parties, defeated the Sandinistas, who promised to respect the mandate of the electorate. In Mexico, the Institutional Revolutionary Party (PRI) has begun to permit greater contestation at the municipal and regional level, but these elections are still characterized by numerous restrictions, fraud, and localized violence.

28. There is little information on the dynamics of regime transition in Costa Rica. See Jacobo Schifter, *La fase oculta de la guerra civil en Costa Rica* (San José: EDUCA, 1979), and Fabrice Edouard Lehoucq, "The Origins of Democracy in Costa Rica in Comparative Perspective (Presidentialism)" (Ph.D. diss., Duke University, 1992), which applies the notion of democracy as a contingent institutional compromise to this case. On the transition in Peru, see Cynthia Sanborn, "The Democratic Left and the Persistence of Populism in Peru, 1975–1990" (Ph.D. diss., Harvard University, 1991).

29. Even where the military retained control over the transition, however, it systematically engaged in a process of consultation with civilian parties. See Anita Isaacs, "The Obstacles to Democratic Consolidation in Ecuador" (paper presented to the Latin American Studies Association, San Juan, Puerto Rico, September 21–23, 1989); Francis Hagopian and Scott Mainwaring, "Democracy in Brazil: Origins, Problems and Prospects," *World Policy Journal* (summer 1987): 485–514; and Manuel Antonio Garreton, "El Plebiscito de 1988 y la transición a la democracia" (Santiago: FLACSO, 1988).

30. On these cases, see Charles G. Gillespie, "Uruguay's Transition from Collegial Military-Technocratic Rule," in *Transitions from Authoritarian Rule*; Jonathan Hartlyn, "Democracy in Colombia: The Politics of Violence and Accommodation," in *Democracy in Developing Countries*, vol. 4; Alexander W. Wilde, "Conversations among Gentlemen: Oligarchical Democracy in Colombia," in *The Breakdown of Democratic Regimes*; Karl, "Petroleum and Political Pacts."

31. I am grateful to Samuel Valenzuela for this point. See Samuel Valenzuela, *Democratización via Reforma: La Expansion del Sufragio en Chile* (Buenos Aires: Ediciones IDES, 1985).

32. The roots of these arrangements can be found in the *Pacto de Punto Fijo* and the *Declaración de Principios y Programa Minimo de Gobierno*, which were signed prior to the country's first elections by all contending presidential candidates. These agreements bound all signatories to the same basic political and economic program regardless of the electoral outcome. These pacts are described more fully in Karl, "Petroleum and Political Pacts."

33. This distinction was originally drawn by Philippe Schmitter in a conference on "Micro-Foundations of Democracy," University of Chicago, March 1988.

34. This agreement served primarily as a mechanism for partitioning state offices and establishing other temporary forms of power-sharing. Because it excluded powerful, well-organized forces on the Left and was never aimed at establishing permanent rules of the game, it does not meet the criteria for a foundational pact.

35. I am grateful to an anonymous reviewer for this observation.

36. Most observers locate the roots of this exploitation in colonial and postcolonial landholding patterns that, slowly or abruptly, concentrated property ownership and dispossessed the majority. Specific social processes not conducive to democratization accompanied these landholding patterns. For example, unlike the reciprocal forms of feudalism that developed in Europe and that may have eventually contributed to widespread norms of reciprocity and community at the local level, the penetration of capitalism altered traditional clientelist relations between landlords and peasants in Latin America from a two-way to a one-way affair. As Paul Harrison, *Inside the Third World: The Anatomy of Poverty* (London: Penguin Books, 1979), 105, remarks, "in Latin America the peasant has only duties, the landowner rights." Such social relations have left little residue of notions of mutual obligation or reciprocity between the rich and the poor.

37. I am referring to indicators of inequality here, not absolute poverty. While most of southern Asia and Africa is far poorer than Latin America, their colonial past, patterns of land tenure, and relations of production are quite different. Parts of Asia that have experienced capitalist commercialization of agriculture are now beginning to approximate these same indicators of inequality, but Asia in general has not reached the regional scale of inequality that marks Latin America.

38. One statistic eloquently demonstrates the depth of the crisis. By 1987, Latin America's debt represented 46 percent of the region's gross national product and more than four times the value of its exports. See IDB, *Economic and Social Progress in Latin America: 1988 Report* (Washington, DC: Inter-American Development Bank, 1988), 541.

39. The notion that especially "successful" authoritarian regimes paradoxically may pose important obstacles for democratization can be found in Anita Isaacs, "Dancing with the People: The Politics of Military Rule in Ecuador, 1972–1979" (Ph.D. diss., Oxford University, 1986), and Guillermo O'Donnell, "Challenges to Democratization in Brazil," *World Policy Journal* 5 (Spring 1988): 281–300.

40. I am grateful to Charles Call for this label.

41. There are important differences here, however, between South America and the Caribbean Basin. Military interventions, which have been confined to this latter region in the past, predated the Cold War and are likely to continue after its demise. As the case of Panama shows, the rationale may simply change.

42. Paul Cammack has argued that a ruling coalition might make strategic concessions in its own long-term interest to help sustain democracy, especially after having experienced the failure of militaries to act as reliable allies. See Paul Cammack, "Democratization: A Review of the Issues," *Bulletin of Latin American Research* 4 (1985): 39–46. There seems to be little evidence for this predicted behavior in the current period, however, and further democratization through mass pressure seems to be more likely.

II

The Political Heritage: Culture, Structures, and Authoritarianism

3

Two Cultures and Political Behavior in Latin America

Glen Caudill Dealy

Scholars have sought to explain the evolution of Latin American political development since the early nineteenth century, often comparing and contrasting it to paths taken by Europe and the United States. Within academic circles, various explanations have been debated, including cultural variables, as playing a significant role. Although declining in importance in the 1970s and early 1980s, values, attitudes, and cultural behavior once again started to receive increasing attention in the late 1980s as the wave of democratization struck Latin America. Glen Dealy, who takes a philosopher's approach to culture both in his earlier work, The Public Man: An Interpretation of Latin American and Other Catholic Cultures *(1977) and in his most recent effort,* The Latin Americans, Spirit and Ethos *(1992), attempts to demonstrate fundamental differences in values and attitudes that influence political behavior and to explain why there is a predilection for some models over others. The two essays in Chapter 3 form only a brief introduction to his larger argument that culture is the major determinant of political behavior.*

Dualistic Society Reconsidered

Latin American civilization has a message of importance for a world increasingly prone to subordinate the individual to the goals and procedures of an administrative state. That message underscores the significant advantages attending a separation between private and public life. When integration of these two domains merges daily existence into one encompassing realm, individuals find neither freedom nor identity apart from that whole an option. From Leningrad [now St. Petersburg] to

From Part I: "Dualistic Society Reconsidered," and Part II: "Latin America's 'Two Morality' Paradigm," in *The Latin Americans, Spirit and Ethos* (Boulder, CO: Westview Press, 1992), 3–15, 33–38. Reprinted by permission of Westview Press.

Peoria, Yokohama, and Chongqing, blended unities are an encroaching reality. But these are also places where concatenated values do not engender socially satisfying communities and where attempts at privatized living apart from the whole do not spell solidarity with family or friends.

Latin America's notable location outside the inclusive grip of this administrative state is placed in perspective by considering political philosopher Hannah Arendt's superb critique of nondualistic modernity.[1] Her unparalleled grasp of the problems afflicting contemporary life makes the choice easy. And by accepting Arendt's interpretive concepts and vocabulary as authoritative, we are at liberty to focus upon Latin America's place vis-à-vis modernity.

According to Arendt, Western ills are exhibited in the current rise of an overarching social domain. By this she means that matters and cares of economic necessity that formerly belonged to the household, and whose private resolution made public freedom feasible, have now unfortunately escalated into collective concerns. The resultant "one-dimensional" world, as Herbert Marcuse calls it, endangers liberty within both spheres. It is "against a constantly growing social realm that the private and intimate on the one hand, and the political . . . , on the other, have proved incapable of defending themselves,"[2] since "mass society not only destroys the public realm but the private as well."[3]

Modern seamless totalities, maintains Arendt, threaten the two most cherished aspects of life on this planet: familialism and public action. She observes an arresting correlation between the rise of society, the decline of family, and a societally "conquered" political arena. As a consequence of these disasters, "behavior has replaced action," since "society, on all its levels, excludes the possibility of action."[4]

It follows that present-day states orient themselves around the impersonality of rules regulating private materialistic accumulation; it is a poor surrogate for the human fulfillment customary in ancient times when political freedom was exercised in viably sized public forums. Lacking "love of the world," or at least a practicable means for expressing it, the modern individual's legitimate pride and desire for an excellence worthy of historical remembrance are thereby sacrificed along with life's aesthetic impulse.[5] Wealth—its accumulation and distribution—has taken center stage, and the "withering away" of the public domain, whether preached by Lenin or laissez-faire Friedmanite capitalists,[6] almost everywhere constitutes a self-deluding good. In short, Arendt bemoans the passing of noncommercial human aspiration through neglect of an adequate setting for that forsworn endeavor. Something vital has been lost when personal behavior and the bureaucratic rule of "no one" supplant former ideals of public freedom and heroic accomplishment.

It is a striking fact that this critique of Western civilization rings false to anyone acquainted with Latin America. Neither the private familial nor the public political spheres have there disappeared, nor have they blended to create one inclusive social mass. Indeed, the historical debate over civilization and barbarism within the area turns upon this precise point: Vulgarity to the Latin American mind equals the privatized brutish existence of a people without public space or voice, the antithesis of ancient standards. Domingo Faustino Sarmiento's seminal essay on the Argentine relates barbarity with country living and civility with urban life. He pursues an ideal commensurate with the classical model Arendt believes lost: "All civilization, whether native, Spanish, or European, centers in the cities," and it was there that "the free citizens of Sparta or of Rome . . . lived in the forum or in the public place of assembly exclusively occupied with the interests of the State—peace, war, and party contests." By contrast, the barbaric Argentine landowners, "having no city, no municipality, no intimate associations, lack the basis of all social development." As they are not brought together, "they have no public wants to satisfy; in a word, there is no *res publica*."[7]

Arendt was aware that one modern theorist, Niccolò Machiavelli, comprehended the aged distinction between private household and public *polis*,[8] the latter being a space where the civic virtue of courage (manliness) reigned supreme. However, Arendt did not realize that an entire *Weltansicht* glorifying that virile excellence had unfolded in this hemisphere; nor that this world view sustains an ethos intermittently competing and mixing with imported eighteenth-century nondualist premises.

Arendt's inadvertence, representative of less insightful liberal thinking and scholarship on this point,[9] is instructive in light of her searching criticism of more-familiar contemporary orders. But once we acknowledge that even a preeminent social commentator "followed the crowd" in failing to uncover Latin America's dualistic uniqueness, fundamental questions arise: Is the United States, as so consistently assumed, an appropriate model for Latin American aspirations, or should it be the reverse? Is Latin America the last clinging representative of a traditionalist backward mentality, or is it, like Holy Island during the Dark Ages, the last sane outpost and beacon for nondualist Western civilization?

Such questions and their implications will sound preposterous to outsiders accustomed to seeing Latin Americans as privately immoral (for example, they have mistresses) and as publicly immature (for example, they have dictators). Yet, almost everyone who studies the area even superficially concedes that the stormy and passionate extended Latin family exudes warmth and shelters its members from the outside world to a degree unmatchable by capitalist countries and, more ambiguously, that the public realm furnishes a sense of political efficacy among ruling classes that is equally remote from ordinary Western experience.[10]

Consider immortality. Arendt maintains modern man has lost his appetite for public remembrance; but that is not universally true. However exceptional his eloquence, G. Cabrera Infante states Latin American platitudes when he writes that man "is avaricious, vain, and lusting for power always, everywhere. . . . All that inner, innate perversity creates his thirst for posterity (and its instant form, success), for immortality and, in political terms, his hunger for history."[11] Or, as Octavio Paz declares, reminding one of Petrarch's "Letter to Posterity," outside history man is a barbarian.[12]

Since the Spanish conquest of the New World, Latin aspiration has been tuned to comparative place in epic time. This ideal is continuously restated: in Hernán Cortés's declaration to his men that "far more will be said in future history books about our exploits than has ever been said about those of the past"; in Simón Bolívar's statement during the Wars of Independence that "history will say: 'Bolívar took command in order to free his fellow-citizens' "; in Fidel Castro's singular speech "History Will Absolve Me"; and in Argentine president Carlos Menem's assertion that "the people and history will judge." How small the picture when that backdrop of history is removed! What is left is nonheroic "process man" living in the present.[13]

A personal telling may be instructive. For twenty years I have asked students of both Americas, "Which would you choose: a statue in Central Park/The Plaza or name entry in the empyreal 'Lamb's Book of Life'?[14] Forced to make a decision, would you opt for immortality among men or eternity with God?"

North Americans demonstrate Arendt's insight. Almost all of them pick the eternity of heaven's roll book over worldly renown—but then, manifesting Protestant-ethic "single morality" attitudes, they disavow any conflict in requisite behaviors geared toward attaining one over the other. (Isn't it possible to be a good capitalist and a good Christian at the same time? Surely those virtues leading to worldly success and those required for Christian afterlife are compatible!)

Latin American students almost automatically respond in favor of immortal worldly remembrance over eternal life—but then, exhibiting dualist premises, they hold that following one path does not necessarily exclude the other. (Although fame secured by acting boldly on behalf of the common good may demand evil means, aren't even these sinners open to salvation? Where is the contradiction in the political heroics or artifice necessary to get one's statue in The Plaza, and the Church's ritual absolution or reward for that community-regarding chicanery?)

It is necessary constantly to keep in mind that the civic virtues cherished by Latin Americans—outlined in ensuing pages—are essentially those perfections prized by classical, especially Roman, civilization. Thus in the case of Latin America, Arendt inappropriately laments vanishment from the public domain of qualities such as manliness, dignity, generosity, and grandeur, just as she decries disappearance from the private realm of an entity remarkably like the stereotypical Latin American extended family attending to its own necessities. Here then, south of the border, are fully functional societies exhibiting earmarks of celebrated excellences Western civilization allegedly let slip away.

One or two juxtapositions will suggest the fecundity of ancient values viewed in contemporary Latin American setting. For example, it will be shown that classical grandeur is frequently displayed in Latin oratory as a means of acquiring followers, a prerequisite for political endeavor. Contrary to that publicly silent and "behaving" nature of most present-day nondualist societies, speech and action as features of an admired Greco-Roman existence are everywhere practiced in the area. If "disclosure" of the individual "is implicit in both his words and deeds,"[15] as Arendt maintains, and if it is this that makes "a life without speech and without action . . . literally dead to the world,"[16] then surely Latin Americans are more alive than North Americans. Among the latter, for example, it is common to pride oneself on being a "strong" and "silent" type, two characterizations that nowhere stand together in the Catholic world.[17]

By comparing the personalistic nature of Latin American life with a privatized, bourgeois, money-making impersonal society, one can place in perspective the rationality of this expansive individual disclosure. (Anyone acquainted with Latin Americans' restrained autobiographies is aware that *private* revelations are quite another matter—further testament to a treasured public-familial separation practically unknown to U.S.-style "bare all" biographical detailing.[18]) Endless alliances, coups, and rigged elections leading to surface political instability and uncertainty should be interpreted as the logical outcome of a status-seeking order where each ambitious male consciously endeavors to impress himself upon a theatrically inspired world through the tangible media of words and deeds. This same effort underlay the normal pattern of ancient Roman society. And during the Italian Renaissance in the sixteenth century, an era to which Latin Americans still look for guidance to a degree largely unnoticed by pluralist-minded foreign model builders, that heroic ideal was resuscitated.

Dualistic premises likewise leave Latin Americans outside that modern proclivity to follow authorless stories of time and meaning. They reject "process" society and rigid procedural government, insisting that all of life should display a human dimension. Not least of their antipathy toward faceless constitutionalism is fueled by a sophisticated understanding that inordinately structured countries like the United States, oriented almost exclusively toward economic allocations and benefits, are incapable of permitting or recording extraordinary feats of singular individuals.[19] They know, as Thorstein Veblen observed, that nonindustrial occupations are inherently more honorable and more honored. "Who has ever seen a statue erected to a successful economic entrepreneur?" Latin students ask. And they are correct: Communities nowhere grant true deference and respect—as opposed to envy—to men who operate upon motives of private acquisitiveness rather than on behalf of the *bien comun* (common good). "If capitalists were genuinely convinced that private greed leads to public good," these students reason, "wouldn't one find monuments erected to robber barons?"

Latin Americans maintain that the future, as was the past, will be forged by outstanding individuals, not by unseen forces. They find inadequate those abstractions by which Christian scholastics and modern philosophers "tried to solve the perplexing problem that although history owes its existence to men, it is still obviously not 'made' by them."[20] Even Latin American Marxists proclaiming "scientific" materialist constructions of prior times usually deny the proposition that noncorporeal deterministic factors such as an invisible hand, providence, nature, "world spirit," or class interest govern their destinies.[21]

Indicative of Western civilization's decline, says Arendt, is its dehumanization of the public realm. Yet in striving, like Friedrich Wilhelm Nietzsche, to revitalize standards of worldly excellence in the face of a Judeo-Christian history of other-worldliness, she overlooked an extant culture where economic and political life are unabashedly human creations. For five hundred years Latin American peoples have been governed by a center-periphery philosophy resembling that which instructed the Roman Empire. First from Spain and then from national capitals, elites at the center, infused and guided by classical, Thomistic, and finally Enlightenment philosophies, have contested among themselves, often with the highest idealism, over the direction of public power.[22] If masses far removed from that apex of power by virtue of class or geography have had little say in the disposition of their affairs, this follows from the understanding that, as in the Roman world, by right only those with education, leisure, or excellence in military command should participate. And further, since this elite was small and exclusive, it was possible to think that politics is legitimately stamped by heroic personality rather than abstract process.

Thus, Arendt's critique of present-day faceless societies when joined with her contempt for authorless interpretations of history would seem to favor the visible imperatives and rationalizations undergirding Latin American governance. These peoples do not share a proclivity for the unseen political and economic principles upon which both the United States and Communist polities stand. For example, Arendt writes: "Nothing in fact indicates more clearly the political nature of history—its being a story of action and deeds rather than of trends and forces or ideas—than the introduction of an invisible actor behind the scenes whom we find in all philosophies of history, which for this reason alone can be recognized as political philosophies in disguise. By the same token, the simple fact that Adam Smith needed an 'invisible hand' to guide economic dealings on the exchange market shows plainly that more than sheer economic activity is involved in exchange and that 'economic man,' when he makes his appearance on the market, is an acting being and neither exclusively a producer nor a trader and barterer."[23]

One should note that Latin Americans have consistently been chastised for penning "action and deeds" political history to the neglect of social science expository accounts based upon "trends and forces or ideas."[24] Also, unlike North Americans, who tend to avoid responsibility for the plight of their fellow man by contending that the poor are victims of their own laziness (Calvinism) or of temporary marketplace "forces" (Adam Smith), few Latin intellectuals have been tempted to attribute the condition of their poor to some invisible source. For them poverty is not reducible to technical problems of supply and demand or to impersonal markets. On the contrary, most have been prepared to acknowledge human evil—individual avarice (Christian) and class oppression (Marxist)—as the cause for unjust allocations. The appeal of these mortal explanations is that both may be discussed in terms of concrete remedial actions by specific figures at the head of parties, movements, or factions. Only a small minority in the area would contend that new laws without the force of individual will could accomplish the goal of redressing injustice. Conservatives and revolutionaries each advocate profoundly human solutions. The swing between right- and left-wing ideological politics in Latin America is perennially redressed by the practicality of a solid center core: an eternal return to *personalismo.*[25]

Or consider the typically "surrounded" aspect of Latin America's *Homo politicus.* In succeeding pages an ideal-typical publicly gregarious individual will be distinguished from the isolated, antisocial private man of the United States. When reflecting upon the diminution of words and deeds in our age, Arendt, like numerous others, takes no note of their utility in that coterie-building mode of life beyond our southern border. The Latin American world exemplifies the multiple ways in which a collectivity intent upon *acting* differs from our own society focused upon *making*. Implicit in theater-inclined living is a people-intensive ethos radically at odds with the thing-intensive ambience of a life aligned with production. Unintentionally, Arendt outlines a major disparity between the United States and Latin America: "Action, as distinguished from fabrication, is never possible in isolation; to be isolated is to be deprived of the capacity to act. Action and speech need the surrounding presence of others no less than fabrication needs the surrounding presence of nature for its material, and of a world in which to place the finished product. Fabrication is surrounded by and in constant contact with the world: action and speech are surrounded by and in constant contct with the web of the acts and words of other men."[26]

Latin Americans, more interested in interwoven human relationships than in the surrounding presence of nature, are endlessly convivial. By extension, public power, not autonomous capital, attracts them since "power, like action, is boundless. . . . Its only limitation is the existence of other people."[27] Thus we will see that through constant networking Latins build not wealth but power conglomerates to shield themselves against contingency.

Unlike private capitalists, who need to believe philosophically that the pursuit of power and the pursuit of riches are one and the same—that is, in the necessity to deny any more exalted form of life than that devoted to money-making—Arendt realizes the vast historical, theoretical, and behavioral chasm separating these two goals. Only power understood within the constancy of its collective dimension, she says, can keep the public realm alive: "The word itself . . . indicates its 'potential' character. Power is always, as we would say, a power potential and not an unchangeable, measurable, and reliable entity like force or strength. While strength is the natural quality of an individual seen in isolation, power springs up between men when they act together and vanishes the moment they disperse. Because of this peculiarity, which power shares with all potentialities that can only be actualized but never fully materialized, power is to an astonishing degree independent of material factors, either numbers or means."[28] To elaborate upon these sentences would be to describe Latin America's unique public ethos and commensurate expectations outlined below. Indeed, it would lead us to explicate that confusion between power and authority so typical in the political realm south of the border, a confusion that conversely undermines private (family) life in the United States.

One could easily expand the foregoing multifarious interconnected themes. Arendt's brilliant observations, most of which seem beyond refutation when thinking about the United States, raise a plethora of questions, problems, and conundrums when considering other peoples in this hemisphere. A preliminary summary conjecture might run along the following lines. North Americans could learn much from Western pre-sixteenth-century dualist antecedents still viable in a Latin America that has patently managed to preserve both its familiar existence and its public space; correlatively, Latin Americans could gain a great deal by going back to that same past for lessons in how to divorce coercive force from legitimate authority, thereby utilizing their political forums for more worthy ends.

Latin America's "Two Morality" Paradigm

It is impossible to make practical sense of Arendt's critique without grasping the fact that Latin Americans live a two-track moral existence while U.S. citizens follow a single moral code. Looking at life south of the Rio Grande, one finds a noticeable lack of social conscience. Within the public realm, tolerance, honesty, humility, frugality with government funds, concern for others' welfare, service to community, all seem to be largely missing—even as an ideal. Inside the home or between friends, however, one encounters qualities of rectitude and caring in abundance. In stark contrast to the rather normless jungle found beyond its walled (figuratively and literally) domicile, the Latin American extended family is characteristically knit together by bonds of love and fraternity to a degree unrealized, and unrealizable, within the prototypical Anglo-American nuclear family.

What cultural meaning is explicit or implicit here? How, for example, should one interpret an ordinary Latin father's outpouring of affection toward his own children as he leaves for work—to speed carelessly past a playground and through a crosswalk endangering other people's children? Or more pointedly, how would one explain Argentine murderers during "the dirty war" waiting to kill ideologically incorrect pregnant young women—a death deferred until they had given birth to babies whom these murderers could adopt and cherish as their own?

The answer is anathema to the nondualist Protestant-ethos conscience. Latin Americans freely, openly, and without noticeable inner qualms operate upon a double moral standard: one religious, the other political. Simón Bolívar sharply delineated the two. Religion, he said, "is by nature indefinable in social organization; it lies in the moral and intellectual sphere. Religion governs man in his home, within his own walls, within himself. Laws . . . are applicable outside the home of a citizen."[29] In a speech to Cubans, Fidel Castro—who has always been more Catholic than

Communist—furnishes a contemporary version. Priests, he said, ought to have in mind "that which Christ said: 'My kingdom is not of this world.' (Applause.) What are those who are said to be the interpreters of Christian thought doing meddling in the problems of this world?"[30]

Catholic peoples may be identified by their choice of a binary life, and Protestant peoples by their choice of a unitary one. Within these pages a broad cultural ethos and spirit (social psychology) flowing from Catholic dualism has been designated by the term *"caudillaje"* and placed in juxtaposition to the spirit and ethos of Protestantism's single morality capitalism. As citizens of Poland, Italy, French Canada, Spain, Portugal, and France live more or less within this *caudillaje* ethical ambience, their experiences have been combined herein to construct a model impregnated with this double moral code, which is the hallmark of Renaissance-affiliated societies. Hence we will turn to nonpareil statements and examples wherever found in this aggregate world. In description of its core aspect, none surpass astute Italian publicist Luigi Barzini. He synthesizes Catholicism's dualistic referent as leading to, permitting, and encouraging piety near the hearth and expediency in the public domain: "There is one code valid within the family circle with relatives, intimate friends and close associates, and there is another code regulating life outside. Within, they assiduously demonstrate all the qualities which are not usually attributed to them by superficial observers: they are relatively reliable, honest, truthful, just, obedient, generous, disciplined, brave and capable of self-sacrifice. They practice what virtues other men usually dedicate to the welfare of their country at large; . . . family loyalty is their true patriotism. In the outside world, amidst the chaos and the disorder of society, they often feel compelled to employ the wiles of underground fighters in enemy-occupied territory. All official and legal authority is considered hostile by them until proved friendly or harmless: if it cannot be ignored, it should be neutralized or deceived if need be."[31]

One can better appreciate that bifurcated norm by examining the habits of exemplary representatives. Members of mafia-like organizations, whether Peruvian druglords or Sicilian crime *syndicatos*, place in relief traditional Catholic moral dichotomy. Family lives of high-ranking mafioso generally appear spotless. "They are good fathers, good husbands, good sons; their word is sacred. . . . They never betray a friend. They are always devoted churchmen who give large sums to the local parish or to the deserving poor. Many have sisters in convents and brothers in holy orders."[32] This praiseworthy principle of "churchmanship," of private moral concern, equally epitomizes ruthless murderers who contributed to *la violencia* of Colombia's 1950s civil war, and it guides contemporary narcotic kings who piously build homes for the poor while slaughtering opponents without compunction. Churchmanship also applies to innumerable recent Argentine, Brazilian, and Chilean military officers, torturers responsible for thousands of *desaparecidos* (disappeareds) and to many members of Central American right- and left-wing death squads.

The importance of this bilevel reality to an understanding of *caudillaje* culture could not be overstated. Here we witness an elemental feature of Latin American life, the separation of the ethical world into public and private domains. One follows an opportunistic ethos of politics and of the street;[33] the other an empathic ethos of religion and of the home. Within that society the ideal father embodies virtues and practices inherent to the ancient public forum; the ideal mother represents values and customs of religiosity.[34] The Virgin Mary, representative of both piety and motherhood, presides over the hearth; the collectivity beyond one's door belongs to the god of power, symbolized by dominance and manliness. Small wonder then that men who cut themselves off from the street by the priesthood are considered effeminate, while women who move freely in the streets are considered prostitutes.[35]

The separation into public and private is revealed in a conceptualized scheme of being. In his novel *El Señor Presidente*, Miguel Angel Asturias writes, "A house makes it possible to eat one's bread in privacy—and bread eaten in privacy is sweet, it teaches wisdom—a house enjoys the safety of permanence and of being socially approved. . . . The street, on the other hand, is an unstable, dangerous, adventurous world, false as a looking-glass."[36]

Reflective of dualistic designs for living, Latin Americans learn early to choose their words carefully and guard self-disclosure, to erect barriers around the private persona. For this they need a construction kit: Formality in speech, dress, and habit are their principal tools. North Americans, by contrast, seem to thrive on self-exposure and informality: They dress as they please and "tell all" even to strangers on buses and airplanes. Few U.S. citizens take kindly to being informed what façades (manners and dress) are appropriate or proper to an occasion. The 1960s expression "Let it all hang out" was quintessentially Protestant. Socially "deviant" behavior or foul language in a one-dimensional world knows no distinctions; a mentality that invented the picture window demands that the neighbors accept me, as the Protestant hymn goes, "just as I am." (Taverns, of course, can have no windows in a Reformation culture accustomed to hiding or denying every historical form of immorality from drinking to poverty.) Consequently, in the United States, public life and private life are enhanced or debased together since nothing can be apart and still sacred.[37] Within Latin America, conversely, torture may go on outside one's window for years without undercutting the norms practiced by family and friends within.

René de Visme Williamson underscores my theme: "The [Latin American] family is the only human institution in which human relations are fully personal, and a house is the physical structure whose protective walls cut off impersonal and therefore alien intrusions. The Spanish word for getting married, *casarse*, is highly significant: it means 'to put oneself into a house,' hence a married woman is *casada* [housed in]."[38] Her husband will presumably spend much of his life on the street, "the public arena controlled by 'the government' or by *destino* [destiny]."[39]

As an aside, foreigners who pity the Latin American woman's "plight" should realize the full implications of their critique. To insist that gender parity should occur is to argue that a historically Catholic two-morality people adopt the priorities and reforming ways of a Protestant one-morality society. While modern feminist movements of egalitarian one-morality countries like the United States plausibly demand that natural (equal) rights be extended to women as fulfillment of constitutional promise, the same call in natural law Latin America is necessarily to ask for the destruction of a culture. However meritorious in themselves, as exports to Latin America U.S. feminism and Protestantism alike are faces of cultural imperialism: Each is dependent upon higher law justifications that absolutely reject the validity of Catholic two-morality society.[40]

Correlatively, the Church of Rome, originator and proponent of significant positive aspects of this dualism—most critically, the inviolability of family and a political realm theoretically devoted to the common good—usually has little success in altering public habits since these are both in theory and by popular agreement beyond the purview of Christian moralizing. When, for example, the Vatican attempts to intervene in a country's governmental affairs, local authorities normally refuse to back the Pope and prelates frequently support their parishioners in this regard. An apologetic note issued on one such occasion is illustrative of a general pattern of thinking: "While of course the Roman Pontiff had the right to speak with authority on faith and morals . . . [surely] he did not intend to interfere with politics nor to injure the national movement."[41]

The words of independent Latin America's sentinel of dualism, Simón Bolívar, bear repeating here. Expounding that principle for newborn republics, he said, "The world is one thing, religion another. . . . The noble warrior, daring and fearless, stands out in sharpest contrast to the shepherd of souls."[42] Or, as that contemporary nationalist Fidel Castro allows, "Priests who do not carry out counter-revolutionary campaigns can teach religion, because religion is one thing and politics another."[43] (When

Brazil's Frei Betto asked Fidel how he felt about Marx's belief that "religion is the opiate of the people," his response was typical of dualistic Catholicism's revolutionaries everywhere: "From a strictly political point of view—and I think that I know something about politics—I think one can be a Marxist without ceasing to be a Christian and to work with Communists in order to transform the world."[44]

Compare countries settled by Anglo-Saxon Protestants. In these societies one observes minimal historical differentiation between public and private morality. Certainly private behavior is inconsistent with desired external image, yet one looks in vain for a double standard of moral conduct per se. If stealing and violence within the family are abhorred evils, so also is theft from the public trough or the use of military airplanes, ships, and tanks for individual political ends. Compromise, frugality, and tolerance constitute virtues equally eulogized in the interior and the exterior spheres of life, however much those qualities portray aspiration rather than fulfillment.

In sum, applying the one-morality/two-morality construct to everyday attitudes and habits in this hemisphere is exceptionally illuminating. The *caudillaje* world demands a separation of private and public probity much as bourgeois capitalist culture necessitates a unified standard. Whether accounting for each civilization's approach to human rights, constitutional government, work, love, or power, other current interpretations—including historical materialism and social science developmental paradigms—fall short in comparison with the force and implications of that distinction.

Notes

1. Although Arendt is now deceased, the currency of her views has led me to continue to write of her in the present tense.
2. Hannah Arendt, *The Human Condition* (Chicago: University of Chicago Press, 1958), 47.
3. Ibid., 59.
4. Ibid., 40–41.
5. Ibid., 13, 54.
6. Ibid., 60.
7. Domingo Faustino Sarmiento, *Facundo: Recuerdos de provincia* (Madrid, Spain: Aguilar, 1963), 70.
8. Arendt, *Human Condition*, 35.
9. Arendt, like Max Weber, believes that European Romanticism made public-private life an either/or matter culminating in a Rousseauian compromise: triumph of the social. In his influential "Science as a Vocation," Weber states the position later adopted by Arendt: "The fate of our times is characterized by rationalization and intellectualization and, above all, by the 'disenchantment of the world.' Precisely the ultimate and most sublime values have retreated from

public life either into the transcendental realm of mystic life or into the brother-liness of direct and personal human relations. It is not accidental that our greatest art is intimate and not monumental." From *Max Weber: Essays in Sociology* (New York: Oxford, 1946), 155.

To read contemporary political science, including critical theory, from the Latin American perspective is to see how dependent upon time, space, and culture are these allegedly scientific paradigms. For example, Jürgen Habermas criticizes Arendt: "The (strategic) acquisition and maintenance of political power must be distinguished both from domination or the employment of power and from the original generation or constitution of power; in the latter case, but only there, does the concept of praxis prove useful." Had Habermas lived in *caudillaje* soci-ety he would not have written the following sentence: "The concept of the politi-cal must extend to the strategic competition for political power and to the employment of power within the political system; politics cannot, as with Arendt, be identified with the praxis of those who talk together for the purpose of joint action" ("Hannah Arendt's Communications Concept of Power," *Social Research* 44 [1977]). For views of Arendt's power suppositions, see Fred R. Dallmayr, *Polis and Praxis: Exercises in Contemporary Political Theory* (Cambridge, MA: MIT Press, 1984), chaps. 3–4.

10. Genealogical trees showing the ongoing influence of conquistador fami-lies throughout Central American political systems are fascinating. Samuel Z. Stone has done impressive work in his *The Heritage of the Conquistadors* (Lin-coln: University of Nebraska Press, 1990), appendixes.

11. G. Cabrera Infante, "Foreword," in Carlos Franqui, *Family Portrait with Fidel* (New York: Vintage, 1985), xvii.

12. Octavio Paz, *One Earth, Four or Five Worlds* (New York: Harcourt Brace, 1985), 23.

13. Bernal Díaz del Castillo, *Historia verdadera de la conquista de la Nueva España*, vol. 1 (México: Editorial Porrua, 1960), 206; Simón Bolívar, *Selected Writings of Bolívar*, ed. by Harold A. Bierck, Jr., vol. 2 (New York: Colonial Press, 1951), 284; Fidel Castro, *History Will Absolve Me* (London: Jonathan Cape, 1969); Carlos Menem, in Foreign Broadcast Information Service, *Daily Report*, June 13, 1989, 37.

14. The term "Book of Life," occurring about six times in the New Testament, refers to a heavenly register of the elect. "Lamb" is a symbol of Christ. The Latin "*Agnus Dei*," Lamb of God, is a formula recited by priests before Communion. Note especially Revelation 21:27.

15. Arendt, *Human Condition*, 178.

16. Ibid., 176.

17. "Silence" is the second of Benjamin Franklin's famous thirteen virtues listed in his *Autobiography of Benjamin Franklin* (New York: Modern Library, 1944).

18. Carreño's popular behavior guide advises against self-disclosure: "It is a vulgarity to speak at length in the company of others about our family, our per-son, our illnesses, our quarrels, our business." Take away these, particularly the latter, and Protestant-ethic man would be tongue-tied! Manuel Antonio Carreño, *Manual de urbanidad y buenas maneras para uso de la juventud de ambos sexos*, 38th ed. (México: Editorial Patria, 1983), 185.

19. Arendt, *Human Condition*, 42–43.

20. Ibid., 185.

21. Ibid.

22. Raúl Prebisch's famous thesis that trade relations between rich nations (the center) and poor nations (the periphery) impoverished the poor and enriched the rich came easily to an Argentine. However valid, Latin America was simply moving from Spain and national capitals to Washington as the source of its problems. Here is a classic example of a people maintaining historical attitudes in the face of a sea change in economic and political circumstances. Prebisch's thesis was set forth in *The Economic Development of Latin America and Its Principal Problems* (New York: United Nations Economic Commission for Latin America, 1950).

23. Arendt, *Human Condition*, 185.

24. Ibid., 40.

25. Fidel Castro is well within the tradition we are describing with his axiom, "La jefatura es básica" (Leadership is basic). Theodore Draper argues correctly that this motto is "far more related to 'leadership-principle' movements such as fascism and Peronism than to an ideology-and-party-conscious movement such as Communism" (*Castroism: Theory and Practice* [New York: Praeger, 1965], 9).

26. Arendt, *Human Condition*, 188. As Marcel Proust noted, "People in society are men and women of action on a minute, a microscopic scale, but are nevertheless men and women of action." From "La prisonnière," in *A la recherche du temps perdu*, vol. 3 (Paris: Librairie Gallimard, 1954), 38.

27. Arendt, *Human Condition*, 201.

28. Ibid., 200.

29. Bolívar, *Selected Writings*, 2:604. Kenneth W. Underwood located similar dualism among Catholic politicos in a North American city: "Since the Roman Catholic leaders start their interpretation of politics from the most systematically and precisely developed metaphysical and ethical position of all the religious groups, they give the greatest attention to efforts to define the 'religious and nonreligious issues' and the 'moral and technical aspects' of problems faced by politicians. Even though the Roman Catholic leaders differ at times in their demarcation of the boundaries, they are diligent in their attempts to maintain and observe distinctions between the spiritual and political spheres" (*Protestant and Catholic: Religious and Social Integration in an Industrial Community* [Boston: Beacon Press, 1957], 304). A good example of the success of such dualism within the United States is the life of Chicago Irish Catholic Mayor Richard Daley (Mike Royko, *Boss: Richard J. Daley of Chicago* [New York: New American Library, 1971], 13, passim).

30. Alice L. Hageman and Philip E. Wheaton, eds., *Religion in Cuba Today* (New York: Association Press, 1971), 132. This scripture can as easily be used by the religious right as the political left. In Brazil, liberation theology ideas and programs of Dom Helder Camara, former Roman Catholic archbishop of Recife, are being dismantled by Archbishop José Cardoso Sobrinho. "Orlando C. Neves, a conservative law professor at the Catholic University here [Recife], said in an interview: 'With the full approval of John Paul II, Dom José is trying to return the church to its primary goal: saving souls. Christ said: My kingdom is not of this world'" (*New York Times*, November 12, 1989, 4).

During the Wars of Independence in Mexico, Spanish royalist troops adopted the Virgin of Los Remedios as their patroness and made her a full general of the army. Defeated by the Mexicans, "she was stripped of her uniform by a Mexican general, and ordered to be deported from Mexico. She was allowed to remain on, only when it was promised that she would stay out of politics." Cited by Jon Manchip White, *Cortés and the Downfall of the Aztec Empire* (New York: Carroll and Graf, 1971), 165.

31. Luigi Barzini, *The Italians* (New York: Bantam, 1965), 202. Nicholas Pileggi, writing about Frank Mari, the Cosa Nostra leader, points to the extreme public-private dichotomy of participants in this archetypal Catholic organization: "Like most mafiosi, Mari did not associate with anyone who was not either a member or related to a member of that exotic subculture. Outsiders—all outsiders—are considered prey who can be lied to, cheated, frightened, robbed and murdered. . . . Selling narcotics to strangers is business to the mafiosi, except when it threatens their homes" ("The Story of T," *New York Times Magazine*, March 29, 1970, 13).

Carlo Sforza, *The Real Italians: A Study in European Psychology* (New York: Columbia University Press, 1942), 56, comments upon the same phenomenon: "The home is loved in Italy, not for itself, but as a symbol of the continuity of the family. Even the most modest peasant hovel is an island among many other islands. Only at family feasts—births or marriages—does one lower the bridge between house and house and then only briefly. Yet this implies nothing like oriental seclusion. The Italians, like the ancient Greeks, feel that they were born for the market place; they are not eaten by the desire for solitude which often besets the Briton or the Scot. Thousands of years of city life together have taught every Italian the art of remaining alone in the midst of the noisy crowd; alone—of course, in the Italian sense of the word—with his wife and children. That is, by the way, the source of the Italian art of living together in harmony, three or four sons under the same roof in farm or palace."

32. Barzini, *Italians*, 268. According to the *New York Times*, July 14, 1991, the Cali drug cartel is more successful than the Medellín cartel because the former "long ago wove themselves into Cali's society as seemingly upstanding white-collar citizens." "In Medellín, the cartel competed with the state," says Alvaro Guzmán, a sociologist. "In Cali, there has been a process of accommodation with the state" (*New York Times*, July 14, 1991).

33. "And deeply ingrained in Nicaraguans are conceptions about how they are most obviously divided—by gender. An outline of this division is suggested by the Nicaraguan expression, 'The man is king of the street; the woman is queen of the house.'" Forrest D. Colburn, *My Car in Managua* (Austin: University of Texas Press, 1991), 60.

34. An anthropological exposition of this truism may be found in Mary N. Diáz, *Tonalá: Conservatism, Responsibility, and Authority in a Mexican Town* (Berkeley: University of California Press, 1970), 76–79. A parish priest in Spain speaks of "the quite undeniable fact, as far as Andalusia is concerned, that men consider the church a 'woman's affair' . . . and by and large leave churchgoing to the women" (Ronald Fraser, *The Pueblo: A Mountain Village on the Costa del Sol* [London: Allen Lane, 1973], 114).

35. See Roberto DaMatta, *Carnivals, Rogues, and Heroes: An Interpretation of the Brazilian Dilemma* (Notre Dame, IN: University of Notre Dame Press, 1991), 107ff. In keeping with this view, sixteenth-century Spanish philosopher Juan Ginés de Sepúlveda defended the *conquista*, arguing that New World Indians are to Spaniards as females are to males: "In wisdom, skill, virtue and humanity, these people are as inferior to the Spaniards as children are to adults and

women to men" (*Democrates secundo: De las justas causas de la guerra contra los Indios* [Madrid: Instituto F. de Vitoria, 1951], 33).

36. Miguel Angel Asturias, *El Señor Presidente* (New York: Atheneum, 1975), 125–126.

37. Our ancestors tried to maintain a unidimensional realm of the sacred by exposing and censoring the individual who "conceives no wickedness great that breakes not forth into open view" (Thomas Hooker, *The Christians Two Chiefe Lessons, viz. Selfe-Deniall, and Selfe-Tryall* [London: Golden Lion, 1640], 218). Many secularized contemporaries would reverse this and censor individuals who object to "immoral" paintings, books, or spoken words that are designedly brought into public view. Yet the similarity is apparent. Although our forefathers staked their "self-evident" religious claim in the name of morality, and moderns in the name of free speech, both exhibit a consuming need for sacralization and authentication of their special beliefs and practices. Thus, today exponents of the first persuasion lobby not so much for the freedom to pray in school as for the legitimacy of their religious premises; and the latter want not so much the freedom to hang "dirty pictures" in the gallery as to thereby transform their work into art. Both reflect the truism that in the United States every claim to the sacred is generalized and, to the extent possible, imposed upon other people and over all of life. Most important, progress in "the cause" is equated less with religious or aesthetic self-transformation than with successful proselytization. Catholic holy men and women retreating from the world into private meditation are incomprehensible from this perspective.

38. René de Visme Williamson, *Culture and Policy: The United States and the Hispanic World* (Knoxville: University of Tennessee Press, 1949), 30.

39. DaMatta, *Carnivals*, 66.

40. See "The Americanization of Latin American Religion?" in David Martin, *Tongues of Fire: The Explosion of Protestantism in Latin America* (Oxford: Basil Blackwell, 1990), 278–281.

41. Walter Bryan, *The Improbable Irish* (New York: Taplinger, 1969), 159.

42. Bolívar, *Selected Writings*, 291.

43. From a speech by Castro in Hageman and Wheaton, *Religion in Cuba Today*, 136.

44. Frei Betto, *Fidel Castro y la religión* (Santiago, Chile: Pehuen Editores, 1986), 271–273. Fear of communism has been much greater in Protestant-ethos societies than in Catholic-ethos societies, no doubt due to the former's understanding that a One Morality system, despite its pluralistic pretenses, cannot accommodate diverse public orthodoxies without private values also being threatened. U.S. political pluralism is singularly nonpluralist, ideologically speaking, when compared with Catholic polities of Europe and the Americas.

Modern Marxists, of course, endeavored to politicize all of life. To maintain their traditional dualism, however, Catholic Marxists readily fixed upon the classical and Christian requirement that a small political elite must lead the large religion-prone masses to an end that provides for their own good. Italian Marxist Antonio Gramsci (1891–1937), who has become Latin America's most admired theorist of the Left in the late twentieth century, in so many ways represents this historical Catholic premise. Like Castro, he gave political tutorials in the necessity to change the world from above ("Critical self-consciousness means, historically and politically, the creation of an elite of intellectuals") in the face of a popular following of rather simple individuals for whom "philosophy can only be experienced as a faith." Preaching in the tradition of other great Catholic political thinkers and actors from Dante and Saint Thomas Aquinas, to Charles V and Machiavelli, to Bolívar and Antonio Nariño, Gramsci creates a two-tier world of those who live by knowledge/understanding on the one hand and those who abide in naive faith on the other. In place of the medieval "Christian prince" who both knows and acts, Gramsci suggests the slightly broader "consciousness of being part of a particular hegemonic force . . . in which theory and practice will finally be one." Just as Latin American leaders of the Right long claimed their mission was to "save the patria" with military force, the Left now lays claim to an ideological expertise to "save the patria" through a higher political consciousness. When Gramsci notes that "[desirable] innovation cannot come from the mass," he is underlining a historical "iron principle" of dualistic Catholicism. *A Gramsci Reader* (London: Lawrence and Wishart, 1988), 334–39.

4

Political Culture and Democratization in Latin America

Mitchell A. Seligson

In the past, most scholars have tried to understand the culture of a society through its historical experience, its political behavior, and its intellectual contributions. Some have even argued that mass political values, if inclined toward democratization, not only provide a fertile ground for its growth but also are essential in producing a democratic model. Seligson—who teaches at the University of Pittsburgh, is coauthor of Authoritarians and Democrats: The Politics of Regime Transition in Latin America *(1987), and has been using survey techniques for two decades to better understand Latin American societal values—presents some of his findings on democratic attitudes in Costa Rica and Mexico. As he suggests, although democratic values alone do not account for the transition to democracy in these countries, they play a significant role in explaining the complex interaction of variables that determine political behavior and systems.*

The shift from dictatorship to democracy in Latin America has been rapid, nearly universal, and almost completely unanticipated by scholars, diplomats, and Latin American politicos themselves. Since, however, this is not the first time that elected civilian regimes have been predominant in the region, many scholars are convinced that we are today observing nothing more than another phase in a cyclical pattern. These observers believe that just as the military regimes of the 1960s and 1970s were replaced by elected civilians in the 1980s, a new wave of *golpes de estado* [coups d'état] will soon return the military to power.

From *Latin America and Caribbean Contemporary Record* 7 (1987–88), ed. James M. Malloy and Eduardo A. Gamarra (New York: Holmes and Meier Publishers, 1990), A49–A65. © 1990 Holmes and Meier. Reprinted by permission of Holmes and Meier.

The reasons for the current pessimism regarding the longevity of electoral democracy in Latin America are many, but the principal ones have to do with the expected adverse impact of the debt crisis on regime stability. The enormity of the external debt, its omnipresence throughout the region, and the steadfast unwillingness of creditor nations to accept any major modification in the terms of repayment, have convinced many that civilian democratic regimes will not long survive.[1] But at a deeper level, however prescient these predictions of the negative impact of the debt crisis turn out to be, they are of little assistance to those who seek to develop more universal theories of democratization and democratic breakdown. Even if one generalizes the debt crisis into a category of phenomena related to severe disruption in national economies, it is quite clear from the historical evidence that democratic breakdown in Latin America has often not been linked to economic breakdown.

While the current debate revolves around the impact of economic crisis on democratic stability, the traditional focus has been on the relationship between economic growth and democratization. It has been in that area of inquiry that the largest volume of highly regarded scholarship has been produced. Economic theories of democratization have taken markedly contradictory positions.[2] Classic Marxist scholarship envisions the advancement of industrial capitalism as ultimately leading to a workers' revolution and the establishment of dictatorship (albeit of the proletariat). Modern empirical democratic theory, on the other hand, sees economic growth as strongly linked to democratic growth. One should add to this synthesis the perspective popularized by O'Donnell, with specific reference to the Latin American region, in which advancing economic growth there would result in neither revolution from below nor democracy from above, but in a special form of military-dominated authoritarianism, which he has termed "bureaucratic-authoritarianism."[3]

The evidence contradicting each of these widely varying predictions is well known. The classic Marxist view has been widely contradicted by the emergence of proletarian revolutions among those countries where industrial capitalism was only poorly developed and its failure to emerge in the highly advanced industrial capitalist states. The O'Donnell hypothesis seems to be relevant only to a limited number of cases and only for a very limited period of time, and therefore is of little help in generating a more inclusive theory.

Far more persuasive has been the evidence for a link between economic growth and democratization. Western Europe and North America seem to be the classic cases that best fit the theory. In Latin America there is some evidence to support the theory as well. Costa Rica and Venezuela are two countries that have advanced economically and have seen stable democracy take root. On the other hand, the pre–World War II break-downs of democratic rule in much of Latin America conformed quite well to a theory that views these democracies as "premature." Throughout most of Latin America, per capita income in the pre–World War II period did not surpass the minimum threshold levels required by the theory.[4]

In the post–World War II period, however, continued economic growth has meant that most Latin American nations have surpassed the GNP (gross national product)-per-capita levels that were associated with the emergence of stable democratic rule in Western Europe and North America. Yet democratic regimes in economically advanced Latin American countries have repeatedly been swept aside by military coups.[5] Thus countries as economically advanced as Argentina and Uruguay saw not only the breakdown of democracy but its replacement by exceptionally brutal military regimes. By the mid-1950s, Chile's level of per capita income was already far above the minimum, and it was enjoying a long period of democratic rule that extended back to 1932. Yet in 1973 a coup terminated elected rule in Chile. Cuba and Panama both enjoyed relatively high levels of economic development, but experienced only short periods of elected government. In sum, economic growth and democratization do not seem to be closely tied together in the Latin American region. One can agree fully with Soares, who after a summary analysis of economic development and democracy in Latin America (including the troubling cases of economically advanced socialist countries that have not democratized) concludes: "The relationship between economic development and electoral democracy is not simple nor universally valid. Empirically, the relationship is strong across all three subsets of countries [included in his study] and within the Core democratic subset. It is weak in the Latin American and socialist subsets. In these subsets, democracy awaits explanation."[6]

One conclusion that could be drawn from the preceding analysis is that a certain level of economic growth is a necessary but not sufficient condition for the establishment of stable electoral democracy. However, a moment of reflection will reveal that there are important exceptions to this notion as well. The case of India immediately comes to mind. As Dahl has noted, India's GNP per capita was only $73 in 1957, one-third to one-half of the threshold normally used in such research, but the nation nonetheless was enjoying a protracted period of stable electoral democracy.[7] Weiner suggests that another variable needs to be entered into the mix in order to explain the case of India: "The British colonial model of tutelary democracy has been more successful than other colonial models in sustaining democratic institutions and processes in newly independent countries."[8] Weiner's evidence for this conclusion is impressive; he

highlights six developing countries with populations of over 1 million
that have had recent colonial experiences, and which currently have stable
electoral democracies; the common denominator for these countries is
that they had each experienced British tutelary democracy.[9] Indeed, Weiner
finds that among the smaller developing countries, most that have remained democratic were also colonies of Britain.[10]

Although Weiner's argument is persuasive, there are too many exceptions to make it totally convincing. Grenada, Tanzania, Uganda, Ghana,
and Nigeria are British tutelary democracies that broke down. Within Latin
America, Costa Rica and Venezuela are two important non-British cases
in which democracy seems to have taken a firm hold. The explanation for
these two Latin American cases, however, it can be argued, rests in the
economic threshold theory rather than the British tradition theory. If so,
then one is still left with exceptions. There is the case of Honduras, a
country that holds the distinction of being the poorest country in Central
America; yet, with the exception of Costa Rica, it is recognized as having
the deepest democratic traditions in the region. Indeed, as I have reported
elsewhere, the GNP per capita of Honduras, always near the bottom in
the Latin American region, remained below the minimum threshold into
the 1980s, when electoral democracy was gaining in strength.[11]

Vanhanen takes a somewhat different macroanalytic approach to the
problem. He focuses on "the relative distribution of economic, intellectual and other crucial power resources among various sectors of the population. Democracy will emerge under conditions in which power resources
have been so widely distributed that no group is any longer able to suppress its competitors or to maintain hegemony."[12] While the explained
variance is impressively high, he nonetheless finds that 14 out of 147
countries in the 1980–1983 period contradict his hypothesis. He argues
that his approach is probabilistic and not designed to produce 100 percent
accuracy of prediction. But among those who eschew quantitative methods, it is these nonconforming cases that are seen as undermining the
utility of the entire approach.

It is worthy of note that 5 out of the 14, or 36 percent of the exceptional cases in the Vanhanen analysis, are found in the Latin American
region, when the Latin American countries comprise only 17 percent of
the total sample of nations.[13] This finding is consistent with that of Soares,
who sees Latin America as one major exception to the worldwide pattern.
Indeed, Soares puts his finger on the core of the problem in Latin America,
namely, the problem of regime stability. As Soares states, "Both democracy and dictatorship are unstable in Latin America."[14] Viewed from this
angle, Latin American exceptionalism may be more a problem of the in-

stability of regime, irrespective of the form it takes, rather than instability of democracy per se.

Instability certainly has been characteristic of Latin America for much of its history. Edward Muller and I have shown that instability (in the form of insurgency) is directly linked to inequality in income distribution.[15] Since income inequality in Latin America is, on the whole, far higher than it is in other developing areas of the world, it stands to reason that instability would be endemic there.[16]

While instability in Latin America can be explained, what is far less clear is the form that the instability takes. Specifically, why is Latin America frequently characterized by an oscillation between dictatorship and democracy? Other variants of the pattern are possible and have indeed occurred in Latin America. For example, Cuba moved from right-wing dictatorship under [Fulgencio] Batista in the 1950s to left-wing dictatorship under [Fidel] Castro beginning in the 1960s. In the 1970s, Nicaragua followed the same path with the downfall of [Anastasio] Somoza [Debayle] and the rise of the Sandinistas. Peru, beginning in 1968, experienced regime shifts from populist-left military rule to more traditional, rightist military rule. But the overall pattern has been one that oscillates between military rule and civilian, electoral democracy.

The problem of explaining Latin American exceptionalism is perhaps best viewed as a problem of understanding the factors that have been responsible for the cyclical pattern for much of this century among countries that have achieved the minimal levels of economic development. In Latin America, no country has sustained electoral democracy for any substantial period of time without having crossed the economic threshold. While most of the nations in the region have crossed the threshold, only Costa Rica and Venezuela have sustained electoral democracy since first establishing it in the post–World War II period.[17] Hence, in Latin America, crossing the economic threshold may be a necessary condition for democratization, but it is clearly far from a sufficient condition. As Inglehart has forcefully argued with reference to the general question of the origins of stable democracy, "There is no question that economic factors are politically important—but they are only part of the story."[18]

According to Inglehart, the other "part of the story" is political culture. This much maligned variable of political analysis has recently begun to regain some of the attention it once received. Serious political culture research has its origins in Almond and Verba's *The Civic Culture*, one of the few books of modern political science that remains an object of discussion and debate a quarter of a century after its publication. As Verba has stated, the many weaknesses in method and theory in the book "derive from the boldness" of the effort.[19] Almond and Verba attempted in *The Civic Culture* to draw a direct micro-to-macro linkage between attitudes and regime type. The leap was enormous and entirely premature given the infant state of survey research at the time. Nonetheless, the challenge it presented is one that remains with us today.

In the literature on Latin America, some of the strongly negative reactions against political culture research are generated by works that are culturally reductionist in the extreme, and which view culture as largely immutable and a constant throughout the region. For such authors, the so-called Iberic tradition is the central explanatory variable for political instability and authoritarian rule.[20] But these perspectives are incapable of explaining cases such as Costa Rica and Venezuela, since constancy of cultures ought not to produce variable political outcomes.[21]

Inglehart's argument is that "political culture is an intervening variable that helps explain why economic development is conducive to, but does not necessarily lead to, the emergence of modern or mass-based democracy."[22] Inglehart's attention is not focused on generalized cultural traditions, but on a specific subset of "norms and attitudes supportive of democracy." His evidence is based upon a two-decade study of a sample of fifteen nations. The overall conclusion of the study is especially important for the Latin American cases. He argues that "a long-term commitment to democratic institutions among the public is . . . required, in order to sustain democracy when conditions are dire."[23] In Latin America, the conditions are almost always dire, and have been particularly bleak during the 1980s debt crisis in which democracies have been struggling to survive.

Inglehart attempts to prove his case for the importance of political culture by using data from a sample of twenty-one nations over the period 1900–1986. His conclusion is that the impact of economic growth on democracy is mediated through political culture. A far more direct relationship has been shown by Gibson, who shows that intolerant attitudes of political elites in the United States are strongly associated with repressive public policy. Gibson found that in the 1950s, states with political elites more intolerant on the issue of the rights of Communists were far more likely to have adopted legislation restricting the rights of Communists.[24]

Although political culture as an important variable determining the stability of democracy is regaining support in the United States and Western Europe, it meets strong resistance in Latin America. There are a number of good reasons for this. First, political culture research is invariably quantitative in nature and therefore reflects the mainstream of the positivist, empirical paradigm of North American social science, an approach which runs against the grain of humanist tradition predominant in Latin American universities. Second, Latin American scholars view such work as having a condescending tone to it, symbolized by studies of modernization and civic culture which place the United States at the most preferred end of the continuum and Latin American countries at the least preferred end. Third, the research is often seen as characterized by "victim-blaming," in which the problems of Latin American politics are a result of their own (pathological) cultures. Fourth, acceptance of the North American paradigm implies a deepening of cultural dependency. Fifth, a residue of suspicion, generated initially by Project Camelot, lingers over the motivations of scholars who probe public opinion in Latin American countries. Finally, there is the reality of the extraordinary difficulties, both methodologically as well as pragmatically, in conducting valid survey research on political opinions in regimes characterized by repressive police and military forces.

While political culture research meets strong resistance within Latin America, it is also unpopular among North American Latin American experts. The masterful critique by Craig and Cornelius of the Mexican component of *The Civic Culture* summarizes the many problems inherent in that study that have come to symbolize the weaknesses of survey research on Latin America.[25] The limitation of the sample to urban areas, the serious errors in translation from English to Spanish, the failure to be attentive to regional variation, and the lack of sensitivity to the authoritarian context in which Mexican politics are conducted are all problems that appear in the Mexican survey. Consequently, when Latin Americanist graduate students are exposed to the notion of political culture, they are likely to be introduced to it via *The Civic Culture* and to be shown why such research is of little use.

A further difficulty is that in the training of area specialists so much effort and time are needed to acquire the requisite language and culture skills that little room is left over in graduate curricula for a heavy dose of statistics, sample design, and survey research methodology.

Finally, Latin Americanist graduate students who are considering a survey research–based approach for their dissertations quickly realize that they do not have access to the functional equivalent of the widely available and highly respected political and social surveys conducted in the United States by the Institute of Social Research at the University of Michigan or the National Opinion Research Center at Chicago. Hence, while their fellow graduate students who are studying American and Western European governments can obtain a gold mine of survey data neatly stored on computer tapes, Latin Americanist graduate students must contemplate the daunting prospect of financing, organizing, administering, and processing a survey all by themselves. Those who forge ahead in spite of these obstacles often end up being forced to content themselves with tiny, unrepresentative samples, and more often than not are unable to find the resources to process the raw data into machine-readable format. In the end, these students often disregard their surveys altogether and base their dissertations on more traditional sources of data such as interviews, archival research, and newspaper clippings. Students who have confronted an experience such as this often end up teaching their own students that good surveys cannot be done in Latin America and hence propagate the bias against political culture research.

Yet, in spite of all of these limitations, there is an unmistakable increase in interest in political culture research in Latin America. The publication of Norbert Lechner's edited volume entitled *Cultura política y democratización*, is one important indication, while another is the recent publication of an article by Enzo Faletto, a primary proponent of dependency theory, on the subject of political culture and democratization.[26] It is worth noting that this advocate of the primary importance of economic factors in determining political outcomes is now arguing that "structural conditions are insufficient for democracy to arise and take effect."[27]

No single factor is more directly responsible for this dramatic shift than the retreat of the military and the emergence of elected civilian regimes. The newly democratic regimes in Latin America are understandably more tolerant of political research than [were] their authoritarian predecessors. But far more important than the liberalized atmosphere is the fact that candidates for public office hope to enhance their chances of winning by making heavy use of public opinion polls to help guide their election campaign strategies. It is not at all uncommon in Latin America today to find political polling consultants from Washington, DC, planning campaign strategies for presidential candidates. Similarly, newspapers and magazines are conducting their own polls in an atmosphere of highly competitive elections; poll results sell newspapers.

Added to the stimulus of polling provided by election campaigns is the use of polls to support or refute key policy positions. There is no clearer case of this phenomenon than that of the United States Information Agency (USIA) polls conducted in Central America. President [Ronald] Reagan opened the debate in March 1986 by claiming that a Gallup poll conducted in Central America showed that Central Americans supported the U.S. policy of aiding the contras in Nicaragua. This announcement immediately generated a flurry of claims and counterclaims about the accuracy of what the president had reported and the quality of the polls themselves.[28] U.S. congressmen began reading into the *Congressional Record* results of these polls to support their position on contra aid. Hence, Central American public opinion polls were being used to help influence public opinion in the United States and, ultimately, to help determine a key aspect of U.S. foreign policy.

Within Latin America, elected officials and opposition parties cite polls supporting their position on numerous public policy issues. This is a phenomenon found not only in the newly established democracies but even in authoritarian Chile. In a country which at this writing is facing a national referendum in which there is only one candidate, General Augusto Pinochet, it is reported that "myriad research groups, consultants, and others are polling Chileans about their attitudes toward the coming presidential plebiscite."[29] Even Paraguay is experiencing a miniboom in public opinion surveys.

In spite of the recent growth of survey research in Latin America, those interested in studying the political culture of the region still face a daunting task. There is no central archive like that found at the University of Michigan or the University of Essex in England, where Latin American surveys are stored. In the 1960s the Center for Latin American Studies at the University of Florida maintained a Latin American Data Bank, but that operation was closed in the 1970s. The London-based Gallup International does not maintain an archive of the polls conducted by its many affiliates in Latin America.[30] The University of Connecticut is reported to be planning an archive of Latin American survey data under the direction of Fred Turner, and one would hope that the effort will take root. At the moment, however, one is limited to studying a small portion of the extant survey data based upon an unsystematic process of contacting those who are known to possess such data.

In the following discussion, a preliminary effort is made to explore some facets of Latin American political culture with specific reference to attitudes related to democracy. The effort begins with a look at the paradigmatic case: Costa Rica. In a comprehensive review of the Fitzgibbon-Johnson-Kelly Survey of Scholarly Images of Democracy in Latin America, Baloyra concludes that despite its many acknowledged weaknesses, it is the best instrument available for comparisons over time of the levels of democratization in Latin America.[31] Based upon the nine surveys that have been conducted every five years beginning in 1945, Costa Rica has been ranked fourth once (1950), second on four occasions, and since 1975 it has held first place in three consecutive surveys. If we are going to find a political culture of democracy anywhere in Latin America, we should find it in Costa Rica.

In 1978, Miguel Gómez and I conducted a small-scale survey of the metropolitan area of Costa Rica's capital city, San José, and the provincial capitals of the major cities in the surrounding central valley.[32] The sample size was 201. Some of the items in that survey were coordinated with two other surveys also conducted in 1978, one in New York and another in Mexico. Edward Muller and Tom Jukam conducted a survey in New York City (N = 618), and Edward Williams, John Booth, and I conducted a survey in selected urban areas of Mexico (N = 430).[33] The survey data from New York provide benchmark data against which the Latin American cases can be measured. After all, *The Civic Culture* did find the U.S. case to be far and away more democratic than Mexico. Finally, Mexico, while presumably at the bottom of this trio in terms of level of democratization, is ranked quite high in the Scholarly Images study cited above; since 1965 it has ranked no lower than sixth, and in 1980, the year of the survey closest to the year in which our survey of Mexico was conducted, it ranked third.

While the surveys included a number of items on different aspects of democratic political culture, here I will focus on only one: tolerance for the rights of dissenters. Since the days of the pioneering research of Prothro and Grigg, it has been clear that while surveys of opinion often produce very high levels of support for general principles of democracy (e.g., freedom of speech, right to vote, etc.), mass publics are far less willing to extend those rights to groups that they do not like.[34] Tolerance of dissent, therefore, has become a central focus of much public opinion research in the United States and abroad.[35] Willingness to extend to opposition groups the right of free speech, the right to vote, and the right to run for office are three key indicators of support for democratic values.

Table 1 presents a comparison of the levels of tolerance for the rights of opposition in Costa Rica, Mexico, and New York. Three rather unremarkable conclusions can be drawn from an examination of this table. First, there is a hierarchy, in a Guttman-scale sense, of activities that are most highly tolerated and those that are least tolerated. In all three countries, there is more tolerance for freedom of speech (and hence opposition to censorship) than there is for the right to vote. The right of dissenters to run for office is the least well tolerated in these three samples. These results are predictable: dissenters can speak out with little effect, while their voting could change the outcome of an election and running for office could result in a dissenter's being elected. The respondents, then, seem to be making rational distinctions among these different aspects of tolerance. Moreover, there seems to be a certain universality in the ways in which these rights are perceived across these three cultures. Second, average opinion consistently falls on the supportive end of the continuum in all cases except in Mexico on the "run for office" item, where it falls slightly into the negative end. While support for the rights of dissenters is not very high in all three countries, it nonetheless averages out to be more tolerant than intolerant. Third, predictably, New York City scores are consistently more tolerant than those in Costa Rica and Mexico. These three conclusions add to our confidence in the validity of the surveys and suggest that they may well be tapping attitudes that can be linked to regime type.

Table 1. Tolerance of Dissent in Costa Rica, Mexico, and New York (Mean Scores)[1]

	Costa Rica	Mexico	New York
Censorship	6.3	6.4	8.3
Vote	5.8	6.3	7.1
Run for office	5.1	4.7	5.7

Source: See note 33.
[1]Means based upon a scale of 1 to 10, with 1 indicating lowest tolerance and 10 highest. The items were:

Censorship: "To what extent would you approve or disapprove of the government censoring radio, TV, or newspaper ads that criticize the government?"

Vote: "To what extent would you approve or disapprove of people who only say bad things about the Costa Rican (Mexican, United States) form of government having the right to vote?"

Run for Office: "To what extent would you approve or disapprove of people who only say bad things about the Costa Rican (Mexican, United States) form of government having the right to run for office?"

What does come as a surprise, and therefore challenges our confidence in the reliability of the data, is that even though Mexico is widely viewed as a less democratic country than Costa Rica, on the voting and censorship items Mexican opinion is more tolerant. The differences on the censorship items are so small as to be entirely within the confidence intervals of the two samples. The differences in the vote item are wider and probably reflect a true difference in perspective. These findings suggest that a more authoritarian political system seems to be undergirded by a more democratic culture. If this were to prove to be the case, then it would go far in undermining our confidence that one can in fact find micro-macro linkages in political culture research.

Closer examination of the items reveals that the marginals reported in the table may be misleading. The items focus on the rights of critics of the system. Those who support the system of government and would nonetheless allow critics to enjoy full civil rights are considered tolerant and supportive of a political culture of democracy. But what of those who oppose the system? Those individuals might well support the rights of dissenters not because they are tolerant but because they are critical of the system. To test for this possibility, it is necessary to compare tolerance for critics only among those who support the system.

Along with Edward Muller, I have developed a cross-culturally valid and reliable set of items measuring system support.[36] The items have been tested in both Costa Rica and Mexico and have been shown to behave as expected. To simplify this presentation, I use only one of those items in this paper, one which asks, "To what degree are you proud of the Mexican (Costa Rican) system of government?" The item has face validity and is highly correlated with the other items in the larger set.[37] What we find when comparing Mexico with Costa Rica in the 1978 surveys is that whereas nearly half the Mexicans (46.4 percent) score in the bottom half of the scale, only one in twenty (5.3 percent) Costa Ricans score in this range.[38] So, the percentage of the sample population with low pride in their nation is approximately nine times greater in Mexico than it is in Costa Rica.

Table 2 divides the Mexican sample into two halves, those with low pride in their political system and those with high pride in it, and then compares the responses on the tolerance items. It is evident from this table that tolerance for dissent is affected by one's support for the system. For each civil liberty, tolerance scores are lower among those with high support than they are among those with low support. While a majority of the sample is tolerant of the freedom of speech and right to vote of critics, among those with high support for the system, a distinct majority would oppose critics running for office. Among those who express low support, a majority would favor the right of critics to run for office. Although the table does not display a similar comparison for Costa Rica because the sample size of those with low support is so small as to place in doubt the validity of percentages, among those with high support 44.2 percent would allow critics of the system to run for office.

The primary conclusion we draw from this analysis is that less than a third (29.9 percent) of Mexicans who express support for their system are willing to allow critics of it to run for office. What seemed to be an anomalous situation of higher levels of democratic political culture in Mexico than in Costa Rica really has turned out to be a spurious result of very different levels of system support in the two nations. Extending this finding to a more general level might provide some insight into the problem of political instability in Latin America. Latin Americans may be tolerant of protest marches, strikes, and the military coups that often follow them not because they are politically tolerant (and democratic), but because they oppose the government in power.

Table 2. Pride and Tolerance in Mexico

	Low pride[1] percent tolerant (N=89)	*High pride percent tolerant (N=154)*
Censorship	78.8	63.8
Vote	63.2	56.4
Run for office	50.6	29.9

Source: See note 33.

[1]Low-pride responses are those in the range of 1 to 5 on the 10-point scale, while high-pride answers are those in the range of 6 to 10.

The evidence presented thus far shows some micro-macro relationship between the political culture of democracy, defined in terms of tolerance for opposition, and the democratic characteristics of the systems in which those cultures operate. But the three nations examined above remained politically stable for a long period before and after the gathering of the survey data. What about systems that experienced breakdown: Can we find evidence of a political culture unsupportive of democracy prior to such events?

Uruguay represents an ideal case for three reasons. First, from 1945 to 1960, Uruguay was ranked first on the Fitzgibbon-Johnson surveys of scholarly images of Latin America. It held on to second place in 1965 and in 1970 was ranked third. So, we are dealing with a case that was indisputably democratic from the point of view of expert observers. Second, Uruguay has long been highly developed economically and socially; therefore, until the breakdown of democracy (which occurred in 1973 with a full military takeover), it was a case that conformed precisely to the theories that link economic development to political democracy. Third, we are fortunate to have relevant data from Gallup Uruguay for the period prior to the breakdown.[39]

In May 1968 a poll of Montevideo with a sample size of 804 was conducted. Since Montevideo contains the bulk of the population of the country, the opinions expressed by its citizens closely reflect those of the nation as a whole.[40] A question asked of the respondents in that poll taps quite closely the tolerance items reported above for Costa Rica, Mexico, and New York City. The item read: "Freedom of speech and assembly should not be denied to anyone." On this item, only 5 percent of the respondents disagreed. By this standard, Uruguayans seemed even more democratic than the New Yorkers. But, as we discovered with the Mexican data, underlying this opinion is another dimension, that of support for the system. Another item in the survey demonstrates this point: "The only road to overcome the problems of the country is social revolution." Only a minority (46 percent) were in disagreement. Hence, over half the adult residents of Montevideo were so lacking in support of their system that they believed that a social revolution was necessary. Even more startling is that fully 12 percent of those polled were willing to admit that they viewed an armed uprising as the way out of the country's economic problems.[41] Since feelings of support for an armed uprising are something to which some individuals might fear to admit, the true level of such support may well have been higher. Finally, 21 percent admitted to preferring a military to a civilian government.[42]

The strong support for freedom of speech and assembly during the late 1960s in Uruguay, in light of the other survey data just presented, may be a misleading indicator of a democratic political culture. Perhaps the best indication of that would be to compare the finding that 21 percent of Uruguayans were ready to support a military government as a solution to the country's problems with the responses of Costa Ricans to a 1987 national probability survey ($N = 927$) directed by the author, Edward Muller and Miguel Gómez. Costa Rica is unique in Latin America in that the national army was disbanded in 1948 and not reestablished. The turmoil in Nicaragua and, to a lesser extent, in Panama led some Costa Ricans to suggest that a national army is needed for national defense. In our survey we asked: "As things are now in Central America, do you think that Costa Rica should begin to start thinking about creating an army?" Fully 88 percent of the national sample answered in the negative. The contrast with the Uruguayan data is clear.

Further evidence of limitations in support for democracy in Uruguay comes from an August 1970 Gallup survey of Montevideo ($N = 250$). In that survey, 48 percent of the respondents agreed that executive power was justified in suspending individual guarantees and allowing arrest and detention without the right to an appearance before a judge. These individuals, no doubt, were concerned about the rising power of the Tupamaro guerrilla group, which was responsible for numerous terrorist attacks in Montevideo. On the other hand, demonstrating that the guerrillas had considerable popular support, 18 percent of those interviewed in August 1970 thought that the Tupamaro movement was justified. Hence, while 48 percent of the population supported antidemocratic actions against guerrilla groups, an additional 18 percent of the population expressed support for such groups. Although we do not have the raw data and therefore cannot determine if these two groups were entirely mutually exclusive as we suspect they largely were, if we add them up we can conclude that over two-thirds of Uruguayans supported the destruction of either their country's entire democratic system or the democratic rights guaranteed by that system.

The Uruguayan data can be contrasted with the 1987 Costa Rican data. Uruguay in the late 1960s was undergoing a severe economic downturn coupled with a menacing guerrilla movement. Costa Rica had undergone its most serious economic crisis of the century in the period 1980–1982. In that two-year period alone, GNP per capita declined by 25 percent and the country racked up the largest per capita external debt in the world.[43] Although Costa Rica was not also suffering from a serious internal guerrilla movement, terrorist cells had been established and armed attacks were occurring. In addition, crime had risen dramatically and fear of entanglement in a Central American war was present in nearly everyone's mind. Yet in an urban sample conducted in 1983 ($N = 501$), only 2.8 percent expressed approval of individuals belonging to groups that sought to overthrow the government and only 1.2 percent expressed negative system support (on the pride item cited above).[44]

We thus have further evidence of a micro-macro linkage between political culture and political regime type. Yet, one can challenge these findings by arguing that survey data is notoriously unstable; anyone who followed the polls in the 1988 U.S. presidential election would conclude that vast shifts of opinion can occur from such nonevents as conventions in which the outcome was predetermined. If opinion data can be so unstable, then what are we to make of the data summarized above? Inglehart responds to this question by stating, "Even when democracy has no reply to the question, 'What have you done for me lately?' it may be sustained by diffuse feelings that it is an inherently good thing."[45] That is, attitudes toward democracy may be far more stable than attitudes toward incumbents and challengers in an election.

To test this hypothesis, we are fortunate to be able to examine the stability of the three tolerance items analyzed earlier in this paper for Costa Rican surveys that were taken in 1978, 1980, 1983, 1985, and 1987. If these are bedrock attitudes that support a political culture of democracy, then they should be relatively stable even when the system is subjected to severe shocks such as the economic crisis which began in Costa Rica in 1980. In 1987, 83 percent of the respondents believed that the economic crisis had been strong or very strong, and 95 percent of those who believed this thought that the crisis was still continuing, seven years after it had begun. Furthermore, 66 percent of those asked thought that the crisis would not be resolved in the coming years. Added to the crisis was the fear of Nicaragua: 88.5 percent of the respondents in 1987 believed that the Sandinista government of Nicaragua was a danger for Costa Rica. Hence, economic pessimism was deep and fear of foreign intervention a reality, factors that might well have eroded tolerance. Yet the evidence presented in Table 3 shows otherwise.

Evidence of the stability of the tolerance items is clear from this table. One indication is that in each year that the survey was administered, the "run for office" item proved the most difficult and the only one in which a consistent minority of the population took the tolerant position. But a more general indication is the stability of the percentages across the years. For a simple random sample of 200 and a 50/50 split, a confidence interval of 7.1 percent is obtained, while for samples of 500 and this same split, the interval would be 4.5 percent. As shown in Table 3, the intersample variation is usually well within the confidence interval. Only in 1987, on the censorship item, does one see a notable decline in tolerance for censorship and some erosion in tolerance for dissidents running for office. Yet, in that same survey, tolerance for the dissidents' right to vote was at its all-time high.

Table 3. Stability of Tolerance in Costa Rica, 1978–1987

| | Percent tolerant (range 6–10) | | | | |
	1978	1980	1983	1985	1987
Censorship	—[1]	51.6	56.3	56.9	49.5
Vote	51.7	59.2	56.3	56.5	60.3
Run for office	42.1	44.7	42.7	44.6	39.2
N	(201)	(280)	(501)	(506)	(388)[2]

Source: See note 33.
[1]Item wording differed in 1978 from other years.
[2]Includes only metropolitan area of San José and capitals of "Meseta Central" (Cartago, Heredia, and Alajuela) as in previous surveys. Entire sample in 1987 was 927.

The overall conclusion that one can draw from this table is that tolerance attitudes can be seen to be remarkably stable even under the impact of economic crisis and perceived foreign threats, at least in Costa Rica. Compare the stability of the Costa Rican data with Inglehart's finding that satisfaction with one's life as a whole, presumably an attitude subject to minor longitudinal variation, declined in Ireland from 53 percent satisfied in 1973 to 35 percent in 1980 and 30 percent in 1987. Belgium saw a decline on this attitude from 43 percent in 1973 to 20 percent in 1983. Denmark, in contrast, experienced an increase from 47 percent satisfied in 1983 to 65 percent in 1986.[46] In Uruguay, the Gallup poll showed that between May 1968 and July 1970, the proportion of people saying that the country needed a "total change" increased from 20 percent to 32 percent. This suggests that attitudes that are more deeply held than are presidential preferences are subject to considerable volatility. Yet, in systems with well-entrenched democracies, support for key civil liberties is largely invariant despite marked declines in macropolitical phenomena.

It has been shown, then, that civic culture may indeed matter after all as an important complement to socioeconomic determinants of regime type. Yet, there remains an important caveat in the literature on democratic attitudes that needs to be explored. Much of the literature has emphasized that while mass attitudes are not irrelevant, it is elite attitudes that are pivotal in influencing policy outcomes. Dahl's *Polyarchy* concerns itself with mass belief systems, but stresses that "it is difficult to see how a polyarchy could exist if a majority of the politically active strata of a country believe strongly that a hegemonic regime was more desirable and could be achieved by supporting antidemocratic leaders and organizations."[47] The tolerance literature on the U.S. case conforms with Dahl's perspective, stressing that, in almost every area of democratic beliefs, elites are more democratic. McClosky and Zaller find that elites are carriers of a nation's creed, and McClosky and Brill report that "elites (as a whole) were more tolerant than the population-at-large even at the same levels of education."[48] The direct link between elite attitudes and policy is provided by Gibson's study, cited earlier, which found that "elite opinion, not mass opinion, determines public policy."[49]

Unfortunately, as limited as our opinion data are for Latin American mass publics, elite data are even harder to come by. Yet, we do have a few important indications that further emphasize the importance of democratic civic culture. In a 1987 sample conducted by the author, Edward Muller, and Miguel Gómez, among a sample of 219 Costa Rican political elites, it was found that elites were indeed more tolerant than the masses interviewed in the 1987 sample.[50] Table 4 provides the relevant comparisons.

Elite tolerance is dramatically higher than mass tolerance in Costa Rica, especially on the critical item of the right to run for office. The percentage of tolerant elites is nearly three times as high as tolerant masses. One can conclude from this that the Costa Rican pattern conforms to that found in the United States: if democratic elites are most directly responsible for democratic politics, then Costa Rican elites are responsible for Costa Rican democracy.

The problem raised by the Costa Rican elite data is that if elites elsewhere in Latin America follow the Costa Rican pattern, then they too may be highly supportive of democratic norms. In that case, it would be impossible to link the attitudes of elites who have a democratic political culture to an authoritarian political system.

Table 4. Mass versus Elite Tolerance in Costa Rica, 1987

| | Percent tolerant (range 6–10)[1] | |
	Mass	Elite
Censorship	56.3	86.3
Vote	60.3	90.4
Run for office	34.6	91.8
N	(927)	(219)

Source: See note 33.
[1]Results for mass sample presented in this table are for the entire national sample, not just the urban areas utilized in Table 3.

There is limited evidence to show that, even at the elite level, there is congruence between political culture and political system. In 1962 and 1963, Daniel Goldrich conducted a survey of the political attitudes of elite youth in Costa Rica and Panama, Costa Rica's neighbor to the south.[51] In 1960, Panama ranked eleventh on the Fitzgibbon-Johnson scale, and Costa Rica ranked second. Hence, one would expect more democratic attitudes among the Costa Ricans than among the Panamanians. Goldrich asked the following item: "More than legislation, more than politicians, what this country needs is a leader in whom the people can place their confidence." In the early 1960s, 46 percent of Costa Rican elite youth agreed with this item, with agreement presumably indicating an antidemocratic proclivity. The Panamanian students, however, were far more antidemocratic as a group: 74 percent preferred a strong leader to legislation and politicians. We included the same item in our elite Costa Rica survey of 1987 and found that only 26 percent of the respondents took the antidemocratic position. This means that either Costa Ricans become more democratic as they mature or that the country as a whole moved in the direction of greater support for democratic norms between the early 1960s and the late 1980s. Since the sample was not a panel design, we really cannot know if either one or both of these explanations have validity. What we do know is that the political system of Costa Rica was supported by an elite political culture far more democratic than its less democratic neighbor, Panama.

Additional items in the Goldrich survey are of interest to the subjects addressed in this paper. Goldrich asked if the students agreed or disagreed with the following assertion: "Freedom of speech and assembly should be unlimited." He found that 61 percent of the Costa Rican elite youth agreed, compared with 45 percent of the Panamanian youth. He also asked for agreement/disagreement with the following item: "If a government is doing a good job, it should be allowed to continue in office even if it means postponing elections." Only 29 percent of Costa Rican elite youth agreed, compared with 54 percent of the Panamanians.

While we do not have the original Goldrich data and cannot investigate them directly, it is quite possible that as in Mexico, those who took democratic positions were more prevalent among those who opposed the political system. One piece of evidence pointing in that direction is responses to an item asked by Goldrich in 1962–63 in Panama and Costa Rica, and which was included in both the mass and elite 1987 surveys in Costa Rica. He asked for agreement/disagreement with this item: "In general, our system of government and politics is good for the country." In Panama, 40 percent of the youth agreed with the item, compared with 91 percent of the Costa Ricans. In 1987, 90 percent of the elites and 93 percent of the masses agreed, indicating virtually no change in support over the twenty-five-year period.

There are additional elite data to support the contention that elite opinion, while generally more democratic than mass opinion, is not supportive of democratic norms everywhere in Latin America. In Brazil, Peter McDonough surveyed 269 elites in 1972–73.[52] In 1970, Brazil ranked seventeenth out of twenty nations on the Fitzgibbon-Johnson scale. He asked for approval/disapproval of censorship of the media based on a 100-point scale, with the higher number indicating the more democratic end of the continuum. The average among all elites was 57, just barely falling on the democratic end of the continuum. The only strong opposition to censorship emerged among the Brazilian Democratic Movement (MDB) (i.e., opposition) party politicians, who averaged 96 on the 100-point scale. These scores, if they can be related directly to those presented in Table 1 of this essay in which a ten-point scale was employed, show that Brazilian elites expressed greater support of censorship than did masses in either Costa Rica or Mexico.

The final pieces of evidence supporting the micro-macro linkage argument made in this paper comes from the recent USIA polls conducted in Central America. In January 1988 comparatively large national samples were drawn in all of the Central American countries except Nicaragua.[53] The following question was asked in each country: "The people of Central America are best off when they live in a democracy. Do you agree strongly, agree somewhat, disagree somewhat or disagree strongly?" Strong agreement was expressed by 80 percent of Costa Ricans and 71 percent of Hondurans, the two most democratic countries in Central America. Only 41 percent of Guatemalans and 38 percent of Salvadorans agreed. These responses conform quite well to our perceptions of the levels of democracy in these countries.[54]

The central implicit question raised by this review of public opinion data in Latin America is that of the direction of causality. Do democratic attitudes cause democratic systems or vice versa? Inglehart argues, based upon his longitudinal analysis of opinion data, that it is attitudes that produce democracies.[55] But the problem is quite complex and not likely to be answered in the near future.

This discussion has attempted to demonstrate that the study of political culture is returning to the forefront of political analysis on Latin America. The inability of economic theories of democratization to predict successfully regime change in the region, coupled with the rapid transition to democratic regimes throughout Latin America, are largely responsible for this shift. While the flaws in earlier efforts to study political culture have become evident, newer approaches may lead to a deeper understanding of the relationship between political culture and regime type, as can be seen in studies of Costa Rica, Mexico, Brazil, and Uruguay. Additional research along these lines may help us better bridge the micro-macro gap that has plagued the analysis to date.

Notes

1. Riordan Roett, "La crisis de la deuda externa y el proceso de democratización en América Latina," *Ideas en ciencias sociales* 3, no. 5 (1987): 13–14.

2. Ary Dillon Glaucio Soares, "Economic Development and Democracy in Latin America" (paper delivered to the World Congress of the IPSA, Washington, DC, 28 August–1 September 1988), 1.

3. Guillermo A. O'Donnell, *Modernization and Bureaucratic-Authoritarianism: Studies in South American Politics* (Berkeley: Institute of International Studies, University of California at Berkeley, 1973).

4. Mitchell A. Seligson, "Democratization in Latin America: The Current Cycle," in *Authoritarians and Democrats: The Politics of Regime Transition in Latin America*, ed. James M. Malloy and Mitchell A. Seligson (Pittsburgh: University of Pittsburgh Press, 1987), 7–9.

5. As a group, the nations of Central America were the last in Latin America to achieve the requisite levels of GNP per capita. In the 1980s these nations all have elected regimes. For details see Mitchell A. Seligson, "Development, Democratization, and Decay: Central America at the Crossroads," in *Authoritarians and Democrats*.

6. Soares, "Economic Development and Democracy," 28.

7. Robert A. Dahl, *Polyarchy: Participation and Opposition* (New Haven: Yale University Press, 1971), 68–69. Dahl classifies India as a "polyarchy," his term for competitive, inclusive regimes.

8. Myron Weiner, "Empirical Democratic Theory," in *Competitive Elections in Developing Countries*, ed. Myron Weiner and Ergun Ozbudun (Durham: Duke University Press, 1987), 31.

9. These countries are: India, Sri Lanka, Malaysia, Jamaica, Trinidad and Tobago, and Papua New Guinea. See Weiner, "Empirical Democratic Theory," 18–19.

10. These include the Bahama Islands, Barbados, Botswana, Fiji, Nauru, Gambia, and Mauritius.

11. Mitchell A. Seligson, "Development, Democratization, and Decay," in Malloy and Seligson, *Authoritarians and Democrats*, 175. For a review of the process of democratization in Central America, see John A. Booth and Mitchell A. Seligson, *Elections and Democracy in Central America* (Chapel Hill: University of North Carolina Press, 1989).

12. Tatu Vanhanen, "The State and Prospects of Democracy in the 1980s" (paper delivered to the IPSA World Congress, Paris, 15–20 July 1985), 5.

13. Argentina, Chile, Mexico, Panama, and Uruguay.

14. Soares, "Economic Development and Democracy," 28.

15. Edward N. Muller and Mitchell A. Seligson, "Insurgency and Inequality," *American Political Science Review* 81 (June 1987): 425–51. This finding has been disputed by Manus I. Midlarski in "Rulers and the Ruled: Patterned Inequality and the Onset of Mass Political Violence," ibid., 82 (June 1988): 491–510; but see Edward N. Muller, Mitchell A. Seligson, and Hung-der Fu, "Land Inequality and Political Violence," *American Political Science Review* (June 1989): 577–87.

16. Mitchell A. Seligson, "The Dual Gaps: An Overview of Theory and Research," in *The Gap Between Rich and Poor: Contending Perspectives on the Political Economy of Development* (Boulder, CO: Westview Press, 1984).

17. Some would include Colombia in this list, but the restricted nature of party competition and the frequent suspension of constitutional guarantees militate against this view.

18. Ronald Inglehart, "The Renaissance of Political Culture: Central Values, Political Economy and Stable Democracy" (paper presented at the American Political Science Association Meeting, Chicago, IL, 2–5 September 1987), 2.

19. Sidney Verba, "On Revisiting the Civic Culture: A Personal Postscript," in *The Civic Culture Revisited*, ed. Gabriel A. Almond and Sidney Verba (Boston: Little, Brown, 1980), 409.

20. Scholars as well as practitioners have stressed the importance of political culture inherited from the colonial period in explaining much of contemporary political reality. See, for example, Glen Dealy, "The Tradition of Monistic Democracy in Latin America," in *Politics and Social Change in Latin America: The Distinct Tradition*, ed. Howard J. Wiarda (Amherst: University of Massachusetts Press, 1974); Richard M. Morse, "The Heritage of Latin America," in Wiarda, ed., *Politics and Social Change*; Howard J. Wiarda, *Corporatism and National Development in Latin America* (Boulder, CO: Westview Press, 1981); Lawrence E. Harrison, *Underdevelopment Is a State of Mind: The Latin American Case* (Boston: Center for International Affairs, Harvard University and University Press of America, 1985).

21. In *Underdevelopment Is a State of Mind*, Harrison attempts to show how the Costa Rican case differs because of idiosyncrasies in its historical evolution.

22. Inglehart, "The Renaissance of Political Culture," 5.

23. Ibid., 7.

24. James L. Gibson, "Political Intolerance and Political Repression During the McCarthy Red Scare," *American Political Science Review* 82 (June 1988): 511–30.

25. Ann L. Craig and Wayne A. Cornelius, "Political Culture in Mexico: Continuities and Revisionist Interpretations," in Almond and Verba, ed., *The Civic Culture Revisited*. See also Gabriel A. Almond and Sidney Verba, *The Civic Culture* (Princeton: Princeton University Press, 1963).

26. Norbert Lechner, *Cultura política y democratización* (Santiago, Chile: CLACSO/FLACSO/ICI, 1987); Enzo Faletto, "Cultura política y conciencia democrática," *Revista de la CEPAL* 35 (August 1988): 77–82.

27. Enzo Faletto, "Cultura política," 77. Author's translation of the Spanish.

28. USIA, "Central American Poll, 1988," 31 March 1988. See William A. Bollinger and Daniel M. Lund, "Mixing Polls and Propaganda," *The Nation*, 7 May 1988, 635–38. A panel session was held at the May 1985 meeting of the American Association for Public Opinion Research in Toronto, Canada, in which representatives of Gallup International, Yankelovich, the USIA, and the Interamerican Research Center (a polling organization critical of the USIA surveys) debated the issue. A report on that meeting can be found in *Interamerican Public Opinion Report*, June 1988.

29. *New York Times*, 27 March 1988, 10.

30. According to Norman Webb, Secretary General of Gallup International, as of April 1988 affiliates have been established in Argentina, Brazil, Chile, Colombia, Costa Rica, Ecuador, Mexico, Peru, Bolivia, and Uruguay.

31. Enrique A. Baloyra, "Democracy Despite Development," *World Affairs* 150 (1987): 75–76.

32. This included the capital cities of Alajuela, Cartago, and Heredia, the three major cities outside of San José in the *meseta central* of Costa Rica.

33. Reports on various components of these surveys can be found in John A. Booth and Mitchell A. Seligson, "The Political Culture of Authoritarianism in Mexico: A Reevaluation," *Latin American Research Review* 19 (January 1984): 106–24; Edward N. Muller, Mitchell A. Seligson, and Thomas O. Jukam, "Diffuse Political Support and Antisystem Political Behavior: A Comparative Analysis," *American Journal of Political Science* 26 (May 1982): 240–64; Mitchell A. Seligson, "On the Measurement of Diffuse Support: Some Evidence from Mexico," *Social Indicators Research* 12 (January 1983): 1–24; and Mitchell A. Seligson and Edward J. Williams, *Maquiladoras and Migration Workers in the Mexico–United States Border Industrialization Program* (Austin: University of Texas Press, 1981). The sample *N*s reported in the text refer only to that subset of the three samples that is directly comparable by socioeconomic class criteria and for which the same questionnaire items were used. The complete samples in New York and Mexico were larger. The Costa Rican and New York surveys were stratified probability samples, whereas the Mexico survey was based upon quota criteria. Mitchell A. Seligson, "Ordinary Elections in Extraordinary Times: The Political Economy of Voting in Costa Rica," in *Elections and Democracy in Central America*; and Steve Finkel, Edward N. Muller, and Mitchell A. Seligson, "Economic Crisis, Incumbent Performance, and Regime Support: West Germany and Costa Rica," *British Journal of Political Science* 19 (July 1989): 329–51.

34. James W. Prothro and Charles M. Grigg, "Fundamental Principles of Democracy: Bases of Agreement and Disagreement," *Journal of Politics* 22 (1960): 276–94.

35. Herbert McClosky and Alida Brill, *Dimensions of Tolerance: What Americans Believe about Civil Liberties* (New York: Russell Sage Foundation, 1983); John L. Sullivan, James Pireson, and George E. Marcus, *Political Tolerance and*

American Democracy (Chicago: University of Chicago Press, 1982); Dan Caspi and Mitchell A. Seligson, "Toward an Empirical Theory of Tolerance: Radical Groups in Israel and Costa Rica," *Comparative Political Studies* 15 (January 1983): 385–404; Edward N. Muller, Mitchell A. Seligson, and Ilter Turan, "Education, Participation, and Support for Democracy," *Comparative Politics* 20 (October 1987): 19–33.

36. Muller, Seligson, and Jukam, "Diffuse Political Support."

37. We have generally used six to eight items in the series. See Muller, Seligson, and Jukam, "Diffuse Political Support," and Seligson, "On the Measurement of Diffuse Support," for full discussions of these items.

38. The two surveys used a different metric for this item. The Mexican survey used a metric ranking from a low of 1 to a high of 10. The bottom half is considered the scores ranging from 1 to 5. The Costa Rican metric ranged from 1 to 7. Hence, there is a neutral point (4) in this scale, but not in the Mexican administration. If the neutral point is included in the bottom half calculation, the percentage with low pride increases from 5.3 percent to 8.5 percent.

39. Gallup Uruguay, various poll reports, 1968–1971. Gallup Uruguay was probably the first Gallup affiliate established in Latin America and has a reputation for producing surveys of exceptionally high quality.

40. In actual fact, comparisons of Gallup's Montevideo data with national data in other studies that they have conducted show very little variation.

41. The actual item read: "Personally, do you believe that armed revolution is the only way to resolve the economic problems of our country, or can the solutions be encountered within the bounds of law and order?"

42. The item read: "Which do you prefer: a democracy like ours, with all of its disorder and crises, or a military government such as exist in other countries in our continent?"

43. Juan M. Villasuso, "Costa Rica: crisis, políticas de ajuste y desarrollo rural," *Revista de la CEPAL* 33 (December 1987): 113.

44. This study, too, was conducted by Seligson, Muller, and Gómez.

45. Inglehart, "The Renaissance of Political Culture," 7.

46. Ibid., 7a.

47. Dahl, *Polyarchy*, 126.

48. Herbert McClosky and John Zaller, *The American Ethos: Public Attitudes Toward Capitalism and Democracy* (Cambridge: Twentieth Century Fund, 1984), 9; McClosky and Brill, *Dimensions of Tolerance*, 251.

49. Gibson, "Political Intolerance and Political Repression," 518.

50. The sample consisted of current and sitting presidents, vice presidents, congressmen, ministers, party leaders, university students, political leaders, party youth leaders, and leaders of the mass media.

51. Daniel Goldrich, *Sons of the Establishment: Elite Youth in Panama and Costa Rica* (Chicago: Rand McNally, 1966).

52. Peter McDonough, *Power and Ideology in Brazil* (Princeton: Princeton University Press, 1981), 176–78. The sample included leaders in politics, civil service, business, labor, the church, and the military.

53. Sample Ns were: Costa Rica, 1,197; Honduras, 1,190; El Salvador, 1,204; and Guatemala, 1,150.

54. Booth and Seligson, *Elections and Democracy in Central America.*

55. Inglehart, "The Renaissance of Political Culture," 13.

5

Lost Promise: Explaining Latin American Underdevelopment

Peter F. Klarén

Many authors have long associated underdevelopment, socially and economically, with political change and, specifically, with democratization. Perhaps more than any other region in the Third World, Latin America has attracted the attention of theorists trying to explain the failure of development in the nonindustrialized world. Peter Klarén, who teaches Latin American politics at George Washington University, foresaw the changing political landscape in Promise of Development: Theories of Change in Latin America *(1986). Here, he examines the major theoretical contributions focusing on the problems of development, first by providing an overview of the works of Karl Marx, Max Weber, and Emile Durkheim and then by exploring the significant sociological and political interpretations since the 1950s. Klarén carefully and lucidly explains the introduction of dependency theory to the Latin American debate, the contributions of modern corporatist theorists, and the bureaucratic-authoritarianism model, all of which have dominated the literature since the 1960s.*

"The development of underdevelopment" is the way one observer, the controversial economist André Gunder Frank, characterized Latin America's evolution since the Iberian invasion of the late fifteenth century. Although many reject Frank's theory of causality, few dispute the stark reality of Latin America's profound underdevelopment in today's world. Once imagined by its Iberian conquerors as a land of "El Dorado," Latin America stands five centuries later at the precipice of economic and social disaster. It is a region wracked by the possibility of collective

From *Promise of Development: Theories of Change in Latin America*, ed. Peter F. Klarén and Thomas J. Bossert (Boulder, CO: Westview Press, 1986), 3–33. Reprinted by permission of Westview Press.

bankruptcy and the reality that most of its people, to borrow from Franklin D. Roosevelt's famous description of the United States in the depths of the depression, are ill housed, ill clothed, and ill fed. Crowded into the sprawling urban slums that surround Latin America's primary cities or locked into a "feudalized" hinterland, prisoners of a decaying economic and social system, Latin America's masses confront an uncertain, increasingly desperate material future.

Explanations for this dismal state of affairs abound. The historiography of the problem reveals numerous interpretations that at best are replete with oversimplification and overgeneralization and at worst are infused with racial stereotype and cultural bias. Prior to this century, for example, Anglo-American writers such as William H. Prescott (1796–1859) viewed the Iberian world through a "glass darkly" and described a world distorted by international rivalry and a collective mythology that stressed religious, cultural, and racial superiority. The image presented by these writers conjured up a "black legend" that attributed Latin American underdevelopment to a brutal Iberian colonialism that mercilessly enslaved and exploited the native peoples of Latin America for metropolitan gain. The object of such hyperbole was, as often as not, wholly self-serving, meant to glorify the emerging democratic experiment of the North by contrasting it to some dark, despotic, Catholic-Latin world in the South.

Another widely held interpretation of Latin American backwardness was the product of nineteenth-century European racist thought that was assimilated by the Creole (Spanish-American) elite after their independence from Spain. A strong sense of racial superiority helped them justify their claim as the new, legitimate rulers of the region. Although implicitly extolling white superiority, they blamed Latin America's lack of progress (defined in European terms) on the Indian, black African, or mestizo masses who were judged inferior and inherently incapable of self-improvement.

In more recent times, these and other equally shallow or warped explanations have given way to more complex, sophisticated interpretations of what many consider the paramount issue of our time. Since the end of World War II, the West has become increasingly aware of the dilemmas of the Third World. This awareness was spurred by three factors: first, the process of postwar decolonization and recurrent wars of national liberation around the world; second, the technological revolution that drew the world closer together and made it more interdependent; and third, the bipolarization of global politics and the rise of the Cold War between East and West, each side with contrasting ideologies competing for influence in every corner of the world. By converging when they did and heightening awareness in the West of the human condition of Third World people, these factors worked in the postwar era, particularly within the emerging social sciences, to focus intellectual resources on finding solutions to the development conundrum.

As a result, four distinct and often opposing theories of Latin American development—modernization, dependency and Marxism, corporatism, and bureaucratic-authoritarianism—gradually emerged during the past few decades. Theorists from each school explained and interpreted Latin American underdevelopment while proposing their own formula for promoting development in the region. Since no theory is produced in an intellectual vacuum and without certain "precursors," let us briefly turn back to the great transformation that forged the European industrial revolution and the rise of modern Western society. Each of the Latin American development theories in one way or another traces its philosophical roots back to that period of complex change and intellectual ferment that occurred in Europe from the sixteenth through the nineteenth centuries.

Classical Sociological Theory: Marx, Weber, Durkheim

Between the sixteenth and nineteenth centuries, a series of developments culminated in modern industrial capitalism, which was to transform not only the West but much of the entire world, including Latin America, by the end of the twentieth century. Fascination with the nature of this vast transition—when, why, and how it occurred—first emerged in the nineteenth century with a corpus of social thought that came to be known as classical sociological theory. The scions of this theory, although by no means its only elaborators, were three towering nineteenth-century thinkers—Marx, Weber, and Durkheim. Thus, the discourse on the problem of modern underdevelopment in the southern hemisphere begins with this triumvirate of European intellectual giants.

Karl Marx (1818–1883)—the great German economist, philosopher, and sociologist—presented an evolutionary view of the development of man and society. According to Marx, society had passed through several stages—tribal (communal); slave (Greece, Rome); and feudal (Europe in the Middle Ages)—and had arrived at modern capitalism, whose industrial phase he personally observed in England (primarily Manchester) in the mid-nineteenth century. For Marx, who regarded the material, economic conditions of life as the basis of societal organization, the central feature of society's great transformation was the emergence of capitalism.

According to Marx, capitalism had several defining characteristics. These included:

- A ruling class;
- the bourgeoisie or capitalists who owned the means of production;
- a production system based on the exploitation of labor;
- the expropriation of labor's "surplus value" by the bourgeoisie to form the "accumulated" capital necessary to drive the system;
- the alienation of the worker from the product of his work;
- the tendency of capital to concentrate in ever-fewer hands, thereby polarizing society into two hostile classes—the propertied or bourgeois class and the propertyless working class or proletariat.

Marx further believed that this polarization would culminate in a final class struggle in which the proletariat would be victorious and capitalism destroyed. The victorious proletariat would then proceed to construct socialism and communism (terms Marx used interchangeably), which Marx viewed as the final or highest stage of society's evolution.

Like other philosophers of his era Marx believed that his theory of society had established the existence of universal laws of evolution and that each stage was a prerequisite for the next. Thus, although societies might evolve at different rates, none could avoid passing through these stages. Capitalism, according to Marx, was a crucial, if transitory, stage in the evolution of Western society. Marx believed that it was primarily a sixteenth-century phenomenon with roots in the medieval cities of feudal Europe. The discovery of America in 1492 and its subsequent colonization, along with the opening of trade to China and India, provided enormous, expanding markets that stimulated Europe's budding industry and commerce.

For Max Weber (1864–1920), the renowned German sociologist and political economist, capitalism was also an important feature of the great transformation. However, Weber was more interested in explaining the uniqueness of modern Western society, which he saw as radically different from the premodern world. For him the core of this distinctiveness lay in modern society's rationality, epitomized by the development of science and the empirical method. This rationalism permeated the entire fabric of Western society, particularly its religious structure (Protestantism and its stress on doctrine and ethics as opposed to ritual and ceremony), polity (the growing importance of bureaucracy with its division of labor and impersonal rules), and economy (the rise of capitalism).

Weber observed in European history a rationalist tendency in the political sphere marked by the slow rise of bureaucratic organizations. Lacking direction, however, bureaucratic rule was periodically eclipsed by the emergence of charismatic leaders who sprang from the masses to seize power from traditional leaders. After periods of unrestrained and unpredictable rule by such leaders, the forces of routinization would reassert themselves. A successor to the charismatic leader would be selected and would reimpose a rationalized and routinized form of rule on society.

As Weber saw it, Western society had alternated dialectically between periods of bureaucratic routine and irrational outbreaks of charismatic rule. In general, however, the tendency toward increasing bureaucratic rationalization of the polity was slow in developing, as was the economy, until the forces of capitalism transformed the organization of production and rationalized the economy.

For Weber capitalism was but one further expression of the process of rationalizing Western society. Unlike Marx, however, who saw the essence of capitalism in the expropriation of surplus value from labor, or the neoclassical economists, who saw capitalism in the pursuit of profit, Weber emphasized what he called the new capitalist spirit among entrepreneurs and workers, which he linked to the advent of the Reformation. Weber made this unique theoretical contribution in his seminal work *The Protestant Ethic and the Spirit of Capitalism*, which stressed the importance of values and ideas as well as strictly economic factors (upon which Marx's theory was based) in the rise of capitalism.[1]

While Weber asserted that the uniqueness of the West derived from the increasing rationalization of society, Emile Durkheim (1858–1917), a French sociologist and philosopher, focused on what he perceived as the breakdown of community that occurred during the transition from a traditional society to a modern society. Under the impact of rapid social change brought about by the increasing capitalization of the economy, the ties of mechanical solidarity that traditionally had bound people in tightly knit communities rapidly unraveled. Urbanization, in particular, had brought about a depersonalization of life, and the traditional authority of the church, the family, and other institutions had eroded, leaving the masses directionless and suspended in a spiritual void. The result of this increasingly soulless individualism was, in Durkheim's view, widespread "anomie," a sense of isolation and alienation from others.

To counteract this tendency Durkheim, using an analogy from biology, advocated the creation of an organic solidarity, composed of new institutions such as the state that would replace older sources of moral authority. Community could be re-formed, for example, at the workplace, where the corporate guild could serve as a new harmonious, if hierarchical, institution anchoring people's lives. Durkheim thus became an advocate of corporatist theory whose idea of the organic state goes back to the political philosophies of Aristotle (384–322 B.C.) and Saint Thomas Aquinas (1225?–1274).

Despite their obvious theoretical differences and emphases, these three nineteenth-century thinkers agreed on one essential point. The West in their view had experienced a profound transition from a traditional to a modern society. Moreover, this transformation had produced a breakdown in community life and the emergence of a more universal and impersonal social structure. It remained for social scientists in the next century to elaborate further this dichotomous view of world development (i.e., the transition from traditional to modern society) in their attempts to analyze the problem of underdevelopment in the Third World.

Reconceptualization of Development after World War II

The preoccupation of the nineteenth-century philosophers with explaining the development of the West shifted in the twentieth century to understanding the lag or lack of development in most of the non-Western, or Third World, countries. The Russian Revolution of 1917 did much to precipitate this intellectual reorientation. Here was a revolution of monumental significance, which, contrary to Marx's prediction, did not occur as a result of capitalist development in Europe, but rather in a backward, noncapitalist, largely agrarian, non-Western country that saw only the beginnings of European capitalist growth. Why had the Third World remained seemingly inpervious to the developmental evolution that had been experienced in the West? It was not until the end of World War II that social scientists, particularly in the United States, became preoccupied with this question in response to the fundamental changes taking place in world affairs during the postwar period.

First, the defeat of the Axis powers in 1945 marked the rise of both the United States and the Soviet Union as world powers and the subsequent polarization between East and West. Second, the postwar period inaugurated a trend toward self-determination, which led to the breakup of the vast colonial empires in Asia and Africa carved out by the West in the nineteenth century. As a myriad of independent nation states emerged from this breakup, their leaders were confronted with two problems. One was how to relate, in a bipolar world, to the two great powers that were intensively competing for influence. The other problem was how to foster development of their backward economies. Most of these leaders shared the nearly universal aspiration for modernity and a better standard of living for their citizens, which they felt could be achieved through rapid economic growth and social transformation.

In this context, U.S. policymakers searched for arguments to counter Soviet claims that Marxism represented a better alternative for development in the Third World than did Western capitalism. At the same time U.S. scholars began to study in earnest the causes of underdevelopment. In particular scholars asked why the West had developed and most of the rest of the world had not.

Whether there was a direct relationship between U.S. national interests and the formulation of modernization theory is not altogether clear. However, critics of modernization suggest that it was no coincidence that as the political and economic power of the United States expanded in the postwar period, so too did the preeminence of liberal, developmental thought in the form of modernization theory. These critics argue that U.S. social science, overtly or subtly as the product of a collective Cold War mentality prone to defend liberal, Western, capitalist values, was put to the service of U.S. policymakers and U.S. national interests. The critics further contend that this use of U.S. social science explains the substantial investment that was made by U.S. foundations and the U.S. government in building a sophisticated social science establishment in the United States during the postwar years as well as the strongly ethnocentric and self-serving world view that they perceive as infusing modernization theory.

Modernization Theory

In any case, modernization theory evolved directly from two ideas about social change that were developed by the nineteenth-century fathers of sociology. One idea was Weber's polar conception of traditional versus modern, which was given a Third World dimension in this century by anthropologist Robert Redfield in his theory of a folk-urban dichotomy. The other idea was the theory of evolution developed by Auguste Comte (1798–1857), the French founder of the philosophical system of Positivism, who also based his thinking on the polar conception. Comte conceived of a theory of social evolution in which modern ("industrial" and "scientific") society was the culmination of a series of stages in human development from a traditional ("theological" and "military") society.[2] The idea that human society had evolved in a series of ever more complex stages, a theory further elaborated by English philosopher Herbert Spencer (1820–1903), came to form an important part of mainstream nineteenth-century thought.

These two strands were combined into a theory of the "stages of growth," which came to form the core of modernization theory in the mid-twentieth century. This theory held that all societies were alike at the "traditional" stage and that eventually they would pass through the same set of changes that had led the West to the "modern" stage.

This polar conception is particularly evident in the work of economist Walt W. Rostow (1960), who elaborated a theory of economic "take-off" in which self-sustained growth involved five stages of development from traditional to modern. Modeled on the experience of the British industrial revolution, Rostow's theory assumed that Third World societies could replicate this experience by developing policies to increase capital accumulation and investment as well as to foster entrepreneurial values or entrepreneurship. For Rostow and other economists who held similar beliefs, modernization for the Third World meant primarily the application of technology to the control of nature as a means of increasing per capita growth.

Dualism, as formulated in the work of economist W. A. Lewis (1955), likewise reflected a polar conception. Lewis distinguished between a dynamic "capitalist" sector and a stagnant "subsistence" sector within the economy. The latter lagged far behind the former in capital, income, and rate of growth. Moreover, interaction between the two sectors was reduced to the unlimited amount of labor supplied by the subsistence sector to the capitalist sector.

The same polar concept of modernization appeared in the work of sociologist Talcott Parsons (1951), a founder of the structural-functionalist approach to social change. A neoevolutionist, Parsons drew from Weber but particularly from the *Gemeinschaft* to *Gesellschaft* (community to association) dichotomy developed by German sociologist Ferdinand Tönnies (1855–1936). Like other sociologists and social anthropologists, Parsons was primarily concerned with the process of differentiation that characterized modern societies.

Parsons believed that forces such as the increasing division of labor were working steadily to divide society. To counteract this tendency toward social disintegration, these new forces had to be accompanied by other forces, pulling society back together again. Here Parsons sought to define the way society reintegrates itself. Differentiation occurred in the economic system and in the social, particularly status, elements of that system. Modernization occurred when economic and technological change made the traditional social and status structures obsolete.

Parsons also suggested that specific characteristics, which he called "pattern variables," distinguished traditional societies from modern societies. He argued that traditional societies contained values often associated with small, local communities: little division of labor and all-encompassing interpersonal relationships. By contrast modern societies were larger and more complex, with greater division of labor and increased mobility. Individual achievements were more important than family background or other inherent factors. In addition the hierarchical, personalistic sources of authority that permeated all aspects of traditional societies were replaced in modern societies by separate political institutions with rational, legal, and impersonal bases of authority.

Parsons viewed the process of modernization as requiring changes in social values toward those associated with the modern "ideal." In particular, diffuse, multifaceted relationships that tied people together in a community had to be replaced by more specific, segmented relationships associated with distinct roles representing separate functions in the new, more complex division of labor. "Collective" traditional values had to be replaced by "individual" modern values. The tendency to treat others according to personal ties—what Parsons called "particularism" —had to be replaced by universally valid, objective, and impersonal criteria.

This typology was based on the assumption that a society's value system, as well as its institutional configuration, was paramount in determining its potential for development. The attainment of self-sustaining growth involved far more than purely economic processes of production, investment, and consumption, as the developmental economists would have it. Rather the values, institutions, and patterns of a society had to be considered. In the case of traditional society, these elements were both a cause and an effect of underdevelopment and constituted obstacles to modernization. For modernizationists the norms and structures of traditional society had to be changed. Traditional society had to give way to sweeping innovations. New ideas, values, techniques, and organizations had to be introduced into the old social order.

There was, however, disagreement over the specific nature of this change. Modernizationists such as Neil Smelser (1963), a sociologist at Berkeley, and Parsons himself affirmed that modernization derived from increasing societal and institutional differentiation and from the rise of new sources of integration (i.e., nationalism, political parties, bureaucracies). Others such as sociologists Everett Hagen (1962) and David McClelland (1962), based on their studies of attitudes in traditional societies, emphasized the assimilation of modern values by individuals.

How this innovation would occur in the Third World was clarified by, among others, political scientist Daniel Lerner (1958) in his in-depth study of the Middle East. Lerner argued that although the West had modernized because of endogenous cultural and institutional changes, non-Western development would be exogenous, brought about by the mechanism of diffusion. Progress was to be diffused from the West—the United States and Europe—to the rest of the world, which would adopt and adapt Western technology, assimilate Western values and patterns of action, and import Western institutions. In short, Third World countries would be able to adopt already established social and economic patterns and would move quickly on the path to development already followed by the West.

The political implications of modernization in Third World countries were drawn by Harvard sociologist Seymour Martin Lipset (1967) and political scientist James Coleman (1960). Westernization, industrialization, and economic growth would generate the preconditions for the evolution of greater social equality and hence, it was assumed, the rise of stable, democratic institutions. Progress, as defined by the West, would in the end transform the underdeveloped world and propel it headlong into the twentieth century and modernity.

As the main lines of modernization theory unfolded, however, such unbounded initial optimism was soon tempered by a troubling question. Was the presumed beneficial impact on Third World societies all that substantial or clear-cut? Political scientist Dankwart Rustow (1967), for example, warned that the effects of modernization were morally ambiguous and that, together with the unprecedented benefits, modernization also brought inevitable hazards and deprivations. Others, such as Harvard political scientist Samuel Huntington (1968) and Princeton historian Cyril Black (1966), saw modernization as disruptive, the source of discontent and social and political conflict. Huntington in particular challenged the idea that modernization led to the emergence of greater equality and democracy in developing areas. Pointing to the growing evidence of revolution, violence, and coups, Huntington suggested instead that rapid development often triggered sociopolitical tensions that led to the breakdown of stable regimes and a form of "praetorian politics." In this scenario the military, not democratic parties, stabilized the polity and created the necessary preconditions for sustained economic growth.

Despite these and other questions, many writers on Latin America, particularly in the United States, applied modernization theory to explain the region's developmental problems. These writers argued that traditional values and institutions that originated in the Iberian colonization of the region in the sixteenth century blocked efforts toward economic and sociopolitical development. They singled out in particular the attitudes of Catholicism, of the large Indian populations, and of the aristocratic landed elite as inimical to the process of modernization and development in the region.

One of the first Latin Americans to apply modernization theory to the problem of Latin American development was Gino Germani. A pioneer of modern sociological analysis in his native Argentina, Germani later came to the United States, where he taught for many years at Harvard with Talcott Parsons and Seymour Martin Lipset. Focusing on the impact of rapid industrialization and urbanization on Argentine society, Germani's most important work, published in 1963, was entitled *Política y Sociedad en una Epoca de Transición* (Politics and Society in an Epoch of Transition).

Germani envisioned Latin America as passing through a series of stages from a traditional to a "mass" or modern society. This was a decidedly disjointed, often accelerated, process punctuated by serious social dislocations that, for Germani, explained the unstable nature of politics. In Parsonian terms the transition in Latin America had produced a rapid process of structural differentiation but not the necessary reintegration to solidify the modern social organism. To a large extent Germani viewed the process as disruptive and negative in its effect on Third World "latecomers" to the process of modernization, industrialization, and development, such as Latin America.

In the United States perhaps the foremost modernizationist writing on Latin American development was Seymour Martin Lipset. His essay "Values, Education and Entrepreneurship" introduced the widely read and influential work *Elites in Latin America*, published in 1967. Lipset was strongly influenced by the ideas of Weber and drew directly on the theories of both Parsons and McClelland in arguing the centrality of differing value systems to explain the disparity between the development of North America and that of South America. For Lipset, echoing Weber, the lack of an entrepreneurial ethic, which he attributed to Hispanic feudalism, was crucial in explaining Latin American underdevelopment. Underdevelopment could be overcome, however, with the spread of a Westernized educational system throughout the region. Unlike Germani, Lipset viewed modernization as beneficial to Latin America, something to be pursued vigorously by the policymakers of both North and South.

Political scientist Kalman Silvert followed a similar line of reasoning in arguing that a "Mediterranean ethos" explained Latin America's historic underdevelopment. "Modernizers," however, were increasingly emerging from the middle and upper classes to challenge this ethos, a fact that gave promise to the future of a more democratic, pluralistic polity. That idea was echoed by Stanford University historian John J. Johnson, whose historical analysis of what he called the "middle sectors" in early twentieth-century society suggested a trend toward greater democracy and modernization. French sociologist Jacques Lambert, on the other hand, took a different analytical tack. Lambert conceived of a dual society in which modernization, diffusing from the urban areas, was impeded by the large landed estates—latifundia—that dominated the rural areas. Only through agrarian reform could structural change unleash the forces of modernity.

Despite the clarity and cogency of the modernization paradigm, it was not long before a number of telling criticisms were leveled against it. One problem involved its use of evolutionary theory and the assumption by modernizationists that all societies moved on a linear, developmental continuum from traditional to modern, as had allegedly happened in the West, passing through a series of universal stages of growth. One difficulty with this idea was that contact between two cultures, Parson's "diffusion" and Lerner's optimistic "exogenous" influences, might well modify such a sequence of stages. More importantly, with respect to the dichotomy between traditional and modern, not all preindustrial societies were or are alike. Social structures vary greatly around the world, and there was no reason to assume that feudal, tribal, or bureaucratic societies would all change in the same way. Furthermore, the word "traditional" conveyed a false image of a wholly static equilibrium, which was simply not the case in many non-Western societies.

Finally, modernizationists, assuming that the Western transition could be mechanically replicated anywhere, insisted on imposing their culturally based model of development somewhat indiscriminately on the rest of the world. Moreover, they emphasized that endogenous more than exogenous factors would stimulate the value changes in traditional Latin American society that would lead to the rise, as in the West, of an entrepreneurial elite that would spearhead development. However, such a view of change largely ignored the powerful economic effects of international trade. As more scholarly attention was focused on the processes of change in the Third World, the modernization viewpoint was vigorously disputed, particularly by proponents of a new perspective that came to be known as dependency.

Dependency and Marxism

The dependency theory or approach began as a serious challenge to modernization theory in the 1960s.[3] The theory originated in the extensive Latin American debate over the problem of underdevelopment, and as such it became a distinctly Latin American contribution to modern social science. Two factors converged to form the dependency school: discussions of underdevelopment that coalesced in the work of the United Nations Economic Commission for Latin America (ECLA) and the revision of orthodox Marxism, which came to be known as "neo-Marxism."

Early discussion of underdevelopment in Latin America was characterized by intense self-criticism and a nearly universal tendency on the part of *pensadores* (thinkers) to apply European thought (eighteenth-century evolutionism, Comtean Positivism, and social Darwinism) to Latin American conditions. It was not until the era of World War I, which saw the Mexican and Russian revolutions as well as a continuation of interventions in Latin America by the United States, that Latin Americans began to attribute their problems to the world at large. The Great Depression of the 1930s intensified this tendency to externalize the causes of Latin American underdevelopment and formed the background for the peripheral theory of economic development. Pioneered by Raúl Prebisch, an Argentine economist and director of ECLA in the 1950s, this theory attributed the causes for Latin America's underdevelopment to the system of international free trade.

To understand why Latin American underdevelopment persisted, ECLA economists focused on the region's relationship with the world economy, which they portrayed as divided into a developed "center" and an underdeveloped "periphery." Departing from the conventional approach of modernizationists, ECLA economists argued that Latin America was adversely affected by its trade relationship with the industrialized countries of the West. In the nineteenth and early twentieth centuries the Latin American periphery increasingly specialized in the production of raw materials (cotton, wool, various minerals) and foodstuffs (wheat, sugar, cattle products) for the industrial center, receiving in return manufactured goods. ECLA argued that instead of benefiting both trading partners equally, according to laws of comparative advantage of neoclassical economics, the terms of trade had turned against Latin America: the prices (hence profits) on exports from the periphery steadily declined, while the prices of manufactured goods from the center conversely increased. Only when trade was cut off between the center and the periphery because of the world wars or depression did Latin America experience a surge of industrial development and thus a more balanced cycle of growth. Whenever trade ties were reestablished between the two regions, Latin American "outward" development resumed, and industrial development again languished.

To reverse this structural imbalance between the center and the periphery, ECLA proposed policies to foster import-substitution industrialization (ISI) and thereby turn Latin America from an outward to an inward pattern of development. A series of measures would be undertaken at the initiative of the state to accomplish this goal. Domestic industries were to be protected from foreign competition by tariffs and stimulated by various government subsidies and a controlled exchange rate. Structural reforms, such as land reform, and income redistribution policies would be pursued in order to expand the internal market for local industry by increasing the purchasing power of peasants and workers.

Initial acceptance of the ECLA strategy, particularly its emphasis on land reform, was slow in unfolding, but by the mid-1950s several Latin American countries had adopted import-substitution industrialization programs based on ECLA proposals. After a short period of success, however, ISI expansion came to a halt during the 1960s as the domestic market reached new limits and became saturated. In addition, to avoid tariff barriers to their products U.S. multinational corporations (MNCs) simply established manufacturing subsidiaries in many Latin American countries. In its analysis of underdevelopment, ECLA had never questioned the role of foreign capital, which it found salutory in the development process; nor had it explored the role of imperialism in this process. This exploration would now be done by a growing number of critics within ECLA who drew upon Marxist theories of imperialism to alter and expand upon ECLA's idea of the center's exploitation of the periphery.

Marxism and the New Left

As with the main nineteenth-century theories seeking to explain the great transformation in the West, early theories of imperialism focused upon its causes in the metropolis rather than its effects on the periphery. Political economist J. A. Hobson (1858–1940) theorized that because of waning demand in the metropolis Western capitalists sought overseas markets for their goods. The great Communist theorist V. I. Lenin (1870–1924), expanding on Hobson's argument, believed that declining profits at home pushed capitalists to find more profitable investments abroad. Lenin also envisioned imperialism as a distinct stage in the world development of capitalism and not as a relationship between two nations or economies. Indeed, Lenin claimed, erroneously as it turned out, that imperialism was the highest stage of capitalism. His predictions were belied by the post–World War II process of decolonization, which did not bring about the collapse of capitalism.

ECLA critics now studied imperialism as part of their analysis of why the ECLA strategy of ISI had gone awry in the 1960s. However, they concentrated their view of imperialism not from the center countries, as Lenin had done, but from the periphery. Contrary to the optimism of some modernizationists, these critics found the effects of exogenous Western influence to be decidedly deleterious to developing nations.

At this point neo-Marxism began to make its imprint on the genesis of dependency. The political context nourishing the neo-Marxist critique of orthodox Marxism was provided by the rise of the New Left in Latin America during the 1960s. Representing the challenge of a new generation to orthodox Marxism, the New Left was particularly critical of the Stalinist tradition adopted by most of the Communist parties on the continent.

According to the Stalinist tradition, Latin America was still in the grip of feudal economic and political relationships. The first stage of what has been labeled the Communist Party's two-stage revolutionary strategy called for an alliance with the national bourgeoisie in order to overthrow the remnant powers of the feudal oligarchy. Once capitalism was brought to full bloom under the aegis of the bourgeoisie, the Communist Party would undertake the second stage—the proletarian revolution that would lead to the overthrow of capitalism and the establishment of socialism.

The success of the Cuban Revolution of 1959 galvanized the New Left throughout the continent. The revolution illuminated a powerful new path in which the peasants were more inclined to revolt than [were] the workers and mobilizing rural guerrillas appeared to be a viable alternative to organizing urban laborers. The revolution also led the New Left to question the Communist Party's historic two-stage strategy. It grew increasingly impatient with the failure of the "objective conditions" for revolution to materialize, as predicted by orthodox Marxist doctrine (e.g., the capitalist stage to be fully developed, enabling the proletariat to be mobilized). As a result, the New Left adopted the ideas of Che Guevara (1928–1967), Latin American revolutionary and leader of the Cuban Revolution, about the ability of the human will to overcome such objective limitations—the so-called voluntarist revolutionary strategy. Boldly proclaiming that the duty of a revolutionary was to make revolution, this new generation set off seismic reverberations in Marxist political and intellectual circles.

A major challenge to orthodox Marxist views on development had already appeared in a work by political economist Paul Baran entitled *The Political Economy of Growth*, published in 1957. In it Baran argued that Western imperialism, rather than initiating the global transition from feudalism to capitalism according to Marxist-Leninist theory, had actually stunted the growth of capitalism in the Third World by draining off capital and killing native industry through unequal competition. Here was a derailment of Marx's evolutionary theory of development. Baran concluded that the Third World had stagnated somewhere between feudalism and capitalism. Imperialism did not represent the highest stage of capitalism in its inexorable march toward proletarian revolution and worldwide socialism. Rather, according to Baran, it had produced a chronic condition of perpetual underdevelopment in the Third World.

Later dubbed the "development of underdevelopment" by economist André Gunder Frank in his analysis of Latin America (1967), Baran's ideas seemed to validate the New Left's revolutionary tactics. Why wait patiently for the "objective conditions" to appear when in fact the Latin American bourgeoisie seemed incapable of bringing about total national capitalist development? If Latin America was indeed doomed to perpetual underdevelopment, the only way to break out of this condition was to mount an immediate revolution with the resources at hand.

Genesis of the Dependency School

At this point these neo-Marxist currents were stirring within a small group of economists and social scientists located in and around ECLA in Santiago who were increasingly dissatisfied with, and critical of, some aspects of ECLA's analysis of underdevelopment. What emerged from their intense debate on the development issue was the new dependency school.

The dependency analysts rejected the modernizationists' contention that certain Latin American cultural and institutional features were the major reasons for the region's underdevelopment. While not totally discounting these factors, these analysts broadened the narrow national focus of modernization to a more global interpretation that linked internal and external factors in a more holistic fashion. For the dependency analysts, Latin America's insertion into the developing world economy during the Age of Imperialism (the sixteenth to the nineteenth centuries) was central to the region's economic stagnation. This global politico-economic system was characterized by the unequal development of its component parts. In this configuration the center, drawing first upon its own resources, began to industrialize and later colonized the periphery to provide the primary goods (mainly agricultural and mineral) that would sustain the process of metropolitan development. This international division of labor imposed by the West did not lead, as the neoclassical economists predicted, to comparative advantage. Rather, the center gained at the expense of the periphery by relegating the Third World to an inferior position in the global system as solely a producer of primary goods. This imposed division of labor constrained the economic potential of the Third World and contributed to its underdevelopment.

Theotonio dos Santos (1970), an important Brazilian dependency analyst, succinctly captured the essence of this condition: "By dependence we mean a situation in which the economy of certain countries is conditioned by the development and expansion of another economy to which the former is subjected. The relation of interdependence between two or more economies, and between these and world trade, assumes the form of dependence when some countries (the dominant ones) can expand and can be self-sustaining, while other countries (the dependent ones) can do this only as a reflection of that expansion, which can have either a positive or a negative effect on their immediate development."[4] It was not only the peripheral economies, however, that were conditioned by the dominant center. The internal social and political structures of Latin America were also shaped so as to reinforce the primary nature of the export economy. In this sense, internal and external structural elements were connected to form an elaborate pattern of structural underdevelopment.

Thus, for dependency analysts it was not so much the cultural or institutional factors that blocked entrepreneurship and therefore development. Latin American entrepreneurs operated in a perfectly rational, profit-oriented manner. However, the structures of dependency caused them to behave in a way that preserved and rearticulated dependency to their benefit—hence the enduring and reinforcing nature of the primary export economy throughout the region. Given all this, it was therefore quite impossible for Latin America, locked into this asymmetrical, interdependent structure, to replicate, as the modernizationists would have it, the evolutionary experience of the West.

In developing what was primarily a historical rather than theoretical model, dependency analysts noted that the pattern of primary exports (gold, silver, dyewoods, sugar, tobacco) established by Spain and Portugal during the colonial period continued in Latin America although the composition of the commodities changed. Even when Spanish America became independent of Spain in the 1820s, "outward development" persisted with export production, which was now directed not toward Spain, but to England and northern Europe. In return for primary products Latin America imported manufactured goods from Europe that flooded the domestic market, often destroying noncompetitive domestic manufacturing.

The Change in Export Structures Within Latin America

Toward the end of the nineteenth century, however, an important difference in the nature of the export structure emerged between various regions of Latin America. In some areas the local elite lost control of export production and were displaced by foreign enclaves. For example, British and U.S. firms moved into nitrate and copper mining in Chile, and U.S. investors began to dominate the Cuban sugar industry. At the same time the state began to regulate and tax these foreign enclaves and became an intermediary between the local economy and the enclaves. Unfortunately, little if any direct stimulation of the local economy occurred since the enclaves remained isolated from the economy at large. Other regional differences developed at this time because of different export products or natural resources, the importance of incipient manufacturing, and the size of the middle and working classes.

The two world wars and the depression of the 1930s produced a succession of crises for the export economy by cutting off foreign markets and throwing Latin America back onto its own resources. To pick up the slack left by falling imports, internal manufacturing was stimulated. The state encouraged this trend by adopting policies (e.g., import substitution) to foment incipient industrialization in industries such as food processing and manufacturing of textiles and other light consumer goods.

Depending on the success in forging multiclass alliances, various countries, such as Argentina, Brazil, and Mexico, were able to attain a considerable level of industrial growth during this period. However, the limits to such growth became evident by midcentury, symbolized by the fall from power of national, populist regimes in Argentina (Juan Perón) and Brazil (Getúlio Vargas).[5]

While these tendencies unfolded at the periphery of the world economy, a major development occurred at the center that gave a new dimension to dependency. The postwar rise of the multinational corporation created what Oswaldo Sunkel (1970), a Chilean economist, called a new "transnational system." Drawing upon large capital, marketing, and technological resources in the West, MNCs established subsidiaries throughout Latin America with the aim of distributing and/or producing products for local consumption, thereby avoiding tariff barriers. For dependency analysts this trend, in effect, undermined (denationalized) the older import-substitution industries within Latin America and created what Fernando Henrique Cardoso (1969), a Brazilian sociologist, and Enzo Faletto (1963), a Chilean historian, called the internationalization of the internal market.

Several individuals made important contributions to the elaboration of the dependency model. Celso Furtado, a Brazilian economist and historian who was associated with ECLA, had become increasingly critical of ECLA's analysis. The inability of ISI to sustain economic growth led Furtado to "radicalize" ECLA's analysis by incorporating elements of Marxism and Keynesian theory.[6] Furtado advocated a greater effort in bringing about structural reforms together with a larger state role in restructuring the entire economy to improve production and income distribution. His main work, *Economic Development of Latin America* (1969), like the work by André Gunder Frank, helped the dependency perspective gain an international audience.

Less widely known outside Latin America but equally important in radicalizing the ECLA perspective was Oswaldo Sunkel. Although not rejecting Marxism, Sunkel worked in a more eclectic fashion within the structuralist tradition of ECLA. He worked with ECLA during the early 1960s, but unlike Prebisch, Sunkel emphasized the internal factors in the peripheral model. "The possibilities of carrying out a national development policy," he wrote, "basically depend on the domestic situation,"[7] in other words they depend on effecting radical structural reforms. This was something that ECLA, as an international agency, had been reluctant, for diplomatic reasons, to advocate. ECLA did not want to offend the conservative governments in power in Latin America during the 1950s.

Dependency and Development

If Furtado and Sunkel radicalized ECLA's analysis of Latin American underdevelopment, Fernando Henrique Cardoso approached the problem from an explicitly Marxist perspective. Cardoso, who took up residence in Santiago after the 1964 coup in Brazil drove him into exile, collaborated with Enzo Faletto on a book entitled *Dependencia y Desarrollo en América Latina* (Dependency and Development in Latin America, 1979) that has become one of the classics on dependency theory. The work was enriched by the lively debate on development taking place at the time within and outside ECLA in Santiago.

Cardoso accepted as a given that Third World countries were conditioned by the global economic system centered in the West. What was crucial to him was how and under what circumstances each dependent economy was linked to the world market. In other words, the key question was one of political power—how class alliances were formed and political decisions taken in each country in a given historical circumstance. Thus, Cardoso's principal contribution to dependency theory was to add an important sociopolitical dimension to ECLA's predominantly economic analysis. The result, which he called a "historical-structural approach," was at once a more sophisticated and complex analysis than ECLA's and captured the interplay of international economic forces and internal political forces.

Although generally acknowledged as a principal formulator of dependency theory, Cardoso himself takes a more modest credit for the intellectual origins of the theory. He declared that dependency "did not represent new methodological propositions. What happened was that a current which was already old in Latin American thought managed to make itself heard in the discussions that were taking place in institutions normally closed to it: ECLA, the universities, some government planning agencies, and—last but not least—the North American academic community." He goes on to say that a critique arose both inside and outside ECLA that presented "alternatives both to orthodox analyses [modernization] and to what we might call the ECLA-Keynesian analysis." Referring to his own role in this process, Cardoso declared that "a few groups of intellectuals in Santiago in the mid-1960s took up the ECLA problematic and tried to redefine it radically, while seeking to avoid 'vulgar Marxism.' "[8]

Frank and the Development of Underdevelopment

If Cardoso deepened and enriched the dependency analysis, André Gunder Frank popularized it beyond the small circle of intellectuals clustered in Santiago, particularly in the English-speaking world. His *Capitalism and Underdevelopment* (1967), according to one commentator, "flashed across the Latin American intellectual horizon like a dazzling, fleeting comet."[9] It was written at a time when Latin America was convulsed in crisis and turmoil. The Castro revolution had triumphed in Cuba in 1959, unleashing a revolutionary storm elsewhere on the continent, only to culminate in a backlash of reaction first in Brazil in 1964 and finally a decade later in Chile in 1973.

Frank's work closely reflected the mood and temper of the times, representing a defiant alternative to both the existing social order in Latin America and the traditional theories and practices of the socialist world. Indeed, according to Frank's publisher, the book's economic and political analysis complemented the political conclusions reached by Régis Debray (1967), the flamboyant French theoretician of the left who had embraced the Castro revolution of 1959. Frank himself stated that the fall of the populist government of [João] Goulart in Brazil in 1964 influenced much of the way he treated Brazilian history. Searching the past for clues to the fall of the Brazilian regime, Frank concluded that any attempt to change the socioeconomic order in Brazil or elsewhere must begin by breaking away from the capitalist order.

This was a conclusion that many on the Latin American left, both at home and abroad, were more than ready to accept. The early Cuban experience with socialism and revolutionary change had provided the left with an alternative to the reformism of earlier populist models as well as the moderate, gradualist tactics and goals long adopted by the Communist parties in Latin America. At the same time social scientists, disillusioned with the linear interpretations founded on a Marxist understanding of the transition from feudalism to capitalism as well as the modernizationist view of society moving from a traditional to a modern order, were also ready to consider Frank's alternative model of dependency theory.

On another level Frank's book as well as the favorable reception (Cardoso called it "consumption") in the United States for dependency theory was the distinct product of the U.S. intellectual climate of the times. Just as modernization might be said to have offered a model of capitalist development that dovetailed with the anti-Communist thrust of American foreign policy during the Cold War era, Frank's work and dependency generally emerged as an alternative, counter model to a new generation in the United States (1960s) that reacted against and rejected that older model. During this period Marxism had, with considerable help from McCarthyism,[10] been virtually eliminated from the U.S. intellectual horizon. The tumultuous decade of the 1960s, culminating in the civil rights movement and the drive to end U.S. intervention in Vietnam led to a general critique of U.S. society and foreign policy and made radical ideas, as during the 1930s, more acceptable to broader sectors of the intelligentsia. It was in this context that dependency theory and Frank's book were readily assimilated into the American political awakening of the 1960s by a public that was "eager to get from the past a confirmation of the lessons the present was apparently offering."[11]

Although closely linked with the Latin American structuralist approach associated with ECLA, Frank's *Capitalism and Underdevelopment* was more than just a recapitulation of dependency theory. While roundly criticized from all sides, Frank's work, nevertheless, made an important contribution to a new formulation of dependency theory. As one scholar put it, "he fused the separate strands of U.S. neo-Marxist and Latin American structuralist thought in a powerful synthesis."[12]

Frank boldly argued that capitalism, by its penetration of Latin America, had caused the region's underdevelopment, rather than its being caused by "traditional" or "backward" structures, as modernizationists maintained. This penetration, which succeeded in incorporating Latin America into the capitalist world system, was characterized by a series of metropolitan-satellite relationships, on both an international and a national level. These relationships worked to drain surplus capital from the region toward the center. Furthermore, Frank rejected the notion of a dualist structure, one traditional and the other modern. Rather he envisioned a linkage between the two systems by way of capitalism, which worked from the modern sector to exploit and expropriate surplus from the traditional sector. Finally, since underdevelopment resulted from close ties to the metropolitan West, Frank reasoned that in order for development to occur those ties should logically be severed.

In one of his more controversial assertions Frank maintained that capitalism had been in force in Latin America since the Iberian conquest. The national bourgeoisie, he argued, had become hopelessly tied to the external economy, which undermined the potential for national development. His conclusion was to promote a nationalist alliance of the peasantry and proletariat and to forsake the national bourgeoisie in the revolutionary process of establishing socialism. Much of his argument drew significant inspiration from the success of the Cuban revolution and posed a direct challenge to the two-stage revolutionary strategy of the Latin American Communist parties.

Renewing the Debate Within Marxism

Frank's argument raised an old debate within Marxism, now brought up to date by the revolutionary fervor of the 1960s. This debate, which surrounded the Russian Revolution (an event unimagined by Marx himself), raised questions about how to define Russia's position in Marx's theory of historical stages: was Russia feudal and therefore in need of a capitalist revolution, or was it already capitalist and therefore able to begin the process toward socialism? Lenin, building on the theory of "permanent revolution" developed by Leon Trotsky (1879–1940), argued strongly and persuasively for most subsequent Marxists that capitalism, though weak, was sufficiently in evidence in Russia for the proletariat to carry out the revolution. Lenin's argument, however, was specific to Russia in the early twentieth century. Stalin was able to establish a new orthodoxy that defined the national conditions in most of the Third World in terms not unlike those of the modernizationists: the Third World was not sufficiently capitalist to achieve socialism without an alliance with the bourgeoisie.

This debate within Marxism emerged again after dependency analysis had gained a significant following in Latin America. The debate focused on both the conceptual issue of how to define the historical stage in the Marxist typology and the strategic issues of whether to ally with the national bourgeoisie or to push directly for socialist revolution. The conceptual issue became defined as how to determine the "mode of production" in Latin America.

Frank had defined the mode of production as capitalist because Latin America was so firmly entrenched in a world economic system that was based on merchant capitalism. The new Marxist criticism of this view was first expressed by Ernesto Laclau (1971), an Argentine political scientist at the University of Essex. Laclau found that Frank's definition of capitalism was not based on Marx's own emphasis on the mode of production but rather on the exchange of goods (commodities) that occurred under many modes of production, such as slavery, feudalism, and capitalism. Laclau and others who followed this "modes of production analysis" argued that precapitalist modes of production persisted in Latin America and that there was no a priori way of determining the dominant mode of production without carefully examining each nation. In particular, the class

structures and the relations between workers and owners in specific production environments needed to be scrutinized. It was likely, Laclau and
his colleagues argued, that several different modes of production existed
at the same time and that in some cases they were reinforced by each
other. For instance, merchant capitalism seemed to reinforce feudal production on latifundia that produced for the world market.

The task for analysis then became one of defining the class and economic relationships within a "mixed mode of production." This focus,
while not denying the importance of external factors for the economic
structure in Latin American nations, suggested that the dominance of the
world economy by merchant capitalism did not necessarily imply the complete penetration of capitalism within each nation and that the central
focus of analysis should still be the internal class and productive relationships. This more orthodox Marxist approach returned analysis to the
dynamics within the nations and suggested that a greater variety of social, economic, and political situations existed in Latin American nations.

The implications of this more complex approach for the strategic issues of revolutionary practice were unclear. It was obvious that such analysis raised serious questions about the optimistic predictions and
prescriptions of Frank and others who argued for more daring revolutionary paths. However, the implications of this analysis were that each
nation's productive force had to be examined on its own terms. No blan-
ket recommendations for strategy were likely to be valid. Unfortunately,
these analysts were not able to develop specific guidelines for strategies
in mixed modes of production, leaving the implications of their analysis
for political practice open to question.

The debate raised by modes of production analysis was widely reflected in several important articles in the *New Left Review*, an influential
English Marxist journal. It was also adopted by several Latin American
scholars, including Agustín Cueva (1977) and Roger Bartra (1975).[13] It
soon became clear that the modes of production analysis, although shifting the dynamics of change within Latin America to the internal productive and class forces, had not sufficiently developed an analytical
framework that could prioritize the relationships and define the political
implications of these more complex relationships. In addition, the modes
of production analysis, while suggesting that more sophisticated dependency analysts like Cardoso did not give sufficient attention to the internal economic and class issues, really did not challenge the general thrust
of these more complex uses of the dependency perspective. Modes of
production analysis remains a general approach that has presented a
major critique of dependency, without developing a clear direction of its
own.

As the foregoing discussion might suggest, the literature on dependency is far from homogeneous. Indeed, numerous debates and disagreements have occurred among its adherents as to what constitutes the main features of the approach. Moreover, whereas the original thrust of dependency addressed the problem of underdevelopment, recent studies,[14] particularly in the United States, have been more interested in explaining international relations than in resolving the problem of underdevelopment. For these scholars, dependency is viewed principally as an asymmetry or imbalance in the international structure of power that exists between two sovereign nation states. These scholars' solution to the problem is the necessary dialogue and negotiation between center and periphery, North and South, over the redistribution of global resources.

In another direction a group of dependency analysts from the United States chose to underscore the role played by U.S. imperialism in forming Latin American dependency and underdevelopment. According to this view the United States not only came to dominate Latin American trade and its financial flow but also exercised political and military hegemony over the region. For example, political scientist James Petras (1974) and sociologist Dale Johnson (1972) focused special attention on the U.S. role in Chile before, during, and after the Marxist government of Salvadore Allende Gossens (1970–1973).[15] Those who see dependency in terms of U.S. imperialism usually advocate its replacement by various forms of socialism.

Corporatism

Let us now turn to a third major approach to the problem of development, one heralded by both Comte and Durkheim. Corporatism is a very old concept of community and of the state. In contrast to modernization and dependency, it traces its origins back to Aristotle. Its particular Iberian form derives from the Roman occupation that lasted over four centuries and imposed a degree of unity and political organization never before experienced. Superceded by the long Moorish occupation, Roman law and imperial achievements were rediscovered, fused, and blended with the Christian, Thomistic-Suarezian[16] conception of the state that supported Iberian society from the sixteenth century onward. It then passed, at least in its essential features, to postconquest Ibero-America, where it took root and endured. There it formed a unique blend of Roman and Thomistic values, an authoritarian political heritage, and a corporatist economic and social organization.[17]

According to modern corporatist theorists, Latin American underdevelopment is a product of this unique and enduring corporatist tradition, which not only stood apart from but rejected the revolutionary spirit that animated the West in the age of capitalism and modernity after 1500. Both anticapitalist and anti-Marxist, corporatists reject what they see as the imposition of foreign, alien developmental models on Latin America. Modernity and development, if it is to come to the region, must be filtered through and adapted to what they see as a uniquely Latin American structure and tradition. For many the core of this distinctiveness is to be found in the authority of the state and the central role it has played in shaping the society and the economy. Some corporatists have thus envisioned a third, noncapitalist, non-Marxist path to modernity and development. This move is directed by a powerful, activist, and interventionist state, but one that is within the essentially Catholic cultural and philosophical framework of Latin American tradition.

The core of corporatist theory lies in what one commentator calls the organic-state tradition.[18] This tradition originated with Aristotle and ran through Roman law, medieval natural law, and contemporary Catholic social philosophy. Organic statism stresses the political community, a specific theory of functional associations called "the concession theory of association," and the central role of the state in achieving the common good.

The starting point for organic statism is the idea that the preferred form of political life is an association of individuals as members of a community. (By contrast liberalism emphasizes the rationale of individual self-interest, and Marxism stresses the dominant mode of production and class struggle.) Since people are, by nature, political beings, political institutions are a natural, organic element of society. But in order to fulfill their proper role, these institutions must be infused with order and power— authority. In this conception the state is viewed as the most perfect form of political community. However, its component parts (individual, family, and private associations such as churches, clubs, and interest groups) all have a proper functioon, a natural sphere of action within the organic whole (i.e., the state) to which they are intimately connected.

The role of the state then is central in the organic-state tradition of corporatism. Equally important is the notion that the state has a moral end, a moral *telos*, which, as defined by Aristotle, is to govern with a view to the common interest and general welfare of the entire community. This view of the common good, together with the organic political community, became crucial to Catholic social philosophy in the nineteenth and the early twentieth centuries. On the one hand, it could challenge the Marxist notion of class conflict, which violated the organic-state ideal of the harmonious community (as, of course, did liberalism's emphasis on the sanctity of the individual). On the other hand, it criticized liberalism, together with modern capitalism, which led to the abuse and antagonism between classes. Also the corporatist idea of an activist state intervening in society to promote the common good contradicted the liberal notion of a weak state. Over the years the idea that the state should play a relatively autonomous, architectural role in the polity had become another central precept of the organic-state tradition.

Finally, the concession theory of association played an important role in organic statism. This theory was derived from the Greeks who believed that the public common interest was dominant and that private interests should be allowed only the freedom consistent with the organic functioning of society. When transferred from the city-state to the bureaucratic state of the Roman Empire, this concession theory took on new significance. According to Roman law, interest groups had to be chartered by the state, thereby reinforcing the idea of the organic state. The interest group, in exchange for the privilege of official recognition, accepted the obligation that in effect made it an integral part of the state. For example, guilds were licensed and granted monopolies in return for maintaining high-quality output and paying taxes to the Crown.

The "new corporatism" represents a revival of this older, time-honored theoretical model of the state. Political scientist Philippe Schmitter has provided the following "ideal-type" definition of the concept: "Corporatism can be defined as a system of interest representation in which the constituent units are organized into a limited number of singular, compulsory, noncompetitive, hierarchically ordered and functionally differentiated categories, recognized or licensed (if not created) by the state and granted a deliberate representational monopoly within their respective categories in exchange for observing certain controls on their selection of leaders and articulation of demands and supporters."[19]

Corporatism provides an indigenous (Iberian) alternative to Western liberal capitalism and Marxist socialism, both of which are viewed by certain Latin American elites as inherently disruptive and as alien threats to the traditional fabric of Latin American society. For its practitioners, who reject both modernization and dependency theory, corporatism provides a model of development that is genuinely Latin American. It is also a means of providing social solidarity and avoiding unrestrained individualism or class conflict in the face of the dislocations of modernity. At the same time corporatism seeks to integrate the masses by providing opportunities for popular participation in local, regional, and functional groups. Above all it stands as a nationalist bulwark to prevent a revolution from below (popular) by initiating a process of controlled development from above (the state) that is at once nationalist and consistent with Latin America's monistic and authoritarian traditions.

Numerous criticisms have been leveled at corporatist theory. Some critics see it primarily as an apology for fascism, designed to repress conflict, tensions, and the general sociopolitical crisis unleashed by modernization. Others with Marxist inclinations reject the corporatists' rigid denial of class conflict, even in supposedly harmonious corporatist settings. Schmitter challenges the notion that corporatism is a uniquely Mediterranean phenomenon and argues that corporatist variants can be found in Northern Europe and even the United States. Finally, social scientists Samuel and Arturo Valenzuela (1978) question the idea that corporatism represents a significant departure from modernization theory. They suggest similarities in the two theories' stress on cultural values and note the implicit acceptance by at least one corporatist (Wiarda) of the modern versus traditional dichotomy proposed by modernizationists.[20]

Bureaucratic Authoritarianism

Our final development theory, bureaucratic authoritarianism (BA), grew out of attempts to understand the emergence of authoritarian and military governments in Brazil in 1964 and Argentina in 1966. Both regimes inaugurated periods of rule by the military as an institution, with the intention of promoting accelerated industrial growth based on massive new foreign investment. In the process they eliminated or drastically controlled elections, restricted the freedom of labor unions, and adopted economic austerity programs that imposed wage controls on the urban popular sector, which was composed of the working and lower middle classes.

The principal architect of BA, who explained these regimes, was the Argentine political scientist Guillermo O'Donnell (1973) who drew, albeit critically, on all three theories: modernization, dependency and Marxism, and corporatism. To O'Donnell and others, early developmental analysis, which suggested a positive connection between socioeconomic modernization and democracy, hardly seemed appropriate for explaining the rise of this new authoritarianism. On the contrary, as O'Donnell saw it, quite the opposite seemed to have happened. He developed a hypothesis that suggested that in late-developing countries more advanced levels of industrialization might actually coincide with the collapse of democracy and an increase in inequality.

O'Donnell argued that economic stagnation, coupled with increasing political demands, led to the breakdown of the progressive populist coalitions of the 1930s and 1940s. At this point sectors of the bourgeoisie (new industrialists and managers), together with new technocratic elements (high-level civil and military bureaucrats and technocrats), that in a Weberian sense emerged from an era of economic expansion, seized power through the military. They then moved to rationalize the economic and social systems by excluding the popular sectors and encouraging economic growth by way of broadening links with foreign capital and technology. Rather than modernization's producing a tendency toward democratization and greater social equality, O'Donnell saw it as moving in the opposite direction toward BA.

O'Donnell's work in effect synthesized several intellectual traditions that had tended to remain disparate. This was particularly the case with his uses of modernization, dependency, and corporatist models. O'Donnell recast modernization theory by arguing that "the processes set in motion by high-level modernization tend to generate authoritarianism."[21] Moreover, O'Donnell's key concept of BA owed much to Weber's theory of bureaucracy and politics, especially Weber's concern with values and roles (reflected in O'Donnell's emphasis on "technocratic roles"). At the same time, as political scientists Karen Remmer and Gilbert Merkx of the University of New Mexico point out, "his [O'Donnell's] analysis had an historical-materialist character because of its focus on the manner in which social and economic contingencies structure political development."[22] Finally, O'Donnell's description of the mechanisms of control in BA regimes drew on corporatist conceptions of authority and functional groups.

The fact that BA, as a hypothesis to explain political change, was limited to the Southern Cone (first, Argentina and Brazil, and later Chile and Uruguay as well) raised certain questions. Could it be extended to embrace other Latin American countries so as to constitute a more global model? Was the political-economic model pursued in these four countries as consistent and coherent as O'Donnell argued, particularly when the levels of industrialization in these countries did not appear comparable? Critics suggested that BA appeared to be simply a restoration of the type of authoritarianism that existed in the 1930s and 1940s. Finally, some critics questioned the economic arguments used in explaining the emergence of BA.[23]

O'Donnell's work on BA marks a good stopping point for our overview of Latin American theories of development. While his analysis has come under considerable criticism, no major theoretical approach has yet emerged to take its place. Moreover, since O'Donnell's theory represents something of a synthesis of the previous theories, O'Donnell charts a path toward a convergence of theoretical concerns that might . . . represent the most fruitful direction for future theory building.

Notes

1. For Weber this new capitalist spirit emphasized ascetic, achievement-oriented values among entrepreneurs. These values extolled hard work and sav-

ing as opposed to more moderate living and working habits. Thus, for Weber, capital accumulation, the key to the emergence of capitalism, was derived not from the expropriation of the peasant-worker, as Marx asserted, but rather through the dedication and self-denial of entrepreneurs and workers. This new capitalist spirit, according to Weber, grew out of the rise of Protestantism, particularly the doctrines of sixteenth-century Calvinism, in which worldly success became a sign for being one of the "elect," those who were predestined for eternal salvation. Driven by their anxiety to ensure salvation, seventeenth-century Puritans, therefore, dedicated themselves to hard work and the acquisition and saving of wealth, which became the moving force in the development of modern capitalism. For Weber this explained why the Protestant countries—England, the Netherlands, and the United States (New England)—developed to a greater extent than did the Catholic countries—Spain, Portugal, and Italy.

2. Comte believed that the development of man's capacity to think, which grew from fetishism to what he called "Positivism," mirrored this transition. Positivism, marked by observation and accuracy, was elaborated by the natural sciences and later the social sciences, particularly sociology. For Comte the task of sociology was to identify the stage reached by society, thereby facilitating the creation of the modern order.

3. Fernando Henrique Cardoso, one of the founders of the dependency school, prefers to use the term "approach" rather than "theory," which he believes others have incorrectly attributed to dependency. See his "The Consumption of Dependency Theory in the United States," *Latin American Research Review* 12, no. 3 (1977): 15–17.

4. Theotonio dos Santos, "The Structure of Dependence," *American Economic Review* 60, no. 2 (May 1970): 231–36.

5. The period of national populism was from 1930 to roughly 1950 when an alliance of the new bourgeoisie, the middle classes, and the working classes succeeded in wresting control of the state away from the export-oriented oligarchy. This state then pursued interventionist economic policies designed to stimulate national industries as well as to incorporate the lower classes into the economy and into society.

6. Economist John Maynard Keynes (1883–1946) reformulated liberal economic theory in his influential *The General Theory of Employment, Interest and Money*, published in 1936. According to Keynes's theory, correct government policies could smooth out the economic cycle. When the economy lags the government should lower the interest rates charged to borrowers, especially businesses, to encourage production. They should also spend money on public works and social welfare to put more money into circulation and thus to stimulate consumption. As the economy expands the opposite policies should be followed to check inflation and excessive speculation. Keynes's theory formed the theoretical foundation for Franklin D. Roosevelt's New Deal program of social and economic reform and is still dominant in the academic and business worlds.

7. Quoted in Magnus Blomstrom and Bjorn Hettne, *Development Theory in Transition, The Dependency Debate and Beyond: Third World Responses* (London: Zed Books, 1984), 59.

8. Cardoso, "The Consumption of Dependency Theory," 9–10.

9. Tulio Halperin-Donghi, "'Dependency Theory' and Latin American Historiography," *Latin American Research Review* 17, no. 1 (1982): 116.

10. Senator Joseph McCarthy (1909–1957) campaigned to root out alleged Communist influence in government during the 1950s. His indiscriminate, often

unfounded, accusations, inquisitorial investigative methods, and sensationalism, ostensibly in the suppression of communism, were widely condemned at the time.

11. Halperin-Donghi, " 'Dependency Theory' and Latin American Historiography," 418.

12. Charles W. Bergquist, *Alternative Approaches to the Problem of Development: A Selected and Annotated Bibliography* (Durham, NC: Carolina Academic Press, 1979), item #118.

13. See Colin Henfrey, "Dependency, Modes of Production, and Class Analysis of Latin America," *Latin American Perspectives* 8, nos. 3–4 (1981): 17–54.

14. See, for example, Robert A. Packenham, *Latin American Dependency Theories*, mimeo (Stanford: Stanford University, July 1974); and David Ray, "The Dependency Model of Latin American Underdevelopment: Three Basic Fallacies," *Journal of Inter-American Studies and World Affairs* 15 (February 1973): 4–20.

15. See Marcelo J. Cavarozzi and James F. Petras, "Chile," in *Latin America: The Struggle with Dependency and Beyond*, ed. Ronald H. Chilcote and Joel C. Edelstein (New York: John Wiley & Sons, 1974), 495–578; and James Cockcroft, André Gunder Frank, and Dale Johnson, *Dependency and Underdevelopment: Latin America's Political Economy* (Garden City, NY: Doubleday, 1972).

16. Thomism refers to the theological and philosophical system of Saint Thomas Aquinas (1225?–1274), the Italian scholastic philosopher and a major theologian of the Roman Catholic Church. Francisco Suárez (1548–1617) was a Spanish theologian and philosopher.

17. The classic example of a corporatist institution is the Roman Catholic church, which is organically and hierarchically organized with some residual autonomy at the level of the individual priest.

18. Alfred Stepan, *The State and Society: Peru in Comparative Perspective* (Princeton: Princeton University Press, 1978), 26–40.

19. "Still the Century of Corporatism?" in *The New Corporatism: Socio-Political Structures in the Iberian World*, ed. Fredrick B. Pike and Thomas Stritch (Notre Dame: University of Notre Dame Press, 1974), 93–94. Another important book on the new corporatism is Howard J. Wiarda, ed., *Politics and Social Change in Latin America: The Distinct Tradition* (Amherst: University of Massachusetts Press, 1974).

20. J. Samuel Valenzuela and Arturo Valenzuela, "Modernization and Dependency: Alternative Perspectives in the Study of Latin American Underdevelopment," *Comparative Politics* 10, no. 4 (July 1978): 542–43.

21. Guillermo A. O'Donnell, *Modernization and Bureaucratic Authoritarianism: Studies in South American Politics*, 2d ed. (Berkeley, CA: Institute of International Studies, 1979), 206n.

22. Karen L. Remmer and Gilbert W. Merkx, "Bureaucratic-Authoritarianism Revisited," *Latin American Research Review* 17, no. 2 (1982): 5.

23. See David Collier, ed., *The New Authoritarianism in Latin America* (Princeton: Princeton University Press, 1979), 7–9 passim.

6

Authoritarianism and Corporatism in Latin America: The Modal Pattern

James M. Malloy

As the analysis of Latin American politics increased in sophistication during the 1970s, scholars began to focus on two broad models, often intertwined, to describe the region's political systems. James Malloy argues, in what since has become a classic article in the collection Authoritarianism and Corporatism in Latin America *(1977), that Latin American politics can be described as numerous variants of authoritarian regimes. He describes individual countries in the region as "corporatist" models, each characterized by somewhat different structural and organizational qualities. Malloy's interpretation of Latin American politics at the high point of authoritarian regimes provides a helpful historical grounding, both conceptually and theoretically, from which to analyze the transition to democratic models a decade later. The author suggests how Latin America moved from a potentially more democratic type of populist corporatism to one dominated by the military.*

For the foreseeable future at least, "modernizing authoritarian" regimes will remain a part of political life in Latin America. This fact has forced a rethinking of much of the conventional wisdom regarding the area, be it based on Marxist or liberal democratic theoretical foundations. The recent experiences of Brazil, Argentina, and Peru, and the discovery that behind the façade, Mexico is really an authoritarian system, have led many to suggest that the region is generating a "new path" to development, which, if it is to be understood, demands the fashioning of new conceptual approaches to the analysis not only of these regimes but of the region as a whole.[1] Central to this rethinking is the recognition that authoritarian regimes are not historically doomed to extinction as societies modernize and develop but are potentially viable (if unpleasant) modes of organizing a society's developmental efforts. Indeed, one author has persuasively argued that authoritarian regimes of a certain type are actually a product of high levels of modernization in the Latin American context.[2] Whichever is the case, it is now generally agreed that authoritarian systems constitute a regime type that must be understood in its own terms and within which it is possible to delineate a number of subtypes.

While the significance of the concept of authoritarianism as a regime type has been largely accepted, there remains some confusion regarding the delineation of subtypes, particularly when one comes to grips with authoritarian regimes that are self-consciously oriented toward the development and modernization of their respective societies. Thus, the terms "bureaucratic-authoritarianism," "populist authoritarianism," and "military populism" have all recently been offered as ways of talking about specific modernizing authoritarian regimes in the area—with Juan Perón and Getúlio Vargas representing populist authoritarianism, Peru since 1968 military populism, and Brazil since 1964 bureaucratic authoritarianism.[3] These distinctions are undoubtedly useful in that they point out significant differences among these regimes in terms of the role of charismatic leadership, group coalitions supporting regimes, and differences in policy emphasis and developmental strategies. These, in turn, have been effectively traced to the varying levels of development achieved by the different countries when the specific regimes appeared.

Despite the important differences unearthed by this approach, others have pointed out an overarching similarity in structure and organizational principles among the regimes just mentioned and other authoritarian systems such as Mexico's. The critical point of similarity is that each of these regimes is characterized by strong and relatively autonomous governmental structures that seek to impose on the society a system of interest representation based on enforced limited pluralism. These regimes try to eliminate spontaneous interest articulation and establish a limited number of authoritatively recognized groups that interact with the governmental apparatus in defined and regularized ways. Moreover, the recognized groups in this type of regime are organized in vertical functional categories rather than horizontal class categories and are obliged to interact with the state through the designated leaders or authoritatively sanctioned interest associations. This mode of organizing state and society has aptly been termed "corporatism."[4] Viewed from this perspective, the conceptual problem in the Latin American context can be broken down to three levels of analysis: (1) a general level of regime-type authoritarianism of which there can be many variants, running from an old-fashioned caudillo such as Anastasio Somoza [Debayle] to a sophisticated regime such as Brazil's; (2) an overarching subtype "corporatism," which is defined in terms of structural and organizational principles; and (3) a series of subtypes within corporatism (those noted above) defined in terms of the roles of leaders, supporting coalitions, and policy strategies. Thus, corporatism can be seen as a major authoritarian theme upon which there can be different variations.

Among those who address themselves to these questions there is considerable disagreement as to the factors, both regional and country-specific, that account for the emergence of corporatist authoritarian regimes. Some authors stress a Hispanic-Catholic tradition that has long lain dormant in the region and is presently asserting itself.[5] Others go a step further and point to a persistent de facto mode of group formation and conflict always present in the region behind the façade of previous liberal democratic constitutional forms.[6] From either of these two perspectives, one might say that the emergence of an authoritarian corporate regime in a given country represents less a breakdown of democracy into authoritarianism than a breakout from a grafted liberal democratic structure of an underlying mode of political organization. Be that as it may, others who recognize the significance of these two factors rightly point out that they alone cannot account for the emergence of authoritarian corporate regimes and particularly their orientation toward the promotion of development and modernization.[7]

For these authors, the problem must be placed in its developmental focus. To do this, one must take into account the level of development achieved by specific countries and the international context of development impinging on the region as a whole and on specific countries. Those who approach the question from this more complex and historically specific developmental context have pointed to two important processes that are closely linked to the emergence of authoritarian corporate regimes. First, they point to the crucial fact that the region as a whole and countries within it began to develop later than the advanced industrial states; therefore, the nations of Latin America confront the process from different vantage points and different perspectives. One critical aspect of this lateness is the fact that all of the nations of the region are based on economies that are to one degree or another dependent on and influenced by the more advanced industrial states. In brief, the first factor of significance is the phenomenon of "delayed dependent development."[8] The second factor is connected with the fact that throughout a large part of the region the most significant political movements that have sought to promote reform and change since the 1920s and 1930s were based, in some fashion or other, on an orientation generally called "populism."[9] The term is no doubt

vague and embraces a variety of political movements. Most agree, however, that the phenomenon of populism has been critical in the region.
Thus, besides the Hispanic tradition and de facto modes of group conflict, two processes rooted in the region's twentieth-century developmental experiences are closely linked to the emergence of corporatist
authoritarianism. These are the phenomena of delayed dependent development and populism.

Delayed Dependent Development

The contemporary trend toward authoritarian corporatist regimes in Latin
America must be viewed against the backdrop of the region's previous
pattern of economic development, which is best described as delayed
dependent capitalist development. In this chapter, then, authoritarian
corporatist regimes are seen as responses to a general crisis of public
authority brought about by the multiple effects of delayed dependent development. More specifically, the problem to which these regimes have
responded has been that of integrating a multiplicity of societal interests
into a decision-making structure that guarantees a minimum of political
stability and allows decision makers to launch development-oriented policies. By and large, formally democratic regimes have been unable in the
Latin American context simultaneously to integrate societal actors and to
sponsor development, thus leading to the predisposition in many countries to adopt authoritarian corporatist solutions.

   In this chapter, we examine in broad terms the major sequences in
the region's development pattern with the aim of linking the phenomena
of delayed dependent development, populism, corporatism, and
authoritarianism. Particular attention will be paid to the phenomenon of
populism, which from the 1930s on was the most significant type of political movement in the entire region and, in my view, is the most important direct link between delayed dependent development and corporatist
authoritarianism. In brief, the argument of this chapter is that populism
was a general regional response to the first crisis of delayed dependent
development. In both orientation and practice, populism was at least implicitly corporatist but left open the question of whether it would establish corporatist structures within a formally democratic or authoritarian
framework. Both variations were attempted at various times in different
countries. By and large, however, not only did populist elites fail to resolve the underlying crisis, but because of internal contradictions within
the movements, in most cases they actually exacerbated the situation. They
thereby contributed to an environment which tended to give rise to the
more blatant authoritarian corporatist regimes we see in the region today.

The phenomena of delayed development and external dependence in Latin America have been examined at length by numerous scholars. In brief, this pattern of development took place during the end of the nineteenth and the beginning of the twentieth century in response to stimuli emanating from the more industrialized capitalist states of Western Europe and the United States. As a result, the various nations of the region were integrated into an international capitalist market system where they functioned mainly as suppliers of raw materials and consumers of manufactured goods. For the most part, economic growth and modernization in the region were the results of an outward-oriented growth model which overemphasized development of the export sectors of the local economies.

The outward-oriented growth model had numerous secondary effects on the nations of the region. In the first instance, the local economies became increasingly dependent on an international market structure over which they had little or no control. In addition, internal development was extremely unbalanced, which in turn led to a local situation of structural dualism: The nations of the region experienced a differentiation into a relatively modern urbanized sphere based on the export sector and a more traditionally organized and more backward agricultural sphere. The former dominated and exploited the latter, thereby recapitulating within the countries of the region the phenomenon of the dependency of a more backward periphery on a more advanced center. Thus, by the 1920s, a major characteristic of the region was an interlocking hierarchy of dependency structures descending from the advanced industrial center, through the various states of Latin America, and into the most backward regions of the various nations.

Development during this period did not eliminate previous societal patterns in the region but added onto them more modern, externally derived patterns, creating the general Latin American phenomenon that Charles Anderson has labeled the "living museum."[10] Internally, the countries of the area were cleft along myriad lines of division and potential conflict that cut along regional, racial, cultural, caste, and class lines. Internally, these powerful centrifugal tendencies were held in check by a powerful local elite of landed, export, and commercial interests—often referred to as the oligarchy—that was able to assert its hegemony through control of the state. The key to this pattern of elite control was a de facto internal structure of vertically organized patron-client networks based on an internal hierarchy of dependency and dominance that pervaded the nations of the region. These vertically ordered patron-client networks, as Julio Cotler has shown for Peru, ran from the local center to the local periphery, cutting across class, caste, and regional lines, thereby fostering highly particularistic orientations and vitiating mobilization along horizontal lines of class or caste.[11] Particularism, along with the multiple lines of cleavage, fostered a columnar social structure which has been excellently described by scholars such as Kalman Silvert and Ronald C. Newton.[12] Thus, in one sense, the various nations of the region manifested the invertebrate social structure that José Ortega y Gasset described in Spain.[13]

The tendency for this type of society to fly apart was held in check somewhat by a hegemonic elite in effective control of authority and the interlocking clientelistic nets descending from national elites down into intermediary and local subelites. Internally interconnected points of dependence created a vertically structured system of interdependence which tended to hold the parts of the system together.

A central social grouping to appear during the first stage of export-based development was a new urban middle class. As a product of delayed export-based development rather than autonomous industrial development, the Latin American middle class differed markedly from the middle class in the industrial center. In the main, it was a class of liberal professionals and public and private white-collar employees who were dependent in the sense that they did not control hard sources of wealth but lived off wages, salaries, and fees. A large sector of the middle class depended on public employment, a phenomenon often referred to as premature bureaucratization: the tendency of the formal governmental apparatus to expand faster than underlying socioeconomic structures. This pattern of premature bureaucratization fostered consumption patterns which in later years outstripped the local economies' ability to sustain them.[14] In any event, the new dependent urban middle class was destined to become a critical political actor from the 1930s on and the human base that spawned populism.

Finally, delayed dependent development significantly affected the position of formal governmental structures or "the state." By the late 1920s, most Latin American state structures vis-à-vis both internal and external actors were characterized by low levels of autonomy and relative weakness. In other words, the general situation of dependence translated into the specific dependence of the state upon a limited number of internal and external actors. The growing need for financial resources to support expanding public employment owing to the incorporation of sectors of the urban middle class into the public bureaucracy increased even further the state's dependence on a limited number of internal and external sources of revenue. Thus, governments in the region were subjected to heavy pressure from the local elite as well as from external private and public interests who were able in the main to shape local public policy to reflect their interests. Again from the 1930s on, a critical political issue was to be the power, effectiveness, and autonomy of the various central state structures of Latin America.

The Emergence of Populism

The 1930s and 1940s are an important watershed in Latin American history. The worldwide depression hit the region with particular ferocity, bowling over the props of the area's export-based economies and causing widespread internal dislocation. The disruption of international trading structures threw the bulk of the Latin American states back on their own resources; the relative economic isolation of the 1930s was reinforced in the 1940s by World War II. Economic depression, sociopolitical disruptions, and relative isolation forced a general rethinking of the region's internal structures and their links to international structures.

Central to the rethinking of Latin America's position was a generalized rejection of the "liberal" concepts of political economy that had been previously dominant and a significant rise in nationalist sentiment expressed as a generalized desire for autonomous national development of individual societies. Nationalism and developmentalism became, and were to remain, dominant ideological themes throughout the region.

The problem, of course, was to give concrete substance to the sentiments of nationalism and developmentalism. Although a variety of groups from left to right vied for power and the capacity to redefine individual societies, the most significant alternative political expression to emerge during the period was populism. Populism is a general and somewhat amorphous concept that embraces a wide-ranging spectrum of political movements and programs. Nonetheless, there is sufficient similarity in terms of group composition among these movements and enough thematic consistency behind their programs to justify considering them *as of a piece*.[15]

In retrospect, it is evident that populism was a specific and indigenous regional response to a general crisis which emerged from the exhaustion of a particular phase of delayed dependent development: namely, the exhaustion of the primary-product, outward-oriented growth model. The inability to sustain this model in the face of the global crisis of a stage of international capitalism reflected itself in Latin America in a general crisis of authority of the internal oligarchic power structures that had previously held sway. The hallmark of this "hegemonic" crisis was the disaffection of large sectors of the middle class from the system of which they had been the bedrock of support.[16] With the collapse of oligarchic authority, sectors of the middle class were thrust to the forefront of the political struggle. However, these disaffected elements of the middle class could not independently carry out basic structural transformations, and to buttress their position they had to seek allies in other social strata. Populism became the guise within which change-oriented segments of the middle class sought to construct multiclass coalitions powerful enough to gain control of the state and underwrite programs of structural transformation. Populism in Latin America was and remains largely the ideological product of the highly bureaucratized and largely dependent Latin American middle class, which found its previously secure position threatened by the multiple effects of the exhaustion of the export-oriented growth model.

Populist movements varied widely from the highly personalized style of Perón and Vargas, who both constructed movements and ideologies from positions of formal power, to the more organized movements such as the Alianza Popular Revolucionaria Americana (APRA) in Peru, Acción Democrática (AD) in Venezuela, and the Movimiento Nacionalista Revolucionario (MNR) in Bolivia, which constructed organizations and ideologies as a means to assault the bastions of formal power. The biographies and relative "success" of these movements varied considerably; but in all cases populism left a deep imprint, both in terms of its concrete impact on the respective systems of political economy and as a potent ideological legacy. Populist rhetoric has played a major role in structuring political debate in Latin America since the 1930s, and in one manner or another all political forces from left to right have been forced to structure their behavior in response to the populist challenge. For good or ill, populism has, since its inception, been the major political force in Latin America.

Rhetoric and self-designation notwithstanding, Latin American populism was never revolutionary in the sense of advocating a radical break with the past and a total overhaul of existing structures. On the contrary, in both theory and practice it was and remains a reformist attempt at limited structural transformations aimed at adapting to new exigencies, while at the same time maintaining basic continuity with past cultural traditions. Populist political doctrine proceeded from a diagnosis of the ills of Latin America which anticipated many later theoretical formulations, including those of Raúl Prebisch of the United Nations Economic Commission for Latin America, and many aspects of the contemporary theory of "dependence."[17]

For the populists, the central problems of Latin America were economic underdevelopment and deformed economic structures. A central dilemma was the lack of internal "integration" owing to the dichotomy between a modern sector and what the populists called a semifeudal agrarian sector. In the Indo-American countries such as Peru and Bolivia, popu-

lists also stressed a lack of geographical and cultural integration reinforced by dualism. These internal structural problems were due to the
structure of the international system—for example, imperialism, particularly that of the United States—and the way the international structures
penetrated local economies, transforming them into semicolonial append-
ages. The mechanism of imperial penetration was the local oligarchy,
which identified its interests with those of the imperial powers, thereby
becoming agents who plundered the local economy for the benefit of their
foreign allies.

The local oligarchy was a nonnational class that aided the imperial
center to exploit the nation as a whole. Thus, the problem was not, as the
Marxists would have it, the internal exploitation of class by class, but the
global exploitation of the "nation" by the "antination." The nation was
made up of all the groups other than the oligarchy (at a minimum, the
middle class, workers, and peasants) who, because they were equally exploited, shared a common set of interests. The task, therefore, was not to
form a class-based party to establish the rule of one exploited class, but
to form a broad multiclass movement to unseat the oligarchy and install
leadership that would represent the entire nation.

The chief declared goals of the populists were: (1) to assert national
economic independence, for example, anti-imperialism; (2) to break local semifeudal structures so as to liberate human and material resources
for economic development; and (3) to promote social justice for all sectors of the nation. The central agency charged with achieving these goals
was the state; central themes for the populists were state, nation, development, and social justice. The task of the multiclass movement was to
seize the state and use it to promote the other goals. Populism was oriented to a system in which the state would control national resources to
assure their local reinvestment and equitable distribution.

Populism was therefore "statist," but it was not socialist: Indeed,
populism rejected in rhetoric both socialism and capitalism and advocated a third route to development which was unique to each nation. While
populism was rhetorically anti-imperialist and anticapitalist, most populist ideologies argued that its backward, semifeudal condition made the
nation's attempt to break completely with internal and external structures
both impossible and foolhardy. Rather, the task was to expand state power
so as to reform and regulate internal and external structures and achieve
an evolutionary process of controlled economic development. In terms of
political economy, populism advocated a system of "neomercantilism" or
what some would call "state capitalism."

Another populist theme was that of "integral" development, an organizational principle to achieve maximum sociopolitical harmony. Having

rejected Marxian principles of class analysis and the "egotistical individualism" of liberalism, and having assumed a community of interests
among all groups of the nation, populism projected the possibility of
achieving development with a minimum of social conflict. The key to
achieving this goal was to construct society around a set of principles
that would foster interdependence and cooperation.

The profound impact of the populist vision can be seen not only in
those countries where populists came to power, but also in the fact that
during this period most Latin American nations either amended or re-
wrote their constitutions in terms that heavily reflected populist concepts.
The process of constitutional revision was so general that some have referred to the period as the "era of social constitutionalism."[18] These ideas
were so widespread that one could argue that there developed, particularly among the middle classes of Latin America, a general consensus
around the image of reform preferred by the populists.[19] The problem, of
course, was to put the image into practice. Latin American politics since
the 1930s can be interpreted in part as a struggle to realize the reformist
image of populism. When the Cuban Revolution transcended this reformist image and created an alternative radical revolutionary image, a sense
of urgency was added which created among many groups, including sectors of the elite and the military, a belief that something resembling populist reform had to be implemented if more radical solutions were to be
avoided.

Looking back at populism from this vantage point, in terms of ideological formulations, constitutional principles, and the kinds of practices
implemented by populist governments such as those of Vargas, Perón,
and the Mexican Partido Revolucionario Institucional (PRI) (the Mexican Revolution anticipated populism and was a major symbol for most
populists), the MNR, and others, it is now evident that populism was and
is based on an implicit *corporatist* image of sociopolitical organization.
With the exception of Vargas, the populist preference for a corporatist
solution to the pressures of modernization was seldom stated explicitly,
but there seems little gainsaying that populism has always shown a high
affinity for corporatist principles of organizing the relations between state
and society.[20] The real issue has been whether it would be a more or less
democratic corporatist solution or a more or less authoritarian solution.

Populism advocated a pluralistic coalition to achieve reform and therefore sought to mobilize the working class and to some degree the peasants. But it is important to keep in mind that populism was primarily a
middle-class phenomenon. Populist doctrine was also founded on the
notion that because of economic backwardness and structural deformity,
the mass of workers and peasants were themselves underdeveloped and

hence ill prepared to define either their own interests or those of the nation. Populists saw the mass of workers and peasants as "human capital" to be freed from semifeudal fetters and more rationally organized as a productive force.[21] Another theme was that the workers and peasants had to be "capacitated" (educated) to play their future role. In short, populism has always looked at the masses of workers and peasants as backward groups whose main role was to follow the lead of the populist elite, that is, the progressive sectors of the middle class. From its inception, populism has been infused with an elitist orientation in which the masses tended to be viewed as objects to be manipulated and controlled (for their own good) and were to remain the passive recipients of paternalistic social policies formulated by the elite. Whatever else it was, populist ideology was at its base nationalist, statist, and elitist.

The Impact of Populism

While populism was a multifaceted phenomenon whose impact varied throughout the region, a number of generalizations hold for most of Latin America from the 1930s to the 1960s. These can be related either to the direct impact of populist governments or to the indirect effect of populist orientations on public policy and/or the need of status-quo elites to respond to the challenge of populist movements.

Populism rejected classical liberal political economy and argued that one of the key problems of the region was the inability of the states of Latin America to limit the influence of external actors and to direct local economic activity so as to promote broad-based economic development. This inability was rooted in the weakness and low autonomy of the state, which in turn was rooted in external economic dependence and local oligarchic control. Thus, populist elites sought to control the state and use it to undermine the power of the local oligarchy, restructure external economic relations, and intervene in the economy to overcome the outward-oriented export model by stimulating economic diversification, mainly through policies of import substitution. In a sense, the real problem was to seize the state and create a base so as to render it capable of acting as an autonomous factor shaping both its internal and external environment rather than as a more or less passive instrumentality reflecting the push and pull of environmental stimuli and pressures.

In coping with this problem, populist regimes sought to expand the support base for more effective and directive governmental decision making by mobilizing broad popular support, not on the basis of "class," but on the basis of "citizenship," that is, the nation (concretized in the state) versus the antination. Throughout the region, populism directly contributed to a significant increase in both the breadth and the tempo of political mobilization, drawing large sectors of hitherto excluded social groups (organized labor, marginal urban residents, peasants, etc.) directly into the political arena. To use E. E. Schattschneider's image, one impact of populism was to expand significantly the scope of political conflict.[22]

In its first phases, then, by emphasizing mobilization, populism was oriented to the inclusion of a very broad set of actors into the political game. The purpose of this "inclusionary" approach was to underpin the power of populist regimes and increase the autonomy of the state. However, to make the state an effective regulatory instrumentality, central authorities had to achieve a degree of independence not only from traditional foci of pressure but from those mobilized by the populists as well. Populist regimes therefore sought not only to mobilize a broad popular base but also to control that base and structure the relationships of its support groups to the state.

The objective need to control and structure the mobilization process fed directly into the elitist and statist tendency implicit in the populist leadership's orientation, which in some cases (Perón and Vargas, for example) mutated quickly into an openly authoritarian governmental style. Populist regimes attempted to structure and control their support base by a combination of three factors. In the first instance, they offered symbolic gratification in the form of charismatic leadership styles, new symbols of dignity (Perón's *descamisados*), nationalist rhetoric, and significant nationalistic acts such as the expropriation of foreign corporations. Populist regimes also offered their supporters material gratification in the form of increased wages and salaries, expansion of public employment, expansion of public services, etc. Finally, populist regimes sought to fashion centrally controlled organizational structures to link their support groups directly into the state structures. The bulk of these organizations were formed on sectoral and functional criteria, thereby fragmenting support groups into parallel primary organizational structures joined at the top by interlocking sectoral elites. The success of populist organizational efforts varied considerably, but they all manifested a clear predilection for corporatist organizational principles; in the case of Vargas, the corporatist bias was made explicit in the constitution of the Estado Nôvo.

A central problem hampering the ability of most populist regimes to maintain control over their own followings was the inherent contradiction between the populist goal of stimulating state-sponsored economic development and the tactic of mobilizing a mass base by increasing the levels of popular consumption. The tension between policies fostering development and those increasing consumption in an environment of relative scarcity was manifested most directly in the problem of inflation, which was chronic in most countries of the Latin American region from the1940s on.

Political mobilization concomitant with a rise in nationalism and increases in levels of popular consumption had two further impacts: the introduction of new principles of legitimacy, and the creation of serious strains on the limited economic resources of most countries in the region. By the 1940s, the principles of a nationalist-oriented welfare statism had become so deeply implanted that even status-quo regimes at least had to pay lip service to them. The problem of meeting an increase in range and intensity of material demands, manifested most directly in chronic inflation, created serious problems of social control which plagued populist as well as nonpopulist regimes. A combination of the inability to unseat traditional elites as well as to control their own followers brought numerous populist experiments to untimely and often violent ends.

By the 1950s, populism had had a profound impact on the area. It had (1) weakened the power of the traditional elites; (2) stimulated import-substitution growth, which increased the relevance of local industrialists and organized labor; and (3) stimulated a general increase in political mobilization and popular consumption. The last factor in particular tended to outstrip both the rate of growth and the control capacity of public institutions, contributing thereby to a general tendency in the direction of praetorian politics.[23]

An important aspect of the praetorianization of Latin American politics during this period was the fact that although the formal state apparatuses in the region grew markedly, this was accompanied not by an increase in the power and efficiency of the states but rather by the reverse. The continuing reality of dependence was a critical factor in the development of states that were formally large and powerful but in practice weak. Another factor was a kind of de facto disaggregation of the state as various particularistic interest blocs in a sense captured relevant pieces of the state which they manipulated to their own benefit.[24] This de facto parceling out of bits of the state was particularly evident in the politics of social security policy. As some analysts have shown, the many funds tended to become the fiefdoms of the interests they served and were used in a manner that actually reinforced socioeconomic inequality even as social security spending fed inflation.[25] Thus, instead of an assertion of the autonomous power of the state apparatus to regulate its internal and external environment, this period saw an increase in the size of the state but a decrease in autonomy, power, and efficiency of governmental apparatuses.

Despite these developments, the pressures generated in the 1930s and 1940s were to a large extent contained during the 1950s and 1960s despite recurrent predictions of violent revolutionary upheavals that would sweep the continent. Anderson has effectively argued that containment was achieved because of the flexibility of established elites who adapted to the new situation by allowing proven power contenders into the political game as long as they did not seek to unseat established power groups.[26] In short, the period saw a kind of de facto politics of informal and nonstructured inclusion that expanded the participants in the political game without any significant restructuring of the game. This process (which Cotler described in Peru and labeled "segmental incorporation") had numerous effects, including an increase in particularism, reinforcement of columnar social organization, and expansion of clientelistic politics.[27]

The ability to maintain a politics of inclusion by co-optation of specific power contenders was a direct function of resources available to meet demands, which, of course, varied widely in the region. The ability to generate resources was in turn tied to the previous nature and degree of external dependence, and the ability to generate horizontal growth based on import substitution—capacities which fluctuated widely. Variations on these factors were important variables accounting for the political patterns in different countries during the 1950s and 1960s. But even in countries with more diversified export sectors and a large capacity for import substitution, the ability to generate resources and maintain a politics of segmental incorporation was not unlimited. By the mid-1960s it became evident that even in nations such as Brazil and Argentina there were both internal and external structural limits on import-substitution growth and that instead of diminishing external dependence, import substitution resulted in new and more onerous forms of dependence.

By the mid-1960s, a new structural crisis developed with the exhaustion of import-substitution growth and the reality of even more pervasive external economic penetration by multinational corporations that assert control over local manufacturing activities. This time the crisis took place against a backdrop of an accumulated public legitimation of nationalism and developmentalism, and societies characterized by high rates of political mobilization. One might also add the existence of revolutionary Cuba, which acted as a specter of what might come if matters were left to drift. In this situation, increased praetorian politicization in a context of large but weak and disarticulated states rendered a civil solution to the accumulated problems and bottlenecks all but impossible.

Thus, acting under the guise of doctrines of national security and national developmentalism, military organizations in several Latin states seized formal power. Again, the effectiveness of these regimes has varied, but in all cases the orientation to state-sponsored rapid industrial development has been paramount. To achieve this general goal, two subsidiary goals have loomed large. First has been a concerted attempt to increase the power and autonomy of the formal state and establish it as the primary regulator and arbiter of political economy. Related to this has been a conscious decision to favor some power contenders and their interests over others. This has given rise to what Guillermo O'Donnell has called the politics of "exclusion," or the forcing of previous players out of the political game.[28] Given the fact that few groups would leave voluntarily, the perceived need to exclude has generated a move to blatant authoritarianism, which consciously seeks to control political participation through a combination of state-imposed structural controls and, when necessary, violent repression. Although the apparent mix of included and excluded varies from system to system (Peru versus Brazil, for example), the structural mechanisms of organizing and controlling participation are more than ever explicitly corporatist in principle and practice. Thus, in confronting this second crisis of delayed dependent development, a large part of Latin America has moved from the implicit and at least potentially democratic corporatism of the populists to the present blatant authoritarian corporatism of the soldiers and technocrats.

Notes

1. Philippe C. Schmitter, "Paths to Political Development in Latin America," in *Changing Latin America: New Interpretations of Its Politics and Society*, ed. Douglas A. Chalmers (New York: Academy of Political Science, 1972), 83–108.

2. Guillermo A. O'Donnell, *Modernization and Bureaucratic-Authoritarianism: Studies in South American Politics* (Berkeley: University of California, Institute of International Studies, 1973).

3. These types are developed by O'Donnell in *Modernization and Bureaucratic-Authoritarianism*.

4. The concept of corporatism has recently been used by a number of scholars when discussing Latin American politics. For an overview of several such usages see Frederick B. Pike, ed., "The New Corporatism: Social and Political Structures in the Iberian World," *Review of Politics* 36, no. 1 (special edition, January 1974). For an exhaustive operational definition, see especially Philippe C. Schmitter, "Still the Century of Corporatism?" in the same issue, 85–131.

5. See, for example, Howard J. Wiarda, "Toward a Framework for the Study of Political Change in the Iberic-Latin Tradition: The Corporative Model," *World Politics* 25 (January 1973): 206–36.

6. Ronald C. Newton, "On 'Functional Groups,' 'Fragmentation,' and 'Pluralism' in Spanish American Political Society," *Hispanic American Historical Review* 50 (February 1970): 1–29.

7. Among the more salient proponents of this viewpoint are Schmitter, "Still the Century of the Corporatism?" and O'Donnell, *Modernization and Bureaucratic-Authoritarianism*.

8. See James D. Cockroft, André Gunder Frank, and Dale L. Johnson, eds., *Dependence and Underdevelopment* (Garden City, NY: Doubleday and Company, 1972); Susanne Bodenheimer, "Dependency and Imperialism," and Theotonio

dos Santos, "The Structure of Dependence," both in *Readings in U.S. Imperialism*, ed. K. T. Fann and Donald C. Hodges (Boston: Sargent, 1971), 155–82, 225–36; and Helio Jaguaribe, *Political Development: A General Theory and a Latin American Case Study* (New York: Harper and Row, 1973), 470–78.

9. See Torcuato di Tella, "Populism and Reform in Latin America," in *Obstacles to Change in Latin America*, ed. Claudio Veliz (New York: Oxford University Press, 1970), 47–74; James Malloy, "Populismo militar en el Perú y Bolivia: Antecedentes y posibilidades," *Estudios Andinos* 2, no. 2 (1971–72): 114–34; Alistair Hennessy, "América Latina," in *Populismo*, ed. Ghita Ionesui and Ernest Gellner (Buenos Aires: Amorrotu, 1969); Ronald C. Newton, "Natural Corporatism and the Passing of Populism in Spanish America," *Review of Politics* 36, no. 1 (January 1974): 34–51; and Jaguaribe, *Political Development*, 440–54.

10. Charles W. Anderson, *Politics and Economic Change in Latin America* (Princeton: D. Van Nostrand, 1967).

11. Julio Cotler, "The Mechanics of Internal Domination and Social Change in Peru," in *Masses in Latin America*, ed. Irving Louis Horowitz (New York: Oxford University Press, 1970), 407–45.

12. See Kalman Silvert, "The Costs of Anti-Nationalism: Argentina," in *Expectant Peoples*, ed. idem (New York: Random House, 1963), 347–72; and Newton, "On Functional Groups."

13. José Ortega y Gasset, *Invertebrate Spain* (New York: W. W. Norton, 1937).

14. The phenomenon of premature bureaucratization has recently been linked to a more general process labeled "premature modernization." One author has argued that this process, which involves the diffusion of modern values to economically less developed societies, is a major impediment to further economic development. See Alejandro Portes, "Modernity and Development: A Critique," *Studies in Comparative International Development* 8, no. 3 (Fall 1973): 247–79.

15. See n. 9.

16. The literature on this period in Latin America is voluminous. One of the best studies of this "hegemonic crisis" in a single country is Julio Cotler, "Political Crisis and Military Populism in Peru," *Studies in Comparative International Development* 6, no. 5 (1970–71): 95–113.

17. See n. 8.

18. For an exhaustive compendium of constitutional changes adopted in this period, see Academia de Ciencias Económicas, *Las clausulas económica-sociales en las constituciones de América*, 2 vols. (Buenos Aires: Editorial Losada, 1947–48).

19. One should remember, for example, that Fidel Castro mobilized broad middle-class support by returning to the Cuban populist constitution of 1940.

20. The constitution of the Brazilian Estado Nôvo decreed in 1937 was explicitly based on corporatist principles.

21. The following statement of MNR leader Víctor Paz Estenssoro is a good example: "It is a general law that the men of the oppressed class are never the ones who achieve gains for their own class, and this for a simple reason: those of the oppressed class do not have the economic means to even raise themselves culturally and develop their personality, let alone be able to make a great reform or a revolution" (*Discursos parlamentarios* [La Paz, Bolivia, 1955], 316–17, my translation).

22. E. E. Schattschneider, *The Semi-Sovereign People* (New York: Holt, Rinehart and Winston, 1960).

23. Samuel Huntington, *Political Order in Changing Societies* (New Haven: Yale University Press, 1968).

24. Eldon Kenworthy, "Coalitions in the Political Development of Latin America," in *The Study of Coalition Behavior*, ed. Sven Groennings et al. (New York: Holt, Rinehart and Winston, 1970), 103–33.

25. Carmelo Mesa-Lago has conducted extensive research on social security in Latin America. See his "Social Security Stratification and Inequality in Chile" (Pittsburgh: University of Pittsburgh, Center for Latin American Studies, 1973); "Social Security Stratification and Inequality in Mexico" (Santa Monica: Fourth International Congress of Mexican Studies, October 1973); and "La estratificación de la seguridad social y el efecto de desigualidad en América Latina: El caso peruano," *Estudios Andinos*, no. 8 (1973): 17–48.

26. Anderson, *Politics and Economic Change*.

27. Cotler, "Mechanics of Internal Domination."

28. O'Donnell, *Modernization and Bureaucratic-Authoritarianism*.

III

Agents of Political Change? Religion, Militarism, Electioneering, and Nongovernmental Organizations

7

Civil-Military Relations in a Democratic Framework

Augusto Varas

The military is undoubtedly the single most important institutional actor in the rise or fall of democracy in Latin America. The relationship between civil and military leaders, specifically, the subordination of the military to civilian authority, has long plagued Latin American efforts to achieve political stability, continuity, and democracy. Augusto Varas, a Chilean specialist on civil-military relations and the author of Check on Democracy: New Military Power in Latin America *(1989), argues that civilian leadership, within the context of democratic governments, must develop fresh ideas and approaches to create the trust and respect necessary to establish a long-standing relationship. At the same time, he suggests that the military itself is undergoing internal changes in its self-conception and autonomy, thereby having significant consequences for civil-military relations and democratic politics.*

The use and abuse of the armed forces in the political realm in Latin America has left a negative balance in terms of their stability and institutional development. In turn, the democratic stabilization projects put into place in the region after military interventions have been basically faulty in the sphere of military policy. To the extent that the Latin American democracies fail to perceive clearly the issue of the armed forces' insertion in the democratic process and to identify the national defense in their reform projects, a key problem will remain unresolved; this, in turn, soon becomes a threat to the democratic institutions themselves, through either new autonomous adjustment forms or renewed military interventions.[1]

From Louis W. Goodman et al., *The Military and Democracy: The Future of Civil-Military Relations in Latin America* (Lexington, MA: Lexington Books, 1990), 199–218. © 1990 Lexington Books. Reprinted by permission of Lexington Books, an imprint of Macmillan Publishing Company.

Theoretical and empirical research of the relations among the armed forces, the society, and the state has thus become a crucial issue for the Latin American democracy. From the findings of such studies, a framework of definitions can be developed, so as to ascertain the role of the armed forces in the internal security and national defense spheres and determine how to insert the armed forces into the state structure and ensure effective civilian control over the armed institutions.[2]

Nowadays, the behavior and interactions among the armed forces, the civilians, and the state occur in the context of three relational systems: *intervention-withdrawal, autonomous adjustment*, and *civilian control*. Each shows specific degrees of underlying state inconsistency, military professionalization, and civil ability to develop a system of linkages among the state bodies in question.

Intervention-Withdrawal

Although there are numerous studies on the causes of military intervention in the Latin American politics, the existence of various viewpoints and the identification of different variables have not led to thorough theoretical presentations.[3] The number of variables, background factors, and explanations of political intervention by the military remains an open question that must be deepened in connection with the major issues of the evolution and consolidation of the region's democratic governmental forms.

In order to get some clues for redefining civil-military relations within a democratic framework, I have chosen to systematize those variables that have been crucial for the armed forces' participation in democratic transition.[4] This will permit us to identify the elements that must be put into place—even though their mere presence may not be sufficient—so that balanced civil-military relations can be established in the future. I will refer to the cases of Argentina (1983), Brazil (1984), Bolivia (1980–1982), Ecuador (1979), Peru (1979), and Uruguay (1984) and compare them to those of Chile (1987) and Paraguay (1986).

Delivery of power to the civilians has been contingent on sets of both social and military factors.

Social Factors

The major social factors affecting the military are the transformation of the system of political relations and the local political culture, mass-mobilization capabilities, the status of the civil-military relationship, and the terms of the armed forces' withdrawal. Overall, these factors constitute what could be called opposition *succession capabilities*. Such social developments challenge the leadership of the armed forces and bring about or increase internal dissent.[5]

A first set of prerequisites for transition, significant for the armed forces, has been the surge of the political system's capability to respond to the issue of *dissident unity*, which creates a new government option. Second, the party system and political-institutional crisis facilitated military intervention in Latin America.[6] However, once such problems were overcome, these forces started to perform a key role in transition toward democracy. Hence, the attempts to develop a new political relationship within the opposition have been effective in creating the prerequisites for transition. This indicates that the greater the transformation of the political system during the authoritarian period, the easier the democratization.[7] Brazil is a case in point.[8] Finally, the isolation of the antiestablishment forces has also helped to deprive the armed forces of political reasons to rule. The degree of consensus for such coactive measures tends to be inversely proportional to the breadth of the dissident front.

Some of the changes that propitiated transition took place at the political culture level. The emergence of more pragmatic approaches and the isolation of fundamentalist-type ideologies have helped substitute genuine national will for sector and group interest-led approaches. In this regard, the defeat of "ideologism" and the explicit nationalistic orientation of the democratizing forces have been important factors. A similar situation has been apparent in Argentina, Brazil, Uruguay, and Peru.

Another important factor has been the opposition's capability to create and mobilize national forces for change. Although such mass mobilizations have been common in economic crisis situations, they have also taken place without such a context; they have been a means to support basically political targets regarding full civil rights—democracy as a value in itself. Mass mobilizations not only have led to the situation in which the military regimes typically find themselves in their terminal periods—when they lose their capability for crisis management[9]—but also have represented the component of majority will, which is one of the few deterrents the armed forces pay attention to.

In the case of Peru, mass mobilizations attesting general readiness for change strongly influenced the military rulers.[10] In Bolivia, domestic resistance to the [Luis] García Meza regime was one of the key factors in the ensuing process of unification of the opposition. In Brazil, the mass protests and the campaign for direct elections in 1984 were crucial.[11] In Uruguay, the defeat in the plebiscite, and the inability to legitimate its political project through social consensus, was decisive for the start of negotiations and transition.

When the armed forces face a legitimation crisis in respect to the main forces supporting them, their situation becomes untenable. The inability to set up a stable order—be it legitimate or not—and develop the positive results of the original insurrectional coalition has also been a factor of democratic transition in the region, as shown by the cases of Argentina,[12] Brazil, and Peru.

In Brazil, the arduous relationship between the military government and its supporting business elites was one of the basic reasons for the military's decision to launch an opening process, which admittedly was an almost unilateral initiative of the armed forces.[13] By then, the armed forces were facing several perils.[14] Hence, we can conclude that the ruling armed forces' estrangement from their business elite supporters left them without any chance to manage both the military internecine crisis and the crisis created by the moves of the opposition forces. The mix of mass mobilizations and the estrangement of the business elites created a favorable climate for a military decision to start a transition process.[15] The same situation took place in Peru, although there, mass mobilization and business elite estrangement tended to coincide briefly.[16]

These four sets of factors have made their influence felt within the army barracks. They have challenged the arguments expounded by the military to remain in power: both the negative one—that of fighting the antiestablishment forces—and the positive one—that of legitimizing a new political order through social consensus or by enjoying elite support. The hinge of the institutional self-attributed images is also put in doubt. As the opposition front widens, there is less consensus for repression, and the costs of using force become higher. Hence, the isolation of the armed forces within the state apparatus and the society becomes apparent, thus enhancing the civilians' deterrent capabilities and creating, in the armed forces, a climate that makes them ready to accept a formula for civilian takeover that includes low levels of uncertainty regarding the institution's future.

Military Factors

Two sets of military factors can be identified: the crisis of the professional function—resulting from the contradiction between the functions of defense and domestic police tasks; and at the governmental level, the management crisis. These factors coalesce into a single result: erosion of the internal consensus and emergence of a new one, aimed at protecting the collective interests of the armed institutions—their institutional continuity being challenged—through retreat to the barracks.

Regarding the first set of factors, the fact can be established that in all the countries analyzed, the professional crisis emerging from the strain between defense and domestic order functions has been detrimental to the armed forces' modernization and professionalization. One of the most evident consequences of this process of the army's becoming a police force has often been the consolidation of an intelligence community that assumes control of the major levers of the military power. This institutional framework tends to freeze professional development and the process of modernization of the armed institutions. The practical effects of this contradiction became apparent in a dramatic manner during the Malvinas [Falklands] conflict. This military defeat can also be explained by the institutional erosion associated with massive violations of human rights.[17]

For these reasons, and because the armed institutions' assumption of police tasks cannot be justified, a political space is created inside the armed forces where the institutionalist groups can demand that the *professional* development be continued. This situation, which was apparent in Argentina, Brazil, and Bolivia, was also noticeable in Ecuador.[18]

The second set of military factors refers to the internal effects of the governmental management crisis of the armed forces. To the extent that the armed forces insert themselves in a different way when they *are* the government, their success or failure ends up affecting their political role.

Thus, the management crisis in Argentina during [Jorge] Videla's term, which was aggravated during [Roberto Eduardo] Viola's and [Leopoldo] Galtieri's administrations, paved the way for the military defeat, as the command line was cut off and its verticality was affected by the emergence of internal groups that put the government's management skills into question and brought forth alternative proposals.[19] Such was also the case in Ecuador and Peru.

This type of crisis has compounded the classic problem that the armed forces confront when they take power—namely, becoming as politically split as the society at large. Such new reality transforms the armed forces "into ambiguous political forces,"[20] which necessarily leads them to a process of internecine conflict and threatens their institutional continuity—a key factor if they are to be able to operate in a unified way in a war scenario.

This type of problem could be only provisionally overcome in Uruguay, where the armed forces themselves became a "substitute political party"[21]—a process that was facilitated by a strategic-political context in which the armed institutions have no deterrent capabilities. Only in this context could the military function be denatured, and the police and political responsibilities proper were hypertrophied. The Uruguayan experience, however—unthinkable as it is in other South American countries—shows the limits of the tension between the defense functions and those of a political-police nature.

The other polar case is that of Argentina, where the attempt was made to turn each branch of the defense services into a substitute political party and, simultaneously, to enhance the country's defense capabilities. The end result was the state's becoming divided in three watertight compartments—one for each defense branch—whereby the management crisis deepened[22] and the military deterrence capabilities themselves were eroded.[23]

Crisis Management Capabilities

Because the military institution's political capabilities are determined by its resources, professional ability, and internal coherence,[24] any crack in that coherence affects both the management capabilities and, basically, the crisis management capabilities of the armed forces.

The importance of internal relations management within the armed forces is compounded by the very repression of internal dissent by high-ranking government authorities,[25] which in many cases permits, if not a solution, at least postponement of a solution to the crisis. In the case of Peru, it was not the disagreement within the armed forces that ultimately prevented the military from tackling the crisis. The leading factor was Velasco's inability to orient the process and organize the various internal factions, because of his precarious health condition.[26]

Rewards and Sanctions

Under the circumstances, it becomes particularly relevant to examine the issue of the impact of military rule on the armed forces' development and their relationships with civilians and the state.[27] I am specifically referring to the need to denounce the effects on national unity of the political power monopoly by the armed institutions.

Use of military force within the processes of modernization or political reform has always been catastrophic for national unity. Even though higher levels of economic growth have been attained—through maintenance of the internal order, repression, and wage compression—the net balance is negative in the mid- and long run. Thus, the administrations of [Raúl] Alfonsín, [Julio] Sanguinetti, [José] Sarney, and even Alán García [Pérez] are still being penalized by the feud between the civilians and the armed forces in Argentina, Uruguay, Brazil, and Peru, respectively. The "full stop" policies in Argentina and Uruguay, "protected democracy" in Brazil, "narco-militarism" in Bolivia, and the Pol Pot-style revolutionary fundamentalism in Peru indirectly stem from the political power monopoly by the armed forces, which failed to produce institutions that served as channels of communication among the elites and among the mass organizations, the social base, and the state's decision-making structure.

Such a historical review of the effects of military rule—through the analysis of specific situations—is a collective "sanction" for those who saw themselves as representing the loftiest concepts of national unity but, in fact, became a factor of national discord. At the same time, it is an institutional "reward" for those armed forces that recognize the fact that national unity can withstand the harshest tests without the need for militarization of the nation's life.

Withdrawal and Democracy

Based on the analysis of the social and military factors that determine the attitude of the armed forces regarding the process of transition to democracy, the following key variables in normalizing civil-military relations can be derived: (1) civil democratic unity, embracing even those elites that, in the beginning, supported the military rule; (2) isolation of the antiestablishment forces that legitimate the armed forces' fulfillment of internal security tasks; (3) effective mass support that does not overflow the institutional framework or generate new crisis; (4) reestablishment of the institutional balance by focusing on professional unity in the armed forces and avoidance of political or ideological fragmentation, as well as governmental and internal security responsibilities that impair appropriate professionalization; (5) moral recovery of the armed forces, which entails recognizing the identity between constitutionalism and democracy; and (6) a change in the sphere of civilian political culture, which makes possible all of the other variables.

Autonomous Adjustment

Between the scenarios of military intervention and civilian control over the armed institutions, there are various midway hypotheses, which I have christened "autonomous adjustment." Such situations reflect a type of civil-military coexistence whereby the armed forces are not fully in control nor are military decisions a province of civilian jurisdiction. Each accommodation scenario can occur in each and every one of the civil-military relationship dimensions or only in some of them. Some compromise represents the relative balance level that the parties have been able to reach in a specific country and under specific historical circumstances—without, however, being able to make the new arrangement a part of the state's structure.

The contention that it is easier to demilitarize the government than the power is fully relevant in such a context.[28] In a number of countries, the autonomous adjustment scenarios have existed for such a long time that they cannot be depicted as transitional forms—they have become new state forms in Latin America. In some countries, the elites have assumed a leading role in the economic development process. In some others, they have become a key power factor; some governmental programs cannot be executed without them. Thus, autonomous adjustment means the maintenance of veto powers by the armed forces to a lesser extent than in intervention periods but to a greater extent than in periods of civilian control.[29] In such a context, the armed forces as a whole become an active power factor, just as the political parties, the church, the trade unions, and other social institutions and organizations are. Thus, autonomous adjustment entails sustained high levels of state militarization, even in cases where the armed forces do not rule directly.

This new reality—which began to make itself felt in Latin America at the end of the 1970s—reflects a particular set of factors, which will be discussed here. Once these factors have been identified, we will be in a position to specify a second set of tools that may be useful in restoring balanced civil-military relations.

Some structural factors explain why the armed forces have become social conflict arbitrators, social reformers, or modernization agents in various countries.

First, some systems of organization of the armed forces and some civil-military relationship structures are not entirely consistent with constitutional democracy. In Latin America, the most common organizational system is a mix of "cadres and conscripts," which cannot be compared to that of civilian militias and appears in association with nondemocratic government systems.[30]

The existence of permanent professional cadres that train a regular contingent of conscripts—that is, people compulsorily recruited under the law—produces interesting sociological dynamics. First, there is the corporative (guild-type) closed situation typical of "professional armies." Second, the compulsory nature of the conscription system reinforces the internal authoritarian attitude of the cadres in respect to the recruits. Third, recruit training focuses on basic military operations. Technical-professional knowledge is reserved for the permanent personnel, whereby their segregation is reinforced. Fourth, this "self-centered" organizational order tends to make the armed forces assume and perform functions progressively differentiated from their military ones, substituting for the civilian institutions in specialized scientific, technological, productive, and even commercial and banking areas. The military world thus secludes itself in an ascending spiral of autarchic self-sufficiency.

Inside the armed forces, the aforementioned factors produce a civil-military relations model that duplicates the military institutional order. Thus, the extension of the organizational categories, and those of internal operation, is projected on the rest of the society, engendering an authoritarian, nondemocratic approach to civil-military relations. The core of this approach is the notion that the civilian element—its categories and values—is irrelevant in terms of the military order and its institutional continuity and, in some cases, is even a threat to the military system itself. Because social change constitutes a more dynamic process in the Latin American countries than in other, northerly regions, social mobilization and demands for participation clash with armed forces that reject conflict, disorder, and sociopolitical diversity or heterogeneity within the state. This structural inconsistency with verticalistic, nondemocratic institutions could well explain some military interventions prompted by social change processes.

Moreover, in most of the region's countries, the integration of the various military branches into one single state organization—the Defense Ministry or the Joint Chiefs of Staff—is an occasional factor. Thus, under the military reforms undertaken in Argentina and Peru, priority has been given to the establishment of a unified command organization for the whole of the armed forces, whereby autonomous bureaucratic dynamics are created that tend to reinforce institutional introspection.

In many cases the relative lack of organic integration in the typical Latin American state[31] prevents the existence of a set of interests that the various social sectors and groups share—a fact that reflects upon the various state organizations. This function has been made even more important by the fact that, historically—from colonial times up to an advanced stage of the independent era—the armed forces have performed a number of political tasks.[32] These conditions facilitate political intervention by the armed forces and simultaneously underpin the military prejudice that civilian politics are "anarchical" and that the military institution should protect itself in their regard.

The military organization is adequate for the performance of functions that are national in scope—that other social organizations or state institutions are unable to undertake, given their fragmentation and basically regional jurisdiction. Within the armed forces as a whole, the army is particularly able to manage adequately defense or any other task of a similar magnitude at a national level because of its structure and the fact that its resources are naturally spread throughout the country. This reality enhances the potential autonomy of the armed forces.

As a result of their permanent interventions in the political realm, the armed forces have been granted a high level of functional autonomy relative to their respective societies and governments. This situation varies from country to country. The degree of autonomy of each Latin American army is the aggregate of a number of simultaneous processes, including a military process of "corporatization" and a civil ability or inability to control the armed forces.

From the military standpoint, the modernization and professionalization processes, together with accompanying situations of sociocultural segregation—some of which I have already mentioned—have unleashed the centripetal forces that "corporatize" (that is, segregate or isolate) the armed forces relative to the civilians. The technological element, specialization in subjects scarcely linked to the civilian life, and the corporative-style accompanying ideologies set barriers and institutional limits between the armed forces and the society. The foregoing would be among the sufficient conditions of the process of autonomous adjustment.

On the other hand, this process has also been affected by the terms of the military ouster from government.[33]

In Argentina, the opposition striving for democracy made military institutional continuity possible through policies that included punishment for massive violations of human rights, but only for the organizers of such actions. The policy of modernization and professionalization of the armed institutions completes a type of civil-military agreement that was not easily reached but set the stage for democratic government—although not for a new civil-military equilibrium.[34]

In Bolivia, the actions against the military narcotics trafficking clique were limited to the most active groups; they received the whole impact of the exemplary measures of the democratic authorities. The implementation of these policies, however, has not been free from problems.

In the Brazilian case,[35] the price of transition has been a remarkable program of enhancement of the country's military capabilities, and no punishment was even considered for those guilty of excesses during the military regime.

A similar case—though a less successful one—has been that in Uruguay, where even though institutional continuity was assured, the approval of a bill of amnesty has encountered serious difficulties.

Withdrawal terms similar to those in Brazil were observed in Peru, where military spending has been dramatically augmented—to the point that the present democratic government has had to take a series of measures designed to set limits to this spending spree.

In Ecuador, however, the civilians striving for democracy were in no position to formulate a consistent initiative. Hence, the armed forces were granted an exceptional statute for institutional insertion into the state, whereby they have reached a level of relative autonomy that can hardly be compared to those of other armed institutions on the American continent.[36]

In sum, although military withdrawal has been the product of a civil and/or military crisis, the terms of withdrawal tend to be highly favorable for the armed institutions, whose institutional continuity has been preserved. However, the greater this protection, the larger their veto power during the transition period and their autonomy during the democratic consolidation period.

In this regard, it is important to stress the need for new conceptual analyses of the phenomenon of autonomous adjustment in Latin America.[37] Such analyses may provide elements for better understanding of the new state forms that are being developed in the region, where the armed forces have an active role. This knowledge would prepare civilians to deal successfully with the task of defining key issues regarding the design of policies of contention—and eventually reduction—of military autonomy.

Civilian Control

As noted before, civilian control over the armed forces should be substantive rather than formal. Though not exclusively, civilian control capabilities are of a conceptual nature; they have to do with the definition of guidelines and institutional goals[38]—in other words, with the restoration of the professional dimension of the military function.[39] Once the necessary conditions for a new armed forces–society equilibrium and new organic relations between the military institutions and the state have been developed, it becomes necessary to identify the sufficient conditions— the contents, the flesh—of the principle of civil leadership over the armed forces.

The armed forces are an integral part of the defense apparatus; they manage the military deterrent component, whereas the government remains in control of other aspects, such as foreign relations. Thus, the possibility of civilian control over the armed forces to a large extent depends on state and government ability to define the wide variety of subjects connected with national defense in a consistent manner. Consistency exists—as witnessed by civil- and/or military-launched state and government policies—when there is an ability to adopt the programs and measures that will be referred to here. Failure or loss of civil initiative in such spheres results in loss of control over the armed forces. The armed forces need to perceive that clear-cut policies are being implemented and, also, that a lack of civilian control over their processes would represent a big threat for the army—a reality that armed institutions do not clearly recognize. The perception of safety or peril for their institutional position is a very important factor in the study of these organizations.

Civil control over the armed forces is contingent on the civilians' being aware of all of the relevant (political, economic, technological, and social) variables in the domestic and international realms. To this effect, a governmental, noncorporatized style has to be in place, so as to permit the government to tackle the issues of the state as a whole in pursuance of the interests of the community.[40] This global approach is crucial for the armed forces to "position" themselves as an institution. Each society must face the main military national defense issues and must use a national, democratic approach to solve them.

Professionalization

The fundamental requisite for redefining the role of the armed forces is to professionalize their institution. Contrary to past decades' military-technological innovations and doctrines, those of the present are highly dynamic. The contents of the profession change every year, along with progress in world military knowledge and practice. This generates demands for modernization, which, in turn, changes according to research and development advances and domestic or foreign weapons availability. All of these changes affect the military doctrines on war, its causes, and its linkages with politics and the society.

The new frontier of technological development has already been drawn. Latin America has to assume the approach of the third industrial revolution.[41] These new challenges cannot be faced, however, with the limited resources of individual countries. Regional cooperation and integration are the new concepts that have started to be analyzed. From the military point of view, the progress demands preparation for a new age. For the Latin American armed forces, the only choice is to reinsert themselves, on a cooperative basis, in the regional context and launch a joint research and development effort whereby industrial and/or commercial projects can be put into place. To attain this goal, the institution's energies cannot be wasted in governmental-political projects. Professional commitment is the only chance of "formal" survival after political interregnums.

Regional integration, national coordination, and a new civil-military relationship are the terms of future regional space—as well as naval and land—sovereignty.

New Concepts

To rely on old-fashioned concepts in the attempt to assume new strategic roles in a world with changed dimensions would be nonsense. It is easier to understand the new approach to strategic-military affairs by comparing the various policies emerging from the reality and the needs of the national defense phenomenon.

The traditional approach to internal security, territorial defense, hemispheric security, and conflict between the superpowers has led to accelerated militarization. This trend has been strengthened by a context of short cycles of relative autonomy in the military sphere. Hence, new definitions of those dimensions should reduce and reverse the process of militarization and create self-centered responses that prevent the reappearance of militarization at other levels.

To proceed from the traditional to a modern approach, the strategic target, as well as the means to attain it, would have to be redefined in light of the new international realities. Modern concepts should be developed other than internal repression, intrastate conflict, military balance, and thoughtless alignment on the Western world defense side.

Both civil and military regional leading elites have remained committed to the traditional definitions of the various security and national-regional defense dimensions, despite the change in the strategic context. Such concepts prevent the emergence of a new, self-centered, nonheteronomous definition of national defense. The current national strategic interests are much broader than the military interests. The military dimension itself should not be specific, unless it is conceived among the national defense interests, which in this context have a continental scope. The traditional oligarchic approach of territorial and hemispheric defense being irremediably confined to the territorial perimeter—one that gives priority to the armed forces' police responsibilities—has been detrimental to the performance of military functions and to democracy,[42] and has hampered the establishment of a common basis for regional military relations. At present, in order to identify a modern strategic role for the armed forces, the police function has to be revamped and limited to that of curbing the types of behavior that deserve penalties under the law, rather than certain ideologies. And police, rather than the armed forces, have to be relied on for the performance of such functions.

Similarly, regarding intrastate defense, higher, regional levels of military cooperation should be reached, so as to identify common regional strategic interests that are consistent with today's national interests. In the realm of global security, the target should, for the most part, be one of neutrality and self-exclusion from the global conflict, together with voluntary defense of regional interests. Rather than defining itself according to extracontinental interests, Latin America should strive to develop a positive strategic role for itself. Not alien interests but its own interests should be the fundamentals of such a definition. In this context, military cooperation will be instrumental in the protection of the region's common interests.

A new, endogenously created regional security system—aimed at regional cooperation and the nurturing of long-run common interests in the field of defense, rather than assumption of an outstanding role in strategic matters—has become a must in the present circumstances.

The ideological and financial weight of the traditional approach prevents the emergence of national defense formulas other than regional military balance—which, in turn, starts new poverty cycles, followed by heavier repression responsibilities for the armed forces and additional, more acute regional military balance needs. However, the region has become militarily more vulnerable, to the extent that conflicts centered in other areas tend to add the land, sea, and space of Latin America to their original battlefield. In the present circumstances—with armed forces committed to police tasks—little, if anything, can be done to prevent this new form of subordination and submission. To reduce military and economic weakness and to control new poverty cycles, new forms of military cooperation have to evolve in the field of regional security. A new definition of security system defense policies would streamline defense policies and give priority to resource allotment and military spending control, which so far have been relatively incoherent and disorderly.[43]

To settle the controversy regarding Latin America's strategic role, the approach has to switch from privileging geographic aspects to emphasizing conditions that grant Latin America the role of a protagonist, rather than a mere territory, in strategic matters. This new approach would not be necessarily or exclusively referred to close protection of a territory. The nation-state protagonist would thus abandon its territorial approach and adopt the modern one, which takes into account other spheres, such as communications, trade, energy, and finance.

No individual Latin American country is in a position to attain new, self-centered strategic targets, such as hinterland, space, and maritime control. This creates a strong need for integration and cooperation as a means of national sovereignty defense. The state's sovereign power is no longer projected only on a territorial space, as new strategic dimensions have been opened that require new responses. Because this scope of sovereignty necessitates regional cooperation—as a requirement for real autonomy and sovereignty—military cooperation is now the most modern and least costly form of national sovereignty protection.

Military-Industrial Integration

Under long-run developmental policies, new regional military capabilities should be established in order to overcome the area's economic and military weaknesses. Modernization would be ancillary to regional security, but not as in the past, when security and the military were diverted from their military functions in order to attain the targets of the development doctrine through labor training or tool production. Overall, these policies produced military "invasion" of all state sectors. Under a new security approach, each Latin American state should be able to fill and occupy a new, independent, nonhegemonic place in the modern world by integrating the armed forces with other institutions and structures and preventing them from becoming the state coordination and consistency axis.

The new strategic issues are a natural outcome of a different perception of the regional interests. Conceivable goals would be setting up a Latin American space agency; or developing a joint nuclear program with a regional program safeguard system of its own; or integrating regional military industries[44] that are able to make use of the existing resources in the framework of civil development.

Hemispheric Relations

The absence of a self-centered, globally designed and managed Latin American system results from a big void in the civilians' strategic concepts. Such voids are always filled by the armed forces as subsidiary participants. They often do this in an inadequate manner.

The new regional defense system must be seen as the beginning of a process whereby higher peace levels would gradually be reached. Through diminishing internal tensions, mutual confidence-inspiring actions, partial military integration, and reduced arm imports and manufacturing, integration and disarmament projects of a larger scope would be within easier reach.

The diversity of conflict formation structures in the region accounts for the difficulties of integrating them all in a single security system and helps us understand the individualistic, specific position of each Latin American country in the global military field.[45] However, within the issue of regional defense systems, we have identified the issues around which new hemispheric military cooperation forms could be developed. Such regional defense systems should protect the hemispheric collective defense interests through a revision of military relations with the United States and a new design for hemispheric defense that is separated from global confrontation. Because world peace depends on regional defense systems,[46] the need for a U.S. presence in them must be recognized. Moreover, U.S. participation can be turned into an asset and, therefore, into a contribution to global peace.

The United States should abandon the idea of using military means to solve problems such as narcotics trafficking or terrorism. Similarly, the use of techniques for low-intensity conflicts[47] or covert operations should be replaced by economic and social policies aimed at the roots of the social problems from which regional armed tensions, narcotics trafficking, and terrorism stem. The effects of these problems should be controlled by police actions, rather than by military actions, which tend to reproduce the phenomena on a larger scale, rather than checking them. This type of confusion erodes inter-American military relations; confusion is sown at various levels, and the perspective of establishing a common security system of some type is impaired. The military linkages should be democratized through renouncement of the use of force as a means for solving internal conflicts.

This set of policies could turn Latin America into a buffer zone in respect to global conflict. In a way, a special "power void" would be gradually created. However, this void, far from being attractive to the USSR, could generate centrifugal forces, provided that the major external participants remain outside its boundaries. As "one's intrusion attracts that of one's rivals,"[48] the military neutralization of the region and its transformation into a buffer zone would activate the centrifugal forces needed in the area.

In sum, an emphasis on military professionalization; development of new concepts on which a new, modern approach to national defense can be based; integration of the fundamental productive functions of the Latin American armed forces; and a new definition of their professional links with the United States constitute a set of components that could create the sufficient conditions for the restoration of civil-military balance in a democratic framework.

Conclusions

A new formula for civil-military relations in Latin America is a crucial issue in an agenda for democracy. Unless such new links between civilians and the military are established, the viability of the regional democracies would be just another utopian idea in a continent where such ideas are the visible face of a deep inability to articulate interests, negotiations, compromise, and consensus.[49]

To a large extent, these new civil-military relations would depend on the capability of the civil society to develop a theoretical framework consistent with the new realities. It should identify the necessary conditions of restored balance: democratic civilian unity, embracing even those elites that originally supported the military government; isolation of the antiestablishment forces that legitimate the performance of internal security functions; effective mass support within the institutional boundaries that does not engender new crisis; restoration of institutional balance by emphasizing the professional unity of the armed forces; abandonment by the military of governmental and internal security tasks; moral recovery of the armed forces, including a clear perception of the identity between constitutionalism and democracy; and a new civil-political culture.

The possibility of restoring civil-military equilibrium also depends on a number of sufficient conditions: a review of the defense institution organization systems and their organic links with the rest of the state and the society, particularly in the nonmilitary spheres; enhanced organic coherence in the state, which must become a "formal" entity, rather than an anarchic body; definition of the state's subsidiary functions; and civil-political agreement so that this new relationship with the armed forces will be feasible. Consequently, civilian control over the armed forces would be assured through the development of new concepts that can be the basis for a new, modern approach to national defense: professionalization, with strong technological contents; integration of the war materiel productive functions of the Latin American armed forces; and a new formula for the military's professional links with the United States.

Finally, it should be pointed out that the issues of defense and the armed forces have traditionally been dealt with by party and/or sectoral approaches. Each group or party has designed defense policies based on its own political interests. If an effective redefinition of civil-military relations and the capabilities for defense analysis and planning is to be put into place, the defense issues have to be approached from a multiparty, pluralistic perspective. In other words, a national approach is required to tackle the issues of the military reform agenda.

Notes

1. In this regard, see Andrés Fontana, "Notas Sobre la Consolidación Democrática y el Control Civil de las Fuerzas Armadas en Argentina" (paper presented to Consejo para la Consolidación de la Democracia, Buenos Aires, May 13, 1986). See also, "Will the Brass Return?" *Newsweek* (April 21, 1986).

2. See Riordan Roett, "Argentina's Army Isn't Corralled Yet: Weak Democratic Institutions Leave Civil Authority at Risk," *Los Angeles Times* (April 22, 1987).

3. See Mario Fernández, "La Intervención Militar en la Política en América Latina," *Revista de Estudios Políticos* (November–December 1985). For a theoretical step ahead in this regard, see Fernando Bustamante, "Los Paradigmas en el Etudio del Militarismo en América Latina," *Documento de Trabajo* (FLACSO) (October 1986). Specifically, the variable "civilian political elites' will" has scarcely been developed.

4. For a comparative analysis of the Latin American cases, see Alain Rouquié, "Demilitarization and the Institutionalization of Military-Dominated Politics in Latin America," in *Transition from Authoritarian Rule*, ed. Guillermo O'Donnell, Philippe Schmitter, and Laurence Whitehead (Baltimore: Johns Hopkins University Press, 1986). My analysis, however, is confined to the South American cases.

5. For a discussion of some social factors, see Ulf Sundhausen, "Military Withdrawal from Government Responsibility," *Armed Forces and Society* (Summer 1984).

6. Alain Rouquié, *El Estado Militar en América Latina* (Buenos Aires: Emecé, 1984), 250.

7. For a comparison of several Latin American cases, see Karen L. Remmer, "Redemocratization and the Impact of Authoritarian Rule in Latin America," *Comparative Politics* 17, no. 3 (April 1985): 253–75.

8. The authoritarian regime thoroughly modified the political divisions, the party organization, the clientele networks, and the electoral loyalties. Ibid., 270.

9. Rouquié, "Demilitarization and the Institutionalization of Military-Dominated Politics in Latin America."

10. "The July 19 [1977] strike was the first national strike in this century. It showed the extreme isolation of the Morales Bermúdez rule." Henry Pease, "Avances y Retrocesos de la Democratización en Perú," in *Transicón a la Democracia: America Latina y Chile*, ed. Augusto Varas (Airavillo, Chile: ACHIP, 1984), 60.

11. See Riordan Roett, "The Transition to Democratic Government in Brazil," *World Politics* (January 1986).

12. See Andrés Fontana, "Armed Forces and Neoconservative Ideology: State-Shrinking in Argentina (1976–1981)" (paper presented at the research conference "State Shrinking: A Comparative Inquiry into Privatization," University of Texas at Austin, March 1–3, 1984). See also, Guido Di Tella, "Fuerzas Armadas y democratización en Argentina," in Varas, *Transición a la Democracia*, 106.

13. See Saturnino Braga, "La Oposición y la Apertura Política en Brasil," in Varas, *Transición a la Democracia*, 99.

14. See Alfred Stepan, *Rethinking Military Politics: Brazil and the Southern Cone* (Princeton: Princeton University Press, 1988); see also, William A. Bacchus, "Development under Military Rule: Factionalism in Brazil," *Armed Forces and Society* (Spring 1986).

15. See Roett, "The Transition to Democratic Government in Brazil."

16. See Pease, "Avances y Retrocesos," 58–59; and the chapters by Peter Cleaves and Henry Pease and those by Cynthia McClintock and Luis Pásara, in *The Peruvian Experiment Reconsidered*, ed. Cynthia McClintock and Abraham Lowenthal (Princeton: Princeton University Press, 1983).

17. Report of the Commission Investigating the Crimes of the Argentinian Military Junta, *Nunca Más* (Buenos Aires: Endeba, 1984).

18. See Anita J. Isaacs, "From Military to Civilian Rule: Ecuador, 1972–1979" (Ph.D. dissertation, Oxford University, St. Anthony's College, 1985), 364.

19. For an analysis of the cases of Argentina and Brazil in this regard, see Peter Calvert, "Demilitarization in Latin America," *Third World Quarterly* 7, no. 1 (January 1985): 31–43.

20. See Rouquié, *El Estado Militar en América Latina*, 337.

21. See Juan Rial, "Los Militares en Cuanto 'Partido Político Sustituto' Frente a la Redemocratización," in *La Autonomía Militar en América Latina*, coordinated by Augusto Varas (Caracas: CLADDE, Nueva Sociedad, 1988).

22. See Andrés Fontana, "Fuerzas Armadas, Partidos Políticos y Transición a la Democracia en la Argentina," in Varas, *Transición a la Democracia*, 117.

23. For a military view of the Argentine campaign in the Malvinas, see "Conflicto Malvinas: Informe Oficial del Ejército Argentino," *Armas y Geoestrategia* (December 1983).

24. In this regard, see Abraham Lowenthal, "Ejércitos y Política en América Latina," *Estudios Internacionales* (July–September 1976): 62. According to Alexandre de S. C. Barros and Edmundo Campos Coelho, the lack of formal succession criteria becomes a genuine threat for the armed forces' discipline, hierarchy, and internal cohesion, as it often leads to confrontations among different military factions. "Military Intervention in South America," *International Political Science Review* 3 (1981): 346.

25. In Chile, there is a high level of intramilitary control. See Genaro Arriagada, *La Política Militar de Pinochet* (Santiago: ICHEH, 1986).

26. Regarding the Peruvian case, see Liisa North, "Perspectives on Development Policy and Mass Participation in the Peruvian Armed Forces," Working Paper No. 22 (Washington, DC: Wilson Center, Latin American Program, 1978).

27. "Silence has been and will be the main accomplice of the abuse and outrages by the dictatorial regimes." Juan Goytisolo, *En los Reinos de Taifa* (Barcelona: Seix Barral, 1986), 45.

28. Rouquié, *El Estado Militar en América Latina*, 417.

29. For a detailed description of the Latin American cases, see Varas, *La Autonomía Militar en América Latina*.

30. See Samuel Huntington, "Tocqueville's Armies and Ours" (remarks delivered to the seminar "Democracy in America Today: A Tocquevillian Perspective," John M. Olin Center for Inquiry into the Theory and Practice of Democracy, University of Chicago, February 15, 1984).

31. In this regard, see Norbert Lechner et al., *Estado y Política en América Latina* (México: Siglo XXI, 1981).

32. See Rouquié, *El Estado Militar en América Latina*.

33. Certainly, these new forms of autonomous adjustment are, to a very large extent, influenced by the terms of the military withdrawal from government. "The role of the terms of the post-militaristic democratization in the democratic development of the Andean South American countries." *Documento de Trabajo* (FLACSO) (January 1987).

34. In this connection, see Augusto Varas, "Democratización y Reforma Militar en Argentina," *Documento de Trabajo* (FLACSO) (1985). See also, Carlos Moneta, "Las Fuerzas Armadas y el Conflicto de las Islas Malvinas: Su Importancia en la Política Argentina y en el Marco Regional," *Foro Internacional* (January–March 1983).

35. Regarding the Brazilian case, see Joao Quartim de Moraes et al., *A Tutela Militar* (São Paulo: Vértice, 1987); and Eliezzer Rizzo de Oliveira, *Militares: Pensamiento e Acao Politica* (Campinas, Brazil: Papirus, 1987).

36. Formal control by civilians must be distinguished from real autonomy. For a comparative discussion of the constitutional mechanisms for civilian control, see Felipe Agüero, "The Military in the Constitutions of the Southern Cone Countries, Brazil and Spain," in *El Papel de los Partidos Políticos en el Retorno a la Democracia en el Cono Sur* (Washington, DC: Wilson Center, n.d.).

37. For a research agenda, see J. Samuel Fitch, "Armies and Politics in Latin America: 1975–1985," in *Armies and Politics in Latin America*, ed. Abraham Lowenthal and J. Samuel Fitch (New York: Holmes and Meier, 1986).

38. Only a few studies conclude with proposals for effective civil control over the armed forces. An outstanding example is Alfred Stepan, *Os Militares: Da Abertura a Nova Republica* (Rio de Janeiro: Paz e Terra, 1986).

39. Such is the approach in General Fred Woerner, "Shield of Democracy in Latin America," *Defense* (November–December 1987); and in J. Samuel Fitch, "The Armed Forces and Democracy in Latin America" (paper prepared for the Inter-American Dialogue, Lima, August 16–17, 1987).

40. At this stage, I would simply like to mention the abundant literature on corporativism in Latin America and its effects. For a comparative analysis, see Fernando Bustamante, "Some Conclusions and Hypotheses on the Issue of Civil Control over the Armed Forces and Democratic Consolidation in the Andean Countries," *Documento de Trabajo* (FLACSO) (April 1987).

41. In this respect, see Carlos Ominami, *La Tercera Revolución Industrial: Impactos Internacionales del Actual Viraje Tecnológico* (Buenos Aires: GEL, 1987).

42. For a similar approach, see Elliot Abrams, "Speech at the Inter-American Defense College," Santiago, August 13, 1986.

43. In this regard, see Augusto Varas, "Limites a las Opciones de Desarrollo: Las Políticas de Defensa Nacional," in *Repensar e Futuro*, ed. Enzo Faletto et al. (Caracas: Nueva Sociedad, 1986).

44. On the benefits of an integrated arms industry, see Edward A. Kolodziej, *Making and Marketing Arms: The French Experience and Its Implications for the International System* (Princeton: Princeton University Press, 1987).

45. By *security system*, I mean a set of express or implicit norms, principles, rules, and decision-making procedures around which the participants' expectations converge in a certain area of international relations. *Principles* are beliefs about facts, causes, and rectitude. *Norms* are behavioral measures defined in terms of rights and obligations. *Rules* are action-oriented specific prescriptions or proscriptions. *Decision-making procedures* are prevailing practices for making collective options. See Robert O. Keohane, *After Hegemony: Cooperation and Discord in World Political Economy* (Princeton: Princeton University Press, 1984), 57.

46. See United Nations, "Report of the Independent Commission on Disarmament and Security," A/CN.10/38 (New York: United Nations, 1983).

47. See Lilia Bermüdez, *Guerra de Baja Intensidad* (México: Siglo XXI, 1987).

48. Stanley Hoffman, *Dead Ends* (Cambridge, MA: Ballinger, 1983), 134.

49. In this context, ideologies and ideologisms could be understood as aborted pragmatism.

8

From Church and State to Religion and Politics and Back Again

Daniel H. Levine

*Given the importance of religion and Catholicism in the culture and po-
litical development of Latin America, few institutions have more potential for influencing political behavior both in the formation of societal
values and in its capacity to make demands on the political system than
does the Catholic Church. Since the 1960s the Church has undergone
significant changes, moving away from being a status quo institution to
becoming more activist on social issues, human rights, and even political
liberalization. Daniel H. Levine, who has written widely on Church affairs for many years, including his classic* Religion and Politics in Latin
America: The Catholic Church in Venezuela and Colombia *(1981), provides numerous insights into why the Catholic Church offers the potential
for introducing new values and attitudes, some of which have possible
consequences for political behavior. He stresses the importance of reex-
amining changes, both in religious philosophy and in the actions of the
rank-and-file clergy and Catholic laypersons, to understand the new directions that Catholicism might pursue.*

> Do I contradict myself?
> Very well then, I contradict myself.
> (I am large, I contain multitudes.)
> —*Walt Whitman*

R eligion and politics in Latin America today often seem a mass of
conflict and contradiction. There is debate over the meaning of events
and bitter struggle to shape and control them. There is also confusion.
Contradictory claims abound, and the evidence to sort them out is scarce

From *World Affairs* 150, no. 2 (Fall 1987): 93–108. Figures omitted. Reprinted by permission of Heldref Publications.

and unreliable, at best subject to very divergent interpretations. All this conflict and contradiction stems from almost thirty years of unprecedented change in both religion and politics. To borrow a religious phrase, these are "signs of the times." They speak of a search for new bases of understanding and call us to careful reflection before deciding what is true.

Reflect for a moment on the meaning of "signs of the times." This Biblical concept (e.g., Matthew 16:3) was revived and given new force in the Catholic Church by Pope John XXIII. Concern for the "signs of the times" runs throughout his pronouncements as pope. It appears in his convocation to the Second Vatican Council, and is arguably central to the tone and character of key Council Documents, and thus to much of the subsequent experience of Catholicism in the modern world.[1] Conciliar stress on "signs of the times" was reaffirmed and magnified for Latin America at Medellín, the landmark meeting of the region's bishops in 1968, in which the church reassessed its own experience and its position in the ongoing transformations of Latin American culture, society, and politics.[2]

This general concern with reading the signs of the times undergirds a position, which is at once open to and hopeful about change, with notable implications for the long-term ties of religion and politics. Traditional distinctions of "church" from "world" are undercut: the church is part of the world, shares in changing circumstances, and must learn from them. Reading the signs of the times affirms the religious value of ordinary experience and in this way opens the door to more egalitarian perspectives on knowledge and action. Alongside the hierarchical, "trickle-down" models of authority and action long identified with Catholicism, more democratic, or "bottom-up," views begin to find expression. Average people have something to offer apart from faith and passive obedience; elites lose their monopoly on truth and inspiration. Optimism is also central to this perspective. Discerning the signs of the times connotes searching, often in difficult circumstances, for evidence of the spirit at work in the world. This does not require blessing all existing structures or events, but does suggest faith in the positive aspects of change.

What signs of the times can be found for religion and politics, and for the ties between them in contemporary Latin America? Change is surely one. Even the most casual glance at recent Latin American experience with religion and politics turns up a lot of change over little time in institutions and areas long seen as static and stodgy. So much change is hard to grasp and absorb under any circumstances. But Latin America is also big and diverse, embracing countries with radically different cultural traditions, social and economic structures, and political histories. Even if we were to argue (for purposes of discussion) that "religion" has only a single sort of influence and impact, it should be no surprise that its expressions vary according to circumstance. Constraints and opportunities, urgent needs and felt imperatives are bound to differ from revolutionary Nicaragua to stolid Colombia or authoritarian Chile. They also vary within nations by region and social level, and over time as well as societies themselves change. A first step in making sense of all this change and variation is to realize how normal and inevitable it is. Change and contradiction abound, but acknowledging them as real does not condemn us to accept confusion as inevitable. To find order in variation, it may be helpful to begin by clarifying a few basic concepts often misused in current discussions. Two in particular warrant separate attention here: the "politicization of religion" and the explanation of sources of change.

Critics often describe the current Latin American situation as one of the "politicization of religion." What does it mean to speak in such terms? Describing developments in this way implies that in earlier (presumably happier) times, religion was not politicized. But in Latin America religion and politics have been joined ever since the Conquest. The common complaint is then less about the relation between religion and politics as such than it is about religiously based challenges to the existing order of things. Concern with "politicization of religion" works from a false premise: that "politics" is only (or principally) a matter of challenges to established arrangements.

Clearly, when we speak of religion and politics, church and politics, or church and state, at issue is not "politicization of religion," as if this were some simple index that rises or falls to levels on a hypothetical religio/political thermometer. Change is less a matter of religion's political involvement or salience per se than of the ideological direction and social location of the whole process. In ideological terms, powerful critiques of capitalism have become commonplace throughout the region, and there is intense struggle over the validity of Marxist analysis in religious discourse. In practice, these debates are often confused with conflict over the legitimacy of Marxist-Christian alliances in social and political life.

Debates of this kind have been accompanied, and often sharpened, by the emergence of religiously inspired popular groups, advancing independent concerns, and often vigorous claims to autonomy. Such groups bring their own agenda to the encounter with institutions, respecting but not necessarily following to the letter directives received from above. There is thus less unquestioned unity around core institutions led by clergy and bishops. As I will show in detail in the next section, the result has been to wrap disputes about authority in the church around fears of Marxism and concerns over undue "politicization."

These reflections raise questions about how best to identify and evaluate the sources of change. Is change primarily internal (rooted in religious structures or ideas) or external (a response to threat or opportunity in society at large)? If there is a mix, what is it like? Does change stem primarily from institutional reorientations (whatever *their* source) or is it a matter of popular movements coming into the institution and forcing a new agenda on it? A necessary first step in answering such questions is to see that change itself is not well addressed in the abstract, nor is it best conceived as a something like flipping a switch. Change is not an event but a process, carried out in fits and starts, advanced and resisted by real people whose loyalties and activities often cut across the lines our conventional expectations lead us to expect.

In any case, change is not all there is to the process, nor is it inevitable or irreversible. There are also important continuities, stemming, for example, from the church's own institutional order and authority structure, and from the continuing commitment average Catholics feel to its leaders and structures. Continuity is also promoted by the daily life of the churches, where ordinary existential problems remain, and people continue to seek help and guidance apart from the ups and downs of politics. In our concern to grasp the relation of religion and politics, we must not forget the autonomous value of religious faith. Attention to politics alone, focusing only on the possible political impact of religious groups, obscures the reason people join such groups in the first place, and why they may remain active in the face of great pressure and personal danger.

All these considerations point up how much complete understanding requires a fresh look at the meanings built into the questions we ask. In the main body of this chapter, I raise a few related questions: what has been done in research; what are central points and tendencies of change; and what can we expect in the future? The next section examines the changes, which give this essay its title: from church and state to religion and politics and back again.

Conceptual Transformations

Over the past three decades, the way people think and talk about issues of religion and politics in Latin America has changed a great deal. The "people" in question include scholars, interested observers, and all those actively involved in the religion and the politics of Latin America at all levels—average people, sisters, priests, politicians, and bishops. All these sorts of people have come to address the issues in different ways because reality itself has altered to the point that conventional understandings of terms like "church," "state," "religion," and "politics" no longer seem adequate to grasp events or to provide a reliable guide for predicting the future.

Scholarly discourse itself has altered beyond recognition. In over twenty-five years of fruitful work, researchers have largely abandoned talk of "church and state" for studies of "religion and politics" broadly conceived. They did so partly in reaction to an older tradition centered on "church and state," considered in terms of the formal relations between ecclesiastical and governmental institutions. Analysis in this tradition was narrow and static, with much time spent looking at documents, laws, and treaties. Exclusive focus on church and state conceived in such terms presumes that formal ties between elites and institutions are all there is to the process. It further takes church and state as fixed entities, linked in identical ways over time and space.[3]

This general perspective has clearly been overtaken by events. The institutions of both church and state have lately been subject to much controversy, redefinition, and expansion, in Latin America as elsewhere in the modern world. Further, religious and political activism has taken new forms and directions, often moving well beyond the formal limits of institutions and the control of traditional elites. New popular groups and movements have developed, with major implications for both religion and politics. To grasp such changes, scholars turned from "church and state" to "religion and politics," reaching for concepts to help make analysis more dynamic and broader in scope.

To make analysis more dynamic, exclusive focus on church and state as set entities was decisively abandoned. New work studied changes in religion, in politics, and in the links between them. From this vantage point, no pattern can be taken as valid once and forever: all are subject to change and variation. To broaden the scope of research, studies moved well beyond institutions, elites, and documents to link up with other levels of reality in systematic ways. After all, religion and politics happen throughout life. Their expression cannot be confined simply to what formal organizations do or say. In any case, the translation of institutional programs and formal doctrines into action is never automatic. Other levels must be studied closely to grasp how the links to institutions which we all presume to be operative actually work in practice. With these goals, academic study has turned with increasing vigor to the analysis of popular classes, grass-roots movements, and their often conflicting ties with high politics and big structures.[4]

Despite these reorientations, the prevailing agenda for research remains centered on formal structures. Central questions are still elite focused, concerned, for example, with the development of church programs for reaching the poor, with intrachurch debates over the meaning of poverty, or with emergence of new ecclesiologies and models of participation in the church. I do not mean to suggest that questions of this kind lack importance. Most popular groups have original and enduring ties with institutions, ties which are valued by elites and average members alike. Understanding such ties is basic to any analysis of the dynamics of group formation and change. Nonetheless, when questions are framed in this way, research takes off from structures and agendas created in the churches and then studies their projection to popular groups. Researchers now commonly ask how institutions view the people and make a legitimate place for them in doctrine, ideology, and structure. But suppose we invert the question and ask *how people view the institution*. How do average men and women see the big structures of religion and politics? How and why do they organize in certain ways? What specific needs and goals do they bring to the encounter with the high politics of power and meaning [that] the institutions of religion and politics embody and project?

Reformulating the issues of research in this way makes for a richer portrait of reality. Much of the force and drama of recent Latin American experience arises from the convergence of issues of poverty, justice, and participation in the churches, with the expansion of military regimes, and thus with political closure, heightened repression, and restricted opportunities for participation of any kind in society and politics generally. New initiatives from the churches thus found a ready and receptive popular clientele. The conjunctures were critical, and gave decisive impulse and direction to religious and political ferment in key cases across the region. Repression often helped to magnify pressures for participation and enhance their legitimacy. Why did it have this result, and not the intended outcome of reinforcing fatalism, apathy, and acquiescence? First, where they took hold, new religious ideas legitimated activism in theory through their translation into innovative forms of grass-roots organization. Second, the very experience of participation provided nets of solidarity which encouraged members in continued resistance. Finally, political closure drove new clients into these structures, which often were the only outlets available.[5]

At issue here is no longer a simple opposition of religion to political power: for this, Latin American history provides ample precedent. What is new is the language of opposition and its carriers: liberation theology as worked out by average people in the grass-roots groups known widely throughout the region as ecclesial base communities or CEBs (from the Spanish, *comunidades eclesiales de base*). Much has been written on liberation theology and CEBs, and I will not go over this familiar ground here.[6] But a few key points may well be noted. Moving beyond condemnation of specific rulers or regimes to challenge whole economic, cultural, and political systems as unjust and sinful, liberation theology has crafted a different discourse about religion, society, and politics. CEBs, in turn, have created new kinds of practice. These are generally small and socially homogeneous groups, mostly of poor people, which meet regularly to read and discuss the Bible and to reflect on community life and problems from this perspective. Their normal practice encourages self-expression, sharing, solidarity, and active participation in the collective affairs of daily life.

Liberation theology and CEBs took on added political meaning from the conjunctures in which they emerged. Each enhances participation and activism; each crystallized in the early to mid 1970s, a time when collective action generally was viewed with deep suspicion; each quickly became a target for repression. Civil and military rulers fear popular organization just as they fear *any* uncontrolled action. They fear it even more when it comes legitimated by the moral and organizational force of religion.[7] A notable result of all this has been to make church-state issues salient once again. Conflict between church and state has arguably been more intense over the last few decades than at any point in the previous century. Conflicts arise and find expression in this format once again because ecclesiastical institutions are drawn into confrontation with states in defense of grass-roots groups. The process is often described in terms of "radicalization," pointing up the repeated escalation of conflict from modest, localized beginnings to general challenges to the logic and legitimacy of authoritarian rule.

While radicalization is clearly present, the concept does not do justice to the events or to the actors. It is too passive, deriving change primarily from reactions to repression. But we are dealing with active, creative subjects, whose particular vision of faith and commitments was open to radicalization from the outset. The stress on activism, participation, and themes of equality and justice in recent Latin American Catholic discourse made them especially sensitive to undercurrents of power and privilege in any situation.[8] Once the cycle of conflict gets under way, such new religious orientations, reinforced by mutual support in different kinds of group structures (more participatory in theory and practice) become self-sustaining in ways unlikely in the past.

So in a curious and unexpected way we are back to church and state. Churches with an expanded sense of mission and a different presence in everyday life find across their paths states striving to control and repress an ever-widening circle of action. Church-state issues are salient again, but note that the axis of dispute has shifted. Traditional concerns over education, marriage and divorce, state subsidies, and the like have largely yielded center stage to disputes over human rights, justice, social criticism, and by broad conflict over the proper role and place of popular classes in the social order.

These summary comments underscore the extent to which conceptual change (from church and state to religion and politics and back) draws on the impact of new ideas about authority and reflects the long-term implications of stress on reading the "signs of the times" in today's Latin America. A look back over the course of this conceptual migration points up a few critical elements for reflection. It appears that conflicts between church and state, politics and religion in Latin America are best addressed along two related dimensions. The first considers interinstitutional disputes, to control the social and political projection of church-related and religious organizations. The second looks within institutions, at struggles to shape and orient popular groups. At stake here is more than control of specific programs and commitments. Conflict is also engaged at all levels to shape the structure and quality of group life, and thus to set the process by which any goals emerge and become legitimate. The second nurtures the first; each is religious and political at one and the same time. The next section traces these developments in finer detail. I outline central tendencies of change since 1958: looking first over time, and then at variation across cases.

Realities: Change and Variation

I date the current period from Pope John XXIII to the present. In the church, this takes us through four popes (John XXIII, Paul VI, and the two John Pauls). It is deeply marked by the Second Vatican Council and its opening to the world, both in general terms and through the impact of reforms in liturgy and ritual, which open religious participation enormously. In social doctrine, the period sets out from Pope John's two encyclicals (*Mater et Magistra* and *Pacem in Terris*) which open doors to learning from the social sciences, to collaboration with Marxism, and generally to an option with the poor. These themes are carried forward in Vatican II and take general shape in Pope Paul's *Populorum Progressio*, which sets them in a context of concerns about "modernization and development." Social and political themes like these soon yield to concern with birth control (*Humanae Vitae*), and later to stress on preaching the gospel (*Evangelii Nuntiandi*), and to concerns over declining unity in the church. The period ends under John Paul II with a burst of conservative activity, devoted in organizational terms to reaffirmation of unity, and summarized doctrinally in attacks on liberation theology. The Extraordinary Synod of late 1985 marks a convenient closure.

If these churchy "events" are set against a social and political time line for Latin America, the conjunctures are suggestive. In political terms, the period is marked by revolutions twenty years apart in Cuba and Nicaragua. The Cuban experience had enormous appeal early on, and spurred a new kind of Catholic political reformism epitomized in Christian Democracy, which reaches its high point with victories by Eduardo Frei in Chile (1964) and Rafael Caldera in Venezuela four years later. But although Christian Democracy offered a new outlet for Catholic political energies in open societies like Chile or Venezuela, in other cases alternative visions of religion and politics began to bubble up at the same time. Only two years after Frei's election in Chile, Camilo Torres was killed in Colombia. Torres was a former priest who moved to revolution as an outgrowth of his general Christian commitment to justice. While he has found few imitators, the ideals Camilo Torres posed remain alive, in a call to change *beyond* reform, and to political action beyond electoral vehicles. In any case, Christian Democracy was not the only "model" to appear on the Latin American scene in 1964. That year also witnessed the military coup in Brazil, which set a standard for the next twenty years of authoritarian rule in the region. The Brazilian example was followed in the 1970s by profoundly reactionary regimes in Uruguay and Chile, and (in fits and starts throughout the period) in Argentina.

The trajectory of Christian Democracy in Chile is central to our story. As it rose to power, the party carried with it a surge of optimism about reform. It helped create a new place and direction for Catholic political energies, breaking with the alliances of the past. Christian Democracy soon divided and ran out of gas in Chile. Electoral defeat itself was less significant than the fact that both Left and Right abandoned the party. The Catholic Left turned to stormy alliances with Marxism, forged in the 1970 [Salvador] Allende [Gossens] campaign and confirmed in tumultuous meetings of Christians for Socialism (Cristianos para el Socialismo, or CpS) in Santiago in 1972. The Catholic Right returned to traditional links with conservative parties, and also to extremists in the military and in organizations like TFP [Society for the Defense of Tradition, Family, and Property]. As the initial Christian Democratic impetus decayed, Catholic political energies divided, reformist optimism faded, and a notable backlash against the "politicization" of religion and the churches got under way throughout the region.

Once presumably united around a reformist agenda (Christian Democracy, Populorum Progressio), Latin American Catholicism now split. On the progressive or revolutionary end, we find Camilo Torres, and close to him movements like Chile's CpS, Colombia's SAL [Priests for Latin America], or the Movement of Third World Priests in Argentina. On the level of theory, it is around this time that a long period of discussion and reflection crystallizes in the publication of Gustavo Gutiérrez's landmark, *A Theology of Liberation*, which gives a name and focus to many of these concerns. The 1968 meeting of the Latin American bishops at Medellín seemed to empower and legitimate many of these elements. But in retrospect Medellín looks more like a peak than a marker on the road to growing commitments with change. Soon after Medellín, there was a changing of the guard. Msgr. Alfonso López Trujillo of Colombia was elected Secretary General of the bishops' conference (CELAM) in 1972 and moved quickly to reorient the organization. The tone and agenda of publications and conferences was altered, and the staff of key CELAM departments and institutes was purged. López Trujillo also promoted an ideological counter to liberation theology, joining with Roger Vekemans to found the journal *Tierra Nueva* in Bogotá in 1972. *Tierra Nueva* immediately became a central voice in the attack on liberation theology and related "progressive" issues and movements.[9]

Reflect for a moment on the contrast between Camilo Torres and Roger Vekemans. They both took off from a similar starting point of social science analysis and Christian reformism, but soon moved in opposite directions. In his brief career, Camilo Torres passed quickly from sociological research and Christian Democratic reformism to general political organization (the ill-fated Frente Unido) and finally to guerrilla struggle. Vekemans began with Christian Democratic concepts and programs, working for many years in Chile in research and also in the creation of popular organizations closely linked to the Christian Democratic party. After Allende's victory in 1970, Vekemans and his team moved to Colombia, founding *Tierra Nueva* and operating what amounted to a continental clearing house for the counteroffensive against the Left. Out of the original Christian Democratic impetus, Camilo Torres quickly moved to the left, giving a foretaste of much that was to come in the twenty years since his death. Vekemans is more complex, because it is less a matter of his move rightward as of general shifts in the ideological spectrum that pushed an originally reformist (*not* even "centrist") position identified with Christian Democracy to the right end of the range of available alternatives.

The polarization embodied in these two careers grew steadily through the 1970s, surfacing again at the end of the decade as the regions gathered again in 1979 at Puebla to weigh changes since Medellín and chart a course for the future. The conference convened at a particularly critical time for church and politics alike. Puebla marks the inauguration of a vigorous new pope (John Paul II), and his appearance in Latin America on the first of repeated visits to the region. This is also the moment of successful revolution in Nicaragua and enormous escalation of violence in El Salvador. Church people played a visible role in both processes, often in close concert with opposition groups.[10]

Since Puebla, these trends have continued, with violence growing and unity declining steadily. Violence has come to the churches in large part through direct attacks by military regimes and their security services. Pastoral agents, CEB members, priests, sisters, and bishops in many nations have been victims of this onslaught. Violence also figures in church debates through the issue of class conflict. A major charge against liberation theology has been its supposed endorsement of violent class conflict through partisan stress on preferential options for the poor.[11] As for unity, if like most bishops we take this to mean obedience to hierarchically constituted authority, then unity has clearly dwindled. Norms of unquestioned obedience, and the general expectations of passivity on which they rest, have all been put into question.

Latin America has lately been a major focus of Vatican concern. John Paul II has clearly made the region a priority, with five visits to the area since his inaugural trip to Puebla in 1979. On these tours, he regularly condemns violence, stresses the "nonpolitical" character of the church's mission, and underscores the need for unity and discipline in the ranks.[12] Some have seen in all this a "Polish model," noting the pope's experience with Polish church traditions of clerical dominance, episcopal unity, and tight authority relations. Ecclesiastical discipline and unity are central to this model, and in Polish experience have clearly been underscored in the face of a hostile environment. The Polish tradition, reinforced strongly in this century, makes the very idea of "church" hinge on bishops, clergy, and dioceses. These hold the "sacred deposit" of truth (to use an old phrase) and give it to masses who also belong, but not in the same way. It is a trickle-down theory of religious life, well fitted for social or political contexts which are themselves elitist and authoritarian in character.[13]

Of course, there is another Polish model, epitomized by Solidarity, which provides suggestive parallels to Latin American experience. From early 1980 until General [Wojciech] Jaruzelski's December 1981 coup, the brief but spectacular career of Solidarity illustrated how an autonomous popular movement can grow, break open hierarchical and closed structures, and pull them into new sorts of commitments and challenges. But this is clearly not the model the pope has in mind. If a Polish model is indeed being advanced for Latin America, it is surely one which reinforces hierarchy and discipline in the church. Autonomous grass-roots groups are to be curbed and "depoliticized," and the role of key prelates like López Trujillo magnified strongly. From this vantage point, "politics" is identified with conflict and violence, withdrawal and neutrality are urged, activism deemphasized, and spiritual values stressed. The "preferential option for the poor," seemingly enshrined at Puebla, is qualified as "not exclusive," and reworked as a "preferential love for the poor and young"—quite a different sort of commitment.[14]

Over the whole course of events, two "moments" stand out, points in time where the weight of thought and action shift direction and new "packages" are conceived and put together. The first runs from Vatican II and Christian Democracy, peaking in the period around Medellín. There is general openness to change, a new critical discourse about society and politics is invented, and significant ideological and organizational innovations get the stamp of religious legitimacy. The fall of Christian Democracy, followed by the experience of CpS, Allende, and military rule in Chile all mark the end of this period. The publication of *A Theology of Liberation* comes near the close. The second "movement" starts to crystallize after deep divisions in the mid-1970s. One end of the spectrum is held by liberation theology and a "radical ideal" of base communities which make them central to the construction of a new order in society, politics, and culture.[15] The confrontation of key episcopal conferences like Brazil or Chile with national security states reinforces this group.

The other end of the spectrum takes form with the change of command in CELAM, and the turn of key Catholic institutions to critical stances on Marxism and politics. The "moment" itself comes together around the time of Puebla and the Nicaraguan Revolution. It continues through the violence in El Salvador, the rise and fall of Solidarity in Poland, and the growing, concerted attack on liberation theology which peaks with the 1984 Ratzinger Instruction and the Extraordinary Synod of late 1985. If we were to draw a curve [from 1958 through 1986], tracing some mythical level of enthusiasm for radical or liberationist ideas and solutions among church officials in Latin America, the line would rise slowly through the 1960s, top off around Medellín, and thereafter drop sharply from the mid-1970s on. This general trajectory holds for key cases like Chile and has been advanced strongly throughout the region by Colombian church leaders. Brazil provides the major counter example.

Of particular interest in this pattern is the changing set of political outlets for Catholicism and the altered meaning given to "politics" itself in Catholic discourse. In the first "moment," the churches stood with Christian Democracy. These parties seemed to offer an ideal way to free the institution from earlier partisan entanglements. Now the bishops could safely leave "politics" to reformist Christian elites, acting "on their own." The "church as such" (the ecclesiastical institution) was not compromised, and specific Catholic political parties seemed a thing of the past. But as Christian Democracy soured and divided, the idea that such an alternative could get the church "out of politics" proved illusory.

Church leaders did indeed strive to "get out of politics" by abandoning older alliances. But pressures for political action of new kinds grew nonetheless. First came cases like Camilo Torres, for whom "politics" was a Christian imperative, part of a generalized revolutionary (but still nonpartisan) challenge to the established order of things. Then, groups like CpS called for partisan political action, but now in alliance with the Left. CpS and similar groups legitimated their "politics" through ideas soon to crystallize as liberation theology. Liberation theology itself brought "politics" to the churches by legitimating explicit political action in religious terms, and further through its expression in the program and daily experience of CEBs.

Through all this, the churches have moved from being unquestioned supporters of the established order through periods of major criticism to a current stance (much contested to be sure) of neutrality. What drives these transformations? As we have seen, part of the answer comes from the way changes in religion are magnified by political pressure or threat. But more is at work. Recall my earlier stress on how people "see" the church, and on the implications of this new "seeing." The outcomes visible across the region cannot be reduced to a simple function of repression turning the churches in one direction or another. There must be a prior ideological change, a decision on where to stand, with whom, and for what. Conflict and violence have been broadly similar in El Salvador and Guatemala, but in the first case Archbishop [Oscar Arnulfo] Romero and a host of grass-roots workers put the Salvadoran church in the midst of conflict, closely aligned with the popular movement. In contrast, under Cardinal Mario Casariego, the Guatemalans pursued "neutrality" and, with rare exceptions, condemned "politics" in and for the churches.[16] Repression has been great throughout the Southern Cone, but only in Brazil and Chile did the churches take a determined and vocal stand in opposition, promoting and defending popular movements as part of their general position. To illustrate this variation more fully, I close this section with a look at Colombia and Brazil, generally considered to hold conservative and progressive ends, respectively, of any ideological spectrum in today's Latin American Catholicism.[17]

First note a few key similarities. Each episcopal conference is highly organized, well staffed, and unified around a coherent program which is pressed consistently both at home and abroad, as Brazilians and Colombians both work to mobilize international support (in CELAM or the Vatican) for their positions.[18] Sharp differences rest above all on the contrasting models of "church" which prevail in the two hierarchies. Colombia's bishops work with an image of "church" rooted in hierarchy. Distinctions of rank and office are maintained and affirmed, and authority as hierarchy is made central to the legitimate constitution of any religious activity. The operative Brazilian model is more communitarian and acknowledges that "church" has constitutive sources and dimensions beyond the hierarchical. Colombia's bishops attack democratization in the church, reserving special fire for liberation theology, the "popular church," and autonomous CEBs. In contrast, the Brazilian position rejects distinctions of popular from institutional church as a false dichotomy: all levels share in and contribute to the same experience.

These differences have deep historical roots. In Colombia, the church has long been dominant, and since the late nineteenth century has been identified with cultural and national unity. Conservative victories in the previous century's civil wars enshrined this dominance in law, practice, and popular expectations. The general position has eroded only marginally, if at all, in recent years. From this starting point, Colombian bishops have strived to preserve, protect, and defend. In Brazil, regalist tradition and a dominant state left the church weak and dependent. These weaknesses were reinforced by Brazil's notable cultural and religious pluralism, and have led the church over the years to search for ways to create and extend links with popular classes.

Recent political changes have also marked each church's overall stance very strongly. Until the 1940s the Colombian church was firmly allied with the Conservative party. This alliance was shaken by interparty violence after 1948, which left hundreds of thousands dead over fifteen subsequent years. The horrors of the political violence in Colombia reinforced hierarchical fears of popular mobilization, which in effect became identified with chaos and slaughter. In the aftermath of the violence, the church moved from proconservative to partisanship to "neutrality" in favor of the established order. Now, officially indifferent between liberals and conservatives, the bishops remain fearful of alternatives: challenging parties and alternative political structures are both ruled out.

Even if new visions were to thrive in the Colombian church, where would they find allies? In political terms, electoral democracy has been the rule through most of this century, and politics remains dominated by the traditional political parties. The system is relatively open, and this openness has served as a safety valve, letting opponents blow off steam. There has been no threat of radical revolution, no sharp turn to repression. Hence, there is no dictatorship to draw opponents together, no major leftist group or coalition, no significant popular movement with which to join forces.[19]

From this heritage and history, a consistent and thorough program has emerged, linking conservative ideas with bureaucratic and organizational growth. The Colombian church does not just sit and sigh for the good old days. It articulates and projects a conservative message with great vigor, sponsoring the "right kind" of groups (carefully monitored and linked to clergy and hierarchy). Independent and thus "unreliable" initiatives are delegitimized, isolated, and, where possible, destroyed.

The contrast with Brazil is very marked. There, initial dispositions to accept change were magnified many times over by the heavy hand of post-1964 military rule. As the Brazilian church experimented with new programs and strategies, repression radicalized its pastoral agents while driving an available clientele into church structures. Clients themselves grew in number and accessibility over the post war years. In sociological terms, Brazil has seen considerably more mobility and popular organization than has Colombia over the same period. One might say that politics was inevitable for Brazil's bishops, thrust upon them by the constriction of alternatives. More precisely, new ideas about popular organization and a general religious enhancement of popular experience converged in Brazil with social and political current espousing a similar project. The conjuncture provided a decisive opportunity, one magnified by the specific conditions of military rule.

The variation between these experiences reminds us that although Catholicism may be one church and one religion, it takes on very different forms in specific contexts and circumstances. Of course, the point of such an exercise in comparison is not just to lay out models of the church in an abstract way, but rather to see how these are worked into normal practice and experienced on a day-to-day basis by real men and women. Models have an impact as they shape practice, and make some kinds of behavior seem right, proper, and possible. Why do activist and democratizing notions take hold and appeal in one context and not another? Why does liberation theology seem welcome in Brazil and condemned in Colombia? One anonymous commentator put it this way: "Liberation Theology is like a tree. If you plant it in the right place, it is good for the place and good for the tree." By the testimony of Brazilians themselves, planted in Brazil it has enriched the church. Planted in El Salvador, it found prophetic leadership and committed activists and flourished. The tree withered in Colombia. The ground is hard and the plant neglected.

The Future

In conclusion, I want to address the future. First, I consider the future in terms of practice: what does the future hold for religion and politics as actually experienced and understood by real people throughout Latin America? After identifying a few central tendencies and likely points of conflict, I then address the future of research and reflection, and ask how we can improve our knowledge of the process and be confident of its accuracy and validity.

In practical terms, no major drop is likely in the prominence of "religion and politics" considered together, as a set of issues. This will continue to confound the expectations of those who associate "modernization" with secularization and thus reduce religion to epiphenomenal status.[20] Although their joint salience will remain high, the nature of the relation between religion and politics will alter. Important changes will accompany the degree of openness or closure in the political system generally. If recent trends to civilian rule and democracy should consolidate and spread, the centrality of religious groups in political organization and action will fade. More outlets will be available: popular groups will be less driven into the churches, and the churches as institutions will no longer stand alone as vehicles for collective action. A major irony of recent Latin American history is surely that the very military regimes which complain so bitterly about "politicization of religion" are major promoters of what they deplore and condemn. As we have seen, the expansion of authoritarian rule clearly magnified tendencies to radical thinking and political confrontation in the churches. Transitions away from military rule will blunt the sharp edges of much dispute.

Although greater political openness should reduce pressures for political action, the churches and religion generally will remain important to the formulation of political issues and phenomena. Part of this presence derives from the continued impact of innovations set in motion over the last fifteen years. A new discourse about justice and equality, rooted in biblical and religious themes, is now very widespread and should remain vital to religious life. There will, of course, be continuing struggle to control the specific texts and images used and discussed, but the center of gravity has shifted. Moreover, even if CEBs are less visible in explicitly political matters, they will continue to play a subtle, long-term role by eliciting and promoting new sources and styles of leadership— making them normal and legitimate. The groups as such may move out of the center of action, but the leaders they develop should diffuse throughout society.

No major formal division or schism is likely to arise in Catholicism. Conflict will, of course, go on, with sharp disputes on the several dimensions noted here: conservatives versus progressives, institutional elites versus popular groups, etc. But despite sharp differences, and occasionally bitter struggle to advance contrasting programs and positions, all remain within the fold. Liberationist sympathizers are prone to recognize the religious legitimacy of Catholic radicals while seeing conservatives as inspired purely by instrumental considerations of power or institutional convenience. At the same time, conservatives often charge radicals with using religion solely for political ends. But the truth is that all these groups work from deep religious conviction, all claim to be "good Catholics" and resist being read out of the church.

I believe a decline is likely in *new* popular initiatives, especially those given to the assertion of grass-roots autonomy. This will result from sustained pressure by the Vatican and most of the ecclesiastical institutions in the region. It is hard for grass-roots groups to resist such pressure indefinitely. They value ties to the church for the religious legitimacy, collective identity, and sense of tradition and moral worth they carry. They also need the institutional church's mediating networks. After all, with rare exceptions these are groups of very poor people, short on time, resources, and allies. All this makes them vulnerable to pressure. In any case, the next ten or fifteen years are likely to see notable struggle between competing models of CEBs, a struggle played out in neighborhoods, towns and villages, religious orders, dioceses, nations, and international forums as well.

What will happen if the new Vatican line should win out and the grass-roots initiatives so highly touted in recent years are radically constricted or eliminated? Will the church "lose" these groups and the classes from which they draw, much as it is often said to have "lost" the working class of Europe in the nineteenth century? It is possible, and many liberationists believe it likely, but it is not inevitable. Hierarchical opposition to radicalized, autonomous CEBs does not mean opposition to grass-roots organization as such. The real alternative is not "CEBs or nothing," but rather a choice between kinds of grass-roots organization. In Latin America today all sorts of groups call themselves "CEBs." Without exception, they meet regularly, study and discuss the Bible, and use biblical texts as a basis for reflection and action. Most also engage in some kind of mutual aid and community improvement.

With all these similarities, how do they differ from one another? The most critical differences arise from the dependent and deferential ties to hierarchy which characterize conservative structures. Such groups work on what might be called a "Colombian model." They are closely monitored by "reliable" clergy or sisters, who provide the texts, set the agenda, and manage all ties and decisions vertically. Independent links to other popular groups are discouraged. If this model of organization and action should prevail, we may expect representative group agendas to be more explicitly spiritual and less political. The typical scope of group action will be more personal and localized, less focused on collective action and structural change.[21]

What about the future of research? Over the last three decades, scholarship on religion and politics in Latin America has changed and improved dramatically. Research has become more dynamic, and more genuinely comparative as well. As a result, we now have a substantial body of excellent work on different cases and issues, with more good studies in the pipeline. But the pervasive conflict and contradiction documented here make it appropriate to reflect for a moment on the future. What should scholars study in the years to come? How should they go about the business of adding to knowledge, and improving understanding of change?

Agendas for future work can be put together in several ways. The easiest is to compile lists of empirical research questions. In all likelihood we will never have adequate coverage of contemporary or historical aspects of religion and politics. One agenda might therefore call for *more facts*: studies of attitudes, documents, leaders, symbols, groups, issues, movements or shrines, cross-referenced data banks, and the like. But building-block approaches of this kind are likely to disappoint. The problem is not simply to get "all the facts." We first need to establish what the relevant facts are, and this is a matter for theoretical clarification, not simple data collection. Agendas for the future must grow out of reflection on the proper lines of research. What are the processes we need to study? Which are the questions to ask?

It seems to me that research must begin by addressing the sources of change in religious ideas. Why do new ideas emerge at a given point in time? For present purposes, this requires study of general changes in Catholicism (e.g., the Second Vatican Council, papal encyclicals) and of specifically Latin American innovations like liberation theology, which bubble up at more or less the same time all across the region. Why then and not at some other time? The appeal of such ideas to concrete groups must also be specified. How do they "fit" the needs and practices of emergent or existing groups? What structural changes in economy, society, or institutional life make certain ideas more or less appealing? In recent Latin American experience, sharp declines in rural isolation, growing proletarianization, massive migration, and the spread of literacy—to name only a few of the more noteworthy trends—have combined to undercut the status and unquestioned power of traditional elites, while empowering new capacities and dispositions for collective action.

With this foundation, competing attempts to shape religion must be specified, and each associated with an identifiable power base and organizational network. It makes a difference who defines group agendas and what sort of structures mediate personal experience and small group action onto larger arenas of action. For example, pastoral agents do much to set the tone and priorities of grass-roots activities. Thus, the training, orientation, and changing conditions of priests, sisters, and lay activists are a prime area for systematic study. More generally, research needs to develop a dynamic view of institutions. There is nothing automatic about loyalty, affiliation, or sustained motivation. Like all human behaviors, they must be renewed and refreshed regularly. Understanding that process requires attention simultaneously to institutions as they reach out to potential members, and to members themselves as they see and use institutions. Having correctly moved beyond formal institutional limits for its subjects, research must now return to institutions in a more open and behavioral way.

The research agenda laid out here takes off from ideas, works outward to social class, structures and institutions, and then back again through ideas, to action. Comparable agendas could be put together on other bases, class for example. But it is a peculiar value of studying religion that the subject itself reinforces our sense of the creative power of ideas and of their ability to move individuals and groups in new and unexpected ways. Of course, this is not a matter of ideas alone, as if ideas were simply "in the air" in some vague way. Ideas are bound up with structures, carried by institutions, and continuously reworked in the daily routines of and expectations of all sorts of groups. Moreover, it is not the same even within what we conventionally define as a single society or culture: these are matters of conflict and struggle.

The key point is not to freeze "religion and politics" in any one form, the same now as in the past or future, identical here as there. Instead, research must address the formation of packages, clusters of elements and legitimations, and then specify who puts them together, under what circumstances, and for what ends. How can we make our concepts and categories fit experience better? The first and most basic step is to listen: to hear what people say and then to consider action and structure, using their own logic as an interpretive guide. This means respecting the autonomy and validity of religious and political categories, and searching for how they influence and draw on one another in institutions as in ordinary life. It also means paying special attention to the relation of popular groups with elites and institutions. Respecting the autonomy and validity of each, we can begin to figure out how in changing each changes the other, and, in the process, together rework the ties that bind them over the long haul.

Notes

1. In *Humanae Salutis*, his formal convocation to the council, Pope John stated: "We should take our own Jesus' advice that we should know how to discern the 'signs of the times.' " Cited in Peter Hebblethwaite, *John XXIII, Pope of the Council* (London, 1984), 397–98.

2. I have commented in detail elsewhere on the significance of Medellín. Among other sources, see my *Religion and Politics in Latin America: The Catholic Church in Venezuela and Colombia* (Princeton, 1981), especially ch. 2; also see my "Religion, Politics, and the Poor in Latin America Today," in *Religion and Political Conflict in Latin America*, ed. Daniel H. Levine (Chapel Hill, 1986).

3. The classic of this genre is J. L. Mecham, *Church and State in Latin America* (Chapel Hill, 1966), rev. ed.

4. Conceptual reorientation in the study of Latin America has gone through several stages. Early work pursued neofunctionalist models which gave religion a key role in forging a new social and political equilibrium. Ivan Vallier's *Catholicism, Social Control, and Modernization in Latin America* (Englewood Cliffs, 1970) was very influential. There was also concern about the link of religious change to "modernization," for example, in Frederick Turner, *Catholicism and Political Development in Latin America* (Chapel Hill, 1971). More recently, scholars have studied the character of churches as complex organizations and their impact on the scope and limits of change, most notably in Thomas Bruneau, *The Political Transformation of the Brazilian Catholic Church* (Cambridge, 1974), and Brian Smith, *The Church and Politics in Chile: Challenges to Modern Catholicism* (Princeton, 1982). Elite mentalities, cultural formation, and organizational change have been considered in Levine, *Religion and Politics*. Recently, several studies have focused on popular religious movements and revolutionary change, most notably in Central America, as in Phillip Berryman, *The Religious Roots of Rebellion: Christians in the Central American Revolutions* (Maryknoll, 1984). The evolving link of popular to institutional norms and actions provides a central thread in much new scholarship. See, for example, Scott Mainwaring, *The Catholic Church and Politics in Brazil, 1916–1985* (Stanford, 1986), and the studies collected in Levine, *Religion and Political Conflict*.

Conceptual reorientation is not limited to the study of Latin America. For more general considerations, see my "Religion and Politics in Comparative and Historical Perspective," *Comparative Politics* (October 1986).

5. The dynamics of this process are considered in detail in the next section.

6. Cf. my "Religion, Society and Politics: States of the Art," *Latin American Research Review* 16, no. 3 (Fall 1981), and also my "Religion and Politics: Drawing Lines, Understanding Change," *Latin American Research Review* 20, no. 1 (Winter 1985) and the studies reviewed there.

7. Church authorities in many countries are also afraid. They fear loss of authority, as grass-roots groups develop a sense of collective identity and press for greater autonomy. It is vital to be clear about what is at issue: loss of authority is taken here above all as loss of *hierarchical* authority and decay of previous expectations of unquestioned obedience.

Leonardo Boff puts the matter sharply, noting parallels and mutual influences between religion and politics in very suggestive ways: "We must recognize that in the past few years, especially after Vatican II, extremely important steps have been taken. Just as the Church previously took on Roman and feudal structures, it is now taking on structures found in today's civil societies that are more compatible with our growing sense of human rights. This is the often-argued 'democratization of the church.' . . . There is no real conflict between the ecclesial institution and the ecclesial communities [CEBs]. The real tension exists between a Church that has opted for the people, for the poor and their liberation and other groups in that same Church that have not made this option, and who have not made it concrete or who persist in keeping to the strictly sacramental and devotional character of faith." *Church: Charism and Power. Liberation Theology and the Institutional Church* (New York, 1986), 44, 126.

8. Cf. my "'Whose Heart Could Be So Staunch?'" *Christianity and Crisis* (July 22, 1985), where I consider the biography of Jean Donovan, one of the four American churchwomen murdered in El Salvador at the end of 1980.

9. I review the origins and trajectory of *Tierra Nueva* and other Latin American religious journals in "Religion and Politics: Drawing Lines, Understanding Change."

10. Much has been written about Puebla. See in particular Phillip Berryman, "What Happened at Puebla" in Levine, *Churches and Politics in Latin America*. As noted in the text, Puebla came at a time of great political upheaval in Central America, which itself coincided with much change and dislocation in the Catholic Church generally. The year of 1978 saw three popes in the Vatican. After fifteen years in office, Paul VI died in late August, and his successor, John Paul I, died scarcely a month later, on September 28. Pope John Paul II was elected on October 16 and soon after travelled to Latin America, coming to inaugurate the Puebla conference in January 1979. See Peter Hebblethwaite, *The Year of Three Popes* (New York, 1979).

11. Michael Novak presses this point repeatedly, for example in his "The Case Against Liberation Theology," *New York Times Magazine* (21 October 1984).

12. But see Juan Luis Segundo's coment on the pope's highly selective criticisms of violence, in Segundo, *Theology and the Church: A Response to Cardinal Ratzinger and a Warning to the Whole Church* (Minneapolis, 1985), 107–36, 151–52.

13. The point has been made sharply by Leonardo Boff in the book which prompted his silencing: "Throughout its history, the Church has defined itself at times with the ruling classes and at other times with the lower classes. The unequal social structures, revolving around ownership of the means of production, slowly came to predominate within the Church itself. An unbalanced structure in the means of 'religious' production was created; in socioanalytical language (so as not to give a moral connotation) there has also been a gradual expropriation of the means of religious production from the Christian people by the clergy. In the early years, the Christian people as a whole shared in the power of the Church, in decisions, in the choosing of ministers; later, they were simply consulted; finally, in terms of power they were totally marginalized, dispossessed of their power.

"Just as there was a social division of labor, an ecclesiastical division of religious labor was introduced. A group of functionaries and experts was created, responsible for attending to the religious needs of all through the exclusive production of the symbolic goods to be consumed by the now dispossessed people. . . . It is clear that a church so structurally unbalanced is in harmony with the social realm that possesses the same biased means of production. The church has often become the legitimating religious ideology for the imperial social order." Boff, *Church: Charism and Power*, 112, 113.

14. This reworking can be seen in the two well-known Vatican documents on liberation theology authored by Cardinal Joseph Ratzinger in 1984 and 1986. The first (dated August 6, 1984) is entitled "Instruction on Certain Aspects of the 'Theology of Liberation.' " The second (dated March 22, 1986) is entitled "Instruction on Christian Freedom and Liberation." Both were issued by the Congregation for the Doctrine of the Faith, of which Cardinal Ratzinger is prefect.

15. I develop this point more fully in "Religion, Politics, and the Poor in Latin America Today."

16. For details see Berryman, *Religious Roots*.

17. The following comparative discussion draws heavily on Daniel H. Levine and Scott Mainwaring, "Religion and Popular Protest in Latin America," in *Protest and Resistance in Latin America*, ed. Susan Eckstein (1989). I also rely on the sources already cited here, and on Thomas Bruneau, "Church and Politics in Brazil: The Genesis of Change," and Daniel H. Levine, "Continuities in Colombia," both in *Journal of Latin American Studies* (United Kingdom) (November 1985).

18. Peter Hebblethwaite details the opposition and strenuous competition between the two in his insightful account of the Synod held at Rome in late 1985. For details, see his *Synod Extraordinary* (London, 1986).

19. One unintended consequence of the hierarchy's success is the characteristic extremism of alternative visions in Colombia. It is hard to get them started, and harder still to make them survive. When they *do* get off the ground, pervasive repression in the churches drives them to extremes: a middle ground is hard to find. In this light, the short and sharp trajectory of Camilo Torres make sense.

20. For detailed comment on this point, see my "Religion and Politics in Comparative and Historical Perspective."

21. See Levine and Mainwaring, "Religion and Popular Protest," for extended analysis and commentary on this issue.

9

Electioneering in Latin America

Alan Angell, Maria D'Alva Kinzo, and Diego Urbaneja

The advent of democratization in Latin America has brought increased attention to the electoral process, given the belief found in democratic theory that elections are a crucial variable in conceptualizing democracy. Alan Angell, Maria D'Alva Kinzo, and Diego Urbaneja have sought to demonstrate that certain similarities exist in the Latin American election process in their case studies of such diverse countries as Venezuela, Brazil, and Chile. They note that elections in the region are more "Americanized," making use of such features as television campaigning and public opinion polls, and that changing levels of urbanization, education, and industrialization have contributed to these technological developments in electioneering. It remains an open question, however, whether electoral techniques and style influence political systems and the persistence or strength of democratization.

Elections in Latin America are held under sharply differing circumstances, ranging from civil war in El Salvador to the peaceful routines that characterize Venezuela. They may be conducted with scrupulous attention to legal regulations, as in Costa Rica, or with flagrant violations of all such codes, as in the recent elections in Haiti. Within the same country, elections in the modern urban areas may resemble a modern North American campaign while in the backward rural areas the politics of clientelism and patronage largely determine and deliver votes. In some countries, parties may have adopted the techniques of modern electioneering, but without much change in policies or organization or

From "Latin America," in *Electioneering: A Comparative Study of Continuity and Change*, ed. David Butler and Austin Ranney (Oxford, England: Clarendon Press, 1992), 43–68. © 1992 Alan Angell, Maria D'Alva Kinzo, and Diego Urbaneja. Reprinted by permission of Oxford University Press.

behavior. In other countries, the modernization of electioneering techniques has been accompanied by the modernization of the overall political system, with the development of new parties, new policies, and new modes of political behavior.

Whatever the differences between the politics and party systems of Latin American countries, there are some observable general trends in patterns of electioneering. Compared to the 1950s, all Latin American countries are more urban, more industrialized, and with a huge increase in access to television. Electoral campaigns are arguably much more Americanized now than in Europe. The dominant form of campaigning is on television; opinion polls are followed with the interest normally associated with football [soccer] results; campaigning emphasizes personalities; and slick television advertisements for politicians blend harmoniously with those for consumer products. In one respect elections in Latin America differ from those of the United States—levels of participation are generally much higher, and elections generate much greater excitement. Elections in Venezuela have an atmosphere of public carnival. In Brazil so much campaigning is conducted with musical jingles that an observer might think he was witnessing a musical competition rather than an electoral contest. These developments contrast with the electoral campaigns of the 1950s in many countries where the core of campaigning was the long and serious set-piece speech of the candidate before a mass public meeting.

Articles dealing with Latin America make disclaimers that not all countries will be covered, and this one is no exception. We will concentrate on elections in Brazil, Chile, and Venezuela, for the good reason that we have individually observed elections in those countries over a number of years. But the three cases also offer interesting parallels and contrasts. Brazil was the only recent military dictatorship to hold regular elections. Admittedly the party system was devised by the regime, and the electoral process was controlled and regulated to serve the government's interests. Yet the very existence of elections which in the urban areas were not distorted by fraud, provided a crucial method of expressing opposition not just to the government but to the political regime. General [Augusto] Pinochet in Chile did not permit elections or party activity, for his intention was a complete restructuring of the political system. However, when there was a free and fair plebiscite in 1988 (as opposed to the questionable ones of 1978 and 1980), it became a verdict on sixteen years of dictatorship. Opposition victory made necessary the holding of competitive elections for president and congress in 1989. Venezuela before 1958 had, by contrast with Chile, little experience of competitive elections. Since then, however, elections have taken place with clockwork regularity, and parties have been voted in and out of office with almost equal regularity.

Before considering these three cases, some general observations are in order. Latin American political systems are presidential and not parliamentary, and most countries use some form of proportional representation (PR) electoral system. The key election is for the president. In some countries—Colombia and Venezuela are examples—simultaneous presidential and congressional elections deter party fragmentation, and in Uruguay electors must vote for the same party for legislative and executive elections. But most countries have PR electoral systems which ensure the representation of a large number of parties in congress, and staggered elections for president and congress frequently lead to minority support for the executive in congress. The coexistence of a multiparty system, powerful presidents, and staggered elections generate tension and conflict between the president and congress.

With the return to democracy in several Latin American countries in the last decade, institutional and electoral reform are subjects of debate as countries attempt to devise political systems that do not collapse in the face of social pressure and economic crisis. Elections are currently of great importance, for they are a way for the electorate to demonstrate not just its preference between parties and policies but also a commitment to the democratic process as such. Rates of electoral participation are generally high, and when they are not the reason may be fear of fraud or of the lack of relevance of the elections. Abstention in Mexico has increased as widespread suspicion of fraud reduced interest in elections. But even Mexico, which for many years controlled elections very closely, has permitted a degree of electoral pluralism. In 1988 the presidential candidate of the official party, the PRI [Partido Revolucionario Institucional], was elected with the smallest majority (50.36 percent) in the history of the party. Moreover, for the first time, the regime allowed a member of an opposition party to win an election for a state governorship.

In Colombia, the political pact between the Liberals and Conservatives, first implemented in 1958, alternated the presidency between the parties, and divided congress equally between them. In these circumstances it is hardly surprising that electoral participation was low, ranging from 68.0 percent in the first election inaugurating the political agreement in 1958 to a low of 33.4 percent in 1978. The average turnout between 1958 to 1986 was 48.5 percent.[1] There are usually several competing lists of candidates within each of the two major parties. The Colombian electoral system allocates seats according to the Hare quota: seats not allocated by quota are distributed according to the largest remainders. This procedure applies first to the parties and is then used within the parties to allocate seats between competing lists. This electoral system encourages a party system in which the major parties are divided into a series of factions constituted around a mixture of personal, policy, and regional differences. Political bosses effectively control the process at the local level. Continuing concern with the low level of political participation in Colombia led to two important reforms intended to increase participation: the direct election of mayors by means of a plurality election in a single-seat district, and a primary election within the Liberal Party. The election of a Constituent Assembly in 1991 is also expected to be the prelude to further reforms intended to modernize the party system. Colombia's political system has in fact been remarkably resilient in the face of terrible challenges—first of interparty violence on a massive scale, then the development of widespread guerrilla activity, then the growth of a huge illegal drugs trade. But there is little doubt that the system of factionalized ill-disciplined parties, however appropriate for an earlier period in the republic's development, is ill suited for the present demands. Hence electoral reform is not merely seeking to improve the system; it may be necessary to the very survival of that system itself.

Even in societies torn by civil strife, such as El Salvador or Peru, elections with genuine, if limited, participation decide who governs. Electors living in areas of those two countries under guerrilla control cannot vote, and sectors of the population who support the guerrillas may choose not to vote, but among the remaining population, which constitutes the large majority, elections proceed, if not exactly normally, at least after a fashion; they do reflect changing opinion and provide for alternative governments. Elections may be used as an inducement to persuade guerrilla groups to lay down their arms and compete at the polls. Electoral reform in Colombia is intended to make easier the seating of minority groups in congress and to attract guerrilla groups into electoral politics. In the late 1980s in some countries which have practically never known competitive elections, such as Paraguay and Haiti, political campaigns were allowed and elections took place. It is true, however, that they were also conducted under conditions that impose serious limits on both parties and candidates, and in Haiti winning an election is no guarantee of assuming office or of remaining there very long.

These are the worst cases. Most countries in Latin America have much longer-established electoral and constitutional traditions: that of Colombia equals many European countries in its almost uninterrupted longevity. Indeed the problem for some republics is not that their elections are too infrequent but that they have too many, with the cost of voter fatigue and boredom, and hence increased abstention.

What explains the recent increase in the importance of elections in Latin America? The collapse of military regimes in a number of countries led to the reestablishment of democracies. But these democracies are still fragile, and elections are a crucial part of the process of consolidation for they serve not only as expressions of popular choice, but as evidence that both the left and the right, whose attachment to democracy in the past has been conditional at best, now accept the rules of pluralistic democracy. The major criticism of the government made by the opposition parties in Mexico is directed, for example, not at its economic policy, but at the lack of democracy in political life, and the absence of safeguards to ensure that elections are free from fraud. Even when the government in Mexico agreed in 1991 after long opposition pressure to draw up a new electoral roll, there were complaints that the government deliberately undercounted the electorate of the capital city where the opposition is strong.

Because of the fragile nature of democracy in a number of countries, and even in Venezuela experience of dictatorship is well within living memory, the legal arrangements for elections assume great importance. It is vital that an independent and impartial regulatory authority should exist and have power. One of the factors that helped to make the 1989 Brazilian presidential elections widely accepted as legitimate was the authority of the Federal Electoral Tribunal, which publicly made clear its independence from executive pressure. The same role was played by the Electoral Commission in Chile in the 1988 plebiscite and 1989 elections. One of the factors that casts doubt on the validity of elections in Mexico is the absence of a body with similar authority.

The issues at stake in Latin America are more urgent and ideological than those of Western Europe—a reflection of the economic recession that has affected the region with the debt crisis of the 1980s. Hyperinflation, increasing unemployment, and poverty help to explain why at the forefront of elections in Latin America alternative ideological systems are on offer. The failure of governments to live up to sometimes exaggerated promises helps to explain the sharp fluctuations in electoral results. In Peru, for example, the economy has been in decline for most of the 1980s with the occasional year of ephemeral recovery. Living standards, already low, have been savagely cut as GDP [gross domestic product] has fallen, and as inflation has risen to dizzy heights: in one twelve-month period in 1988–89 it reached an annual rate of close on 11,000 percent. In addition a guerrilla war has cost the lives of an estimated twenty thousand Peruvians since 1980. It is hardly surprising that outgoing governments have been sweepingly rejected in favor of a very distinct alternative.

President [Fernando] Belaúnde [Terry] was elected with 45.4 percent of the vote in 1980 only to see his party reduced to 6.3 percent in 1985; and President Alán García [Pérez], elected with 45.7 percent in 1985, saw his party fall to 19.1 percent in 1990, ousted by an almost completely unknown candidate whose appeal seemed to be based largely on the fact that he was unknown, that he was of Japanese origin, and that he was supported by the evangelical churches.

Peru is an extreme case of electoral volatility. Yet, in spite of the economic decline, political uncertainty, and guerrilla conflict, elections are held regularly; they are conducted as fairly as can be expected in the circumstances; and they produce a change of government and of governing ideology. It is no exaggeration to say that the basis of legitimation of the fragile democracy that exists in Peru is founded more than anything else upon regular and competitive elections, and participation is high, given the circumstances—62 percent in 1980 and 70 percent in 1985.

Another reason for the increasing importance of elections in Latin America is that the political right is presently committed to seeking power through elections. In the past the right frequently sought power through support for military intervention. Following the wave of military governments in the 1960s and 1970s, the right tried, though not always successfully, to exercise influence through cooperation with authoritarian governments. With the failure of those governments, and the return to democracy, the right has entered the electoral arena. It has done so with some confidence beause of its new found belief in neoliberal ideas, a doctrine that is seen to be in international political ascendancy, and because it sees the left struggling to assemble its own ideology following the collapse of international communism.

The right, with its access to finance and its international links, has further contributed to the modernization of electoral techniques. Television now plays a vital role in election campaigns. Campaign advisers from the United States and elsewhere play an active role in devising campaign strategies, and the tactics of American campaigns—from motor cavalcades to brief and personalized political messages on television—have become widespread. The use of such techniques is widespread across the political spectrum. In campaigning for the plebiscite in Chile in 1988, President Pinochet sought the advice of British public relations consultants who had advised Mrs. [Margaret] Thatcher, and although clearly uneasy with his new role as a candidate for office, spoke on television in the intimate tones assumed necessary to inspire public confidence. What was remarkable about the campaigning in Chile was the similarity in electioneering techniques used by proponents of very different ideologies. Unfortunately for Pinochet, the opposition campaign was better than that of the government, and it is not unreasonable to argue that the better use of electioneering techniques by the opposition was a powerful factor in explaining their 55 percent share of the vote.

Electioneering in Brazil

Brazil was unique among the Latin American military dictatorships in holding regular elections for congress, the state legislatures, and municipal offices. But those elections hardly conformed to democratic practices. There was no direct election for the president, who was chosen in theory by an electoral college composed by members of congress and delegates from the state legislatures, but in practice by a restricted group of senior military officers. Neither were there elections for state governors, for the mayors of the capital cities of the states, nor for cities considered to be "areas of national security." The government created and allowed only two parties to operate, a progovernment party, ARENA [Aliança Renovadora Nacional], and an opposition party, the MDB [Movimiento Democrático Brasileiro]. The government did not hesitate to use intimidation against opposition candidates. After 1973, when a process of controlled liberalization began, the opposition used television to its advantage in electoral campaigns. The response of the government was to impose further restrictions on the opposition's access to the media, and constant attempts to devise electoral systems that would disadvantage the opposition. But for all these restrictions, the opposition vote continued to grow, especially in the modern urban areas, and this steady growth undermined the military regime's claim to legitimacy, for each election was in effect a plebiscite on the military government.

Restrictions on suffrage have been substantially removed since the return to democracy in 1985. All citizens now have the right to vote: illiterates were enfranchised in 1985, and in accordance with the 1988 Constitution, the age limit for voting has been lowered to sixteen (women were given the right to vote in 1932). Voting is compulsory for electors aged between eighteen and seventy years. This requirement, and the declaration of election days as public holidays, undoubtedly increases the level of participation in a country with a relatively low level of politicization.[2] But it also helps to explain the high proportion of blank and null ballots—in part indifference to the result, in part a substantial protest vote, in part genuine errors in completing what is a complicated ballot. Blank and null votes amounted to 19 percent in 1978, 13 percent in 1982, and 6 percent in 1985 and in 1989. Abstentions were 18 percent in 1978, 17 percent in 1982 and 1985, and 13 percent in the presidential elections in 1989. In 1990 there was a sharp increase in abstentions, and blank and null voting, because of boredom with elections that had been held every year since 1985 except for 1987, because of increasing criticism of the way that the congress had been behaving, and because of the excessive number of candidates and a very complicated ballot paper.[3]

Brazil has used a majority voting system as well as proportional representation. Under the new constitution, the president, state governors, and mayors are elected by a runoff ballot between the two leading candidates if neither receives an absolute majority on the first ballot. Federal senators are elected by a simple plurality system, and federal deputies by a system of PR.[4] Candidates are selected by delegates to party conventions. The Workers' Party (PT) has begun to experiment with primaries, but normally the choice of candidates is made by the party leadership, though this can be challenged if an aspirant for office controls a large bloc of party delegates.

To be elected, candidates need to have votes equivalent to the electoral quota; unallocated remaining seats are shared out among the winning parties by the D'Hondt system. Most importantly, the system is not based on a predetermined party list order. Rather, the number of individual votes each candidate obtains determines the order in which he or she appears on the party list. This voting system has the advantage of allowing voters, rather than parties, to choose the winning candidates. But it tends to disrupt party organization and discipline in so far as it encourages competition between individual candidates for the same party rather than between parties. At this time in the uncertain political development of Brazil, disciplined and accountable parties could help to strengthen the political system. One can imagine how confusing it is for voters to choose candidates when some party lists contain almost a hundred candidates.[5] It is almost inevitable that many votes are either casual, because of the impossibility of assessing the merits of so many candidates, or based upon personal links with local political bosses whose clientelistic style remains a common device to capture support in the rural areas. In short, as Shugart writes of the Brazilian (and of the similar Colombian electoral system), "candidates run against members of their own party as much or more than against members of other parties, central party leaders do not determine who will be elected, and members of the assembly seek out 'bailiwicks' wherein they have personal followings cultivated by the provision of services. Such systems thereby hinder the development of campaigns based upon ideology and program."[6] It is hardly surprising that politicians once elected frequently switch parties. In the congress elected in 1986 about one-third of the members switched parties in the following three years.

Electoral campaigns begin once the party's convention has nominated candidates—and the convention must be held at least six months before election day. No campaigning is allowed forty-eight hours before and twenty-four hours after election day. Parties have free television and radio access for two months before the election. Two hours daily at peak evening time are reserved for the parties, who are allotted time proportionate to their representation in the Federal Chamber. No other television or radio political advertising is permitted. Broadcasting must be transmitted simultaneously on all television channels or radio stations. This provision has been hotly opposed by the television companies, but the absence of choice has been quite effective in disseminating political information among the largely politically indifferent Brazilian electorate.

Television was important even in the period of military rule. The remarkable performance of the opposition MDB in the 1974 legislative elections was due partly to effective use of the medium.[7] Before 1974, television campaigning was widely regarded as uninspired and of little importance, consisting mostly of politicians reading long texts promoting their personal qualities. The opposition MDB campaign in 1974 transformed the use of television. Speeches were cut short and the emphasis was now on criticizing the economic and social policies of the government. Short films were prepared to drive home, with vivid images, the message of the opposition. Perhaps most important of all, the opposition MDB came to an agreement with the television companies to exchange a continuous twenty-minute broadcast for twenty clips of thirty seconds each shown at regular intervals during prime viewing time. The MDB stressed that it wanted to reach out to the new and undecided voters.

Since 1974 television has been the main instrument used by the parties to attract voters, or, more precisely, used by candidates to attract voters. The four leading newspapers in Brazil do not reach more than 10 percent of the population, whereas television is received by over 90 percent of urban and 70 percent of rural households. Soap operas are hugely popular on Brazilian television. Since 1982 the parties have used actors from these series, and popular singers, to reinforce their popularity. The television programs of the PT have been particularly colorful and humorous, even though some members of the party regarded these tactics as suitable for selling soap powder but not for promoting a serious left-wing party. All parties make extensive use of musical songs and jingles to try to promote party identification in a country where such identification is very low.

The importance of television in campaigning, and the emphasis on personal qualities, has placed a premium on professional use of the medium—often to make effective personal attacks on rival candidates. However, there is one crucial message that must be put across: that is, that the candidate cares about, and, even more important, is capable of doing something about the social and economic deprivation that affects the great majority of the Brazilian population, and also of dealing with the corruption that is held to be endemic in Brazilian politics. Most Brazilian voters are poor. Even in the most developed state of the country, São Paulo, three-quarters of the electorate have had education only up to the elementary level, and have salaries on average less than U.S. $100 per month. Effective political campaigning has to address issues that affect the majority of voters, especially as compulsory voting increases the participation of the poor. Candidates are increasingly making use of opinion polls to assess what particular issues are of greatest concern.

Campaigning on television is effective only for elections to the presidency, governorships, certain elections for mayors, and the Senate—all elections based on majority voting systems. For the elections for the Federal Chamber and state assemblies, based on PR, campaigning on television is not possible given the huge number of candidates. This deprives voters of information about candidates at this level, and accounts in part for the higher proportion of blank and null votes. In the second round of the 1989 presidential elections, the debates between the two contenders, [Fernando] Collor de Mello, and the candidate of the Left, Ignácio da Silva [Lula], were widely followed, and Collor's better performance in the debates was important in convincing undecided voters to vote for him. Collor was helped by the way that the most important television company, Rede Glóbo, backed him from the beginning and deliberately reported on the television debates in a way that favored Collor.

Public meetings have become less important since the development of television campaigning, but are still held, especially in the rural interiors of the states. Mass meetings seem to serve largely to provide images of the television broadcasts, and in the capital cities there is normally only one big public meeting. Meetings have also been displaced by motor cavalcades which certainly make a lot of noise, but whose utility must be doubtful given the resentment they arouse when they cause traffic jams. Telephone canvassing has recently been introduced but is not very common. Doorstep canvassing is less frequent than before, but is still used in the interior of the country and on the outskirts of the big cities. Candidates commonly walk the streets at busy times of the day to try to meet the electorate. Poster advertising is in theory strictly regulated, but in practice the restrictions are ignored.

Details of party finance remain obscure, but costs are very high both because the campaign methods have become more sophisticated and professional, and because candidates are covering a huge territory and electorate. One estimate put the average expenditure of successful candidates for the congress for São Paulo state in 1986 at over U.S. $600,000.[8] Attempts by the Electoral Court to control expenditure have had little success, partly because most comes from personal funds rather than from the party. Parties do receive some funds from the government, but these cover only a small proportion of total expenditures. Candidates have to raise their own funds, and a great deal comes from companies with contracts with the public sector, hoping to benefit by electing a friendly congressman or governor.

Public opinion polling has become widespread and important. Given the weakness of party identification in Brazil, a considerable proportion of voters say that they take into account whether a candidate has a chance of winning. In the last month of the campaign three private opinion polls publish their results weekly, and these receive widespread attention and comment. Candidates also make use of private polls and employ them in their television propaganda.

The Brazilian electorate is very volatile. The party system in Brazil is weak, and party identification is low. Surveys indicate that only about 30 to 40 percent of the population expresses a spontaneous party preference—much lower than the European average, and much lower than in Chile or Venezuela. Organizing national parties in a country as large and diverse as Brazil would be difficult enough in the best of circumstances. But when those circumstances have included a twenty-one-year period of military dictatorship, near hyperinflation, economic recession, a military still powerful in politics, and a young and rapidly growing electorate it is hardly surprising that the electorate of Brazil swings abruptly between parties and between candidates.

Electioneering in Chile

Chile is in many ways a mirror image of Brazil. Unlike Brazil, Chile has a firmly based and long-established party system and a history of representative government in which very competitive elections were a regular and important feature until interrupted by the military government from 1973 to 1989. Unlike the Brazilian military government, however, Pinochet did not permit any elections until he was constitutionally obliged to hold competitive elections for the presidency and congress in December 1989 following his defeat in a plebiscite in October 1988.

Elections in Chile before 1973 resembled elections in European countries. They were fought along party lines, with a relatively close association between social class and support for a particular party. The presence of a strong ideological left—the most powerful Communist Party in Latin America, and an even more popular and radical Socialist Party—was matched by strong ideological parties of the center and right, most notably the Christian Democratic Party (PDC). Ideological issues were central to elections in which, with one or two exceptions, such as [Carlos] Ibañez in 1952 and, to a lesser extent, Jorge Alessandri in 1958, independent personalities had little electoral impact. Television became important in the 1960s and played a vital role in the 1970 campaign by showing the initially most popular candidate, the right-wing Alessandri, in a very unfavorable light. Nevertheless, the core of party activity was mass public meetings, smaller reunions with local and representative groups, and rallying the party faithful by door-to-door canvassing. The electoral system was a modified version of the D'Hondt PR system, similar to the one used in Finland. Each party presented a list which could include as many candidates as seats, but voters had to cast their single vote for one candidate. The total vote for all candidates on each list decided how many seats each party received, and those were distributed among those candidates receiving the highest individual votes. Candidates were challenging not only other parties, but members of their own party on the same list.

The electoral system imposed by Pinochet for the 1989 elections was very different. His government had thought of adopting the British first-past-the-post system, to force Chile into a two-party system. The idea was discarded when it became clear that the right would not necessarily command majority support. The electoral system for the presidency is straightforward. If no candidate receives more than 50 percent in a national poll, then there is a runoff ballot. That was unnecessary in 1989, for the Christian Democratic opposition leader Patricio Aylwin received 55.18 percent, the right-wing candidate associated with the Pinochet government Hernán Buchi 29.39 percent, and a right-wing populist businessman Francisco Errázuriz 15.43 percent.

The system adopted for congress was designed to ensure that the right, now recognized to be a minority, would secure representation way beyond its share of the poll. In the Senate there are nine designated senators, chosen by the outgoing Pinochet government, and thirty-eight elected senators. In the lower house there are 120 members. Each constituency, whether for Senate or Chamber, returns two members, though each voter has only one vote. Parties are allowed to form alliances to present lists of two candidates per constituency. If a party alliance gains more than twice the votes of the next most supported list, it takes both seats. If it takes less than that, it returns one member and the next most voted list takes one. Thus, if there are only two lists contesting a constituency, a list with two-thirds of the votes plus one would return two members. If it had one vote less than two-thirds, then it would only return one member, and the minority list with one-third of the votes plus one would return one member. In one of the two Santiago contests for the Senate, a prominent Socialist candidate was not elected even though he came second in the poll with 29.2 percent of the vote. The second seat went to the leader of a right-wing party identified with the Pinochet government, though he won only 16.4 percent of the vote.[9] Parties that were not included in one or other of the two major coalitions had no chance of representation in congress: hence the Communist Party, traditionally a powerful bloc in congress, elected no representatives. The new government wishes to return to the traditional Chilean PR system. However, it lacks a majority in congress sufficient to implement this reform.

The major similarity between the elections of 1989 and those before 1973 was the central role played by well-organized programmatic parties. In the case of the opposition, even the parties were the same as before 1973—Christian Democrats, Socialists, Radicals, and Communists. On the right, the major party, National Renewal, had a different name, but there were many continuities both in personnel and policies with the old National Party. The only really new contender was the neoliberal party, the UDI [Independent Democratic Union], closely identified with the policies of the Pinochet government. What was different, compared to elections before 1973, was that the ideological gap between the parties was far narrower, and that the competition was less bitter and sectarian. There was, for example, considerable agreement about economic policy, and almost complete consensus about the need to consolidate democracy.

As in the past, in 1989 mass rallies and canvassing were important. However, there is no doubt that television played the dominant role in the campaign. As in the plebiscite the year before, a fifteen-minute slot each night for three weeks before the election was divided equally between the three presidential candidates. During the day, there was another fifteen-minute period when the parties were able to appeal for congressional votes. There was only one major debate between the two main presidential candidates, but there were many televised interviews with them. The impact of television on the plebiscite had been dramatic. For fifteen years Chileans had seen nothing but government propaganda on their screens: suddenly the opposition was allowed to put its case. Moreover, it put its case brilliantly, and far better than the government, to an audience which rarely fell below 60 percent of an attentive electorate. The government could command much greater financial resources than the opposition, and was advised by leading public relations consultants from the United States, and by some of Mrs. Thatcher's advisers. But there are limits to what such advisers could do with an unattractive message. There was clear and overwhelming poll evidence both in the plebiscite campaign and in the electoral campaign that the opposition would win by a comfortable margin, and that the television campaigning brought considerable benefit to the opposition.

Opinion polls were used on a very modest scale before 1973. In the campaigns of 1988 and 1989, however, they were given enormous publicity, partly because in the absence of congress and a free press, there was no other way in which the electorate could inform itself about public opinion. The press was at least able to publish opinion poll findings, and they had a novelty akin to the opposition television programs. Virtually all gave the opposition an advantage over the government both in 1988 and 1989, and played an important role in convincing the electorate that the opposition could win and could form a credible government. The opposition used opinion polls internally to target its message to certain groups, and to change tactics in the light of opinion-poll findings.

Mounting electoral campaigns in such a short period of time clearly was very expensive. Where did the money come from for an opposition that had been illegal since 1973? The answer is, largely from abroad. Chile received a remarkable amount of international attention, and the Pinochet government was widely condemned while the opposition, much of it in exile, was widely supported. This financial support was absolutely crucial in keeping the opposition alive in the long years of the Pinochet dictatorship, and in financing the campaigns of 1988 and 1989.[10] Much of this support was channeled through church-based groups. In some countries—such as Chile—when parties are banned or controlled, the Church is prepared to use its authority to defend the right to oppose. This was also true in Brazil, where church-based groups were important in the creation of the Workers' Party.

The opposition was worried that voters would believe that the vote was not secret, and that they would be unable to resist the various kinds of pressure employed by the government, especially at the local level, to ensure a vote favorable for the government. The role of the Church was crucial in persuading the electorate to go out and vote, and not to be intimidated by threats or pressure.

Possible fraud by the government was also a constant worry for the opposition. To minimize this, the opposition set up no fewer than three parallel computer systems linked to an intricate network of fax machines. Support came from the United States and elsewhere both for the long-term campaign to register voters, and for computer counting systems on the date of the poll. The United States Agency for International Development [AID] made a grant of $1.2 million to the Center for Free Elections

(CAPEL) in Costa Rica in December 1987. In turn CAPEL made the grant over to Civitas, a church-linked group in Chile, to campaign for voter registration. At the same time the U.S. Congress approved a $1 million grant to the National Endowment for Democracy to support the activities of the opposition. In the Chilean elections of 1989, AID made a grant of $470,000 to CAPEL to help the church-sponsored Participa organization do what the Cruzada Civica had done in the plebiscite, that is to encourage the registration and participation of the electorate. At least U.S. $5 million went to Chile from U.S. sources to help prepare the plebiscite and the election. European support for the opposition was on an even greater scale, but had been given to the opposition during the long years of dictatorship. Such support was crucial in keeping the parties viable.

International press coverage of both events was intense, and there is no doubt that the government saw the foreign press and television as biased against them. Moreover, there were about a thousand observers present at the plebiscite and during the elections, half from various parliaments and half from a variety of other associations. The presence of these observers was not welcomed by the government, but certainly was by the opposition, who believed that their presence would make fraud more difficult and would lend much needed encouragement to the opposition, especially at the local level.

In the end, there was little fraud. Over 90 percent of the total potential electorate was registered to vote, and over 90 percent of those actually voted. The winning margin was almost identical in both plebiscite and election, with the opposition winning 55 percent of the vote, to 43 percent for Pinochet in the plebiscite, and the combined right-wing vote in the election. The government enjoyed so many advantages—years of political propaganda, control over television, state resources—that at first the opposition's task looked overwhelmingly difficult. But there was a strong desire to return to the tradition of competitive party politics.

Participation has traditionally been high in Chilean elections—usually around 80 percent—but the plebiscite and the elections were exceptional. Clearly the contests of 1988 and 1989 were special elections, one overtly a plebiscite, and the other still with characteristics of a plebiscite. Yet there are reasons for expecting that elections will continue to attract high levels of interest. Parties in Chile are well organized and disciplined with firm social roots and long historical traditions. There exists a very small antiparty vote. Antisystem parties hardly exist any more as both the extreme left and the extreme right have joined the electoral game. There is agreement across the political spectrum about maintaining the successful economic model. There is less reason than in Brazil to expect wide swings in voter preferences, and in these conditions the techniques of modern electioneering will be important at the margins—but in a multiparty system, which may well return to its traditional PR electoral system, the margin can make all the difference between winning and losing.

Electioneering in Venezuela

Venezuela has a relatively long and uninterrupted electoral history compared to most Latin American countries. Since the fall of the dictatorship of [Marcos] Pérez Jiménez in 1958, there have been seven presidential and congressional elections held at five-year intervals. The Venezuelan electorate has considerable experience of electioneering, and combines enthusiastic support for democracy with increasing skepticism about the electoral promises made by the political parties. Indeed, concern about the firm hold of the two major parties on political life in Venezuela has led to the proposal of electoral reforms aimed at reducing the power of the party leadership by moving from closed to open list forms of PR.[11]

Two major parties dominate the electoral scene, Acción Democrática (AD) and the Comité de Organización Política Electoral Independiente (Copei).[12] Both have an extensive and effective organizational structure that reaches all levels of political, administrative and social organization. Until 1973 there were other important parties, but since then, the AD and Copei have shared 80 percent of the total vote.[13] Moreover, the parties now resemble each other in terms of social and regional support; both are multiclass national parties, which have moved toward the center of the political spectrum. The electoral domination of these two parties has created a strong feeling that not to vote for one or the other is a wasted vote.

Electoral campaigns revolve around the work of these two parties, which mobilize their huge memberships in a patient process of meetings, conversations, interviews with candidates, and publicity at the local level. The parties mobilize their links with innumerable social and political groups to bring out their vote. With such intensive campaigning it is not surprising that abstention is low. Until 1978 it never reached 10 percent, and though it has increased with the economic recession of the 1980s its peak was still only 18 percent in 1988. The vote is compulsory in Venezuela for an electorate whose voting age begins at eighteen years.[14] But it is doubtful if this explains the low level of abstention.[15] We would prefer to emphasize the intensity of party electioneering which creates an atmosphere simultaneously of political competition and of political carnival. Elections become a festival of democratic politics, and it is difficult for even the most isolated electors to ignore what is happening.

Until 1978 the choice of candidates was a party matter, decided internally. Such decisions could affect party unity, and the AD choice of presidential candidate led to a damaging split in the party in 1968. But in general, little public attention was paid to the internal party choice, which was made by a variety of methods from primary elections to different forms of delegate selection. Since 1978, however, and linked to the increasing professionalization of electioneering in Venezuela, precandidates for nomination for the presidential elections mount public campaigns to generate support in order to influence the party's choice of candidate. Until 1983 the campaign for nomination, and then the campaign for the presidency, lasted no less than eighteen months, but recent regulations have separated the two campaigns and have ensured that they last no longer than six months in total.[16]

Elections in Venezuela have been conducted regularly and fairly. Four elections of the seven since 1958 have seen the victory of the then opposition party: one of them in 1968 by a tiny margin of 1,083,000 votes to 1,050,000.[17] Governments have the advantage in Venezuela of control over national finances, and there is always the temptation to use public works to manipulate public opinion, or to create a preelection economic boom. But against that has to be set the decline in support for the government which seems to occur regularly in Venezuela: as one minister of the interior lamented publicly, in Venezuela "governments do not win elections." Electoral credibility is one of the basic pillars of Venezuelan democracy.

The electoral system has changed since the establishment of democracy in 1958. Until 1973 the president, national congress, state, and local officials were elected simultaneously. Since then presidential elections have continued to be held every five years; but from 1973 to 1989 municipal councils were elected six months after presidential elections. Since 1989 state governors, mayors, and councilors are elected every three years, separately from presidential and congressional elections; previously state governors were appointed by the president, and the office of mayor did not exist. Presidents are elected by a simple majority. Congressmen and local councilors are elected by a system of PR: the D'Hondt method using closed party lists.[18] The system of closed party lists helped to consolidate democracy in Venezuela by creating strong and disciplined parties. However, the emphasis has now shifted to the need for greater democratic accountability of the parties, and a recent reform means that in the future only half of the lower house of congress will be elected by PR: the rest by a simple majority system. The two senators returned by each state are elected at present, and will be in the future, by the parties that gain the two largest votes, unless one party has more than double the votes of the next most popular party, in which case it takes both seats.

The Supreme Electoral Council (Consejo Supremo Electoral) has played an important role in guaranteeing fair elections. It is composed of representatives of the five most popular parties in the elections, and the president is an independent, elected by congress. It lasts for five years, is in permanent session, and has authority to settle matters of internal party disputes as well. However, there is little fraud in Venezuelan elections, and little use of negative personal attacks beyond the level of rumor and gossip. The most sensitive time in the electoral process is when the votes are counted in the thousands of voting booths all over the country. Small parties that cannot provide representatives at all the polling stations run the risk of having their votes stolen by representatives of the big parties. But the problem is a minor one, limited to rural areas where the absolute number of votes for minor parties is in any case very small. Nevertheless one of the electoral reforms to be adopted is the automatic counting of votes.

It is difficult to generalize about the extent to which elections in Venezuela have been issue oriented. Different elections have revolved around different issues. Those of 1958 and 1963 were about affirming democracy in the face of armed subversion. That of 1968 revolved around the need for a change from the ruling AD government. [The year] 1973 saw the emergence of modern electioneering techniques and the personal appeal of the flamboyant AD candidate, Carlos Andrés Pérez. Personal appeal obviously helps a candidate and his party, but has not been sufficient in Venezuela to reverse a generally unfavorable verdict on the party in government. The elections of 1978 and 1983 were basically a judgment on the policies adopted by the relevant government and confirmed a tendency, clearly apparent in 1988 of both parties to emphasize governing ability rather than differing programs and ideologies. In 1988 the AD won because of its wider organizational base and because of the personal popularity of its candidate, the former president Carlos Andrés Pérez. However, the adoption of IMF [International Monetary Fund]-style adjustment policies by the present government—a radical break from previous economic policies—has brought the debate over economic policies and alternatives to the forefront, and these issues are likely to play a more prominent role in future elections.

Since 1973, Venezuelan elections have made intensive use of modern publicity techniques. Until then publicity was relatively simple. In 1973 the AD used intensive publicity to convert the image of its candidate, Andrés Pérez, from that of the sober and unappealing interior minister who had dealt with the guerrilla uprising to that of a more relaxed and attractive personality. Copei also used intensive publicity in this campaign, and thereafter all parties paid close attention to modern methods of political publicity, so that the advantage that the AD gained in 1973 was canceled out. Both parties make extensive use of foreign advisers in these matters and also seek advice from their international political allies in the Socialist International in the case of the AD, and the Christian Democratic International in the case of Copei. By now local politicians have acquired extensive experience, and both parties have effective electoral commands which direct the campaign of the candidates, making such use of external advice as they think appropriate. Both parties make a great effort to have as rapid a system as possible of electoral returns from the polling stations so that they possess their own independent results.

Electoral costs rose gradually from 1958 to 1968, but with the election of 1973 and thereafter, the costs have risen in a dizzy fashion—aided of course by the huge increase in the value of Venezuelan exports with the oil price increases of the 1970s. It is difficult to give accurate figures of electoral expenditures, and figures in U.S. dollars can be misleading as the Venezuelan bolivar has fallen from 4.30 to the U.S. dollar in 1982 to 50 to the dollar by 1991. But in recent years it is generally estimated that the electoral expenditures of each of the two main parties exceed 1 billion bolivars or U.S. $20 million. The campaigns are financed in three ways. First, by quotas from party members, and by commissions that are paid to the party for its good offices in securing public sector contracts. Second, from state grants, as the Supreme Electorate Council reimburses a part of the costs of parties who gain more than 5 percent of the vote. Third, there is private finance from the wealthy supporters of the party and of the candidate. There is no regulation on financial contributions apart from those coming from the state. This obviously favors the candidates of the two major parties, and there is pressure to limit campaign costs and contributions. But as the two major parties resist this reform it is unlikely to be enacted. Moreover, as there is rough equality in the contributions given to each of the two major parties, electoral expenditure does not give one party a significant edge over the other, and the extravagant promises that are made in the campaign are received with increasing skepticism by the electorate.

Electoral campaigns in Venezuela are intense and prolonged. Each candidate will organize huge meetings in the four or five major cities. Candidates make use of television and radio as much as possible, though the major private television channels try to be balanced between the candidates (but it is obvious that they have their favorite), and the state television channels are obliged to give equal treatment to the candidates. Newspapers are inclined to be more partisan, and some have, in the past, made deals with candidates, pledging support in return for favors.

Television debates between candidates have not been important in electoral campaigns, with a couple of exceptions. And neither has there been much use in Venezuela of door-to-door canvassing, telephone canvassing, or mailing of party propaganda. Much more frequent are the innumerable forums of specific groups such as farmers, cattle ranchers, students, businessmen, and so on, where the candidate or his representatives are expected to debate the issues that concern the audience.

Public opinion surveys are intensively used by the parties and have been since 1973. The campaign teams poll constantly to see what issues are held to be important, and what impression the candidate is producing. Such polls have been influential in changing campaign strategy. But the committed or captive vote is very large in Venezuela, and there is little evidence that opinion poll findings have influenced voting behavior. The AD can count on a stable 35 percent of the vote, and Copei a little less, with 27 percent. It is true that recent polls show some disenchantment with the major parties, which is hardly surprising given the economic crisis, but the effect so far seems to be that the vote for the major parties is relatively stable, but less enthusiastic. The problem is that there is no credible alternative for the electorate to support.

Electoral behavior may change in response to the new staggered timetable for elections, and the new electoral system for part of congress, but there is no doubt that elections will continue to be one of the basic pillars of political legitimacy of the existing regime. One of the firmest political convictions both of the political élite in Venezuela and of the great mass of the electorate is that elections should be free of fraud, and that the results should be respected.

Conclusion

These three cases illustrate how in very different political systems, electioneering has developed in similar fashion. This is hardly surprising. All three countries, and indeed most countries in Latin America, saw important social and economic transformations in the decades after World War II. They became much more urbanized, more industrialized, and their populations more educated. In Brazil, for example, the proportion of the population living in cities of over twenty thousand inhabitants increased from 20 percent in 1950 to 55 percent in 1990. In Chile and Venezuela the proportion of the population living in towns is even higher. The Americanization of electioneering is one aspect of the general Americanization of consumer standards in Latin America, even if for many poor Latin Americans such standards represent a dream rather than a reality. But the dream is constantly reinforced by television, which is now almost as widespread in Latin America as in Europe, at least in terms of viewers.

In the 1950s a great deal of electioneering took place in rural areas, with the candidates as often as not arriving on horseback or in a Jeep, addressing a small audience in the presence of the local political boss, who could faithfully deliver votes on election day. Serious issues were debated seriously in campaign meetings in towns, but restricted suffrage and limited access to media reduced the overall impact of elections on the population. In the 1990s, by contrast, elections in Latin America are impossible to ignore, if only because of the noise and litter that accompany campaigning. But the core of electioneering is now conducted on television with techniques as modern as those in the United States, and with considerably more interest and enthusiasm than elections in that country.

Democracy is still fragile in Latin America, and much depends on the evolution of party and electoral systems. In societies suffering from acute social and economic crisis, as in Peru, the very survival of democracy is at issue in every election, and it is doubtful whether the most modern electioneering techniques would have made a substantial difference to the result in 1985 or 1990. The more settled and legitimate the political system, as in Venezuela, then the greater the importance of modern electoral techniques in influencing political outcomes. Paradoxically, one could argue that electioneering techniques do matter in Brazil, but not because the major issues of democratic consolidation are settled, as in Venezuela, but rather because the party system is so weak and its roots so shallow that publicity and electioneering are necessary for the voters simply to be able to identify the candidates.

Debates on electoral and party reform seem to be taking place in almost every republic. They are linked to another debate: the virtue of the parliamentary as opposed to the existing presidential systems. The argument of those who favor parliamentary systems is that it would help to produce responsible and disciplined parties, and that potential crises would be resolved more quickly than in presidential regimes, where by contrast, it is argued, political impasse can lead to regime breakdown. Advocates of parliamentarianism argue that élites in some Latin American countries have adopted institutions and practices that have favored strong presidents and weak parties and have encouraged personalistic and clientelistic practices.

In opposing dictatorships, opposition parties stressed their commitment to democracy without being specific about the form that democracy would take. Now in power, opposition politicians are finding that issues of electoral and party reform are crucial to the consolidation of those democratic regimes. Substantive political issues rather than questions of presentation and persuasion are likely to be the core of politics in Latin America for some time to come. But parties and politicians across the political spectrum are acutely conscious of the need to influence voters, and the trend toward the adoption of modern electioneering techniques is likely to intensify.

Notes

1. Ronald McDonald and J. Mark Ruhl, *Party Politics and Elections in Latin America* (Boulder, CO: Westview Press, 1989), 85. They point out that the actual proportion of eligible voters who do vote may be 10 percent higher than the official figures because official figures include adults who cannot vote (the armed services), Colombians abroad, and so on. The Colombian electoral system is well described in Matthew Shugart, "Electoral Systems and Political Reform in Colombia and Venezuela," *Electoral Studies* (March 1992).

2. Electors who do not vote, and who do not justify their absence in the Electoral Tribunal within thirty days (a period of grace which applies only to those who were absent from the city where they were registered to vote), have to pay a fine ranging from 3 to 10 percent of the legal minimum salary. In addition, if one cannot produce the document proving that one has voted or the legal exemption from voting, it is not possible to apply for a job in the public sector, nor to borrow money from banks and saving associations controlled by the government, nor obtain a passport or identification card, nor be matriculated in a state school.

3. In São Paulo state the percentage of abstention rose from 3.5 to 8.5 percent between 1985 and 1990, but the percentage of null and blank votes rose from 11.5 to 21.2 percent for the gubernatorial elections, and an even higher 22.9 to 41.7 percent for the national congress.

4. The senatorial mandate lasts for eight years, but there are elections every four years: once for one-third of the Senate and once for two-thirds. Seats in the lower house and in state assemblies are changed every four years.

5. For example, in the last legislative elections in São Paulo state, no less than 610 candidates competed for the state's sixty seats in the Federal Chamber of Deputies, and 1,182 candidates for the eighty-four seats in the State Assembly.

6. Shugart, "Electoral Systems and Political Reform."

7. See Maria D'Alva Kinzo, *Legal Opposition Politics under Authoritarian Rule in Brazil: The Case of the MDB, 1966–1979* (London: Macmillan, 1988).

8. This compares with an estimated $393,000 spent by winning candidates in the 1988 elections for the U.S. House of Representatives.

9. Because of this system, although the opposition alliance came first and second in nine of the senatorial contests, in only two of them did it poll the two-thirds plus one votes necessary to return two candidates. For the right-wing alliance this form of discrimination operated only twice.

10. On the elections of 1989 see Alan Angell and Benny Pollack, "The Chilean Elections of 1989 and the Politics of the Transition to Democracy," *Bulletin of Latin American Research* 9, no. 1 (1990): 1–23. On the general question of foreign funding of political activities see Michael Pinto-Duschinsky, "Foreign Political Aid: The German Political Foundations and their U.S. Counterparts," *International Affairs* 67, no. 1 (1991): 33–63.

11. For the 1993 congressional elections the plan is to adopt a system similar to the West German model.

12. The AD has some 2 million members and Copei one million in a population overall of 20 million.

13. The AD and Copei usually gain about 40 percent each of the overall vote: the principal party of the Left, the Movimiento al Socialismo, normally averages between 5 and 10 percent, and other parties of the Left a total of 5 percent; an antiparty independent can count on 2 percent of the vote, and there are usually a considerable number of insignificant parties.

14. The exception is the Armed Forces, who may not vote. But they play an important part in the electoral process, ensuring public order near the polling stations and overseeing the moving of the ballot boxes to the Supreme Electoral Council.

15. In any case, the sanctions that theoretically exist to encourage voting are rarely applied.

16. However, there is almost incessant electoral activity in Venezuela in the choice of union leaders, professional associations, and community associations, all of which are influenced to some degree or other by party affiliation. (Even in beauty contests it is claimed that the parties have their candidates.)

17. This election was also significant because it was the first one gained by an opposition candidate for the presidency.

18. At present it is not possible to choose between the candidates offered by the party, nor to select different parties for the different bodies being elected at the same time. In effect the party leadership determined who was elected, and as a result parties are very disciplined in congress, for to deviate from the party line is to risk expulsion or to be placed on the list in what amounts to a nonelectable position.

10

Nongovernmental Organizations in Latin America

Leilah Landim

The stimuli for democratic developments come from a variety of sources and levels in society. What might contribute most fundamentally to the strength of democracy are organizations at the grass-roots level, which share participatory values and teach their members how to make demands on government institutions. These local bodies, the origins of which might be social, economic, or political, have been placed under the general umbrella of nongovernmental organizations (NGOs). As Brazilian scholar Leilah Landim argues, these organizations in the Latin American context developed in response to authoritarian and repressive regimes. She identifies their general characteristics domestically and internationally, as well as their origins, relationships to other institutions, and the manner in which they make demands. Landim suggests that these groups will have a fundamental role to play in the consolidation of democratic regimes in Latin America.

Introduction

Analyzing nongovernmental organizations (NGOs) in Latin America in just a few pages implies working from an assumption that must be taken with a grain of salt, i.e., that this "subcontinent" can be treated as an undifferentiated whole. While in the eyes of the advanced, industrialized world Latin America appears to constitute a united bloc because of "underdevelopment" and "dependency," such an approach simplifies and reduces the diversity of national realities, and the differential power of the economies, societies, and states vis-à-vis international power centers.

From *World Development* 15, supplement (1987): 29–37, trans. Charles Roberts. Reprinted by permission of Pergamon Press, Oxford, England.

There is a similar colonial past, in Latin America, but the national societies have evolved along quite different paths. The differences stand out especially when one compares the cultures, shaped by the colonial encounter with societies as diverse as white Europeans and Amerindians; even the Amerindian societies varied significantly from region to region. The African influence left a profound mark on the culture of some societies, while practically none on others. The diverse forms that capitalist development assumed generated social structures that varied significantly in complexity and composition from one country to the next. From this point of view, how can we compare, for example, Brazil and El Salvador?

One basic characteristic of NGOs is that their actions are very much based on the social, political, and economic contexts of the countries in which they operate, in a very close and privileged relationship with grassroots movements. This is all the more reason to bear in mind the diversity among Latin American societies in carrying out a detailed analysis of NGOs.

These observations are but an introductory caveat. They render all the generalizations set forth below relative, also relativizing a perspective "from outside," which may underplay differences that are quite significant, especially for those who live them.

This is, thus, the first difficulty to be confronted. It is impossible to work, in this text, with the particularities of that world of diverse social situations that is behind the category "Latin America."

I am thus going to deal with those features that are common and general. Therefore, I focus not so much on the social contexts in which the NGOs exist and to which they adapt in different ways, but rather on the NGOs themselves, as specific institutions, understood in terms of their own characteristics.

This simplifies our task, for there is no question but that NGOs are a relatively new and widespread phenomenon in Latin America, a sort of "institutional novelty" bringing together a set of social actors who have been present and influential in those societies for the last twenty years. Their characteristics—among which ambiguity of their modes of insertion in the different social contexts and of relating to other social actors stand out—enable them to survive short-term transformations and redefine their roles and functions.

We must also define at the outset just what we are talking about. After all, what is it that we are referring to when we speak of a "nongovernmental organization?" The name seems inadequate, for it does not define the phenomenon empirically. "Nongovernmental" encompasses recreational and charity organizations, trade unions and clubs, among others. Moreover, the term has been imported, having been coined in the countries of the North, where, no doubt, the relationship between civil society and the state has a different dynamic, and where NGOs' projects and functions differ from those in the Third World.

Nonetheless, the very "emptiness" of the term may be positive insofar as it designates an entity with ambiguous characteristics. More than that, NGOs constitute a phenomenon whose identity in Latin America is still taking shape. Indeed, until a short time ago, the term "nongovernmental organization" did not have any particular meaning in that context, either for members of such institutions or for politicians, academics, or the general public. Lack of familiarity with the term certainly reflected a failure to recognize what we call "NGOs" as a social phenomenon, i.e., the failure to recognize a shared identity among a set of institutions with specific characteristics. It is only of late that NGOs have thought of themselves and their role as NGOs in society, as part of a complex social fabric involving international relations. Such reflection is still in its initial stages.

I even believe that there has been a certain resistance on the part of NGOs to take up this discussion and accept this shared identity, which is revealing of their nature. They are entities that think of themselves largely in terms of autonomy and individuality, stressing their direct relationships with social groups and movements within which they act: NGOs are not an end unto themselves, existing rather "at the service" of the exploited and underprivileged sectors of the population. In addition, as will be discussed below, the fact that in large measure they have developed under authoritarian regimes has meant that their actions have unfolded within legal bounds for long periods, since they dealt with the perilous terrain of social issues and subaltern groups. Discussing identities, coordinating work, becoming visible were simply not appropriate in certain contexts.

"Nongovernmental organization" is a category that is being forged in Latin America. Conferences, discussions, preliminary networks, publications, research, are all processes that have been expanding of late, constituting building blocks of this identity. For the purposes of this paper, I shall use a definition that encompasses a set of organizations which have evolved since 1970. In the words of Mario Padrón, an author who has studied NGOs in Latin America, "these are, in general, private non-profit organizations that are publicly registered (i.e., have legal status), whose principal function is to implement development projects favoring the popular sectors, and which receive financial support. The sources of financial support are almost always non-governmental organizations themselves, based in industrialized countries, operating in the framework of international development cooperation."[1] It is this type of organization that will be discussed here.

It is difficult to find thorough surveys on NGOs in any country. This is a task yet to be undertaken. There must be thousands of such organizations throughout Latin America. For example, documents indicate the existence of 250 such entities in Mexico[2] and 300 in Peru.[3] A survey we carried out in Brazil in August 1986 listed 1,041 NGOs in Brazil alone![4]

All indications are that NGOs in Latin America are here to stay. While they emerged in the 1950s and took on their present characteristics during periods of dictatorship, the winds of redemocratization blowing across Latin America appear to have given them an extra boost. The growth and increasing complexity of social movements, new spaces for participation, and reorganization of civil society all represent new challenges for the NGOs. They have responded by significantly multiplying and diversifying their activities, forming a growing universe of nuclei for social initiatives, small cells of power dispersed throughout society, actors with a specific role in the Latin American sociopolitical setting.

Studying NGOs in Latin America implies identifying the specific types of relationships between NGOs and other social actors, their mission, and their ability to intervene politically, both nationally and internationally. It is hoped that the following data will contribute toward answering these questions.

Origins

NGOs and Developmentalism

The 1950s marked a sort of prehistory of NGOs as studied in this paper. Latin American NGOs took shape at that time; but their outlook and role then differed significantly from what they are today.

During the 1950s nongovernmental cooperation agencies supported the developmentalist ideology being promoted by the modernizing elites of Latin America. Having experienced processes of import-substitution industrialization, countries such as Brazil, Argentina, and Mexico had begun to develop heavy industry. While some countries continued—as today—to experience the classical structural dependence of agrarian economies, others were already entering a new phase of industrialization. The more industrialized countries would be affected by the growing internationalization of capital, at first through multinational corporations, and later through subordination to the more encompassing global logic of the international financial system.

The NGOs played a role in forms of cooperation that emphasized "aid" and "industrialism." Institutions such as the churches and United Nations-related organizations would take the first steps in encouraging the action of such institutions, i.e., NGOs based on the idea of "promoting development." "Development" in this context was understood as support for economic growth so as to overcome "backwardness." The problem was one of transferring resources and technology, securing investments for development that would yield results measurable in general indicators such as per capita income. The "welfare approach" (*assistencialismo*) was another feature of these institutions, especially those linked to the Catholic Church, in which charitable actions were geared to transferring food surpluses from countries of the North. As Rodrigo Egaña says: "There was no questioning, in the initial processes of cooperation, of the way in which production was carried out in the so-called developing countries, nor of how that product was distributed and consumed."[5]

The above observations suggest the ideological frameworks towards which the NGOs would start to move in the mid-1960s: criticisms of developmentalism, which were emerging from social thought and within opposition forces in Latin America. More structural analyses pointed to the negative effects of the traditional development model, in which growth and industrialization generated and coexisted with poverty, social marginality, and economic dependence.

That was the period of political and economic crises generated by authoritarian regimes in Latin America. New NGOs emerged and grew during the periods of dictatorship in the context of that critical spirit, redefining their role and creating new forms of social intervention. It is in that period that the outlook and work style particular to the NGOs that were to proliferate to the present day in Latin America took shape. Henceforth, much has changed in terms of the practices and social role of the NGOs. But their origins have left their mark, especially since they are so recent; studying them is part of the process of understanding these institutions.

The NGOs "at the Service of the Popular Movement"

NGOs in Latin America developed during the periods of political authoritarianism, their basic role being one of resistance and denunciation. Their backs completely turned away from the state, they affirmed during that period one of their fundamental characteristics, i.e., their orientation to civil society. The NGOs thus sheltered a set of social initiatives linked to the grassroots; such initiatives, in turn, were oriented to movements at the intermediate and lower levels of the body politic and society that stood for autonomy and independence vis-à-vis the state.

This was the period of "antlike work," work on a very small scale, involving small projects to support the economic and political resistance of the poor. It was at the stage that the welfare (*assistencialismo*) perspective was dropped in favor of "participation," one of the crucial components of the "development projects" implemented. The category "development" was perforce being redefined, becoming increasingly identified with structural social transformation and the pursuit of citizens' rights.

The political aftershocks of dictatorial regimes coming to power in Latin America, and especially the 1973 military coup in Chile, awakened the international community to the need to revise development cooperation policy. In this context, the 1970s were marked by international recognition of the importance of NGOs in Latin America; the NGOs, imbued with this "new outlook," became interlocuters for nongovernmental entities, above all from Europe and linked to the churches, especially the Catholic Church. The growing number of Latin American exiles no doubt contributed to the search for alternative forms of development cooperation, independent of the authoritarian regimes.

Some very characteristic features of the NGOs date back to that period, and are worthy of mention, especially if we wish to understand some of the impasses NGOs were to come up against later in "adapting" to the period of redemocratization.

The NGOs developed in close relation with religious circles, especially the Catholic Church. In contexts of closed political space the Church is generally powerful enough to safeguard its scope of action. In some cases the Church became the main arena for the popular sectors, deprived of any political channels for expressing themselves and participating in society, for speaking out and articulating their needs. The consolidation in certain regions, during the 1970s, of the current that has been called "the Popular Church," is of particular importance. Religious sectors—both clergy and laity—who embrace a common discourse (sociological, political, theological: the theology of liberation) and a series of practices with specific characteristics, left a profound mark on the social movements they supported, and alongside which they worked, through "capillary action," attending to the everyday needs of the popular sectors. At a time of closed political space, the NGOs in many countries took shape with this fundamental relationship with the Church's work: they operated under the auspices of the Church, carrying out their activities primarily alongside the pastoral work. While the NGOs have since become increasingly secular, their proximity to the Church has left its mark on them.

The voluntary and committed character of the work carried out by NGO actors can be understood as related to their religious roots, together with the contexts of political authoritarianism. Many entities even began to operate discreetly as informal groups, only later taking on institutional identities. This, indeed, is a critical issue that would come to confront the NGOs: how to maintain their voluntary and militant character vis-à-vis the growing need for institutionalization brought on by the increasingly complex nature of their activities.

General Characteristics and Criteria for Differentiation

Institutional Relationships

Although the Church played a key role in the origin and development of NGOs in Latin America, it was not the only institution to affect their nature and actions.

As the processes of democratization advance in Latin America, and as the societies become more modernized and complex, the greater the range of actors to which the NGOs relate. The growth and consolidation of popular organizations (such as neighborhood and peasant associations) and trade unions, the fragmentation among political parties, the rise of social movements linked to the so-called minorities (ethnic groups, women), and "alternative" issues, such as ecology, have brought a series of actors onto the scene in Latin America, alongside which the NGOs have developed their work, with either integrated or informal working relations.

These diversified forms of institutional linkages are at the core of the nongovernmental organizations. Indeed, they move within their own space, but profoundly oriented toward other institutional contexts, such as churches, political parties, universities, trade unions, and the state.[6] They unfold in a field of relationships, the poles of which mark their limits.

Thus a favorite term in the NGO world, "alternative," which means to do that which is done, but in another place, using other methods. To do research, politics and, in a sense, religious work, but not as the universities, political parties, or churches would. "Alternative" implies a certain ambiguity, both affirming and negating, simultaneously, the sacred cows of our civilization. It affirms them insofar as they are still taken as a point of reference which, though criticized, is fundamental. It negates them in claiming to pose an "alternative."[7]

As we already indicated, the NGOs initially distanced themselves from the state, the relationship often being antagonistic. They opted in a radical fashion for civil society, acting at the grass-roots level of society, behind the back and beyond the reach of governmental authority. Nonetheless, with the advance of democratization, NGOs have adopted a new posture regarding this relationship. One of the current debates among the NGOs revolves around the questions: "Should we work in cooperation

with state programs? Should state financing be sought? Should we occupy within the state apparatus? In sum: at what level of activity, and
under what conditions, should NGOs relate to the state?"[8]

These are the questions currently being put forth; the answers have
been many. In this regard, a resolution passed at a January 1987 pioneer
meeting of thirty NGO leaders from nine Latin American countries declared: "In terms of relations with other social actors, the relationship
with the state has been accorded priority, based on the assumption that
the division between civil society and the state should not be seen as
absolute. The Centers define as one of their functions permanent denunciation and criticism. But the Centers also consider that they are in a
better position than state entities for developing creative proposals that
respond to the most fundamental social problems."[9] The resolution
carefully examines old positions, but seems to have a certain degree of
ambiguity.

Ambiguity is indeed one of the characteristics of NGOs, situated as
they are in this context of relationships. On the one hand, autonomy is
their trademark, independence one of the cornerstones of their discourse;
and they are oriented toward individualization, as nuclei of power in civil
society. On the other hand, however, they tend to revolve around other
institutional contexts and projects, social movements, and political currents, taking on the character of "satellites" that are "at the service of."
Often (and this stands out clearly when we carry out any survey on NGOs)
it is difficult to establish criteria for precisely classifying just what is and
is not an NGO, for their profile is fluid. There are many organizations
that oscillate between being "independent" and being "para-religious"
groups, "para-party" entities, "para-trade union" organizations, and so
forth. Loyalties and basic alliances, officials, principal interlocutors, origins, sources of financing are all discreet indications of certain links, links
which create ties of dependency that are perfectly compatible with institutional independence.[10]

In this network of ambiguous relationships, relations with financing
entities are a matter unto themselves, and will be taken up below.

I believe that the differences determined by the institutional relationships that have been accorded greatest priority can be an important crite-
rion for distinguishing among NGOs, including among NGOs from
different Latin American countries. Such institutional linkages vary enormously in accordance with the political situation, in which the numerous
actors play different roles with varying degrees of influence, in each society and at each point in time. A more detailed research project on this
range of linkages, based on the reality of each country, would certainly

lead us out of the realm of common features and into that of the specific differences detected in the universe of Latin American NGOs.

The Actors

An important set of individuals engaged in NGO work comes, naturally, from the Catholic Church (and, secondarily, from some Protestant churches). Many working in NGOs have a traditional Christian left background, often having been persecuted during periods of dictatorship, or hindered in their social work via direct control exercised by the Church hierarchy. At the same time, the "new pastoral mission" of the Church beginning in the 1970s, committed to grass-roots work, gave rise to a new generation of activists, who may act both pastorally and politically— as well as professionally—within the NGOs. One thus finds a certain number of priests, former priests, former nuns, and people who became involved in social action through "popular pastoral" work, active in NGOs.

Former members of traditional left organizations also form an important group within NGOs. Whether because of lack of other outlets for their political commitment or because of a crisis in their past activities, they find that they can continue working for social transformation alongside the popular sectors through the NGOs, which represent new and alternative organizational forms. The fact that many people exercise "dual militancy" does not threaten NGOs as institutions with their own work styles and realms of action, in which there may also be tension with clandestine parties, in an ambiguous dynamic of convergence and separation.

In general, all these people have university degrees, and often maintain their links with the academic community. Nevertheless, in the world of Latin American NGOs it is common to come across the concept of "isolation" from academic circles insofar as they fail to address social issues or produce knowledge in function of structural social change.

The NGOs thus took shape as institutions in which agents with somewhat different histories of organizational commitment would interact, institutions in which a variety of histories and points of reference would come together, with their own chemistry. Yet another contradictory aspect of NGOs is that they have increasingly come to present a professional option for those intellectuals who emerged from the middle class.

Between highly committed volunteer service and professionalization; between the Church, universities, and political parties; between Christianity and Marxism; between a conspiratorial brotherhood and institutional relations: it is amidst these contradictions that the agents of these *sui generis* entities make their way.

Outlook and Forms of Intervention

As was already mentioned, NGOs are outward-oriented, i.e., their existence is predicated on the relationships they establish with social sectors
and movements. They exist not in function of their own members (as would
be the case with associations or clubs), but rather "to serve," i.e., in function of other "beneficiary groups." Such service is carried out through
development projects or programs. "A development project is a planned
set of activities geared to satisfying the needs of poor sectors of the population. A development program includes several projects. Both imply the
availability and use of financial resources earmarked for this purpose,"[11]
such resources being provided by other entities.

These are the characteristics common to NGOs in Latin America, the
general basis of their actions. Nevertheless, the NGOs can be differentiated in some respects: the ways in which they relate to groups, i.e., the
various ways of "serving," can differ; the emphases they place on their
activities, depending on their ideas of just what constitutes an action for
development, may be different; and the groups they work with as well as
the types of projects they implement vary.

Relationships between NGOs and social movements take on two basic forms. Using the categories preferred by the NGOs themselves, their
work may take place either through "direct action" or through "external
advising" of the group. While most NGOs incorporate both of these forms
into their work, debates persist as to which is most appropriate for the
goals they pursue.

Direct intervention seems to be the most common and widespread
line of work. It is "grass-roots work," as "popular education" is called,
which presupposes living side by side on a daily and long-term basis with
the sectors to whom the work is reaching out. The promoters should be
open to learning with the group, adopting an egalitarian posture that com-
bats and questions the authoritarian traditions of relations with popular
sectors in Latin America that is typical not only of the dominant social
sectors but also of the traditional left. Motivating participation and autonomy of popular groups is a key objective of this method of work, which
is sensible, especially in a context such as Latin America, where there is
a strong authoritarian tradition and exclusion of popular sectors from
decision-making and full citizenship.

From the standpoint of the NGOs, issues relating to the role of promoters in their direct relations with the popular sectors have generated
much debate. These promoters are seen as new intellectuals who leave
academia to insert themselves, as part of an existential commitment, in
poor communities, intellectuals whose "purpose is no longer to lead a

process, but to place themselves at the service of the process. Their methods are no longer to teach, but learning-teaching-learning. They began to realize that theory is not only a task for intellectuals. The people (*o povo*) can and must create theory."[12]

These basic principles of "popular education," which, unfortunately, I can only treat superficially given the brevity of this chapter, have been questioned both among and from outside of the NGOs. "Populism," for example, by analogy with classic Russian populism, has been one of the accusatory terms set forth in this debate.

Based on postures critical to the current set forth above, or arising from other factors, there is another set of entities—clearly the minority—that dedicate themselves exclusively to what is called "external advising." These entities aim to promote service activities for the benefit of the grass-roots groups without this implying daily insertion of its members. They respond to requests for courses, lectures, and seminars on specific topics, usually for grass-roots leadership, but also for promoters from outside the groups. Many such organizations prioritize documentation and informational work geared to the immediate interests of social movements, understanding that democratization of information is an important task in Latin American processes of participation and popular autonomy. We must recognize that in general "external advising" and "direct intervention" are not mutually exclusive within a given NGO.

NGOs can also be distinguished by reference to the differential emphases of their work. They may place emphasis on activities aimed at directly meeting the needs of or improving conditions for their target population, be these material or cultural conditions and needs. Or their action may be geared to long-term structural transformation of society.

The first case, addressing living conditions, includes economic projects, such as initiatives regarding alternative forms of production and marketing in rural areas, establishment of artisan workshops in the city, work with cooperatives, and even projects involving improved health care, as alternative medicine and preservation of traditional treatments and cures. In the second case, work for structural change, emphasis would be on organizational and training activities.

Generally speaking, these two types of action are both found in a single entity. One of the current debates regarding NGOs revolves around the possibility of setting up economically-oriented projects—which perforce are small-scale and local—in such a way as to have a broader impact on the society. Often the usefulness and meaning of these small projects is questioned in terms of the lack of organizational benefits or of a change in consciousness of the sectors where the projects are carried out, in addition to their limited scope in terms of the very purposes they set for themselves, i.e., improving the material living conditions of the group. Evaluations of these activities are often negative from the standpoint of popular education, to the extent that they turn inward and in several cases compete, only to accentuate differences within the sector in which they work, since they promote material improvements just for small groups. Latin American NGOs have questioned the encouragement of such projects, with evaluative parameters based on productivity or measurable material results.

Some popular education organizations have sought to integrate these two levels of activity, linking the economic projects to the more general objectives of organization and leadership training, apparently with considerable success. One example—and there are many—would be the implementation of community fields for raising crops in the case of smallholders without legal titles (*posseiros*) who are threatened with land seizures, and whose collective defense of their lands is at stake. In this case, the necessary economic resistance is closely linked with the establishment of organizational forms that have a positive impact on the political resistance effort.

Thus, various types of projects are implemented by the NGOs; one could differentiate among them based on their diverse specializations. Projects directly affecting material living conditions, involving economic activities, and improving public health were all mentioned above. Some entities also work in communication, publishing information on current political events, or analyses of various social issues; publishing primers written in an easily accessible style on a variety of problems confronted by popular sectors; or producing videos, films, or other educational audiovisual materials. Other entities specialize in promoting initiatives related to human rights. Some opt to work in advising and motivating popular organizations, while others place a greater priority on leadership, education and training. Research, generally of a participatory nature, is also carried out, although this is a more limited field among NGO activities.

NGOs also differ from one another as regards the sectors that benefit from their activities. It is easy to imagine that there is no lack of dominated and needy groups of various sorts throughout Latin America. NGO actions are aimed primarily at rural workers, industrial workers (in certain countries), and slum dwellers living in marginal areas of the large cities. But there are other beneficiaries, including women, minors, blacks, Indians, fishermen, and migrants.

Clearly there is a wide range of activities; but this seems not to correspond to a similar number of "types" of NGOs. In effect, specialization in a single area seems not to be the rule among NGOs, most of which combine several kinds of projects.

There seems to be greater specialization among beneficiary groups. Our research on NGOs in Brazil is revealing in this regard. We found three main categories of population to which Brazilian NGOs' projects are geared: "popular sectors" (peasants, rural wage earners, industrial workers, *favela* dwellers, etc.); women; and blacks. This categorization, while constructing and reinforcing the social existence of certain categories ("the people," "blacks," and "women") refers to different practices, to specific conceptions concerning the realm of "the political," and to diverse institutional forms.

We believe that here too there must be additional and more profound research to account for the different "specializations" of the NGOs in each country and region of Latin America. Such research must bear in mind the ethnic and social differences among these countries and regions.

International Relations

Latin American Networks

Forming linkages among NGOs working in social promotion in Latin America is a top agenda item for such entities.

The establishment of relations among NGOs is part of their operational tradition in Latin America. Nonetheless, relations among NGOs have always been based on particular and short-term matters: promoting conferences, establishing more or less permanent fora for discussing common practices, exchanging information, and the like. Such networks are generally issue-oriented, or functional, with only an incipient degree of institutionalization. There are also networks that form naturally around institutions that are common points of reference, such as churches.

We may think that it is in the nature of NGOs to resist formal networks and coordination: NGOs are jealous of their autonomy and independence, and plurality is a basic aspect of their existence. Establishment of networks could imply centralization and control, which are contrary to their very outlook.

Nevertheless, it seems that such skepticism is being overcome of late. The NGOs are going through a process of self-knowledge and self-affirmation, as a set of institutions with common interests and perspectives. They are beginning to perceive the importance of coordinating their efforts in a more permanent fashion, even on the basis of general projects for social transformation.

Although there is clearly a trend in this direction, as of yet there are no specific results in terms of establishing those more formalized networks. That process is in its initial phase. Indeed, the recent research projects aimed at better understanding the world of NGOs constitute an important step in establishing such an identity and making possible such linkages.

Promotion of large conferences of NGO leaders in Latin America is a recent phenomenon, reflecting such concerns. At stake in this effort are linkages that not only go beyond specific common projects, but are based on more general issues. The discussions have revolved around issues such as institutional problems of NGOs; relationships with funding agencies; relations with other social actors, in each context; and the contribution of NGOs to the process of democratization or to deepening democracy.

Another discussion also in its initial stages attempts to identify NGOs' capacity for opening the way for participation in international relations. This discussion raises the possibility of NGOs acting in the sphere of what is called "informal diplomacy" establishing specific channels and conditions for international relations separate from relations among states, governments, corporations, and other powerful institutions, such as churches and political parties.[13]

Relations with Funding Agencies

Relations with funding agencies are, of course, key in determining the actions of NGOs in Latin America. They deserve a more profound analysis that is beyond the scope of this chapter. I have chosen to simply point out a few operational matters as they are currently posed by Latin American NGOs themselves.

First, the NGOs criticize the lack of coordination among the international cooperation agencies, on the one hand, and between them and Latin American NGOs, on the other.[14] There is a need for a more systematic and institutionalized financing policy. Linkages among the institutions are based on individualized, personalized relationships between representatives of both the financing agencies and the NGOs. The need for greater institutionalization in the NGO world has also been raised.

The bilateral relations between foreign and national entities have been criticized for being superficial and short-sighted: financing granted does not correspond to individual projects, visits of supervisors from foreign projects are short and superficial, and their knowledge of the national context is generally quite limited.

All this has an impact on evaluation methods for the work carried out by the NGOs; such methods are often criticized for being unsuited to the objectives claimed by the entities being "judged." A communication breakdown results at that level, with the local entities finding their way out of the problems by failing to reveal the full implications of their activities. Establishing greater space for dialogue at this level has been discussed. Structurally affecting all these issues is the asymmetry inherent in these relations. The Latin American NGOs' dependency on external financing programs over which they have no control gives rise to profound insecurity in terms of the possibility of undertaking projects in which interests of sectors outside the NGOs come into play. Postures reflecting the "political arrogance" that is frequently the norm in relations between agencies from the North and Latin America—despite the good faith of funding agency representatives and the good intentions of their discourse—have been discussed in this context. The counterpart attitude is the posture of acceptance and passivity generally found in third world organizations, as traditional relations of inequality are reproduced at other levels.

The resolutions approved at the conference of Latin American NGOs mentioned above deal with these issues, concluding that the NGOs should stand before the international financial agencies "in a dignified position, as equals, demanding respect for national sovereignty and institutional autonomy. The Centers strive to serve as means through which the developed countries return to the developing countries part of the resources taken from the developing countries, and which continue to be taken from them year after year. The Centers shall endeavor to win the cooperation of the agencies and even of the center countries in bringing about more just international relations."[15] These are but a few of the main issues currently being discussed among Latin American NGOs regarding their relations with funding agencies in the North.

Final Issues

What is the role of NGOs in the current Latin American sociopolitical scene? What is their future given the transformations under way in Latin America?

We return here perforce to the matter of regional diversity within Latin America. On the one hand, there are countries with liberal democratic regimes, and those experiencing redemocratization, as in the Southern Cone (Brazil, Argentina, Uruguay). There are still some regimes based on political authoritarianism, such as Chile. Finally, there are countries with revolutionary situations, such as Nicaragua. Different political situations no doubt determine diverse functions and forms among NGOs.

NGOs' actions, however, appear to be guided by a basic characteristic: they are always oriented to the strengthening of civil society. This takes on special meaning when dealing with societies that have strong authoritarian traditions, and which traditionally exclude most of the population from access to participation, cultural expression, indeed to the minimal material living conditions.

The vocation of pluralism and autonomy characteristic of the NGOs in Latin America indicates the importance of their role in the consolidation of democratic forms of government. Their specific forms of taking action, their proliferation, and their recent trend to forming more permanent networks and forms of exchange raise the question as to their weight as actors in the sociopolitical panorama within the various countries of Latin America and internationally.

Notes

1. Mario Padrón, "Los centros de promoción y la cooperación internacional al desarrollo en América Latina," mimeo (Buenos Aires, Argentina: Europe–Latin America: Political Relations and Development Cooperation, international seminar, 1986), 1.

2. Joaquín Esteva, "Situación y perspectivas de las redes de organizaciones no gubernamentales que operan en México, apoyando al desarrollo rural y las organizaciones populares," mimeo (Mexico City, April 1985).

3. Padrón, "Los centros de promoción."

4. Rubem Fernandes and Leilah Landim, *UM Perfil das ONGs no Brasil* (Rio de Janeiro, Brazil: Comunicacões do Iser, Year 5, No. 22, November 1986).

5. Rodrigo Egaña, "Las ONG de cooperación al desarrollo en las relaciones Europa-América Latina," mimeo (Chile: PET, n.d.), 3.

6. Rubem Fernandes, *Sem Fins Lucrativos* (Rio de Janeiro, Brazil: Comunicacões do Iser, Year 4, No. 15, July 1985).

7. Ibid., 15.

8. "Encontro Nacional de Centros de Promocão Brasileiros" (National Conference of Brazilian Centers for Promotion) (1986), 36.

9. "Encuentro Sudamericano de Centros de Promoción" (South American Conference of Centers for Promotion), unpublished document (Statiaia, Brazil, 1987).

10. Fernandes and Landim, *UM Perfil das ONGs no Brasil*.

11. Mario Padrón, *Cooperación al Desarrollo y Movimiento Popular: Las Asociaciones Privadas de Desarrollo* (Lima, Peru: DESCO, 1982).

12. Marcos Arruda, *El Papel de las Organizaciones no Gubernamentales en la Perspectiva de la Democracia Participativa* (Rome: Third International Consultation FFHC/AD, 1985), 9.

13. Sergio Spoerer, "Cooperación política en América Latina," mimeo (Buenos Aires, Argentina: Europe–Latin America: Political Relations and Development Cooperation, international seminar, 1986).

14. Edmundo Garafulic, "Grupo de trabajo funcional: Interrelación entre las ECDIS-NG y las ONGDs," mimeo (Cochabamba, Bolivia, 1986).

15. "Encuentro Sudamericano de Centros de Promoción."

IV

Consequences of Democratization:
Case Studies in Change

11

Brazil under Collor: Anatomy of a Crisis

Ben Ross Schneider

To better understand the consequences of reintroducing the democratic model in Latin America and the difficulties that democratic leadership faces, it is useful to explore democratic regimes in practice. Few governments have received more attention in the United States and the region than that of Fernando Collor de Mello, who took office as president of Brazil in 1990. Ben Ross Schneider, a professor of political science at Northwestern University and the author of Politics within the State: Elite Bureaucrats and Industrial Policy in Authoritarian Brazil *(1991), has analyzed the Brazilian case in considerable detail, suggesting in this chapter that the disorganized masses were largely responsible for electing Collor to office. At the same time, however, Schneider argues that unless these groups form stronger linkages and organize themselves formally, it will be difficult for them to maintain the political pressure necessary to keep social justice, an important ingredient in Latin American democratization, at the forefront of the government agenda.*

On March 15, 1990, Fernando Collor de Mello became president of a country on the verge of collapse. Inflation—the most easily measured indicator of economic chaos—had reached a monthly rate of 80 percent. Conditions for sustainable development, meanwhile, were completely lacking. In politics, the indicators were less precise but the crisis no less severe. The preceding government of José Sarney had left office in universal disrepute and, since his was the first civilian government after twenty-one years of military rule, the fledgling civilian regime suffered by association. Moreover, the first round in Brazil's presidential elections had eliminated the centrist candidates, and the winners—Collor and

From the *World Policy Journal* (Spring 1991): 321–23, 325–47. Reprinted by permission of the *World Policy Journal*.

Lula (Luis Ignácio da Silva), the candidate of the Workers Party (PT)—
subsequently polarized and inflamed electoral politics. Still less visible
and measurable was the nation's corrosive social crisis. The root causes
were numbing poverty and glaring inequality, manifested in headline stories about rising homelessness, disease, and violence.

Any of these crises would be daunting to a new president; together
they could easily be overwhelming. Yet, paradoxically, they could also
give an energetic, innovative, new government greater leeway. Runaway
inflation generated a consensus that the incoming government would have
to take drastic measures. Collor's austerity program consequently provoked less opposition than comparable measures had in the past, even
though the social costs were higher. Similarly, the successive and accumulated failures of policies throughout the 1980s opened the possibility
for (and weakened resistance to) a profound shift in development strategy. The risks in March 1990 may thus have been enormous, but so were
the opportunities. A new president could go down in flames—or in
history.

By the close of Collor's first year in office, the former prospect seemed
more likely, though not inevitably so. The calendar year ended with one
of Brazil's worst recessions of the century and with an all-time record for
inflation (1,795 percent, though only about 300 percent since Collor took
office). Collor's plan to revive the country's economy had not succeeded,
and this failure, in turn, revealed how shallow his political support was,
especially among the political and economic elite. Business interests might
still remember how glad they were that he had defeated Lula, but mostly
they were complaining that Collor and his team were arrogant, inexperienced, technocratic, and intransigent. Congress was increasingly unwill-
ing to be railroaded into abdicating its legislative functions in deference
to Collor's emergency decrees. Collor thus entered 1991 in a very isolated position.

The most that could be said for the new government as it neared the
end of its first year in office was that it had pulled the country back a bit
from the brink. But the yawning chasm was still dangerously close. Although inflation was no longer completely out of control, the resumption
of economic development was nowhere on the horizon. The government
enjoyed greater legitimacy than had Sarney's, but its initial popularity
and credibility were fast receding. Democracy itself was not in immediate jeopardy, but it could hardly be deemed robust. And in social terms,
those who were hit hardest by stagflation were the ones least able to
afford it.

Although the news coming out of Brazil in 1990 was mostly economic (and mostly bad), the real story was Collor's inability to muster

sufficient political force at any level—through popular mobilization, party alliances, or elite compacts—to tackle inflation, recession, and inequality. Collor had dashed hopes that he would deliver a single knockout, karate blow (Collor's preferred metaphor) to Brazil's intractable and intertwined social, economic, and political crises. The reasons for his government's failure are numerous; they include errors in style, inexperience, technocratic excesses, miscalculations in negotiation, and distortions in the country's political system and social organization.

Although Collor was not the best thing that could have happened to Brazil at the opening of the new decade, 1990 was not the story of failure foretold. The new government missed important opportunities and misdiagnosed the severity of the crises. (To be fair, the crises themselves may not be solvable in the space of a year to two using conventional policy instruments. But if that's the case, it is the government's responsibility to fashion tools adequate to the task of long-term economic revival.) The prospects for the future are not bright but could be otherwise. Those in the Collor government have margin to rethink, regroup, and replan. What remains to be seen is how much Collor and his collaborators are able and willing to adjust, and how effectively other social and political actors can force them to do so. . . .

Conservative Modernization

Collor has tried to avoid labels and cultivate an aura of mystery about his ultimate intentions. But by July 1990 it was possible to start patching together an answer to the question of what his long-term project was. In its first three months the new government's output of programs, promises, rulings, and provisional measures (which permit the president to rule by decree) was impressive. Most emergency measures formed part of the Collor Plan to reduce inflation, but other policies began to give concrete shape to Collor's longer-term strategy and project.[1]

Some have defined Collor's project as liberal or neoliberal.[2] Collor, by this reckoning, is just the tardy backwash of the liberal wave that swept the world in the 1980s. The usual agenda would include dismantling the state; eliminating protection; and destroying unions, cartels, and other impediments to markets. Indeed, indicators of liberalism are not hard to find in Collor's discourse, the arguments of his economic advisers, and many of his longer-term policies. He is an open admirer of former British prime minister Margaret Thatcher and has promised to bring "true capitalism" to Brazil. Among his early measures were personnel cuts, tariff reductions, and the removal of many wage, price, and exchange controls.

These and other policies were market oriented, it is true, but it would be an exaggeration to read into them any abiding ideological beliefs. Collor and his team were too pragmatic and instrumental to merit the label liberal, especially in comparison to radicals such as the Chicago boys in [Augusto] Pinochet's Chile. Most of Collor's policies were gradual, partial, and reversible. The economic team was also heterodox enough to resort to very unliberal measures when deemed necessary for other purposes, such as reducing inflation. The major feature of the March 1990 stabilization program, for instance, entailed the largest confiscation ever of financial assets in Brazil. Further deviation from pure liberalism is evident in the government's verbal commitment to an expanded welfare role for the state.

In fact, social democracy is another label sometimes applied to Collor's project.[3] From this perspective policies such as deregulation and privatization are seen to relieve the state of its development responsibilities so that it can better perform classic welfare functions. Yet it is a mistake to read too much into Collor's support of the state's welfare role. Every political campaign takes up the liturgy of health, education, and housing, if only because these areas are so woefully underfunded, and no one in Brazil would publicly defend a retraction of the state's welfare functions. In part because it is so consensual, the social welfare state cannot be said to constitute a project in the same way it did in postwar Europe. In Brazil it is not based on the triumph of leftist parties and affiliated unions, nor does it yet imply any significant redistribution of wealth. To the contrary, the Collor government's short-term stabilization measures have been highly regressive, and its efforts to rein in the developmental state have yet to translate into an expansion of the welfare state.

Conservative modernization is the most appropriate label for Collor's project.[4] What makes it conservative is the absence of any indication that Collor wants to alter basic property and power relations. Agrarian reform is off the agenda, as are radical proposals for income redistribution. And Collor shows little interest in empowering popular or worker organizations.

Collor's project is modernizing in the sense that it takes selected items (new for Brazil) from the liberal, ecological, and social democratic agendas. It also appears modern in its attacks on oligarchs, oligopolies, and clientelism. In principle it seeks to redistribute power within the elite away from the old to the modern; from protected, inefficient, paternalistic capitalists to new dynamic managers; from clientelistic, good ol' boys in congress to young independents. The modernizing policies—administrative reform, privatization, trade liberalization, deregulation, and debureaucratization—largely bear on the state and its intervention in the economy and the polity. Many of these policies would be priorities for a neoliberal government, but the slow pace and restricted scope of implementation in 1990 betrayed a different motivation: the goal was the creation of a lean, agile state that relied more on indirect forms of intervention.

The design of the privatization program, a policy dear to liberals and even some social democrats, illustrates the modernizing but conservative impulses in the Collor government. The government announced early on an ambitious program for selling off state-owned firms, but then slowed implementation and ultimately did not sell anything in 1990.[5] The core of the program was the sale of large steel firms. Many of these firms had already been targeted for sale by the Sarney government, and a majority of elite respondents in a 1990 survey favored turning them over to private owners.[6] Hence, privatization—Collor-style—did not represent a dramatic departure from Sarney's program, as a truly liberal course would require; nor has it alienated developmentalists. In fact, those in charge of the program claim to want to reform (and thereby conserve) rather than destroy Brazil's developmental state. Sales are designed in principle to generate maximum revenues to contribute to the pragmatic goals of deficit reduction and the retiring of government debt rather than to increasing welfare spending or redistributing share ownership, as is the case with more radical programs in other countries.

The privatization program also clearly reveals the government's tendency toward technocracy and the limitations of such a tendency. The government's goal is to "technify" and depoliticize the process as much as possible. This has resulted in the elimination of potential allies (in congress, state governments, the private sector, and unions) from the decision-making process—allies who might otherwise compromise a coalition of supporters for the program. The government has gone so far as to "privatize privatization": consulting firms have been called in to determine who gets to buy how much of each firm and at what price. The strategy met with little real opposition in 1990 because the government did not sell anything. When actual sales begin imposing real losses and gains, as any privatization inevitably does, the issue will become far more emotionally and politically charged. Then the isolation the government cultivated in 1990, rather than serve as protection for the planners, will be a political liability.

In order to succeed, a project also has to work well as a medium-term political strategy. Although Collor has not yet used his project as the basis for building a dependable coalition, conservative modernization has great potential in this regard, as suggested by the support (albeit ambivalent) the government attracted in its first year. The project appealed to opposing groups, with different groups supporting different pieces of it.

The conservatives, established clientelistic politicians, and large business groups, on the one hand, were "trapped" in the government camp. Collor was by no means their first choice, but he was certainly preferable to Lula. Initially, therefore, they tolerated Collor's occasional attacks on them and their bases of support as long as he forestalled more radical alternatives. Collor is, after all, one of them. The modernizers, on the other hand, were willing to ignore occasional right-wing lapses as long as Collor continued to promote reforms.[7] Though internally contradictory, this strategy is one of the few that could work politically for Collor. A completely modern, liberal, social democratic, or green project could not attract more than minority support; given the high expectations for change, a more explicitly conservative project would also be untenable.

The composition of Collor's cabinet was a clear reflection of the contradictory elements that make up conservative modernization. The cabinet comprised a mix of young modernizers, old conservatives, and assorted cronies and colleagues. The heads of the major economic agencies are predominantly thirtysomething and gung-ho on modernizing capitalism.[8] The conservatives include several older men in economic policymaking and several who were associated with the military regime, such as Ozires Silva in infrastructure, Carlos Chiarelli in education, and Jarbas Passarinho in justice. (The nomination of Passarinho to the Justice Ministry in October put to rest any remaining doubts about Collor's strong ties to conservatives. Passarinho served as minister in three military governments; in particular, he signed the Institutional Act No. 5, the formal act that in 1968 inaugurated the most repressive phase of the authoritarian regime.)

Administrative reform—one of the most significant reforms of 1990—reveals how politically delicate modernization can be and how little sensitivity the Collor government showed when implementing reform measures. In an attempt to marry administrative reform to the goal of reducing the fiscal deficit, Collor in his first months ordered all government agencies to cut 30 percent of their employees. Modernizers—many of them in the executive bureaucracy—recognize the need to cut unproductive personnel, increase efficiency, and generally overhaul Brazil's public administration. But Collor's across-the-board cuts were indiscriminate, affecting the best and the worst of agencies alike. Consequently, Collor alienated productive bureaucrats—many of whom are responsible for implementing other modernizing policies—without visibly improving efficiency. By the end of 1990, although the government had eliminated less than a third of the 360,000 jobs it promised to cut, it had nonetheless managed to lower morale, motivation, and productivity throughout the executive branch.[9] Modernization requires a stronger, more qualified, better paid, and more engaged bureaucracy, not an anemic one.

Collor also eliminated half of the sixty-five thousand political appointments in the federal bureaucracy and excluded politicians from filling most of the rest.[10] In so doing he antagonized his clientelist conservative supporters who had built their careers on such patronage.[11] "How," they asked (publicly at times), "can we continue to support your legislation if you are destroying our political bases?" Previous conservative modernizers solved this dilemma by demarcating modern and clientelistic parts of the government. Collor has yet to make an equivalent arrangement, and has consequently lost support from conservative clientelists.

Conservative modernization has worked before in Brazil, both as a project for capitalist industrialization and as a strategy of government. Getúlio Vargas and Juscelino Kubitschek—two of Brazil's more popular presidents—were both adept modernizers. In the 1940s and 1950s they created a developmental state, modern at the time, without disrupting underlying power and property relations. Governing with the support of the landed elite, they used tariff protection, subsidies, and state enterprises to drive industrialization. And the country's long-lasting military regime (1964 to 1985) was also explicit in its desire to further rapid capitalist industrialization without disrupting social relations. Conservative modernization has succeeded in Brazil because it builds bridges between groups in nominally opposing camps and inhibits the formation of a united opposition. These historical examples demonstrate that economic stability and political acumen, especially in negotiation and coalition-building with elite groups, are essential factors in this strategy—factors that were lacking in Collor's first year.

Conservative modernization has worked before and it could work again. The immediate obstacle is political. Collor was unable in 1990 to patch together a coalition of reliable supporters of the project, despite clear signals that powerful groups were willing to join such a coalition. Collor's offensive style and the technocratic urges of those implementing modernizing reforms alienated most potential supporters. As one observer noted, the Collor administration "knows what to do but does not know how to do it."[12]

Another problem is that conservative modernization requires reasonable macroeconomic stability and debt relief, both of which are at least a year or so away.[13] Thus, as a development strategy it is difficult to know what Collor's project might be able to deliver, although recent Mexican experiences offer a sobering glimpse of a likely outcome. While President Carlos Salinas [de Gortari], and Miguel de la Madrid [Hurtado] before him, both managed to reorient state intervention in the economy, reduce inflation, and slow the outflow of resources to service the debt,

Mexican-style conservative modernization has yet to deliver any improvement in per-capita income or social equality. If in both Mexico and Brazil excessive and archaic state intervention became a major obstacle to growth in the 1980s, then modernizing the state is now necessary. It may not, however, be sufficient to attract the requisite private investment.

Stabilization and Elections

When Collor first assumed office in early 1990, the severity of the economic crisis gave him a free hand in stabilization policies. He shocked many supporters—especially liberals and the middle class—by confiscating (officially "freezing") financial assets worth close to a quarter of the country's gross domestic product (GDP). But the Collor Plan initially enjoyed great popularity. The freeze and other drastic measures—such as tax increases, suspension of subsidies, and budget cuts—drove monthly inflation down to single digits for the first three months. Later, Collor's economic team added a traditional monetary squeeze.

By September, however, inflation had climbed to 12.6 percent and the economy was plunging headlong into recession—much to the government's surprise and dismay. Before taking office, Collor had stated that he wanted to make the right indignant and leave the left perplexed. The March stabilization package initially had just that effect. However, by year end the left was not quite so confused, many more than those on the right were indignant, and according to ex-finance minister Bresser Pereira, it was Collor's economic team that was perplexed.[14] GDP by then had fallen 4.4 percent (the second worst decline on record), led by sharp declines in construction, agriculture, and industry (–8.9 percent). Per-capita income had dropped to the level of 1979. Business was laying off hundreds of thousands of workers (200,000 in São Paulo, or about 10 percent of the work force), and the average real salary in industry and commerce had dropped 29 percent between January and September.[15]

Several factors were responsible for pushing monthly inflation back into the high teens. Foremost, in the government's view, was the oil-price shock resulting from the Persian Gulf crisis. Economists outside the government were more likely to single out errors in policy design and implementation, however. The freezing of financial assets was excessive at first, unnecessarily paralyzing a lot of economic activity. The government then overreacted and unfroze too many assets, thereby allowing the deflationary pressures of reduced liquidity to dissipate. Overall control of the money supply was also erratic in 1990, with huge increases in the later months of the year.

The lifting of many long-standing price controls was another factor contributing to inflation. Although the government attempted to use jaw-boning, the threat of imports, and the courts to stop the monopolies and oligopolies from taking advantage of the new climate, these measures were insufficient to discourage further price increases. For one thing, the commercial opening failed until the end of the year to promote an influx of imports. High interest rates, like the 100 percent real rate of interest Collor introduced in December 1990, also failed to curb inflation. Rather than serve as an incentive to reduce consumption and investment and thereby ease pressure on prices, the high rates became a cost component that firms simply passed on to their buyers.

Expectations also worked against lowering inflation. Business, for instance, feared a price freeze (rightly so, as it turned out), and reckoned that the best way to prepare for it was to have prices as high as possible in relative terms when the freeze hit. In addition, the measures the government employed to alleviate budgetary pressures on inflation—freezing public sector salaries and confiscating assets—produced a budget surplus of one-half of 1 percent of GDP (not the 2 percent Collor promised in March). Since these measures cannot be repeated again in 1991, inflationary fiscal pressures are expected to return.

Diagnoses differ, but by November even monetarists were warning that a monetary and fiscal squeeze was not enough. The government had held a marathon meeting in June to try to work out a "national under-standing" among business associations, unions, and the government, but then dropped the idea in the face of what it considered to be unacceptable union and business demands, and in light of the early success of the Collor Plan. In September, Collor, with the encouragement of the progressive wing of São Paulo industry, directed his ministers of economy and justice to reconvene tripartite discussions. From September through December, representatives of business, labor, and the government met five times, with time out for the elections in October and November.

When triparite negotiations appeared deadlocked, capital and labor met separately and hammered out an agreement, but the government found the terms unacceptable. Basically, negotiations fell apart over the issues of salaries and interest rates. The unions wanted some form of indexation to protect workers from continuing inflation, which by December had climbed to 19 percent. Business wanted some relief from high interest rates. Collor and his economic team, however, refused to open their monetary policy to negotiation and adamantly opposed indexation. By Christmas, negotiations had collapsed.

The failure to achieve an agreement demonstrated most clearly the fundamental flaw of the Collor Plan: the lack of negotiated mechanisms to induce economic agents to collaborate. The breakdown of negotiations was, however, one of the more expected results of the year.[16] Overall, societal organizations in Brazil speak for only a minority of business and labor interests and lack internal unity. Only around 15 percent of the labor force is organized, and the labor movement is highly fractured. The Central Única dos Trabalhadores is the country's largest labor confederation, but it has been a reluctant and infrequent participant in the round table discussions. While business confederations represent a larger proportion of the business community, they are split along sectoral lines and between old corporatist structures and new dissident groups.

The government bears more direct responsibility for the failure of the talks, however. Many in the economic team evinced a liberal aversion to organized capitalism. Moreover, government inexperience and ineptitude, which caused many embarrassments in 1990, were particularly damaging to the negotiations. Government spokespersons, for instance, were wont to engage in fruitless verbal abuse of business leaders. This took its toll. So much confidence was lost in the government as a good-faith negotiator that when, in December, Collor responded to the demands negotiated separately between labor and capital with a proposal of a mere 3 percent wage bonus, the other participants concluded [that] Collor was not seriously interested in achieving a negotiated settlement. Generally speaking, the government simply refused to compromise its policies, so there was ultimately little to negotiate.

Surprisingly, failures on the stabilization front did not translate into major defeat for the government in the October elections. Although the ineffectiveness of the Collor Plan was by then becoming apparent (and was quite clear by the time of the second-round gubernatorial elections in mid-November), Collor succeeded in keeping his plan and his government from becoming major campaign issues. The structure of power in Brazil facilitated Collor's efforts. Governors, especially in the large, rich states, have throughout this century been far more powerful than senators and deputies. The gubernatorial campaigns therefore overshadowed the legislative races and, for the first time in decades, these were local contests rather than referenda on the president and the regime, as they had been during military rule.

It may also have helped that the public was easily overwhelmed by the number of contests: 27 governorships, a third of the Senate (31 seats), all of the Chamber of Deputies (503 deputies), and 969 state deputies were up for election in October. All told, more than 70,000 candidates vied for office.[17] Turnover was high—close to two-thirds of the old congress did not return—and yet the composition of the new congress was still favorable to Collor. The PRN (Party for National Reconstruction), the convenience party Collor used for his presidential campaign, gained some seats (41) in the lower house. The real winners, however, were the parties of the right and center: the PDS [Democratic Social Party], the PMDB [Brazilian Democratic Movement Party], and the PFL (Liberal Front Party). The PDS and the PFL will presumably continue to support Collor, and together with the PRN, the PTB (Brazilian Labor Party), and half a dozen other minor parties, they give Collor a slim majority in the Chamber of Deputies and close to a majority in the Senate. In the previous congress these parties scored high in terms of *governismo* (willingness to support the executive), and, with the exception of the PTB, high in their support of conservatism.[18]

The major opposition parties, the PT and the PDT [Democratic Labor Party], increased their small numbers significantly, demonstrating continuing national strength after the strong showing of their presidential candidates in 1989. However, with 82 deputies between them, these parties are still very much in the minority. Furthermore, they proved to be a surprisingly ineffective opposition to Collor in the previous congress.[19] The unexpected loser was the center-left Party of Brazilian Social Democracy (PSDB), down from 60 to 37 deputies, which many had expected would enter into some accord with Collor had it fared better.

Parties that have voted with Collor before won enough seats to give him a majority, but this does not mean that Collor goes into his second year with a reliable legislative coalition. Color has no formal alliance and has shown little willingness to engage in the unrestrained horse trading that Sarney relied on with the same parties. Nonetheless, the fact that Collor came through the legislative elections without facing a preponderance of uncompromising opponents has to be considered a major political success. It remains to be seen whether he will be able to capitalize on it.

The results of the gubernatorial elections were nominally less favorable, but they did not translate into implacable opposition to Collor. In the most populous and industrialized cities (São Paulo, Rio de Janeiro, Rio Grande do Sul, Minas Gerais), Collor's supporters lost or his declared opponents won. Some in the opposition celebrated the results as a resounding defeat for Collor and his recessionary stabilization policies. There was likely some vote of general discontent, especially in the second-round elections in November, but most candidates shied away from basing their campaigns on national issues. Most pro-Collor candidates were underdogs or lost by small margins, and the fact that they lost a midterm election can hardly be called a resounding defeat. Moreover, even declared opponents began making conciliatory gestures after their victories.[20] Collor still has a lot of room to maneuver and negotiate with the new governors who took office in March.

On January 31, 1991, the day before the new legislature convened, Collor's economic team announced a new package of measures immediately dubbed Collor Plan II. Inflation for January was about 20 percent and the expectation in the financial markets was that it would climb to 30 percent in February. The government's response was to de-index more fully the formal economy and to freeze wages and prices, despite its almost weekly promises throughout 1990 that it would never adopt a freeze. The government forbade the use of indexing clauses in contracts and devised a new instrument for the monthly adjustment of savings accounts, the Taxa Referencial de Juros (Reference Rate of Interest), based on expectations in the financial markets of future inflation. The idea, long defended in principle by many economists, was to do away with indexation that is based on past inflation—a practice that never allows the economy to escape or "forget" past inflation.

The reaction to this fifth shock plan in six years was mostly negative. The largest daily newspaper, the *Folha de São Paulo*, published a biting editorial on February 2 and gave it particular emphasis by putting it on the front page. It also published a snap survey showing that many more people disapproved of Collor Plan II than [of] its predecessor plan. Another poll conducted in the country's major cities one week later found that 40 percent considered the measures "bad" versus 29 percent who thought they were "good," and 58 percent felt the measures left them worse off compared with the 56 percent in March 1990 who felt better off under Collor I.

Although it will take months for the economy to digest Collor II, there were few early indications that it would contain inflation more than temporarily. Credibility is crucial to the success of any price freeze. Otherwise, retailers will ignore the restrictions (the government cannot police them all) and consumers will rush to buy goods in the belief that the freeze will not last, thereby provoking shortages and fueling inflationary pressures. A week after the decrees, 49 percent of the public surveyed felt the freeze was not working; another 36 percent thought it was only partly working. A month later the proportions increased to 57 and 38 percent respectively. Surprisingly, the rejection of the plan had little impact on Collor's popularity; it suffered only a slight decline. Despite repeated economic reverses, Collor's approval rating has remained remarkably stable since June 1990.[21]

Since his election, then, Collor and his political Calvinism have enjoyed survey and electoral success, though more through omission than commission. The return of local politics kept Collor out of the limelight and helped elect a potentially sympathetic legislature, though Collor has yet to figure out how to turn this potential into solid congressional support. The same shortcoming was even more evident in the failed attempt at "national understanding," but the short-run consequences in that case were more dire. Collor II was an attempt to substitute a technocratic decree on incomes and sacrifices for a negotiated social pact. Past experience in Brazil suggests, however, that without a broad collective agreement on stabilization, individuals will find ways to get around top-down decrees.

Democratic Consolidation and Social Apartheid

Enough time has passed since Collor assumed the presidency to be able to assess how well his government is tackling the legacy he inherited: weakened democracy and staggering poverty. Collor is the first directly elected president in twenty-nine years. His inauguration in 1990, as opposed to Sarney's in 1985, marks the true end of the authoritarian era. As one might expect, therefore, Collor's legitimacy is a source of enormous strength. Yet, Collor has sometimes used this legitimacy in ways that could inhibit the consolidation of democratic rule.

Collor's exercise of power, though within the bounds of the new constitution, may very well be weakening Brazil's legislatures and party system and slowing the institution-building required for democratic consolidation.[22] The constitution allows the president to decree "provisional measures" that take effect immediately and remain in effect until congress amends, rejects, or turns them into ordinary legislation. When Collor entered office, he used the economic crisis as justification for virtual rule by decree, forcing congress into a reactive role. By the time congress went into summer recess in December 1990, Collor had forced it to consider 143 provisional measures. This executive bombardment kept lawmakers from enacting the enabling legislation necessary to put into effect 160 articles of the constitution, not to mention fulfilling other important legislative responsibilities.[23]

Collor sought to improve relations with congress by nominating Senator Passarinho to the Justice Ministry. He saw in Passarinho a respected legislator who might weave together a supportive congressional coalition. Passarinho's predecessor, Bernardo Cabral, was also famed for his brokering skills in congress, but as minister he committed serious legal and constitutional mistakes, and also carried on an ill-fated love affair with the economics minister, Zélia Cardoso de Mello (no relation to Collor).[24] What eventually cost Cabral his credibility with congress, however, was his inability to deliver anything to congressional supporters of the government. Thus, while Collor is willing to nominate congressional standouts, he is not yet ready to undertake negotiations to share executive power with parties in exchange for their support in the legislature.

Collor has also weakened the country's party system, which is the critical political intermediary between leader and citizen in most polities. The depth of his own party loyalty—three different parties in four years—is an indication of how seriously Collor takes Brazil's party system. He ran not only against existing parties but against parties in general. His PRN is largely a reflection of the fact that electoral laws require a candidate to be affiliated with a party. Collor showed little interest in trying to use the October elections to strengthen the PRN, and while some candidates ran under the PRN banner to indicate their support for Collor, neither they nor Collor made any real effort to build party identity. Despite Collor's attacks and neglect, some traditional parties rebounded from their poor showing in the presidential elections. The PMDB and the PFL rose from the ashes, allowing them to organize the largest delegations in congress (109 and 82 deputies respectively) and to win most of the gubernatorial elections.

Nevertheless, Brazil does not boast a strong party system. The resurrection of the PMDB and the PFL, the rise of the PT as the only real party (in terms of lasting organization and programmatic appeal), and a few other points of light, including the vibrance of the São Paulo PMDB and its leader, Orestes Quércia, have managed to counter some of the debilitating effects of Collor's campaign and governing style. Strong, stable parties, however, are not likely to emerge in the current context, in which politicians do fine without paying attention to parties and the party system suffers as a consequence.

Collor's preferences and performance will have a decisive impact on the plebiscite in 1993, when voters will be asked to decide between a presidential and parliamentary system for the country. Defenders of the current presidential system argue that Brazil needs the firm hand of a strong president to resolve the country's many economic and social problems. Those who favor shifting to a parliamentary system argue that Brazil needs a more flexible political system to keep government crises from becoming regime crises. Parliamentarism would also avoid a situation in which the national leader lacked support in congress—a situation that has caused severe political crises before. Although Collor has availed himself fully of the powers at his disposal as president, he claims to be a parliamentarist at heart (this may be related to the fact that he cannot be reelected as president in 1994 but he could be chosen as prime minister). Opinion polls show strong support among the elite in favor of a parliamentary system.[25] The outcome of the gubernatorial elections, however, appears to have impeded movement in that direction. Two strong candidates with the potential to succeed Collor—each eager for the job—won resounding victories. These and other political figures may attempt to swing opinion in favor of a presidential system to further their own ambitions.

The dilemmas of democratization in Latin America always raise questions about the military, yet what was striking about Brazil in 1990 was the scarcity of uniforms in the political news.[26] Collor scrapped his campaign pledge to fuse the four military ministries into a single Ministry of Defense headed by a civilian. However, he did demilitarize the Office of the Presidency and reorganized the military intelligence service (formerly the SNI, now called the Secretariat of Strategic Affairs), adding civilian staff and placing a civilian at its head. Collor, it is true, spent a great deal of time visiting military installations (and donning uniforms), but he appears to have been interested in media exposure rather than political negotiation. Certainly the impression created by a civilian leader visiting the military's backyard was quite different from that created when men in mufti parade through the political arena.[27]

The relative decline of the military's influence was particularly evident in the press commentary on the October elections. Gone were the perennial worries about whether the military would allow the election to occur or those elected to take office. Instead, the concerns were not unlike those of a presidential contest in the United States: voter apathy, uninspired campaigning, and low blows and uncivilized attacks.

On balance, then, Collor has been a mixed blessing for the consolidation of democratic rule in Brazil. On the positive side is the simple fact of his coming to power through direct elections. In addition, he has respected court rulings (even when they did not favor him), sped the withdrawal of the military from politics, and overseen some of the most peaceful elections in the country's brief democratic history.

On the negative side, Collor's authoritarian style, his impatience with congress, his sometimes cavalier treatment of the constitution, and his distaste for parties have all undermined the institutional bases for democracy. As a candidate, Collor was partly justified in his criticism of parties and politicians as unrepresentative, but as president his attacks on them have hit Brazilian democracy at one of its weakest points. These attacks have also inhibited the emergence in congress of a supporting coalition, which Collor needs if he is to confront effectively Brazil's multiple crises. Collor may not be able to institutionalize democracy single-handedly, but he can promote the process rather than working against it, as he did so effectively in 1990.

In broader social terms the Collor Plan, too, may have exacerbated the fragility of the political system. When asked about the risks of failing to reduce poverty and inequality, 85 percent of those responding in a recent poll of elite opinion said they thought a state of chronic social convulsion was either likely, highly likely, or almost certain in the next ten years. More than half felt the same way about the risk of political takeover by an extremist movement (63 percent) or the military (55 percent).[28]

These concerns reflect awareness of the fact that through the 1980s and into the present decade, Brazil's social fabric has frayed. Consequently, increasingly violent though still isolated conflicts have erupted. Rio de Janeiro was so afflicted by urban violence (much of it fueled by a recent drug boom) that the U.S. consulate felt compelled to issue a travel advisory in July. Rio de Janeiro also suffered a wave of kidnappings in 1990 (on average, three per month) in which rich businessmen paid out million-dollar ransoms. In July, striking workers at a Ford plant went on a rampage, destroying machines, cars, and buildings. In August, a demonstration of landless peasants in the wealthy state of Rio Grande do Sul turned violent and a policeman was hacked to death with scythes. And in December, police in São Paulo killed two squatters as they cleared a shantytown from land belonging to a developer.

It is not difficult to locate the root causes of these outbursts. Income disparities in Brazil are among the worst in the world, while the level of social spending is among the lowest. Worse, the government metes out proportionately more of its social budget to the middle and upper classes than to the poor. Moreover, only about a third of what the government spends actually reaches the targeted beneficiaries; the rest goes to administering the programs.[29] All of the decade-end figures released over the course of 1990 reveal that the situation is worse than imagined and has been deteriorating steadily since 1960.

If the 1980s were a lost decade for the country in general, they were a catastrophe for the poor. According to the United Nations Economic Commission for Latin America, 58 percent of all Brazilians (or almost 90 million out of a total population of 150 million) are either poor or indigent (having an average monthly family income of less than $58 or $28, respectively). And most of these people have full-time jobs.[30] If they seceded, this impoverished mass would constitute the largest country in Latin America. One thousand children under the age of four die every day in Brazil, most from preventable causes.[31] According to the Brazilian Institute for Geography and Statistics, Brazil has the third-highest rate of infant mortality in Latin America after the much poorer countries of Peru and Bolivia. UNICEF, the United Nations Children's Fund, estimates that 15 million children are living in the streets of Brazil's cities.[32]

As elsewhere in the world, this grinding poverty is tragic; the associated income inequality, however, makes it appear criminal. In the 1980s, Brazil experienced a 5 percent decline in per-capita income (or less, depending on how the informal sector is factored in). This compares favorably with other countries in Latin America. Yet, at the same time, income inequality worsened. By 1989 the top 10 percent of the population received 53 percent of the nation's income, while the bottom half lived on only 10 percent, and the bottom 10 percent on less than 1 percent.[33] The World Bank ranked Brazil third worst in terms of income inequality, after Honduras and Sierra Leone.[34]

Most of this poverty is scattered throughout the country and is regularly ignored. Few studies, for instance, probe the implications of these distressing conditions for social, class, and political relations. In those that do, "social apartheid" is a common theme—a class gulf so wide that interaction ceases, except in domestic service and on the shop floor.[35] Social apartheid is the motive force behind the spread of closed residential communities in São Paulo—one of the few going concerns in an otherwise sluggish real-estate market. According to the advertisements, these communities are enclosed behind walls five meters high, protected by sophisticated security systems, and patrolled by round-the-clock guards who also carefully screen all visitors. Maids and other day laborers are searched every time they enter or exit. Inside are gracious homes and children playing in the street as in any affluent suburb in the United States, except that this is an island in a sea of squalor.[36]

No one publicly denies that the situation requires immediate remedy; in fact, Collor and Lula had remarkably similar platforms in terms of health, education, housing, and other welfare programs. But in actual deeds the Collor government subordinated social policy to overall fiscal austerity and thus accomplished little in 1990. It remains to be seen whether Brazil's tattered social fabric and fragile democracy can withstand even a brief and shallow recession. Recent opinion polls reveal impatience with democracy and only an instrumental attachment to it. Already in 1988, 40 percent of those polled in São Paulo favored the return of the military. The proportion of people who consider it more important for a leader to be competent than to be elected rose from half in 1974 to three-quarters in 1988.[37] The current threat to democracy in Brazil is not forceful overthrow so much as creeping disaffection.

Looking Ahead

The shortcomings of Collor, his government, and Brazil's political system operated in perverse synergy to impede economic and political progress in 1990 and to dim prospects for any improvements in the near future. Collor's technocratic political Calvinism weakened the polity in two areas where it most needs strengthening: procedural democratic governance and intermediate political organization (of which the party system is a critical element).

Economists use the clumsy term "disintermediation" to describe the phenomenon whereby savers withdraw funds from discredited institutions, such as banks and stock exchanges, and put them in dollars or physical assets—the modern equivalent of the mattress. Collor promoted an equivalent process of political disintermediation. By circumventing congress, parties, and civil groups, he encouraged these intermediate organizations to withdraw from interaction with the government. Citizens, in turn, had little incentive to participate in parties, unions, business associations, or other organizations because these were no longer agents of intermediation. In social science language, Collor undermined collective action and encouraged free riding. In proverbial terms, it was every man for himself and God against all.

Put differently, the impact of Collor's style and policies is centrifugal and has tended to further fragment the polity at a time when the challenges of democratization, social justice, development, and stabilization require greater cohesion. Disintermediated political Calvinism may work, albeit poorly, in a rich, highly institutionalized democracy with manageable cyclical ills—a fair description of the United States under Ronald Reagan, who perfected the direct, televised relationship with voters that bypassed Congress, parties, and organized groups. However, disintermediated democracy is surely unsuited for the restructuring of a country on the verge of social, economic, and political collapse.

In other countries either threats from abroad (real or perceived) or integrative cultural norms may provide a degree of cohesion that enhances political capacity, as they have in the case of successful industrialization in East Asia. Brazil has neither of these factors at its disposal. Economic and social recovery therefore require more complex and time-consuming efforts at conciliation and bridge-building—what we might call centripetal governance. This is not the place to attempt the story of what might have been. It is possible, however, to imagine a counterfactual virtuous circle in which Collor's reliance on parties, congress, and organized society would have strengthened their credibility and thus made them better able to represent, negotiate, and compromise. Instead, Collor promoted a vicious circle: by belittling these institutions he promoted popular disaffection and individual rather than collective solutions to Brazil's concatenated crises.

Some would argue that the fault lies not with the government but with Brazilian society. It may be true that parties, unions, and employers' associations are too unrepresentative, inexperienced, and intransigent to participate in a national recovery effort involving genuine cooperation and coordination. But given that technocratic, disintermediated governance does not work—as the experiment of Collor's and previous plans makes clear—it is time to start building organizations capable of participation in such an effort. The impetus for constructing such political intermediaries ultimately can come only from civil society. Because of the dominance of the state in Brazil, however, the initiative for creating a favorable environment for institution-building must come from the government. After decades of interventionist and authoritarian rule, individuals, citizens, and economic agents have learned to take their cues from the government. Clear signals from the government that it is willing to listen to sectoral and elected representatives would begin to alter the current disincentives to collective action.

As far as the immediate future is concerned, the prospects are gloomy. Even if the Collor government corrects the many errors of its first year, it is unlikely to provide the salvation that many expected from it a year ago. The problems are more intractable, the solutions more complex and time consuming.

Inflation will remain a principal concern of the Collor government. Collor Plan II had some initial success, as emergency packages of this sort generally do, but it lacked the credibility and the consensus on sacrifices necessary to tackle inflation in a sustained way. Collor II may have damaged irreparably the credibility of the current economic team but the government as a whole still has a legitimacy that under different circumstances—if there were a negotiated agreement with congress or a social pact—would permit a renewed attempt at stabilization. Reports in early March [1991] of discussions among party leaders, and between business and labor about possible negotiated settlements demonstrate that interest in social and political pacts still runs high outside the government.

Another scenario, of course, that could also lead ultimately to lower inflation would be a more orthodox, top-down stabilization plan that relies mostly on wage compression. The Chilean experience with monetarist stabilization in the 1970s suggests that if wages fall far enough for long enough and if unemployment stays high enough for long enough, then inflation will gradually decline. Such a scenario is difficult to contemplate, let alone justify, in a country with Brazil's inequality and tattered safety net, and the consequences for medium-term democratization and development could only be negative, perhaps calamitous. Yet in a country inured to heterodox shocks and whose government has proved inept at negotiating a social-pact solution, this option, unfortunately, remains a real one.

Progress in implementing conservative modernization depends on several factors. New investment is essential, but it is unlikely from any quarter without greater confidence in future stability—including confidence that the government will not intervene as dramatically as it has in the economy. Renewed investment at levels close to those before 1980 will also require debt relief to stem the hemorrhage of resources out of Brazil. This is the area where U.S. policy can make the greatest contribution. But while conservative modernization is quite compatible with the Bush administration's own interests in Brazil, significant debt-relief assistance is not near the top of its agenda.

Conservative modernization, if it is to succeed, will also require a greater effort on the part of the Collor government to hold together its inherently antagonistic base of support. In 1990, Collor made overtures to his conservative supporters (who, in any case, are more firmly rooted in the coalition) but stalled on many of his promises to modernizers. Unless Collor begins to show concrete results, he risks losing their support, which has been hesitant and selective thus far. The modernizers in the government know, furthermore, that their position in the government is precarious; Collor can fire the economic team at any point and replace them all with conservatives. But with just conservative support and conservative policies, the government would no longer have a project. It would then begin to resemble the sad saga of the later Sarney years.

While the requirements for stabilization and development are herculean, those for democratization are surprisingly simpler to fulfill, at least in immediate formal terms, largely due to the absence of powerful groups bent on extraconstitutional takeover. Given the bleak prospects on the economic front, and hence a greater possibility of united opposition to Collor, paralysis and ungovernability are a more serious threat to Collor, if not to Brazilian democracy. Congress could, for instance, move up the 1993 plebiscite and, assuming an outcome in favor of parliamentary rule, adopt the parliamentary system before the scheduled end of Collor's mandate in 1994.[38] Such a scenario would make the institutional rules of democracy more tentative because they would be subject to wholesale revision from one government to the next. But the adoption of a parliamentary system could well be the best step in the medium run to stabilize Brazilian democracy.

Social justice is where the prospects are gloomiest. Unemployment and wage compression are already core weapons in the government's ineffective arsenal against inflation. Whatever redistributive measures might be adopted in an eventually successful conservative modernization project would likely be gradual and marginal (for instance, they would probably affect new growth but not existing wealth). Redistribution was low on the policy agenda in 1990, after stabilization, privatization, fiscal surplus, and administrative reform.

On the campaign trail, however, redistribution and social welfare had been prominent issues. What this shows is that continuing pressure from the poor is unnecessary to keep social justice near the top of the agenda. Governments in the short term have an almost irresistible incentive to impose sacrifices on those without political voice. Disintermediation is a pitfall for all sorts of policy initiatives, but it is probably most grievous in redressing inequality. Furious organizing of workers, urban squatters, rural laborers, blacks, women, and others at the bottom of the social pyramid might, by the close of Collor's term, produce a political force with which the government would have to reckon. Admittedly, this is not easy. With the help of activists in the Church, labor, and the left, these groups have been organizing for years, and while the results are impressive, they are so far insufficient to mount a serious challenge to a government like Collor's. Yet absent organized pressure, the government may well at some point have to respond to spontaneous, mass violence. The *descamisados* elected Collor, but they have yet to find a way to put their concerns back at the top of agenda.

Notes

1. A project is a blueprint for the balance between state and market, and for the market and the political position of major economic actors such as unions, business associations, state enterprises, or exporters. By such a definition many leaders lack either a project or the ability to implement one. Outstanding recent examples of projects would include those by Reagan, Thatcher, the Sandinistas, Gorbachev, and Pinochet. A project is a proposal, not necessarily a solution, as is often implied in debates in Brazil over *projectos*. See Bolívar Lamounier, "Antecedentes, Riscos e Posibilidades de Governo Collor," in *De Geisel a Collor*, ed. Lamounier (São Paulo: Sumaré, 1990), 23–29. To say that Collor has a project does not mean that the diagnosis on which it is based is correct or that it is the best of the projects available for Brazil.

2. See, for example, José Luis Fiori, "O Projeto Neoliberal Encurralado," *Indicadores Econômicos FEE: Análise Conjuntural* 18, no. 2 (August 1990): 88–94; and *Jornal do Brasil*, June 3, 1990, Caderno Ideias/Ensaios, 7–9.

3. Interview with Antônio Kandir, the economics minister's chief adviser, August 30, 1990. Oded Grajew, one of the coordinators of a new business association (PNBE), admired Collor as a nonleftist progressive (see *Folha de São Paulo*, January 10, 1991, B2). César Maia, deputy and leading economist for the left-of-center PDT, applauded Collor's stabilization plan and claimed to have suggested something like it to Collor during the campaign (see *Isto É/Senhor*, March 28,

1990, 30). See also Marcos Antônio Coimbra, cited in Eli Diniz, "O Governo Collor: Social-Democracia ou Neoliberalism," *Cadernos de Conjuntura*, no. 30 (July 1990): 70.

4. César Guimarães uses the label "conservadorismo modernizador" to describe a wing of Collor's electoral alliance. See his article, "Social-Democracia: O que Dizer," *Cadernos de Conjuntura*, no. 30 (July 1990). Barrington Moore applies a concept similar to this notion of conservative modernization to the Meiji Restoration in Japan and to Bismarck in Germany, and distinguishes these countries' development from that of England, France, and the United States. See his *Social Origins of Dictatorship and Democracy: Lord and Peasant in the Making of the Modern World* (Boston: Beacon, 1966). Good examples of conservative modernizers in the twentieth century include de Gaulle and Franco.

5. See Ben Ross Schneider, "Privatization in the Collor Government: Triumph of Liberalism or Collapse of the Developmental State?" in *The Right and Democracy in Latin America*, ed. Douglas Chalmers, Maria do Carmo Campello de Souza, and Atílio Borón (Westport, CT: Praeger, 1992).

6. Instituto de Estudos Sociais, Econômicos, e Políticos de São Paulo, "As Elites Brasileiras e a Modernização de Setor Público" (São Paulo, 1990).

7. Collor appropriated the term "modern," and nearly all social and political groups supported at least some modernizing policies in 1990. In party terms, the leftist PT and PDT most consistently opposed Collor, but even they occasionally voted with the government. The center-left PSDB has had a very difficult time deciding where it stands, in part because Collor has courted it so assiduously, in part because he sometimes seemed modern and social democratic, and in part because so many of the party's voters opted for Collor in the second round.

8. Progress on the modernization agenda depends on the core economic team: Zélia Cardoso de Mello (no relation to Collor de Mello), minister of economics; Antônio Kandir, secretary for economic policy; João Santana, secretary of federal administration; Eduardo Modiano, president of the National Bank for Economic and Social Development; and Ibrahim Eris, president of the Central Bank.

9. The government managed to cut 107,000 workers and put another 65,000 on call. See *Folha de São Paulo*, December 22, 1990, 5.

10. Interview with Marcus Vinicius Brei, director, Departamento de Modernização Administrativa, Secretaria de Administração Federal, August 30, 1990.

11. Deputy Amaral Netto of the PDS, a staunch old-guard supporter, got fed up with Collor's young technocrats (he called Santana a bum) and demanded that Collor reverse his neglect of his allies.

12. José Arthur Giannotti in *Folha de São Paulo*, January 13, 1991.

13. Collor maintained the moratorium on debt repayment and by the end of 1990 Brazil had accumulated arrears of around $9 billion. The government resumed negotiations with private creditors in October, but made only slow progress through the end of Collor's first year.

14. *Folha de São Paulo*, December 13, 1990, 3.

15. GDP and per-capita income figures from *Folha de São Paulo*, January 12, 1991, A2; job loss figures from *Brazil Report*, February 14, 1991, 3; and wage decline data from a study conducted by Istvan Kasznar of Fundação Getúlio Vargas as reported by the *Jornal do Brasil*, December 2, 1990.

16. On the difficulties of negotiating an incomes policy in a country with state corporatist organizations and a large informal sector see Edward J. Amadeo and

José Márcio Carmargo, "Choque e Concerto," *Dados* 32, no. 1 (1989): 5–23; and José Luis Fiori, "Transição Terminada: Crise Superada?" *Novos Estudos CEBRAP*, no. 28 (October 1990): 137–52.

17. Number of candidates reported by *Veja*, August 8, 1990.

18. Maria D'Alva Gil Kinzo, "O Papel dos Partidos," *O Estado de São Paulo*, October 28, 1989, 9–10.

19. One of the political surprises of 1990 was the absence of the PT. After nearly winning the presidential elections, Lula and the PT virtually disappeared from the national scene and reappeared most frequently in the press when internal differences erupted into public squabbles.

20. Governors receive a lot of money from the central government, and it makes good political sense for them to be at least civil. Some of the strong governors are already candidates to succeed Collor. Leonel Brizola, the populist firebrand and perennial presidential pretender, won handily in the first round in Rio de Janeiro. The less notorious current governor of São Paulo, Orestes Quércia, helped take his handpicked successor from complete obscurity to victory. These men and their associated political forces (some of the most organized and potent in the country) will want to keep the preidentialist option alive. Paradoxically, this goal implies ensuring that the Collor government does not get into such trouble that the fear of ungovernability encourages congress to move up the plebiscite on the future of Brazil's political system, scheduled for 1993.

21. *Folha de São Paulo*, February 9, 1991, B4, and March 7, 1991, 1–12.

22. See Samuel P. Huntington, *Political Order in Changing Societies* (New Haven: Yale University Press, 1968). While congress and other instruments may suffer under Collor, one bright spot in terms of institutionalization has been the new constitution. Many have successfully challenged the constitutionality of government measures, thereby demonstrating the document's force.

23. *Isto É/Senhor*, December 26, 1990, 35; and *Folha de São Paulo*, December 19, 1990, A10. The congress that took office in February 1991 set about immediately to draft legislation that restricts the use of "provisional measures."

24. Brazil received very little international press coverage in 1989 and 1990 despite the major developments in its political economy (see Lawrence Weschler, "The Media's One and Only Freedom Story," *Columbia Journalism Review* (March/April 1990): 26–31. One of the few incidents that made it into the major dailies in Europe and the United States was Cabral's romance with Zélia, which provoked front-page stories about tropical libidos. To Collor's chagrin the international press paid little attention to his many trips abroad, though not for lack of photo opportunities.

25. A survey of elites in early 1990 revealed that 69 percent favored parliamentarism over presidentialism (fn. 6).

26. One might be tempted to argue that military influence continues although it has been civilianized and now wears a suit. Two of Collor's top ministers, Ozires Silva (Infrastructure) and Passarinho (Justice), were both colonels. However, since the 1960s both have made their careers outside the military, in state enterprises and politics, respectively.

27. Military discontent flared up again in the news in November and December, as officers, especially retired ones, became more vocal in their criticism of the government's refusal to adjust their salaries for inflation. However, the tone was more of collective bargaining than saber rattling.

28. See fn. 6.

29. Interview with João Santana, secretary of the Federal Administration, *New York Times*, May 15, 1990, D8.

30. *Veja*, November 21, 1990, 42, 44.

31. *Folha de São Paulo*, December 19, 1990.

32. *Isto É/Senhor*, December 26, 1990, 49.

33. *Veja*, November 12, 1990, 42–45.

34. *Isto É/Senhor*, December 26, 1990, 49.

35. See Luis Werneck Vianna, "Despotismo e *Apartheid* Social," *Caderno de Conjuntura*, no. 30 (July 1990); and Francisco C. Weffort, "A América Errada," in *Lua Nova*, no. 21 (September 1990): 5–40.

36. Teresa Caldeira is currently completing a research project on these communities and other private, exclusionary responses to the social crisis. In one survey in Rio de Janeiro she found that hundreds of middle-class respondents feared kidnapping, even though the statistical probability was minuscule. Such fears serve to justify exclusion from middle-class communities of all those with the stereotypical traits of kidnappers—poor, dark, slum dwellers.

37. Judith Muszynski and Antônio Manuel Teizeira Mendes, "Democratização e Opinião Pública no Brasil," in Lamounier (fn. 1), 53, 71.

38. José Luis Fiori, "Transição Terminada: Crise Superada?" *Novos Estudos CEBRAP*, no. 28 (October 1990): 137–52.

12

The Political Impact of Free Trade on Mexico

Peter H. Smith

The long-standing association that scholars have attributed to economic liberalization and capitalism as essential ingredients or causal variables in the introduction of political democracy in Latin America received the most attention in the Mexican case. Anticipating a free-trade agreement with the United States, many analysts argued that Mexico, the last country to resist most features of democratic politics, could be pushed more rapidly along the democratization path through economic liberalization. Peter Smith, director of the Center for Iberian and Latin American Studies at the University of California, San Diego, develops a number of potential scenarios to explain the influence on Mexico's political model of economic liberalization through free trade. He suggests that the arguments for and against a linkage between political and economic development in Mexico are inconclusive but that free trade could encourage an environment more favorable to political liberalization if the country's leadership sought to move in that direction.

> The rule of free trade, taken by itself, is no longer able to govern international relations. . . . Freedom of trade is fair only if it is subject to the demands of social justice.
>
> —*Pope Paul VI*
> Populorum Progressio

Current debates over North American free trade focus almost exclusively on economic issues. Advocates claim that a trilateral agreement will provide impetus for sustained, long-term economic growth in Canada, Mexico, and the United States—and that it will provide a

From the *Journal of Interamerican Studies and World Affairs* 34, no. 1 (Spring 1992): 1–25. Reprinted by permission of the *Journal of Interamerican Studies and World Affairs* and the author.

regional counterweight to the European Community (EC) and to Japan. Critics in the United States claim that the North American Free Trade Agreement (NAFTA) will encourage the export of U.S. investment and employment to Mexico. Canadians fear accelerated debilitation of vulnerable sectors of the national economy, from natural gas to automobile parts. Skeptics in Mexico predict that NAFTA will perpetuate low wages for the Mexican working class and transform the entire country into a massive *maquiladora* [assembly industry].

There is much less attention to the *political* side of this question. And most political discussions, scant as they are, have concentrated on the process of achieving a free-trade accord. Observers have noted the impressive leadership of Carlos Salinas de Gortari and his willingness to jettison nationalistic shibboleths in pursuit of a viable economic model for Mexico. Commentators have dissected the apparent transformation of conservative U.S. Republicans, who have discarded their Mexico-bashing tactics of the mid-1980s in exchange for uncritical support of NAFTA, and the evident discomfort of U.S. Democrats, unable to reconcile their liberal traditions on foreign policy with protectionist sentiments on economic matters. In my own estimation, the approval of "fast-track" negotiations by the U.S. Congress in June 1991 has already had significant political fallout: it has stifled public discussion about the outcome of Mexico's 1988 presidential elections, it has enhanced the personal legitimacy of President Salinas, and it has tended to neutralize international criticism of fraudulent electoral practices in Mexico.

What about the political consequences of free trade? What are the long-term implications? The purpose of this discussion is to examine alternative scenarios for the potential impact that a free-trade agreement may have upon the Mexican political system. To this end, this chapter outlines current ideas that have been advanced on the subject, tries to unravel the logical premises inherent in existing debates, and focuses on problems of cause and effect. Above all, it attempts to clarify the conceptual terms of current debates on the political implications of free trade. Thus far, at least in my opinion, contemporary discussions have tended to be too economistic in substance, too technocratic in tone and, in the political realm, too simplistic and imprecise. Prospects for NAFTA raise fundamental issues about the dynamics of political change, especially for Mexico. These issues require serious, sustained examination.

Caveats are vital here. First, there is no full-fledged NAFTA as of this writing (April 1992). Therefore, for purposes of discussion, approval of an agreement will be assumed. However, since many of the NAFTA's implications will emerge from specifics and details, it remains hazardous to speculate about effects. Second, and partly for this reason, the inquiry will be broadened to focus on the implications, now emerging, of the overall strategy of economic "liberalization" which was initiated in Mexico during the 1980s: lowering of trade barriers, privatization of parastatal corporations, encouragement of foreign investment, and redefining the economic role of the state. As a culmination of this general approach, NAFTA would have distinctive implications of its own; yet it would be a mistake to attribute far-reaching political changes to NAFTA alone. Third, it seems apparent that a free-trade agreement will have meaningful, but limited, political consequences for Canada and the United States. In Mexico, on the other hand, the political consequences of NAFTA (and of liberalization) are likely to affect the regime, already experiencing significant rearrangements and realignments, in meaningful ways. It is the *systemic* quality of the political changes that gives special salience to the Mexican case.

It has been widely asserted, especially in the United States, that a free-trade agreement will accelerate the process of "democratization" in Mexico. For the sake of clarity, this commentary is organized around a cluster of commonplace hypotheses or propositions. One characteristic of the current debate, however, is that these postulations are usually tacit, implicit, or off-hand.[1] By presenting them in schematic, perhaps oversimplified, fashion, I seek to emphasize and explore their logical and theoretical foundations.[2]

Mexico is still a long way from democracy. To be sure, the political system has been undergoing a steady process of evolution and reform ever since the late 1960s. The number of parties has increased, the ranks of the opposition have swelled, and elections have become less one-sided and fraudulent. Official results from the presidential election of 1988 gave Carlos Salinas de Gortari just over one-half the vote. Since then, the Partido de Acción Nacional (PAN) has earned two state governorships and could well win more in the future. Fundamentally, however, Mexico continues to have an "authoritarian" system—much milder and more tolerant than the repressive military regimes that asphyxiated the Southern Cone in the 1960s and 1970s, but authoritarian nonetheless. In Mexico, there is little doubt that power resides in the presidency, that the official Partido Revolucionario Institucional (PRI) can still dominate elections, and that the state imposes limits and restrictions on the opposition. Dissidents, especially on the Left, suffer frequent harassment and abuse of human rights. Recent reforms of the electoral system may contribute to "liberalization" of the authoritarian regime, but they do not necessarily indicate a commitment to "democratization."

Proposition 1: NAFTA Will Contribute to the Democratization of Mexico

The assertion that the North American Free Trade Agreement will promote Mexican democracy takes multiple forms. One assumes that the United States can, and should, exert direct pressure on Mexico during the course of the free-trade negotiations. The *Journal of Commerce* spoke for many when it urged President Bush to take action: "The Bush administration must make it clear that it will pursue free trade only with a country that permits free and fair elections. One of the strongest arguments for the proposed trade agreement is the promise of political stability in Mexico through economic growth. Mr. Bush should remind Mexican leaders that democracy is the best way to ensure long-term stability" (1990: 8-A). In other words, democratic reform represents an efficient means for achieving the long-term U.S. goal of political stability in Mexico.

Support for this position comes from a curious mélange of political bedfellows. U.S. conservatives, jingoists, and self-congratulatory nationalists regard the imposition of political change on Mexico as the natural expression of a new-found hegemony for the United States. Especially remarkable is the fact that many dissidents in Mexico, long suspicious of North American intervention, lend support to the idea of a trade-for-reform exchange. According to this view, the NAFTA negotiations provide an exceptional amount of leverage on the Salinas administration, and it behooves the opposition to take advantage of the opportunity. Besides, the prerequisites imposed by the European Community (EC) on Greece, Portugal, and Spain in the 1970s offer a respectable precedent; the participation of Canada in the trilateral negotiations lends further legitimacy to the process. As a result, there has emerged a convergence of U.S. conservatives with Mexican dissidents.

The assessment rendered here is that the United States will refrain from exerting significant pressure. The end of the Cold War has wrought a pervasive change in Washington's perceptions of Mexico. Ultimately, the Mexico-bashing of the 1980s derived from U.S. frustration over differences of opinion over Central America. However, with the disappearance of the "Communist threat" and the debilitation of the Castro regime, there is less reason for diplomatic disagreement. U.S. lawmakers are more inclined to grant Salinas the benefit of the doubt. As one observer has described their outlook during the debate over the fast-track approach in mid-1991: "Most seem to have decided that while Mexico's political system is far from perfect, it is not a pariah state that warrants imposition of sanctions . . . Mexico's political situation ultimately was not a decisive issue for most members of Congress" (Baer, 1991: 143).

This tends to confuse the issues a bit since the question is not whether or not Mexico constitutes a "pariah state" deserving of "sanctions" but, rather, whether it meets sufficient political criteria to justify a long-term, free-trade agreement. Nonetheless, it seems highly unlikely that U.S. negotiators or legislators will apply significant pressure in favor of political reform.[3]

A second version of the idea that NAFTA will promote democracy focuses not on short-term negotiations but on long-term consequences. The basic assertion, in one form or another, is that the implementation of a free-trade agreement will unleash social forces that will ultimately lay the foundation for democratic development in Mexico. President Salinas has spelled out this contention on numerous occasions. Challenging the assertion that he has fostered *"perestroika* without *glasnost,"* he has told one interviewer that:

> Freedoms of what you call the *glasnost* kind have existed for decades in Mexico. What hasn't existed is the freedom of productive activity because the government owned so many enterprises.
>
> So, actually, we have been more rapidly transforming the economic structure while striving along many paths of reform on the political side.
>
> But, let me tell you something. When you are introducing such a strong economic reform, you must make sure that you build the political consensus around it. If you are at the same time introducing additional drastic political reform, you may end up with no reform at all. And we want to have reform, not a disintegrated country . . . *as we move along the path toward consolidating our economic reforms, political reform will continue to evolve in Mexico* [emphasis added]. (*New Perspectives Quarterly*, 1991: 8)

Others have echoed this claim. Mexico's minister of the treasury Pedro Aspe has also advanced the view that you cannot have an open economy and a closed society (Aspe, 1992). And Enrique Krauze, using almost identical language, even added a timetable: "A closed political system cannot survive long in an open economy. . . . After the signing of the [NAFTA], the unfinished chapter—long-postponed democracy—is for us Mexicans to write. With solid economic foundations, *the transition will take months, not years or decades* [emphasis added]" (*Wall Street Journal*, 1991). Ultimately, economic change is the causal agent of political change.

This contention is, essentially, an article of faith. There exists a body of ideas, the long-outmoded theory of "modernization," which contends that economic development creates social forces—in particular, an expanded and autonomous "middle class"—that seek political democratization. Applied to the Mexican context, modernization theory suggests that free-trade will diversify the location of economic power in Mexico and thus create the bases for political as well as economic competition.[4] As Delal Baer has put it: "A free-trade agreement may help reinforce decentralized economic decision-making, erode the dirigiste tendency of an authoritarian state, and decouple the economy from exclusive party control. Liberalized politics thus tends to accompany liberal economics" (Baer, 1991: 136).

In fact, economic policy has never been under the "exclusive"control of the PRI given the party's subordinate relationship to the executive bureaucracy. Nonetheless, Baer's point is clear: one way or another, NAFTA will support the forces of democracy.

Empirical reality casts doubt on this happy assertion. Some of the most "open" economies on the contemporary scene have fairly closed political regimes: Taiwan, Singapore, and South Korea come quickly to mind. And these are not atypical cases. There exists a substantial literature which argues that "bureaucratic-authoritarian" regimes comprise logical instruments for economic strategies designed to achieve growth through capital accumulation instead of justice through income distribution. Especially where labor is highly organized, repression is needed to impose law and order on deprived, but populous, masses. Hence, the imposition of military regimes in the 1960s and 1970s on such advanced Latin American societies as Brazil, Argentina, and Chile.

The currently democratic dénouement in the contemporary Southern Cone implies, however, that the basic question involves a deliberate *sequencing* of strategies. Here the rule would be: economic reform first, political reform later. The spectacular implosion of the once-mighty Soviet Union would appear to confirm the need for prudence. According to this view, Mikhail Gorbachev made the fatal error of attempting to bring about *perestroika* and *glasnost* at the same time. (Be it said, en passant, that there may be other, and more convincing, explanations for the breakup of the erstwhile USSR.) By the same token, it has been argued that Chile's recent transition to democracy has been facilitated and strengthened by the economic liberalization carried out under General [Augusto] Pinochet (Weintraub and Baer, 1992: 187–88).

In actual practice, the strategy of economics-first/politics-later becomes a rationale for government inaction. This approach makes no immediate demand for progress on the political front. The responsibility of policymakers is to devote themselves to economic reform, not to political maneuverings. However, this stress on sequencing raises a related question: How long is the short run? When will it be time for political reform? How will it be apparent? Seen in this light, Brazil and Chile offer troublesome examples since, in each case, the generals ruled for well over half a generation. How long must Mexico wait?

Proposition 2: NAFTA Will Contribute to the Consolidation of Authoritarianism in Mexico

A contrasting proposition insists that free trade will revive and fortify authoritarian rule in Mexico. One formulation envisions NAFTA as a cynical, bilateral compact with the United States. As Cuauhtémoc Cárdenas, leader of the Partido de la Revolución Democrática (PRD), has asserted:

> The [Mexican] Government hopes to manage the dilemma of separating political and economic reform by relying on U.S. financing and on Washington's political support. The regime is gambling that it can buy off the country's middle classes and neutralize popular discontent with the help of American resources, thus containing demands for democratization that are only skin deep. . . .
> Americans should be aware of one essential fact: The new Mexican administration offers the U.S. an implicit deal, of which the free-trade agreement is the latest step. Mexico will indiscriminately put in place the type of economic reforms that the U.S. always wanted for Mexico, but the U.S. will accept and protect the existing political system. (*New York Times*, 1990: E-19)[5]

In other words, NAFTA offers Mexican elites a means of preserving their power—and their authoritarian system of rule.

This interpretation rests upon two key assumptions. One is that economic reform in Mexico constitutes a genuinely high priority for the United States, and thus gives Mexico a meaningful bargaining chip. The other is that Mexican leaders seek to sustain the status quo. It is a vision of political paralysis, not of change over time.

A second version of this proposition takes more complex form. It asserts that NAFTA will contribute to a reformulation and *accentuation* of authoritarian politics in Mexico, that the consequences of free trade will lead not to the perpetuation of the system but to its "hardening" or *derechización*.

Stripped to its essentials, the argument holds that economic liberalization entails a social restructuring that will (a) facilitate centralization of authority, and (b) require increasing repression. Basic elements of this social process—what Adolfo Gilly calls "an economic and juridical restructuring of Mexican capitalism" (1991)—include:

- Consolidation of an oligopolistic business class, as small and medium-size entrepreneurs suffer decimation (a position drawing support from recurrent forecasts that less than 10 percent of

Mexico's entrepreneurs would be able to withstand the rigors of open competition).[6]

* Dislocation in the countryside, especially in grain-growing areas, where campesinos will be unable to compete with wheat and corn from Canada and the United States. (As noted by Jorge Calderón of the Universidad Nacional Autónoma de México [UNAM]: "This treaty would mean putting 2.7 million communal farmers and 1 million small farmers—all undercapitalized—in direct competition with the most advanced agricultural system in the world" (SourceMex, 1991c).)

* Immiseration of the working class, through the perpetuation of low wages and emasculation of the union movement.

In short, the tacit social compact outlined in the Constitution of 1917, and sustained by the Mexican welfare state, is nearing an ignominious end. Economic liberalization will accentuate social inequality and polarization.

It is in this context that the Programa Nacional de Solidaridad (PRONASOL) assumes fundamental significance. Essentially, it is said, PRONASOL represents a neopopulist measure whose ultimate goal is preservation of the social peace. It is a top-down, paternalistic strategy that dispenses favors in discretionary fashion for clear-cut political goals. (In anticipation of the August 1991 elections, for instance, PRONASOL distributed pork-barrel benefits in order to bolster electoral prospects for the PRI [*Los Angeles Times*, 1991].) Denise Dresser has taken caustic note of this process: "Just like the wife of the industrialist who organizes soup kitchens to benefit the poor that her husband creates, the Salinas government distributes selective subsidies to the population its economic policies impoverish. . . . Social spending through PRONASOL is to be credited, but PRONASOL's existence cannot compensate nor hide the continuation and deepening of a restructuring program that further skews the country's income distribution" (Dresser, 1991b: 13).

Reinvigoration of the PRI thus fits into a fundamental realignment of the party system. Essentially, according to this view, the political strategy has three basic components: (1) fortification of the PRI, (2) debilitation of the PRD, and (3) co-optation of the PAN. There is reason to believe that progovernment elements have subjected *perredistas* to systematic campaigns of intimidation and harassment, while the PRI has struck a tacit alliance with the PAN in common cause against the PRD. It has also preempted the pro-business stance of the PAN, challenging its base within the entrepreneurial community and restricting its electoral possibilities.

(In response some *panistas* have attempted to shore up support within the private sector by warning that unrestricted free trade could inflict serious damage on small- and medium-size business in Mexico [comments of José Angel Conchello reported in *El Universal*, 1991: 1].)

At bottom, the *salinista* strategy entails a high-stakes gamble: that liberalization will generate and sustain sufficient economic growth to forestall social unrest. More specifically, the hope is that enhanced trade will create enough jobs to offset interim dislocations of labor and lead, ultimately, to higher levels of employment. Increased employment, even at modest wage levels, would yield positive social benefits for Mexico and contribute to political tranquility.

Failure of this strategy could have profound long-term implications. As Adolfo Gilly has warned:

> The destiny of the political regime dominated by the PRI has become linked to the fate of the FTA. Integration is the grand historical program that the regime is offering to the country.
> If the treaty does not come about, or if it does not improve the economic situation in a relatively short run, the political regime will once again be seriously threatened by growing demands for elections without fraud, for respect for human rights, and for a genuine multiparty system. . . .
> With this restructuring of Mexico, the PRI is seeking to conserve power, but it runs the risk of unleashing an electoral mobilization greater than that of 1988, yielding the government to the opposition and watching its neoliberal policy frustrated in mid-course. But if the official party regime resorts to authoritarianism, fraud, and corruption, it is difficult to imagine how Mexico will advance along the road to economic modernization within a North American market (recall that Spain and Greece had to move toward representative democracy in order to enter the European Community). Among countries with comparable levels of culture and development, Mexico is one of the last political regimes under state-party domination. (Gilly, 1991: 15)

Implicitly, it seems, the economic failure of liberalization could have either of two differential effects: it could incite protest from the masses and repression by the regime, or it could instigate the eruption of "civil society" that would lead toward genuine democratization. The actual prediction is ambiguous.

Paradoxically enough, economic success could also produce contrary political results. Applied to the Mexican social structure, the liberalization strategy has tended to exacerbate, rather than to reduce, income inequality. Continuation of this pattern under NAFTA could intensify the perception of "relative deprivation" and social injustice among the masses—and ignite sparks of turmoil and/or rebellion. According to this interpretation, in other words, realization of the liberalization strategy is likely to result in protest and reaction. Success, like failure, raises the specter of turmoil and repression.

Proposition 3: NAFTA Will Have No Meaningful Impact on Democratization in Mexico

In differing ways, our first two propositions drew tight causal connections between economics and politics. An alternative argument stipulates the autonomy of the political arena. According to this view, political change results from decisive political action, not from the mechanistic processes of macroeconomic transformation. As a corollary, this approach tends to focus on human political actions and actors—on decisions, tactics, compromises, trade-offs—rather than on abstract social forces.

Interpretations in this vein tend to view democratic transitions in contemporary South America not as the culmination of economic strategies imposed by authoritarian regimes, but as the artful achievements of skilled and calculating dissidents. It was the courage and tenacity of Raúl Alfonsín in Argentina, the flexibility of the Partido do Movimento Democrático Brasileiro (PMDB) in Brazil, and the tactics and determination of the "No" campaign in Chile—not the free-market economics of the generals—that brought about successful installations of democracy. Indeed, free-market policies may have eased the process of consolidation in Chile; but this could not be said for Argentina and Brazil, where democracy continues nonetheless.

Applied to NAFTA, this argument postulates a null hypothesis: economic liberalization will have no discernible impact on the likelihood of political democracy in Mexico. On the contrary, the course of democratization in Mexico would depend upon political decisions—by those in command of the state, by leaders of "civil society," and by members of the opposition. These decisions might be reached via agreement (as in post-Franco Spain) or via rupture (as in post-Malvinas Argentina), but democratic change would come about as a result of interaction among political sectors.

Hints of this argument emerge from some analyses of Mexico's midterm elections held in August 1991. On that occasion, the PRI staged a remarkable electoral recovery by winning 61.5 percent of the total votes cast, and President Salinas stunned the nation by annulling questionable results in Guanajuato and San Luis Potosí. Nonetheless, as Wayne A. Cornelius has observed, the reversal of state-level contests by presidential intervention does not offer a stable solution to problems of vote-rigging and fraud. A key element in this equation is the fragmentation of the elite, including continuing estrangement between *políticos* and *técnicos*. In a word, the chief executive cannot impose electoral transparency:

> The loss of central control means, if electoral transparency is ever achieved in Mexico, it is less likely to result from a supreme exertion of presidential will than from the slow accretion of municipal and state-level conquests by opposition parties. Having won control of the electoral machinery, the opposition parties can proceed to reform state electoral laws, clean up voter registration rolls, and extend poll-watcher coverage, as the PAN has done in Baja California Norte and may now have an opportunity to do in Guanajuato and San Luis Potosí.
>
> It was no coincidence that, in the recent mid-term elections, the fewest irregularities, as well as the only opposition victory for a federal Senate seat, occurred in Baja California Norte, where the elections were presided over by a state government controlled by an opposition party. The long march has begun. (Cornelius, 1991: 4–5, 8)

Democratization will thus depend upon the ability of the opposition to capture local elections, take office, and utilize power to transform the political system. It is the dissidents, not the rulers, who control the country's political fate.

All of this is far removed from NAFTA. It might be argued that a free-trade agreement would discourage Mexican *políticos* from denying electoral victory to dissidents, if only to avoid international embarrassment, but that seems highly uncertain. Once free trade is achieved, in fact, the international community—especially the United States—might well be disinclined to pay much attention to electoral irregularities in Mexico since that would raise awkward questions about the wisdom of the NAFTA enterprise.

Postulation of an indirect connection between economic liberalization (through NAFTA) and political democratization can emerge from a reformulation of the general argument: that is, fulfillment of a free-trade agreement could establish an economic context that would encourage a political decision to establish democracy in Mexico. As in Proposition 1, the economic forces unleashed by NAFTA would constitute a primary variable; and as in Proposition 3, the proximate source of political change would be an act of political will, a voluntary choice on the part of the national leadership. The connection is not one of straightforward cause and effect. Instead, the economic results of free trade would create an environment that would facilitate, encourage, or enable—but not determine—a decision to move toward democracy.

According to one variation on this theme, economic liberalization can bring about economic growth—and this, in turn, could create a climate for political change. As Delal Baer has suggested: "Successful economic liberalization is an important ingredient in easing democratic transitions" (Baer, 1991: 136). Assuming that "success" refers to the attainment of consistent, self-sustaining growth over a period of several years, we might even deduce from this logic a hypothetical timetable for the installation of genuine democracy: around the mid to late 1990s at the earliest, perhaps after the turn of the century.

The practical difficulty with this idea is that political leaders have proved reluctant to surrender power during periods of economic prosperity. On the contrary, continued growth has typically offered a rationalization for perpetuating authoritarian regimes, rather than discarding them. Certainly the generals in Brazil drew political sustenance from the "economic miracle" of the late 1960s and early 1970s, as did Pinochet in Chile throughout the mid-1980s. In short, the idea that economic growth will encourage far-reaching political reform flies in the face of elementary logic and popular wisdom: If it ain't broke, as the saying goes, there is little temptation to fix it.

As a matter of fact, political transitions throughout South America have tended to occur in response to economic crisis, rather than prosperity. This pattern clearly applied to the cases of Peru, Argentina, Brazil, and—to a lesser extent—Uruguay; the evidence was somewhat mixed for Chile, where the economy was strong, but Pinochet did not leave office voluntarily. This is not to say that Mexico would "benefit" from yet another economic crisis; its people have already suffered far too much from the painful costs of poverty and deprivation. It is simply to observe that, in comparative terms, crisis has proved more conducive to transitions from authoritarianism than has prosperity. And it is to assert, once again, that ultimate agency derives from political volition, not from abstract social forces. In one way or another, according to this general proposition, political change in Mexico will result from political actions in Mexico, not from NAFTA or free trade itself.

Proposition 4: NAFTA Will Contribute to the Debilitation of the Mexican State

A fourth proposition deals not with the question of democratization but with the power and role of the Mexican state. As stated here, the argument may appear circular or tautological, since it was the apparent reduction in the role of the state during the late 1980s—via lower tariffs, fewer regulations, and privatization—that enabled Mexico to initiate free-trade discussions with the United States in the first place. It might seem self-evident that an increased reliance on the economic market would reduce the opportunities for state intervention. Nonetheless, the NAFTA and free trade are likely to have some subtle, even counterintuitive, impact on the evolution of the state apparatus, which merit close attention.

First of all, I should like to declare, at the outset, personal skepticism over the idea that the Salinas administration is voluntarily surrendering large portions of state power. My understanding is that the intent of the regime is to streamline the state, to improve its efficiency, to redefine its role, and, overall, to revitalize the state (Dresser, 1990a). As Denise Dresser has observed:

> In terms of its intervention in the economy and its use and channeling of resources, the public sector is not shrinking. Why is this so? Because the public sector is necessary to the construction and maintenance of the Center-Right coalition. Its ability to control or neutralize strategic blocs of organized labor and white-collar employees, to supply key private enterprises, and to service geographically dispersed constituencies is essential. Thus, in Mexico we seem to be witnessing not the retreat of the state but a new form of "statism." (Dresser, 1991b: 5)

After all, it takes a strong state to design and implement drastic reform.

Eventually, however, implementation of a free-trade regime could impose significant constraints upon this redefined state. It has been widely noted that NAFTA would consolidate and institutionalize the *salinista* reforms, a prospect that represents a major attraction for the United States. This may also be a deliberate goal of the Salinas administration. It has been less widely noted, however, that the existence of a NAFTA will sharply narrow the available range of policy options for Salinas' successors. Global and/or national circumstances could undergo considerable change sometime after 1994, but Mexican presidents will not enjoy complete control over all the classic instruments of economic policy, such as trade, investment, exchange rates, wage levels, and so forth. Major redirections will prove difficult, if not impossible. This could restrict the ability of government to respond to changing problems, conditions, and public preferences (Sheahan, 1992: 58–61). In fact it was often said that Mexico, from the 1940s through the 1980s, derived some of its stability from the ability of its various regimes to swing, pendulum-like, from Left, to Center, to the Right, and so on in their social and economic policies. For better or worse, that option will not exist any more—whatever the nature of public opinion.

Emerging relationships between the government and the country's newly vitalized business sector will pose another restraint on state action. It appears that the Mexican state now engages in a kind of partnership with the business class on more or less equal terms, which represents a sharp departure from previous eras, when the private sector was either subordinate, or hostile, to the regime in office. In principle, this new partnership could result in a positive-sum game for both sides (presumably at the expense of someone else), but it also appears that the growing power of the entrepreneurial class could set genuine limits on the "relative autonomy" of the Mexican state. In a sense, it was the autonomy of the state that enabled it to carry out such far-reaching reforms. Ironically, one consequence of this strategy may be the surrender of this autonomy vis-à-vis the business class.

Finally, NAFTA may set tacit, but strict, limits on Mexican foreign policy. It seems unlikely that, under NAFTA, Mexico will be able to express serious disagreement with the United States on major issues of international diplomacy. In fact, this point was made by none other than U.S. ambassador John D. Negroponte himself, in his controversial—and originally confidential—memorandum to Washington in April 1991. As he wrote to U.S. assistant secretary of state for Latin America Bernard Aronson:

> Mexico is in the process of changing the substance and image of its foreign policy. . . . It has switched from an ideological, nationalistic and protectionist approach to a pragmatic, outreaching and competitive view of world affairs. The compelling factor in this change was the failure of the previous approach to respond to the real needs of the Mexican people, but better and more responsible leadership was also clearly an indispensable factor. . . .
>
> The prospect of an FTA must be seen in the context of these reformist trends, which started in the mid-1980s and were dramatically accelerated by Salinas after he came to office in 1988. The proposal for an FTA is, in a way, the capstone of these new policy approaches. *From a foreign policy perspective, an FTA would institutionalize acceptance of a North American orientation to Mexico's foreign relations.* Just think of how this contrasts with past behavior. Previously, as now, 60 or 70% of Mexico's business would be with the United States; but if you listened to us in the UN [United Nations] or debating Central America, you would have thought we were archenemies. The fact that the preponderance of Mexico's foreign dealings were with the United States was carefully masked through various defensive mechanisms. In a way, therefore, adoption of an FTA would help put on an open and legitimate footing what many feel should have been the reality of US/Mexico relations a long time ago. [emphasis added] (quoted in English original in *Proceso*, 1991b: 7)

That Negroponte made this statement does not necessarily mean that it is correct. But it does, at the least, convey a sense of expectations within the U.S. government (*Proceso*, 1991b: 6–11; and 1991a: 6–16).

There is some evidence to indicate that Mexico's foreign policy has already begun to line up with U.S. positions: on Panama, on El Salvador, on the Persian Gulf, as well as in other areas (*Proceso*, 1991a). There may be at least three reasons for this:

1. Mexico may be seeking something in exchange—for example, approval of a suitable free-trade agreement;

2. With the collapse of the Cold War, Mexico's objective foreign-policy interests may have shifted—and thus, in spontaneous fashion, fallen into line with the outlook of the United States;

3. A change in perspective may have led to a subjective redefinition of Mexico's national interests, placing more emphasis on tangible economic goals than on abstract political principles.

The fundamental question, however, is whether NAFTA would give the United States inordinate leverage over Mexico's foreign policy, whether—in this sense—Mexico would become subordinate to the United States. This can only be determined if and when the two countries face a situation where they have unambiguously differing interests, a situation that has not occurred in the past couple of years, but which will almost certainly arise at some time in the future. (Cuba could present an issue of this kind, for example.) One possibility is that, with NAFTA in hand, Mexico will have more freedom in setting its foreign policy, since the United States will not be able to resort to economic blackmail. My own suspicion, however, is just the opposite: the United States will exert more and more leverage over Mexico, which will pose serious dilemmas for, if not actual constraints on, Mexican policymakers. As Elliott Abrams has reportedly remarked: "Conceding sovereignty is the price of leaving poverty: prosperity has its cost" (Gilly, 1991: 14). Under NAFTA, in other words, we won't see anything like Contadora [autonomous initiatives among Mexico and other Latin American countries toward U.S. Central American policy] again.[7]

Conclusion: On the Need for Political Imagination

One striking characteristic of public discussions on this subject is their inconclusiveness. Virtually every proposition about the political consequences of NAFTA has an equally plausible counterproposition. There is little basis, empirical or theoretical, for rejecting any of the arguments set forth in the current debate. Nor is there any solid confirmation.

A second feature of this discourse is its partisan (not to say ideological) quality. Those who favor NAFTA tend to marshal any and all arguments in support of the notion that free trade will lead to democracy in Mexico (Proposition 1). This often leads to logical inconsistencies in reasoning. By the same token, those who oppose the agreement tend to insist that it will perpetuate authoritarian rule (Proposition 2). There is relatively scant consideration of the possibility that NAFTA will have few political consequences at all (Proposition 3), or that it might have more subtle implications for the role and autonomy of the Mexican state (Proposition 4).

My own opinion on these matters is that free trade and economic liberalization could loosen the social moorings of the present political system in Mexico and, thus, create objective conditions for a far-reaching political transition. However, whether and how this opportunity is used entails the exercise of political will, skill, and management at the uppermost levels of power—especially the presidency. Given a realignment of social forces, it would be just as conceivable for Mexico's leaders to resort to repression and install some new form of authoritarianism as it would be for them to embark on a quest for authentic democracy. In Mexico, as elsewhere, the ultimate achievement of democracy will require acts of political determination and volition.

Opposition victories in state and local elections would, in my view, help lay the groundwork for redefinition of the regime. No doubt such victories would accentuate processes of geographic variation within Mexico; indeed, there may well emerge a broad range of party systems (from single party to multiparty) at the regional level. Nonetheless, I doubt that electoral advances by the opposition would be decisive in and of themselves. Ultimately, they would serve primarily to increase the pressure on the ruling establishment. It is the response of that establishment that would then set the course for long-run change, whether toward either genuine democracy or a refurbished authoritarianism.

A third characteristic of the debate is its concentration on the process of political *transition*, rather than on its ultimate destination. There is a tendency to focus on the mechanics of liberalization instead of upon the hoped-for shape and substance of democracy in Mexico—more attention to means than to ends. As a result, there is considerable need for political vision.

In this spirit, let us look at a range of conceptual alternatives for democracy and democratization in Mexico. At bottom, democracy entails three basic principles: participation, competition, and accountability. It requires genuine respect for human rights and the right of political self-expression. This means an unfettered press, freedom of speech, the right to associate and organize, the right to support independent unions and opposition parties. Needless to say, these broad principles can take a wide variety of institutional forms.

Among a host of institutional issues, there are at least two central questions for Mexico: the role of political parties, and the means of presidential succession. Notwithstanding recent adjustments, Mexico continues to have a "one-plus" or dominant-party system, in which the PRI controls the electoral scene against modest opposition. Regardless of cosmetic alterations, the process of presidential succession still follows the *destape*, in which the outgoing president names the successor (Smith, 1989).

Connecting both these questions, the matrix shown here identifies a series of sites, or "settings," for institutional reform in Mexico, which currently occupies the upper lefthand cell (traditional *destape* with a one-plus party system). Sequential movement from one cell to another could, by extension, trace out alternative paths toward genuine democracy. A series of calculated, deliberate movements toward a final goal could comprise a strategy for democratization. On the other hand, partial and limited moves would amount to liberalization.

Channels for Democratization
Party Structure and Presidential Succession

	Party Structure		
	Dominant Party (1+)	*Two Party* (2 or 2+)	*Multiparty* (3 or 3+)
Presidential Succession: Destape	Contemporary Mexico		
Primary Within PRI			
Interparty Competition			Democratic Mexico

As presented here, the matrix invites speculation about the dynamic relationship between party structure and presidential succession. In the abstract, it is possible to imagine a limited connection between the two variables: parties might engage in vigorous competition for state-level and legislative office, for instance, while the *destape* might continue as before. In practice, this would require a tightly segmented electoral system, with a sharp separation between political arenas. Alternatively, there might emerge strategic interaction between the two variables: according to this conception, significant changes in party structure could have causal effects on presidential succession (and vice versa). Intermediate cells in the matrix would thus be unstable points of transition, not durable sites for political action.

Ultimately, the specific cells (and choices behind them) identify institutional locations for citizen participation. Competitive parties offer means for expression and aggregation of preferences and interests. At the moment, Mexico has a one-plus party system which does not foster true competition. (Some might insist that there could be genuine competition *within* the PRI, but this argument is simply not convincing for a society as diverse as Mexico's.) In principle, at least, it would seem feasible for Mexico to develop a durable three-party system—with the PRI in the Center, the PAN on the right, and the PRD (or its descendants) on the Left. Certainly this pattern has proved workable in Europe.

In an authentic democracy, competition must involve the allocation of genuine power, including—and especially—executive power. To put it bluntly: Mexico cannot achieve democracy so long as it relies upon the long-standing *destape*. Some form of presidential primary within the PRI would provide at least partial opportunity for participation and competition, but the ultimate solution (in the judgment of this author) requires interparty competition. For such competition to be meaningful, a non-PRI opposition contender must have an equal, and authentic, opportunity to win. In order to achieve full-fledged democracy, therefore, Mexico would have to move to the lower righthand cell of the matrix: not only multiparty politics, but also interparty competition for the presidency. It will be some time, I think, before that comes to pass.

In the meantime, it is essential for students of Mexican politics—observers and participants alike—to construct, consider, and contemplate plausible visions for the country's political destiny. It is time to think of long-run goals, not only short-term means; it is time to evaluate the direction of political transition, not just the rate of change. It is time, in other words, to engage the political imagination.

Notes

1. One explicit treatment of this subject appears in Camp (1993); see also Sheahan (1992: especially 55–75).

2. For an overview of relevant theoretical literature, see Smith (1991).

3. On this general question, see also Thorup (1991).

4. It is also alleged that increased exposure to the workings of U.S. democracy will exert a "demonstration effect" on Mexican politics. I regard this as fanciful thinking.

5. For additional comentary, see also Cárdenas (1990 and 1991) and Aguilar Zinser (1990).

6. For example, José Luis Solleiro Rebolledo, technical secretary for the technological innovations center of the Universidad Nacional Autónoma de México (UNAM), has estimated that only 6,500 of 100,000 manufacturing enterprises are equipped to compete with U.S. firms in a free-trade environment. Roberto Hernández Hernández of the Confederación de Cámaras Industriales (COMCAMIN) has declared that micro- and small-scale businesses (92 percent

of all firms) cannot survive free trade because of inadequate credit. And Javier Aguilar García, of the Instituto de Investigaciones Sociales at UNAM, has concluded that only large companies—2,365 out of nearly 1.3 million in total—would be able to survive (SourceMex, 1990, 1991a, and 1991b).

7. Regardless of the judgment on the merits of Contadora itself, it represented an independent Mexican initiative on an issue of grave importance to the U.S. government.

References

Aguilar Zinser, A. (1990) "U.S.-Mexico Free Trade: Looking Down the Road." *Los Angeles Times* (September 30): M-2.

Aspe, R. (1992) "Economic Restructuring in Mexico." Public lecture delivered at University of California, San Diego, January 17.

Baer, D. (1991) "North American Free Trade." *Foreign Affairs* 70, no. 4 (Fall): 132–49.

Camp, R. (1993) "Political Liberalization, the Last Key to Economic Modernization in Mexico?" In Riordan Roett (ed.), *Political and Economic Liberalization in Mexico: At a Critical Juncture?* Boulder, CO: Lynne Rienner, 17–34.

Cardenas, C. (1991) "Free Trade Is Not Enough: The Politics of Salinastroika." *New Perspectives Quarterly* 8, no. 1 (Winter): 21–22.

————. (1990) "Misunderstanding Mexico." *Foreign Policy* 78 (Spring): 113–30.

Cornelius, W. (1991) "Mexican Elections: A Salinas Solution" (unpublished manuscript). (A shortened version of this article appeared in *Hemisfile* 2, no. 6 [November] under the title "Mexico's Mid-Term Elections: About Face, Forward March.")

Dresser, D. (1991a) *Neopopulist Solutions to Neoliberal Problems: Mexico's National Solidarity Program.* La Jolla, CA: University of California-San Diego, Center for U.S.-Mexican Studies.

————. (1991b) "The Three Faces of Salinas: Perspectives on Economic and Political Reform in Mexico," Seminar presentation at Center for U.S.-Mexican Studies, La Jolla (CA), March.

Gilly, A. (1991) "Mexico: La restructuración en marcha." *Nueva Sociedad* 113 (May–June): 10–15.

Journal of Commerce (1990) "Free Trade, Fair Votes." (March 19): 8-A.

Los Angeles Times (1991) "Salinas' Pork-Barrel Politics Revives PRI Primacy at Polls." (October 22): H-2.

New Perspectives Quarterly (1991) "North American Free Trade: Mexico's Route to Upward Mobility." 8, no. 1 (Winter): 8.

New York Times (1990) "For Mexico, Freedom Before Free Trade." (April 1): E-19.

Proceso (1991a) "Cambios en política exterior, economía, trabajo y ecología, para complacer a Washington." No. 759 (May 20): 6–16.

————. (1991b) "Conclusión de Negroponte: Con el Tratado de Libre Comercio, México quedaría a disposición de Washington." No. 758 (May 13): 6–11.

Sheahan, J. (1992) *Conflict and Change in Mexican Economic Strategy: Implications for Mexico and for Latin America*. La Jolla, CA: University of California-San Diego, Center for U.S.-Mexican Studies.

Smith, P. (1991) "Crisis and Democracy in Latin America." *World Politics* 43, no. 4 (July): 608–34.

————. (1989) "The 1988 Presidential Succession in Historical Perspective," in Wayne A. Cornelius, Judith Gentleman, and Peter H. Smith (eds.), pp. 391–425, *Mexico's Alternative Political Futures*. La Jolla, CA: University of California-San Diego, Center for U.S.-Mexican Studies.

SourceMex (electronic newsletter) (1991a) "Free Trade Agreement Developments and Debate, September 2–14." (September 18): 11–13. Albuquerque, NM: Latin American Data Base, University of New Mexico.

————. (1991b) "Chronology of Debate on Free Trade Accord, March 19–31." (April 3): 9–13. Albuquerque, NM: Latin American Data Base, University of New Mexico.

————. (1991c) "Chronology of Free Trade Accord Developments, February 20–March 19." (February 27): 11–15. Albuquerque, NM: Latin American Data Base, University of New Mexico.

————. (1990) "U.S.-Mexico Free Trade Agreement Debate: Recent Expression of Opposition, Reservations." (November 21): 7. Albuquerque, NM: Latin American Data Base, University of New Mexico.

Thorup, C. (1991) "México-EU: La democratización y la agenda bilateral." *Nexos* 162 (June): 57–61.

(El) Universal (1991) "Voces disidentes en el foro senatorial de libre comercio." (March 15): 1.

Wall Street Journal (1991) "The Historic Dimensions of Free Trade with Mexico." (May 24): A-11.

Weintraub, S., and M. Baer (1992) "The Interplay Between Economic and Political Opening: The Sequence in Mexico." *Washington Quarterly* (Spring): 187–201.

13

Democracy and Economic Crisis: The Latin American Experience

Karen L. Remmer

Throughout the literature on democracy and development, scholars have long linked economic growth and progress to democracy, more specifically the ability of democracy to survive in Latin America with successful economic policies. But as Karen Remmer, a professor of Latin American politics at the University of New Mexico and the author of numerous works on authoritarianism and democratization, suggests in this chapter, an analysis of the 1980s demonstrates the striking conclusion that democratic regimes, despite the fragility of democracy in Latin America, survived amid economic policy failures and disappointing growth. Remmer explores three important hypotheses: that the type of regime is an important determinant of policy decisions under conditions of economic crisis; that democracies respond to economic crises less effectively than do authoritarian regimes; and that new democracies are less effective than old ones in responding to economic crises. She concludes that authoritarian regimes have not outperformed democracies in the management of economic crisis.

S ince 1979 the politics of Latin America have been transformed by the longest and deepest wave of democratization in the region's history. At the same time, the continent has been confronting its most serious economic crisis since the Great Depression. The confluence of these two trends has raised serious concerns about the future of democratic governance in the region.[1] The prevailing assumption is not merely that economic decline undercuts prospects for democratic consolidation. Because of their vulnerability to popular political pressures, democracies—

From *World Politics* 42 (April 1990): 315–35. Reprinted by permission of Johns Hopkins University Press.

particularly new democracies—are also seen as incapable of mounting effective policy responses to critical economic challenges.

In this chapter, the relationship between democracy and economic crisis is examined with specific reference to the question of policy response. Are democracies less likely than other regimes to address economic crises with appropriate policies? Do they tend to intensify rather than ameliorate economic challenges to their survival? How important are political regime characteristics for explaining varying policy responses to common economic difficulties? A comparative study of policy outcomes in Latin America after the outbreak of the debt crisis in 1982 suggests that the conventional wisdom about democracy and economic crisis not only exaggerates the relationship between political regime characteristics and policy choice; it also fundamentally misconstrues the strengths and weaknesses of democratic forms of governance.

Regime Characteristics and Public Policy

For nearly three decades, comparativists have been arguing over the determinants of policy choice. The debate is far from closed, but a growing body of research has generated considerable skepticism about the importance of regime variations for understanding policy performance.[2] Not only are policy choices constrained by socioeconomic realities, but the political similarities and differences among nations appear to be far too complex and multifaceted to be captured by simple distinctions among types of regimes. As a result, knowing that a regime is civilian rather than military, democratic rather than authoritarian, or even inclusionary rather than exclusionary establishes only a limited basis for making predictions about policy outcomes. The reasons are obvious. What counts in the formation of policy is not merely the rules of the political game, but the composition of governing coalitions, the ideological orientations of government leaders, and the structure of decision making. Recent literature on policy formation in Latin America and Western Europe has accordingly stressed such issues as the ideology of the dominant party, differences between presidential and parliamentary rule, national policy commitments, the belief systems of policy makers, the role of technocrats, union organization, relationships between the state and business groups, and corporatist forms of interest representation.[3]

Policies designed to cope with acute economic crises stand out as a key exception to these generalizations about research trends. Beginning with Thomas E. Skidmore's seminal study of economic stabilization,[4] scholars have repeatedly stressed the significance of regime characteristics for understanding the capacity of governments to manage serious economic disequilibria.[5] Either because economic austerity is seen as posing different kinds of risks for democratic and authoritarian governments or because the capacity to impose unpopular adjustment programs is assumed to vary with regime type, authoritarianism has been repeatedly linked with the successful management of economic crises, and democracy with failure. The first line of theoretical argument is represented by a recent work on the debt crisis, which asserts that "a democracy which is not accompanied by social and economic betterments for the population at large is putting its survival at risk."[6] A quotation from another recent work on Latin America illustrates the complementary argument—namely, that democracies are unable to administer the economic medicine required by crisis conditions. "Present economic policy . . . demands decision-making centers able to impose policies resisted by almost all segments of society. This is a task that prior cycles show is beyond the capacity of open democratic regimes in Latin America."[7] Authoritarian rule, which implies less dependence on popular support and more capacity to override political dissent, is consequently seen as more compatible with economic crisis than democracy.

To date, comparative research has provided only limited support for this line of analysis, and most of that support has been drawn from the historical experience of the three largest Latin American states. To the extent that researchers have considered a broad variety of cases, evidence of any strong linkage between regime characteristics and policy performance in the area of economic stabilization has remained distinctly elusive. A 1986 study, which presented both diachronic and cross-sectional analyses of IMF [International Monetary Fund] standby programs in Latin America over a thirty-year period, concluded that democratic regimes have been no less likely to introduce stabilization programs than authoritarian ones, no more likely to break down in response to their political costs, and no less rigorous in their implementation of austerity measures. If anything, the evidence suggested that the edge with respect to program implementation was with the democracies.[8]

Studies encompassing other areas of the third world have arrived at similar findings. According to Stephan Haggard's study of IMF Extended Fund Facility programs between 1975 and 1984, the capacity to adjust to economic crisis depends less on regime characteristics than on other variables, including the economic ideologies of governing elites, the importance of political clientelism, and the existence of a cohesive group of economic technocrats.[9] Joan M. Nelson's analysis of Third World stabilization programs reached similar conclusions.[10]

Despite this evidence, the economic policies and performance of Latin American states continue to be analyzed in terms of regime characteristics. The reason is twofold. First, either implicitly or explicitly, regional specialists have dismissed the relevance of prior research on the grounds that the current economic crisis is qualitatively different from any in the past. Thus, in their recent book on the debt crisis, Barbara Stallings and Robert Kaufman argue that "political regime type has been an important determinant of policy choice in the 1980s, even if it was not necessarily crucial in the more affluent 1960s and 1970s." In their view, "regime type weighs more heavily in conditions of crisis, when there are sharply contrasting views about how to allocate costs."[11] The argument parallels that of Peter Gourevitch, whose comparative analysis of responses to economic crises stressed that "the moments of greatest freedom are crisis points."[12]

The recent origin of most Latin American regimes has provided a second reason for dismissing the results of past research. Questions about the capacity of the region's democracies to manage the current crisis have been articulated specifically with respect to "newly emerging," "fledgling," "nascent," "struggling," or "incipient" democracies,[13] and not necessarily with reference to the generic properties of democracy as a system of governance. New democracies are singled out because of their supposed fragility or lack of legitimacy; indeed, the adjectives "new" and "fragile" have been used almost interchangeably to describe democratic governments in such countries as Argentina and Brazil.[14] The operative theoretical assumption is that, "in postauthoritarian situations, political legitimacy is very fragile and strongly contingent on material payoffs."[15] In a similar vein, Seligson and Muller have argued, "demands of labor unions, middle-class groups, and peasants must all be at least partially satisfied if these regimes [the new democracies] hope to build their legitimacy."[16] Fragility, however, is not merely seen as a reflection of the contingent nature of popular support. New democracies also harbor strong antidemocratic forces, which may take advantage of widespread political unrest.[17] As a result, political leaders in recently established democracies are portrayed as facing unusually intense pressures to resist economic orthodoxy and to pursue policies that are likely to push their economies in the direction of total financial collapse.

Economic Constraints and Political Instability

Neither the depth of the post-1982 crisis in Latin America nor the recent origin of the majority of the continent's democratic regimes establishes an altogether compelling basis for dismissing prior research findings. First, the magnitude of the recent crisis has limited the choices open to Latin

American countries far more severely than in the past. Regardless of their ideology or institutional base of support, leaders have been forced to choose between losing access to international financial markets and making concessions to the IMF and the international banking community in the form of orthodox policy measures and market-oriented programs of economic restructuring. Under such conditions, it seems plausible to assume that regime characteristics have become less rather than more important than in the past. What has counted is international bargaining position, not domestic politics.

Second, the assumption that new democracies will succumb more readily to economic challenges, or will handle them differently from old democracies, is also questionable. New democracies are not necessarily more fragile than old ones, nor do they necessarily enjoy less legitimacy or support. To assert otherwise is to argue by tautology. Myron Weiner errs in this direction when he states, "when countries have remained democratic for a generation, they appear more likely to remain democratic."[18] To the extent that this and similar statements take us beyond the conclusion that stable (or "institutionalized") democracies are stable (or institutionalized), they hardly comport with the Latin American experience.

Up until the recent wave of democratization, the peak year for democracy in the region was 1960. The correlation between democratic age in 1960 and subsequent durability is statistically insignificant ($r = .0181$). Table 1 illustrates the point. In 1970 there were seven liberal democracies in Latin America, three of which (Chile, Uruguay, and Costa Rica) had been established for a generation or more. Two of these three had collapsed by 1973. The breakdown rate for the "new" democracies was actually lower. Only one of the four (Ecuador) was overthrown by the wave of militarism that swept over the continent in the 1970s. The results are similar if 1960 or 1965 is chosen as a base year. If anything, past Latin American experience thus suggests that old democracies are more unstable and fragile than new ones.

Table 1
Breakdown Rates of Latin American Democracies
(in percentages)

	1960	1965	1970
"New" democracies[a]	66.7 (9)	40.0 (5)	25.0 (4)
"Old" democracies	100.0 (2)	66.7 (3)	66.7 (3)

[a]"New" democracies are defined as those under a generation old at the relevant date.

The experience of Latin America since the outbreak of the debt crisis also raises questions about the supposed fragility of new democracies. Despite repeated prognoses of collapse, every Latin American democracy, whether old or new, weathered the first eight years of the debt crisis. The fate of authoritarian regimes was different: of the six authoritarian governments that existed in South America in 1982, five had been overthrown by mid-1989. The sixth (Chile) was defeated in a national plebiscite in 1988, paving the way for a democratic transition. In Central America and the Caribbean, the situation was similar. There were no instances of democratic regime breakdown, but the twenty-eight-year Duvalier dictatorship [of François and Jean-Claude] was displaced in Haiti, and Guatemala underwent a partial transition from military to civilian rule. Based on this record, it might be more appropriate to emphasize the fragility of "old" authoritarianism rather than the weakness of "new" democracy.

The assumption that new democracies lack the support or legitimacy to see them through a protracted crisis also appears unwarranted. Albert O. Hirschman has pointed out that democratic governments that displace highly repressive or widely discredited authoritarian regimes can count upon a special reserve of political support and trust that may carry them through economic crises.[19] As a result, new democracies may be at a distinct advantage. The transition from authoritarianism to democracy, which allows "political goods" to compensate for declining per capita incomes, provides new democracies with a breathing space not enjoyed by older regimes, whether democratic or authoritarian.[20]

Policy Performance in Latin America

The policy performance of Latin American countries between 1982 and 1988 provides a basis for evaluating the conventional wisdom concerning the linkage between regime and policy. During this seven-year period, the region existed in a condition of continuous economic crisis characterized by net outflows of capital, lowered standards of living, high unemployment, and depressed levels of investment. At issue is the relevance of regime characteristics for understanding varying responses to these common economic difficulties.

Three principal hypotheses are examined:

1. Under conditions of economic crisis, regime is an important determinant of policy choice.

2. Democracies respond to economic crises less effectively than authoritarian regimes.

3. New democracies respond to economic crises even less effectively than old democracies.

For the purpose of this analysis, regime differences have been defined in relatively conventional terms. Governments selected on the basis of popular and competitive elections have been classified as democracies. Governments based upon military power or noncompetitive elections have been classified as authoritarian.[21] To address the theoretical issues posed by the relatively recent origin of many Latin democracies, a distinction has also been drawn between "new" and "old" democracies. All the democratic regimes that emerged after 1979 have been assigned to the former category.

Policy performance has been assessed on the basis of six indicators, which were selected to minimize problems of data availability as well as to circumvent a variety of theoretical controversies. Three of the indicators represent fairly conventional measures of economic performance: the annual GDP [gross domestic product] growth rate, the annual percentage change in the rate of inflation (logged to achieve distributional normality), and the annual percentage shift in the ratio between total external indebtedness and export earnings. A fourth indicator was designed to provide a direct measure of policy choice as distinct from policy outcomes— namely, the annual percentage change in the ratio between the central government's deficit and GDP. Taken together, these four indicators establish a relatively uncontroversial basis for assessing policy success and failure. Whether inspired by orthodox or unorthodox thinking, efforts to cope with the debt crisis have consistently placed a high priority upon limiting deficit spending, controlling inflation, restoring economic growth, and reducing the burden of debt servicing.

The two remaining indicators of policy performance reported in the subsequent tables pertain to labor conditions and are more ambiguous with respect to the question of policy success. These are the indicators of changes in real wages and unemployment, which were included in the analysis primarily to assess the supposed vulnerability of democracies to popular pressures. Much of the existing literature on the relationship between democracy and economic crisis assumes that democracies will attempt to protect real wages and employment levels, even at the risk of courting economic disaster. Hence, to the extent that regime type affects economic performance in line with the hypotheses derived from the literature on the debt crisis, the evidence should indicate that authoritarian regimes outperform democratic regimes, and that "old" democracies outperform "new" democracies, except with respect to the indicators of wages and employment, which should exhibit the opposite pattern.

Because the subsequent analysis is designed to explore variable responses to a common set of crisis conditions, the case base is limited to the ten Latin countries of South America, plus Mexico. The study thus encompasses all of the region's principal debtor nations, but excludes Central America and the Caribbean, which are conventionally considered part of the Latin American region. The reason for this exclusion is that the causes and dynamics of economic crisis in the Caribbean Basin have differed fundamentally from those of the rest of the region. The key problem has not been international indebtedness, but the regional political crisis originating with the struggle to oust the regime of Anastasio Somoza Debayle in Nicaragua. Likewise, the capacity of political actors to manage economic difficulties has been shaped more heavily by military conflict and outside intervention than by pressures from the international banking community and associated outflows of capital. Heavy U.S. aid flows to countries such as Honduras, El Salvador, and Costa Rica, for example, have compensated (and in some cases more than compensated) for the cost of servicing the foreign debt; while the performance of economies such as the Nicaraguan has reflected guerrilla warfare and external intervention. The magnitude of the economic problems posed by the onset of the debt crisis also differed significantly in Central and South America. In 1982, debt-service ratios in countries such as El Salvador, Haiti, and Guatemala were less than one-third of the regional average.[22]

Data on the policy performance of the eleven states have been drawn from official sources as reported to the Economic Commission on Latin America (ECLA) and the Inter-American Development Bank.[23] To augment the case base and to avoid classification problems posed by regime transitions, the statistical analysis has been conducted in terms of pooled data rather than on a country-by-country basis. The data on Argentina for 1982 and 1983, when the military still governed the country, have thus been treated as cases of authoritarian program administration, while those of the five subsequent years have been coded as instances of democratic performance. The same procedure has been followed in the cases of Brazil and Uruguay, which also shifted regime categories in the middle of the period under consideration. The "new" democratic administrations thus include Argentina (1984–1988), Bolivia (1982–1988), Brazil (1985–1988), Ecuador (1982–1988), Peru (1982–1988), and Uruguay (1985–1988). Authoritarian program administrations include Chile (1982–1988), Mexico (1985–1988), and Paraguay (1982–1988), in addition to Uruguay (1982–1984), Argentina (1982–83), and Brazil (1982–1984). Colombia and Venezuela have been coded as "old" democratic. The resulting breakdown yields fourteen years of "old" democratic policy administration, thirty-four years of "new" democratic program administration, and twenty-nine years of authoritarian program administration.

Tables 2 and 3 summarize the effects of regime differences on policy performance. The evidence in Table 2 demonstrates that no major differences separate democratic and authoritarian regimes in Latin America. Not one of the indicators listed in the table points to a contrast that is remotely significant in statistical terms. What is more, the indicators are inconsistent with the hypotheses drawn from the literature inasmuch as they point in the direction of more effective democratic rather than authoritarian crisis management.

Table 2
Democratic and Authoritarian Regime Performance[a]

	Democratic (N = 48) percentage	Authoritarian (N = 29) percentage	F	Significance
GDP growth	1.6	0.3	1.3994	.2406
Rate of change govt. deficit/GDP[b]	3.6	9.9	.0231	.8796
Log percent change inflation rate[c]	4.8	4.7	.1938	.6611
Rate of change debt/exports[d]	6.5	10.4	.5088	.4779
Real wages (annual percent change)[e]	−0.5	−2.4	.2950	.5888
Unemployment rate[f]	8.9	9.0	.0138	.9067

[a]Calculated on the basis of preliminary data for 1988.
[b]Based on the ratio between the central government deficit and GDP. Because some data were missing for 1988, calculations are based on 63 observations.
[c]Based on consumer price index.
[d]Calculated on the basis of the total disbursed debt divided by total exports of goods and services.
[e]Based on average manufacturing wage. Brazilian data represent averages for Rio de Janeiro and São Paulo.
[f]Urban unemployment only. Data for Argentina, Bolivia, and Venezuela represent national urban averages; data for other countries are based on one or more major cities.

A similar picture emerges from Table 3, which analyzes the differences between new and old democracies as well as the contrasts between these regimes and authoritarian ones. These differences are statistically significant with reference to only one of the six indicators of economic performance—the rate of unemployment; and even that indicator fails to

conform to the literature on the management of economic crisis. New
democracies in Latin America have turned in the best record in the area
of employment, but old democracies have not evinced greater sensitivity
to unemployment levels than authoritarian regimes. Contrary to the expectation that authoritarian regimes and new democracies represent the
two ends of the policy spectrum, with the performance of old democracies falling somewhere in between, the best and worst performances in
the area of employment belonged, respectively, to the new and old democracies. What is more, no statistically significant differences separate
the average annual unemployment rates of new democracies from those
of authoritarian regimes ($p = .7889$).

Table 3
Regime and Policy Performance[a]

	"Old" Demo-cracies (N=14) percentage	"New" Demo-cracies (N=34) percentage	Authori-tarian Regimes (N=29) percentage	F	Significance
GDP growth	2.4	1.3	0.3	.9690	.3842
Rate of change government deficit/GDP	−3.7	7.2	9.9	.0296	.9708
Log percent change inflation rate	4.7	4.9	4.7	.5649	.5709
Rate of change debt/exports	7.0	6.3	10.4	.2546	.7759
Real wages (annual percent change)	0.2	−0.7	−2.4	.1625	.8503
Unemployment rate	11.6	7.8	9.0	5.1583	.0081
Debt/exports	251.2	411.4	340.3	13.9313	.0000
Interest payments/ exports	24.3	35.3	32.6	4.7000	.0120
Annual percent change purchasing power of exports	3.6	1.1	10.2	1.6238	.2041
1982 debt/ export ratio	216.0	322.1	321.7	10.6656	.0001

[a]Calculated as indicated in notes to Table 2.

A similar pattern emerges with respect to the other indicators. Not one points in a direction consistent with the literature on economic crisis. In terms of economic growth, real wages, and the rate of change in government deficits relative to GDP, the two extremes of the spectrum correspond to the old democracies and the authoritarian regimes rather than to the new democracies and authoritarian regimes. In terms of the indicator of inflation, new democracies have turned in the worst average record, but no differences separate the other two regime types. The average figures for changes in the debt-to-export ratio also run counter to prediction inasmuch as new democracies have outperformed the other regime types, with authoritarian governments turning in the worst average records. As a result, not only are none of the differences between the newly established democracies and authoritarian regimes statistically significant, but newly established democracies have outperformed authoritarian regimes in promoting growth, containing the growth of fiscal deficits, and limiting the growth of the debt burden. Overall, the old democracies appear to have adhered to the most orthodox line of policy and compiled the strongest records of economic performance.

The last set of indicators in the table, which measures the severity of the economic constraints confronting policymakers, provides some basis for understanding these patterns. Old democracies outperformed other regimes in managing the debt crisis because they faced the fewest economic constraints. As suggested by Table 3, the old democracies— Colombia and Venezuela—entered the crisis in 1982 with debt-to-export ratios that were significantly lower than those of the new democracies and authoritarian regimes, while the authoritarian regimes began at a slight advantage relative to new democracies. Indeed, in terms of linear measures of association, the only indicator presented in Table 3 that is significantly correlated with regime is the 1982 debt-to-export ratio ($r = .3681$), which is also significantly correlated with the post-1982 debt-to-export ratio ($r = .7081$) and the ratio between interest payments and exports ($r = .8017$). When controls are introduced for the debt burden at the outset of the crisis, any relationship between regime and policy performance disappears.[24] In short, the fundamental problem confronted by competitive regimes in such countries as Argentina and Brazil in the 1980s has not been caused by the pressures or constraints of democratic governance, but by the sheer magnitude of the debt burden bequeathed to them by their authoritarian predecessors.

The Impact of Regime Change

In view of the unusually high level of indebtedness of the new South American democracies, is there any basis for arguing that new democracies have actually coped with crisis conditions more effectively than other regimes? The cross-national data establish no support for such an argument; however, because three South American countries shifted regime categories after the outbreak of the debt crisis, it is possible to compare the policy performance of democratic and authoritarian regimes within national units.

Although the results of these comparisons are mixed, they do provide some basis for arguing that a shift to democracy can actually strengthen, rather than weaken, the capacity to cope with economic challenges. Particularly striking in this regard is the case of Uruguay, where a new democratic regime managed not only to increase real wages and reduce unemployment, but also to accelerate growth, limit the expansion of the debt burden, cut the government deficit as a percentage of GDP, and put the brakes on an inflationary spiral. In the other two cases, the economic impact of the transition to democracy was less positive. As indicated in Table 4, short-term improvements in several key economic indicators followed the regime transition, but these improvements appear to reflect the policy ineffectiveness of disintegrating authoritarian governments rather than the policy effectiveness of democracy. The diachronic comparisons thus reinforce the results of the cross-sectional analysis, concretely underlining the diversity of performance patterns encompassed by broad regime categories and the resulting lack of clear contrasts among them.

Even in terms of policy choice (as distinct from performance), major contrasts do not emerge between authoritarian and democratic governance in the three countries that changed regime categories after 1982. As suggested by the figures on changes in deficit spending, in Brazil a lack of strict policy orthodoxy characterized the management of the economy both before and after the election of a civilian president. In neither period did policymakers impose strict fiscal and monetary constraints or pursue a program of restructuring through privatization and liberalization—all of which constitute basic elements of an orthodox program in the 1980s. Probably the closest Brazil came to orthodoxy was in 1982, when its net international reserves dropped by U.S. $5.3 billion, forcing the military's economic team to introduce a series of austerity measures and to open negotiations with the International Monetary Fund. Far from heralding a major shift in the direction of orthodoxy, however, the letter of intent that was signed with the Fund in January 1983 was never fulfilled. Within six months, IMF support had been suspended. As indicated in Table 4, part of the problem was the fiscal deficit, which was allowed to increase from 2.5 to 4.0 percent of GDP; but the rate of growth of domestic credit, which rose by more than 50 percent in 1983, also points to a lack of concern with orthodoxy.[25] Between 1983 and 1985, five more letters of intent were signed with the IMF—and all of them were suspended for noncompliance. Thus, the program of the military in the face of economic crisis can at best be characterized as halfhearted orthodoxy—an approach not clearly distinguishable from the halfhearted heterodoxy of its civilian successor.

Under the leadership of Minister of Finance Francisco Neves Dornelles, the civilian government of José Sarney began with an orthodox economic orientation. It subsequently embraced heterodoxy in the form of the Plan Cruzado, which was announced in early 1986. The failure of that plan, in turn, paved the way for the restoration of a more orthodox approach under the leadership of Finance Minister Mailson Ferreira da Nóbrega. Policies arguably varied within the 1985–1988 period as much as they did between the periods of military and civilian rule, emphasizing the weakness of the link between regime and policy choice. In any case, the evolution of international conditions dilutes the significance of any contrasts that might be drawn between the wavering orthodoxy of the military and the wavering heterodoxy of Sarney's civilian government. Through time, perceptions of the debt crisis changed significantly, as did Brazil's economic position, thus increasing incentives and opportunities for departures from policy orthodoxy. In 1982, Brazilian policymakers had been worried about short-term liquidity problems rather than long-term constraints on growth. Moreover, dramatic improvements in the level of international reserves created possibilities for experimentation between 1985 and 1988 that did not exist at the outset of the crisis.[26]

Uruguay represents the opposite end of the political spectrum: it pursued a relatively orthodox set of policies both before and after the transition to democracy. Indeed, among the countries of Latin America, only Chile—long identified as a paragon of economic orthodoxy—could be described as adhering more consistently to orthodox precepts. A key difference between the two countries is that in Uruguay the military response to the crisis of 1982 was ineffective and vacillating. During the last three years of military rule, the fiscal deficit averaged 6.0 percent of GDP, while the average annual rate of growth of domestic credit exceeded 60 percent. Nevertheless, basic elements of the orthodox approach that had dominated the management of the economy between 1973 and 1982, such as international opening and economic liberalization, were retained and carried forward into the late 1980s under civilian leadership. In Uruguay, regime transition entailed more effective policy implementation rather than major changes in policy orientation.

The case of Argentina resembles that of Uruguay in that authoritarianism proved incapable of mounting a coherent response to the outbreak of the 1982 crisis. In Argentina, however, the lack of policy coherence

Table 4

Democratic Transition and Policy Performance[a]

(percentages)

	GDP Growth	Government Deficit/GDP	Change Government Deficit/GDP	Inflation	Change Rate of Inflation	Change Debt/ Exports	Change Real Wages[b]	Unemployment Rate[c]
Argentina								
1982	-5.8	-3.9	-26.3	209.7	59.8	44.4	-10.4	5.3
1983	2.6	-14.9	261.5	433.7	106.8	2.1	25.4	4.7
1984[d]	2.2	-7.2	-48.9	688.0	58.6	0.6	26.4	4.6
1985	-4.5	-4.5	-37.5	385.4	-44.0	-1.4	15.2	6.1
1986	5.8	-3.1	-31.1	81.9	-78.7	26.8	1.6	5.2
1987	1.6	-8.0	158.1	174.8	113.4	10.3	-5.9	5.9
1988	0.5	n.a.	n.a.	372.0	112.8	-19.6	-5.0	6.5
Brazil								
1982	0.9	-2.5	0.0	97.9	-2.7	33.2	7.3	6.3
1983	-2.4	-4.6	60.0	179.2	83.0	-0.2	-9.8	6.7
1984	5.7	-5.8	26.1	203.3	98.7	-12.5	-1.3	7.1
1985[d]	8.4	-11.8	103.4	228.0	12.1	5.8	15.1	5.3
1986	8.1	n.a.	n.a.	58.4	-74.4	18.7	16.7	3.6

1987	2.9	n.a.	n.a.	365.9	526.5	-5.9	-10.5	3.7
1988	0.0	n.a.	n.a.	816.1	123.0	-25.3	-4.1	4.0
Uruguay							
1982	-10.1	-8.6	85.0	20.5	50.8	-30.3	-0.3	11.9
1983	-6.0	-3.7	-57.0	51.5	17.4	151.2	-20.7	15.5
1984	-1.3	-5.0	35.1	66.1	11.7	28.3	-9.2	14.0
1985[d]	0.2	-1.9	-62.0	83.0	8.0	25.6	14.1	13.1
1986	7.0	-1.4	-26.3	76.4	-10.7	-8.0	6.7	10.7
1987	5.3	-1.3	-7.1	57.3	8.6	-25.0	4.8	9.3
1988	0.0	n.a.	n.a.	68.5	-6.6	19.5	2.3	9.2

[a]Calculated as indicated in notes to Table 2.
[b]Average manufacturing wage; Brazilian figures represent averages for Rio de Janeiro and São Paulo.
[c]Data for Argentina are for all urban areas. Data for Brazil are calculated on the basis of the metropolitan regions of Rio de Janeiro, São Paulo, Belo Horizonte, Porto Alegre, Salvador, and Recife. Data for Uruguay are based on unemployment rates in Montevideo.
[d]First year of democratic administration.

under authoritarianism was more pronounced. Confronted with a rapidly deteriorating international position in 1982 and 1983, the Argentine armed forces wavered between state interventionism and more orthodox approaches, but they were too divided and discredited to implement any effective policy response. The agreement reached with the IMF in January 1983, for example, committed the military government to limiting its fiscal deficit to 2.1 percent of GDP, but the actual figure for the year reached a level of 16.8 percent.[27] The democratic government of Raúl Alfonsín consequently inherited an extremely difficult situation. Its initial response was one of policy drift, but in mid-1985 it announced a bold economic plan, known as the Plan Austral, which combined conventional orthodox measures with a heterodox wage and price freeze. After a brief period of success, however, the economy began to deteriorate again, leading to a progressive drift away from orthodoxy. Hence, as in Uruguay, regime change initially enhanced rather than diluted policy orthodoxy, but the policy shift in the Argentine case was less decisive and less durable.

Analysis of the impact of regime change thus casts further doubt upon the conventional wisdom regarding democracy and economic crisis. The performance of the new democracies in the three countries that changed regime categories during the debt crisis was not markedly worse than that of their authoritarian predecessors. In one of the three cases, democracy was linked with improved rather than diminished policy effectiveness; in the other two, it brought a temporary respite from deepening crisis. The longitudinal evidence also indicates that the way in which governments responded to economic crisis was not a function of regime characteristics. Contrary to the literature crediting authoritarianism with the capacity to administer the harsh medicine of orthodoxy, no sharp differences can be delineated between the approaches of democratic and authoritarian governments in the three countries.

Overall, the evidence points less in the direction of domestic determinants of policy choice than to the relevance of international conditions. Of the three countries that shifted regime categories, Brazil had the strongest international bargaining position and evidenced the least propensity to adhere to orthodox precepts or IMF recommendations either before or after the transition to democracy. Moreover, such shifts as occurred in its policies through time can be linked to the changing international situation. Uruguay, the country with the weakest international bargaining position, adopted a relatively orthodox set of policies both before and after regime transition. Argentina occupied the middle ground, both in terms of its bargaining position and its level of policy orthodoxy.

Conclusion

The experience of Latin American countries since the outbreak of the debt crisis establishes no basis for asserting that authoritarian regimes outperform democracies in the management of economic crisis. When we control for the magnitude of the debt burden at the outbreak of the crisis, no statistically significant differences emerge between democratic and authoritarian regimes or between new democracies and more established regimes. The importance of regime characteristics for explaining differing responses to economic crisis has been exaggerated, as have the inadequacies of new democratic regimes. Despite debt burdens that were significantly higher than those of more established regimes, the supposedly fragile new Latin democracies performed just as effectively as their authoritarian counterparts in managing the debt crisis. Longitudinal data support the same point. The experience of countries that shifted regime categories after 1982 suggests that the inauguration of a democratic regime does not necessarily undermine, and may actually enhance, the capacity of political actors to cope with economic challenges.

The weakness of the link between regime and policy performance can be related to external constraints on policy choice. As suggested by the longitudinal analysis, large countries—particularly those with dynamic export sectors—have enjoyed a much broader array of policy options than smaller ones. In countries that shifted regime categories, the continuities in policy performance over time also point to the possible relevance of factors such as economic structure or national policy commitments, which may not change with regime transitions.

More fundamentally, however, the paucity of evidence linking regime and policy speaks to the wide array of ideologies, political coalitions, and decision-making structures that are encompassed by broad regime categories such as "democracy" or even "new democracy." In countries such as Ecuador, the right dominated the recent process of democratic transition, giving rise to decision-making structures that protected business interests and shielded economic policy-making from electoral pressures.[28] In neighboring Peru, however, democracy unleashed populist forces, threatening the access of business to the decision-making process and pushing policy in more nationalistic and less orthodox directions. Because of important variations in orientation, base of social support, and regime structure, the policy performance of authoritarian regimes has also differed considerably from one case to another.

The problem is that prevailing conceptualizations of regime characteristics do not leave room for such variations. As a result, the potential fragilities and policy costs of authoritarianism have been understated, whereas those of democracy have been exaggerated. Particularly intriguing in this regard are the sharp contrasts that emerge between the debt burdens of the new democracies and authoritarian regimes on the one hand, and of old democracies on the other. In the 1980s, Latin American democracies not only handled economic crises as effectively as authoritarian regimes; they achieved a far better record at avoiding acute crises in the first place.

The findings thus address questions about democracy that transcend the issue of crisis management. Like scholars of other third world regions, Latin Americanists have spent most of the past two decades explaining the instability and rarity of democratic rule. While virtually every aspect of Latin society—from international structures of dependence to cultural values—has been seen as an obstacle to democracy, the dominant theoretical frameworks have emphasized the role of economic performance. In Guillermo O'Donnell's influential formulation, socioeconomic modernization failed to enhance the probability of democracy in the Latin American context because popular-sector pressures came increasingly into conflict with socioeconomic constraints on policy choice.[29] James Malloy, while taking a more cyclical view of political change in the region, has similarly linked the fragility of democracy with public policy, arguing that "since the 1930s the problem has been to found a government capable of solving key economic problems." He views the root of the problem as a tension between the need to accumulate capital for economic development and the need to build political legitimacy by meeting demands for increased consumption.[30] Similar arguments concerning the role of policy failure have been applied to Southeast Asia as well as to areas of the world characterized by comparatively low levels of modernization and popular-sector mobilization.[31] A recent volume on Africa, for example, attributes democratic decay and delegitimation to "the poor, often disastrous, economic performance of democratic regimes."[32]

Although the political face of Latin America has been dramatically transformed since 1979, the process of theoretical reorientation has hardly begun. Emphasis continues to be placed on the link between democratic fragility and policy failure. The puzzle of the 1980s, however, has not been the fragility of democracy, but its surprising vitality in the face of overwhelming economic constraints. To understand this vitality, it is necessary to set aside the assumptions that have been made about the operation of democracy in Latin America. At issue is not merely the question of pseudo-democracy, in which democratic institutions mask authoritarian realities, or even of exclusionary democracy, in which a restricted suffrage undergirds oligarchical control, but also the broader debate about the ways in which capitalism has accommodated democracy. In emphasizing the fragility of democracy in Latin America, scholars have conjured up systems in which the "privileged position of business," the "iron law of oligarchy," "private government," and other related constraints on popular control disappear, leaving policy responsive to the unmediated demands of peasants and workers.[33] Such systems have no empirical counterpart in the North Atlantic, much less in the highly inegalitarian societies of Latin America.

The strengths and weaknesses of Latin American democracy have been further distorted with respect to the political calculus of democratic political leaders. Contrary to the assumption that elected officials will attempt to enhance their legitimacy by delivering material payoffs to the bulk of the population, even at the cost of financial disaster, the lessons of the past have induced considerable political caution. Political leaders are aware that the rise and the fall of democracy in Latin America have corresponded less to the whims of the voting majority than to the concerted opposition of business and military elites.

Notes

1. Jimmy Carter and Howard Baker, "Latin America's Debt and U.S. Interests," in *Latin America's Debt Crisis: Adjusting to the Past or Planning for the Future?*, ed. Robert A. Pastor (Boulder, CO: Lynne Rienner, 1987), 2; U.S. Congress, House Committee on Foreign Affairs, *Global Debt Crisis*, 99th Cong., 2d sess., 1986, pp. 57, 59, 76; Inter-American Dialogue, *The Americas in 1989: Consensus for Action* (Aspen, CO: Aspen Institute, 1989), 1–2; Pedro-Pablo Kuczynski, *Latin American Debt* (Baltimore: Johns Hopkins University Press, 1988), 146; Mitchell A. Seligson and Edward N. Muller, "Democratic Stability and Economic Crisis: Costa Rica, 1978–1983," *International Studies Quarterly* 31 (September 1987): 323; "Bush Aides Are Likely to Offer a Plan Soon on Third World Debt," *Wall Street Journal*, March 9, 1989, 1; "Third World Debt Won't Wait," *New York Times*, October 1, 1988, 4; "Latin Debt Crisis Seen as Threat to Continent's New Democracies," *New York Times*, January 17, 1989, 3.

2. For a summary and review of this literature as it pertains specifically to Latin America, see Karen L. Remmer, "Evaluating the Policy Impact of Military Regimes in Latin America," *Latin American Research Review* 13, no. 2 (1978): 39–54.

3. David Cameron, "Social Democracy, Corporatism, Labor Quiescence, and the Representation of Economic Interest in Advanced Capitalist Society," in *Order and Conflict in Contemporary Capitalism*, ed. John H. Goldthorpe (Oxford: Clarendon Press, 1984); Francis G. Castles, *The Social Democratic Image of Society: A Study of the Achievements and Origins of Scandinavian Social Democracy in Comparative Perspective* (London: Routledge and Kegan Paul, 1978); William Coleman and Wyn Grant, "The Organizational Cohesion and Political Access of Business: A Study of Comprehensive Associations," *European Journal of Political Research* 16 (September 1988): 467–87; Catherine M. Conaghan,

Restructuring Domination: Industrialists and the State in Ecuador (New Haven: Yale University Press, 1988); Merilee S. Grindle, *State and Countryside: Development Policy and Agrarian Politics in Latin America* (Baltimore: Johns Hopkins University Press, 1986); Stephan Haggard and Robert Kaufman, "The Politics of Stabilization and Structural Adjustment," in *Developing Country Debt and Economic Performance*, Vol. I: *The International Financial System*, ed. Jeffrey D. Sachs (Chicago: University of Chicago Press, 1989), 209–54; Douglas A. Hibbs, Jr., "Political Parties and Macroeconomic Policy," *American Political Science Review* 71 (December 1977): 1467–87; Robert R. Kaufman, *The Politics of Debt in Argentina, Brazil, and Mexico* (Berkeley: Institute of International Studies, University of California, 1989); Peter Katzenstein, *Small States in World Markets* (Ithaca, NY: Cornell University Press, 1986); Stephen McBride, "The Comparative Politics of Unemployment: Swedish and British Responses to Economic Crisis," *Comparative Politics* 20 (April 1988): 303–23; Ronan Raddison, *The Fragmented State* (Oxford: Basil Blackwell, 1983); Philippe C. Schmitter, "Reflections on Where the Theory of Neo-Corporatism Has Gone," in *Patterns of Corporatist Policy-Making*, ed. Gerhard Lehmbruch and Philippe C. Schmitter (London: Sage Publications, 1982).

4. Skidmore, "The Politics of Economic Stabilization in Postwar Latin America," in *Authoritarianism and Corporatism in Latin America*, ed. James M. Malloy (Pittsburgh: University of Pittsburgh Press, 1977), 149–90.

5. Christian Anglade and Carlos Fortín, eds., *The State and Capital Accumulation in Latin America*, Vol. I (Pittsburgh: University of Pittsburgh Press, 1985), 8; Alejandro Foxley, *Latin American Experiments in Neoconservative Economics* (Berkeley: University of California Press, 1983); Robert Frenkel and Guillermo O'Donnell, "The 'Stabilization Programs' of the International Monetary Fund and Their Internal Impacts," in *Capitalism and the State in U.S.-Latin American Relations*, ed. Richard R. Fagen (Stanford: Stanford University Press, 1979), 171–216; Robert R. Kaufman, "Democratic and Authoritarian Responses to the Debt Issue: Argentina, Brazil, and Mexico," *International Organization* 39 (Summer 1985): 473–503; Riordan Roett, "The Foreign Debt Crisis and the Process of Redemocratization in Latin America," in *A Dance Along the Precipice: The Political and Economic Dimensions of the International Debt Problem*, ed. William N. Eskridge, Jr. (Lexington, MA: Lexington Books, 1985), 207–30; John Sheahan, "Market-Oriented Economic Policies and Political Repression in Latin America," *Economic Development and Cultural Change* 28 (January 1980): 267–91; Barbara Stallings, "Peru and the U.S. Banks: Privatization of Financial Relations," in Fagen, 217–53; Rosemary Thorp and Laurence Whitehead, "Introduction," in *Inflation and Stabilization in Latin America*, ed. Thorp and Whitehead (New York: Holmes and Meier, 1979), 11, 18; Jorge Dominguez, "Political Change: Central America, South America, and the Caribbean," in *Understanding Political Development*, ed. Myron Weiner and Samuel P. Huntington (Boston: Little, Brown, 1987), 83.

6. Institute of Latin American Studies, *The Debt Crisis in Latin America*, Monograph No. 13 (Stockholm: Institute of Latin American Studies, 1986), 11.

7. James M. Malloy, "The Politics of Transition in Latin America," in *Authoritarians and Democrats: Regime Transition in Latin America*, ed. James M. Malloy and Mitchell A. Seligson (Pittsburgh: University of Pittsburgh Press, 1987), 249.

8. Karen L. Remmer, "The Politics of Economic Stabilization: IMF Standby Programs in Latin America, 1954–1984," *Comparative Politics* 18 (October 1986): 1–24.

9. Haggard, "The Politics of Adjustment: Lessons from the IMF's Extended Fund Facility," in *The Politics of International Debt*, ed. Miles Kahler (Ithaca, NY: Cornell University Press, 1985), 157–86.

10. Nelson, "The Politics of Stabilization," in *Adjustment Crisis in the Third World*, ed. Richard E. Feinberg and Valeriana Kallab (New Brunswick, NJ: Transaction Books, 1984).

11. Stallings and Kaufman, "Debt and Democracy in the 1980s: The Latin American Experience," in *Debt and Democracy in Latin America*, ed. Stallings and Kaufman (Boulder, CO: Westview Press, 1989), 203, 220.

12. Gourevitch, *Politics in Hard Times: Comparative Responses to International Economic Crises* (Ithaca, NY: Cornell University Press, 1986), 240.

13. Seligson and Muller, "Democratic Stability and Economic Crisis," 322, 323; House Committee on Foreign Affairs, *Global Debt Crisis*, 76; "Third World Debt Won't Wait," *New York Times*, October 1, 1988, 14; William C. Smith, "Heterodox Shocks and the Political Economy of Democratic Transition in Argentina and Brazil," in *Lost Promises: Debt, Austerity, and Development in Latin America*, ed. William L. Canak (Boulder, CO: Westview Press, 1989), 156.

14. See, for example, "Brazil's Democracy in the Balance," *COHA's Washington Report on the Hemisphere* 9 (December 7, 1988), 4; see also the statement of James A. Baker, III, the secretary of state-designate, at his confirmation hearings before the Senate Foreign Relations Committee, January 17, 1989, reprinted in U.S. Department of State, Bureau of Public Affairs, *Current Policy*, No. 1146 (January 1989), 1.

15. Smith, "Heterodox Shocks," 156.

16. Seligson and Muller, "Democratic Stability and Economic Crisis," 322.

17. Institute of Latin American Studies, *Debt Crisis in Latin America*, 11.

18. Weiner, "Empirical Democratic Theory," in *Competitive Elections in Developing Countries*, ed. Myron Weiner and Ergun Ozbudun (Durham, NC: Duke University Press, 1987), 18.

19. Hirschman, "The Political Economy of Latin American Development: Seven Exercises in Retrospection," *Latin American Research Review* 22, no. 3 (1987): 28.

20. The concept of "political goods" in this connection is drawn from Kuczynski, *Latin American Debt*, 147.

21. These criteria are utilized solely because they pose few classificatory problems for the time period and the set of countries in question. The only ambiguous case is that of Brazil, which made less than a complete transition to democracy during the period under consideration. For other purposes, a more complex set of operational indicators might be preferable in order to separate inclusionary and exclusionary forms of competitive rule and to differentiate between limited and open competition. For recent efforts along these lines, see John A. Booth, "Elections and Democracy in Central America: A Framework for Evaluation" (paper prepared for the Southwestern Political Science Association meeting, Little Rock, AR, March 30–April 1, 1989); Karen L. Remmer, "Exclusionary Democracy," *Studies in Comparative International Development* 20 (Winter 1985–86): 64–85; Evelyne Huber Stephens, "Capitalist Development and Democracy in South

America" (paper presented at the Midwest Political Science Association, Chicago, April 1988).

22. World Bank, *World Debt Tables, 1984–85* (Washington, DC: World Bank, 1985), 158–227.

23. CEPAL, "Balance preliminar de la economía latinoamericana, 1988" (Preliminary balance of the Latin American economy, 1988), *Notas sobre la economía y el desarrollo*, No. 470 (December 1988); ibid., No. 387 (December 1983); Inter-American Development Bank, *Economic and Social Progress in Latin America* (Washington, DC: IADB, 1982–1988).

24. It may be noted that the results are virtually identical if the analysis is limited to the nine larger and more modern economies of the Latin American region, upon which Stallings and Kaufman focus their discussion of the link between regime and policy [chap. 12]. The only difference with the findings reported here is that the relationship between rates of unemployment and regime remains significant at the .04 level after controlling for the 1982 debt burden. Again, however, that relationship does not conform to the hypotheses presented in the literature inasmuch as (a) the highest rates of unemployment are found in the old democracies rather than in the authoritarian regimes, and (b) the unemployment rates of new democracies and authoritarian regimes are not significantly different.

25. Inter-American Development Bank, *Economic and Social Progress in Latin America: 1987 Report* (Washington, DC: IADB, 1987), 246.

26. Johanna Sharp, "Regime Type and Economic Policy Formation: The Case of Brazil, 1982–1989," unpublished manuscript (Albuquerque, NM, 1989).

27. IADB, *Economic and Social Progress in Latin America: 1987*, 214; *1983 Report*, 148.

28. See Conaghan, *Restructuring Domination*, 120–44.

29. Guillermo O'Donnell, *Modernization and Bureaucratic-Authoritarianism: Studies in South American Politics* (Berkeley: Institute of International Studies, University of California, 1973). See also O'Donnell, "Reflections on the Patterns of Change in the Bureaucratic-Authoritarian State," *Latin American Research Review* 13, no. 1 (1978): 3–38; O'Donnell, "Tensions in the Bureaucratic-Authoritarian State and the Question of Democracy," in *The New Authoritarianism in Latin America*, ed. David Collier (Princeton: Princeton University Press, 1979): 285–318.

30. Malloy, "The Politics of Transition," 239.

31. See, in particular, William Crowther, "Philippine Authoritarianism and the International Economy," *Comparative Politics* 18 (April 1986): 339–56, and Hyug Baeg Im, "The Rise of Bureaucratic Authoritarianism in South Korea," *World Politics* 39 (January 1987): 231–57.

32. Larry Diamond, "Introduction: Roots of Failure, Seeds of Hope," in *Democracy in Developing Countries*, Vol. 2: *Africa*, ed. Larry Diamond, Juan J. Linz, and Seymour Martin Lipset (Boulder, CO: Lynne Rienner, 1988), 15.

33. Charles E. Lindblom, *Politics and Markets: The World's Political-Economic Systems* (New York: Basic Books, 1977); Robert Michels, *Political Parties: A Sociological Study of the Oligarchical Tendencies of Modern Democracy* (New York: Collier Books, 1962); and Grant McConnell, *Private Power and American Democracy* (New York: Knopf, 1966), chap. 5.

Suggested Readings

The rise of democratization globally has produced a plethora of literature on the transition to democracy, on democracy and economic development, and on political development in Latin America specifically. An initial place to start for anyone interested in exploring this topic further is the *Journal of Democracy*, edited by Marc F. Plattner and Larry Diamond. Established in 1990, this journal focuses exclusively on democratic change, transition to democracy, and democratic institutions. Many of its contributors are listed as authors and editors of the works cited in this bibliographic essay. An excellent, comprehensive compilation of works on Latin American democracy is also available in Peter Hakim and Abraham Lowenthal, *Latin American Democracy in the 1990s: The Challenges Ahead* (Queenstown, MD: Inter-American Dialogue, Aspen Institute, 1991).

It is helpful to obtain a more complete understanding of how scholars conceptualize democracy in order to clarify the debate on the actual process of democratization. In addition to Terry Lynn Karl's excellent chapter in this volume, she also has coauthored a lucid interpretation with Philippe C. Schmitter, "What Democracy Is . . . and Is Not," *Journal of Democracy* 2, no. 3 (Summer 1991): 75–88.

Much of the literature on democratization concerns the transitional phases from nondemocratic models to democratic systems. One of the works that has had a major impact and provides a larger international context in which to place the Latin American experience is Samuel P. Huntington, *The Third Wave: Democratization in the Late Twentieth Century* (Norman: University of Oklahoma Press, 1991), in which he argues that the present pattern is the third of three historical waves of world democratization. Students interested in democratic patterns in the Third World specifically should read the four-volume series by Larry J. Diamond, Juan J. Linz, and Seymour Martin Lipset, eds., *Democracy in Developing Countries* (Boulder, CO: Lynne Rienner, 1989), which includes a volume on Latin America.

Comparisons between Latin America and Europe can be found in Juan Linz and Alfred Stepan, "Political Crafting of Democratic Consolidation or Destruction: European and South American Comparisons," in *Democracy in the Americas: Stopping the Pendulum*, ed. Robert A. Pastor (New York: Holmes and Meier, 1989); in Enrique A. Baloyra, *Comparing New*

Democracies: Transition and Consolidation in Mediterranean Europe and the Southern Cone (Boulder, CO: Westview Press, 1987); and in the multivolume series edited by Guillermo O'Donnell, Philippe C. Schmitter, and Laurence Whitehead, *Transitions from Authoritarian Rule*, 4 vols. (Baltimore: Johns Hopkins University Press, 1986). An excellent overview of transitions in general and a series of comparisons among regions is presented in Terry Lynn Karl and Philippe C. Schmitter, who critically discuss the literature in their "Democratization Around the Globe: Opportunities and Risks," in *World Security: Challenges for a New Country*, ed. Michael T. Klare and Daniel C. Thomas (New York: St. Martin's Press, 1994), 43–62.

Works that analyze the Latin American case more specifically are also quite numerous. One of the most comprehensive and balanced collections is James M. Malloy and Mitchell Seligson, eds., *Authoritarians and Democrats: Regime Transition in Latin America* (Pittsburgh: University of Pittsburgh Press, 1987). Two of the most useful broad interpretations for Latin America in this collection are those by the editors: James Malloy, "The Politics of Transition in Latin America"; and Mitchell Seligson, "Democratization in Latin America: The Current Cycle." Martin C. Needler, who has long explored the issues of political development and stability in Latin America, provides a unified interpretation in *The Problem of Democracy in Latin America* (Lexington, MA: Lexington Books, 1987).

For a more specific analysis of the role of elections in the process of political change, focusing on the Latin American case, several collections are useful. Paul W. Drake and Eduardo Silva explore the early 1980s in the edited volume *Elections and Democratization in Latin America, 1980–1985* (La Jolla, CA: Center for Iberian and Latin American Studies, University of California at San Diego, 1986). Students interested in the Central American experience will find an excellent collection in John Booth and Mitchell Seligson, eds., *Elections and Democracy in Central America* (Chapel Hill: University of North Carolina Press, 1989). The most up-to-date and comprehensive account of the entire region can be found in Kurt von Mettenheim and James Malloy, eds., *Deepening Democracy and Representation in Latin America* (Pittsburgh: University of Pittsburgh Press, 1996).

To understand the background of the linkage between economic development and politics, a useful place to begin is Seymour Martin Lipset, "Some Social Requisites of Democracy: Economic Development and Political Legitimacy," *American Political Science Review* 53 (March 1959): 69–105. An interpretation that identifies historical and cultural variables to explain the difficulties of Latin American economic and political development is presented in Kendall W. Brown and Lissa Roche, eds., *Political and Economic Pluralism in the Third World* (Hillsdale, IL: Hillsdale College Press, 1986), 85–102. A clear discussion of various potential scenarios of the impact of capitalism on political liberalization is given in Gabriel Almond, "Capitalism and Democracy," *PS, Political Science and Politics* 24, no. 3 (September 1991): 467–73. The most comprehensive account of development as well as political and economic linkages in Latin America is Peter F. Klarén and Thomas J. Bossert, eds., *Promise of Development: Theories of Change in Latin America* (Boulder, CO: Westview Press, 1986).

The cultural approach to understanding political behavior in Latin America, including its resistance to democratic models, is explored in many writings. A general foundation for some of these arguments, focusing on individual attitudes and values, is established in the classic work by Gabriel Almond and Sidney Verba, *The Civic Culture* (Princeton: Princeton University Press, 1963), which includes Mexico as one of five featured countries, and their useful follow-up study, *The Civic Culture Revisited* (Boston: Little, Brown, 1980). These studies, however, rely heavily on survey research to document citizens' values. The most comprehensive accounts of Latin America, but largely nonempirical, are the works of Glen Dealy: *The Public Man: An Interpretation of Latin American and Other Catholic Cultures* (Amherst: University of Massachusetts Press, 1977); and his recent book, from which Chapter 3 of this volume is excerpted, *The Latin Americans, Spirit and Ethos* (Boulder, CO: Westview Press, 1992), 3–15. Another recent interpretation that takes this approach but links culture to economic development in the region is Lawrence E. Harrison, *Underdevelopment Is a State of Mind: The Latin American Case* (Lanham, MD: Madison Books, 1985).

Finally, for those readers interested in the relationship between societal institutions and groups, and the influence of each on democracy, numerous articles can be found in the journal literature. Institutions have received the most attention. For a superb collection of essays focusing on the potential role of religion and on nongovernmental organizations with religious roots see Edward L. Cleary and Hannah Stewart-Gambino, *Conflict and Competition: The Latin American Church in a Changing Environment* (Boulder, CO: Lynne Rienner, 1992). Stewart-Gambino also provides a detailed interpretation of the recent literature on the topic in her helpful review of "New Approaches to Studying the Role of Religion in Latin America," *Latin American Research Review* 24, no. 3 (1989): 187–99. For an assessment of the culmination of the influences wrought by liberation theology see Paul E. Sigmund, *Liberation Theology at the Crossroads: Democracy or Revolution?* (New York: Oxford University

Press, 1990). On the military and the changing relationship in civil-military relations within the democratic context, the most useful works are Louis W. Goodman, Johanna S. R. Mendelson, and Juan Rial, eds., *The Military and Democracy: The Future of Civil-Military Relations in Latin America* (Lexington, MA: Lexington Books, 1990); and Paul W. Zagorski, *Democracy versus National Security: Civil-Military Relations in Latin America* (Boulder, CO: Lynne Rienner, 1992).

About the Editor

Roderic Ai Camp joined the Tulane University faculty in 1991. He has served as a visiting professor at the Colegio de México, the Foreign Service Institute, and the University of Arizona. He carried out research as a fellow at the Woodrow Wilson International Center for Scholars, Smithsonian Institution, from 1983 to 1984, and has been awarded a Fulbright Fellowship on three occasions and a Howard Heinz Foundation Fellowship for research on Mexico from 1990 to 1991. Camp is a contributing editor to the Library of Congress's *Handbook of Latin American Studies* and to the *World Book Encyclopedia* and serves on the Editorial Board of *Mexican Studies*. His special interests include Mexican and Latin American politics, comparative elites, political recruitment, church-state relations, and civil-military affairs. His most recent publications on Mexico include: *Politics in Mexico* (1993), *The Successor* (a political thriller) (1993), *Generals in the Palacio: The Military in Modern Mexico* (1992), *Entrepreneurs and Politics in Twentieth Century Mexico* (1989), and *Memoirs of a Mexican Politician* (1988). Presently, he directs the Tinker Mexican Policy Studies Program at Tulane and chairs the Political Science Department.